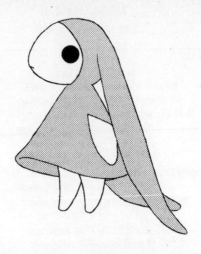

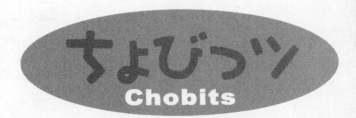

ちょびっツ
Chobits

CLAMP

Satsuki Igarashi
Nanase Ohkawa
Mick Nekoi
Mokona Apapa

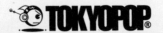

HAMBURG // LONDON // LOS ANGELES // TOKYO

Chobits Vol. 3
Created by CLAMP

Translation - Shirley Kubo
English Adaptation - Jake Forbes
Associate Editor - Paul Morrissey
Retouch and Lettering - Fawn Lau
Cover Design - Anna Kernbaum

Editor - Jake Forbes
Digital Imaging Manager - Chris Buford
Pre-Press Manager - Antonio DePietro
Production Managers - Jennifer Miller and Mutsumi Miyazaki
Art Director - Matt Alford
Managing Editor - Jill Freshney
VP of Production - Ron Klamert
President and C.O.O. - John Parker
Publisher and C.E.O. - Stuart Levy

A 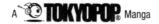 Manga

TOKYOPOP Inc.
5900 Wilshire Blvd. Suite 2000
Los Angeles, CA 90036

E-mail: info@TOKYOPOP.com
Come visit us online at www.TOKYOPOP.com

ISBN: 1-59182-006-5

First TOKYOPOP printing: October 2002
15 14 13 12 11 10 9 8 7 6
Printed in the USA

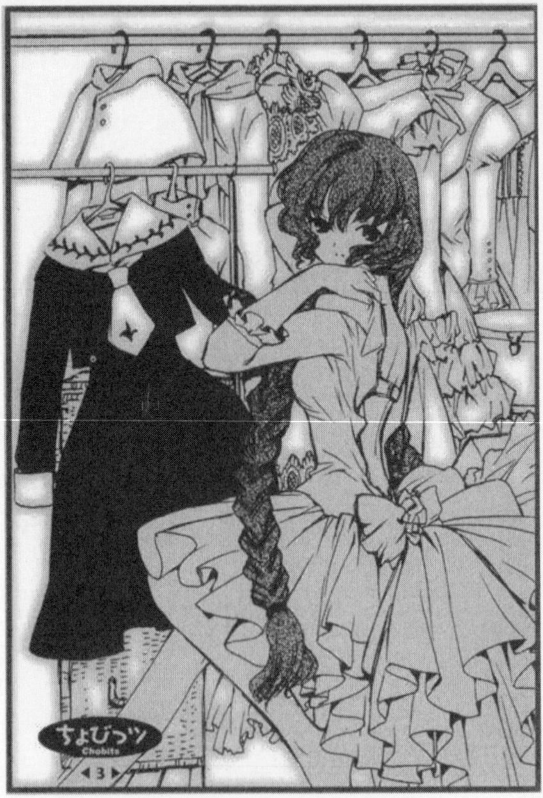
ちょびっツ
Chobits
3

www.Contents.com

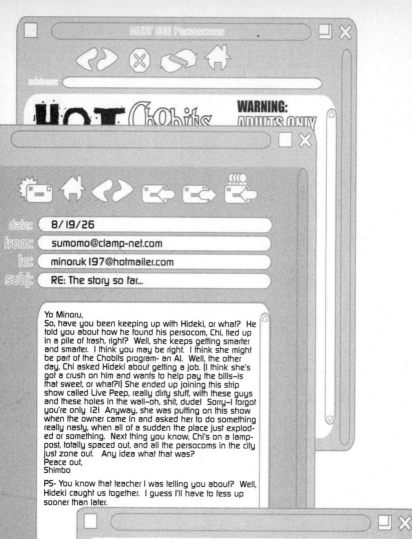

MUST SEE Persocoms

HOT Chobits

WARNING:

date: 8/19/26

from: sumomo@clamp-net.com

to: minoruk197@hotmailer.com

subj: RE: The story so far...

Yo Minoru,
So, have you been keeping up with Hideki, or what? He told you about how he found his persocom, Chi, tied up in a pile of trash, right? Well, she keeps getting smarter and smarter. I think you may be right. I think she might be part of the Chobits program- an AI. Well, the other day, Chi asked Hideki about getting a job. (I think she's got a crush on him and wants to help pay the bills–is that sweet, or what?!) She ended up joining this strip show called Live Peep, really dirty stuff, with these guys and these holes in the wall–oh, shit, dude! Sorry–I forgot you're only 12! Anyway, she was putting on this show when the owner came in and asked her to do something really nasty, when all of a sudden the place just exploded or something. Next thing you know, Chi's on a lamp-post, totally spaced out, and all the persocoms in the city just zone out. Any idea what that was?
Peace out,
Shimbo

PS- You know that teacher I was telling you about? Well, Hideki caught us together. I guess I'll have to fess up sooner than later.

HOT XXX ACTION!
Real girls and persocoms NUDE, READY, and in your bedroom! FREE TRIAL!

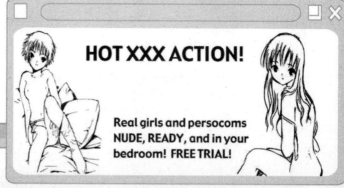

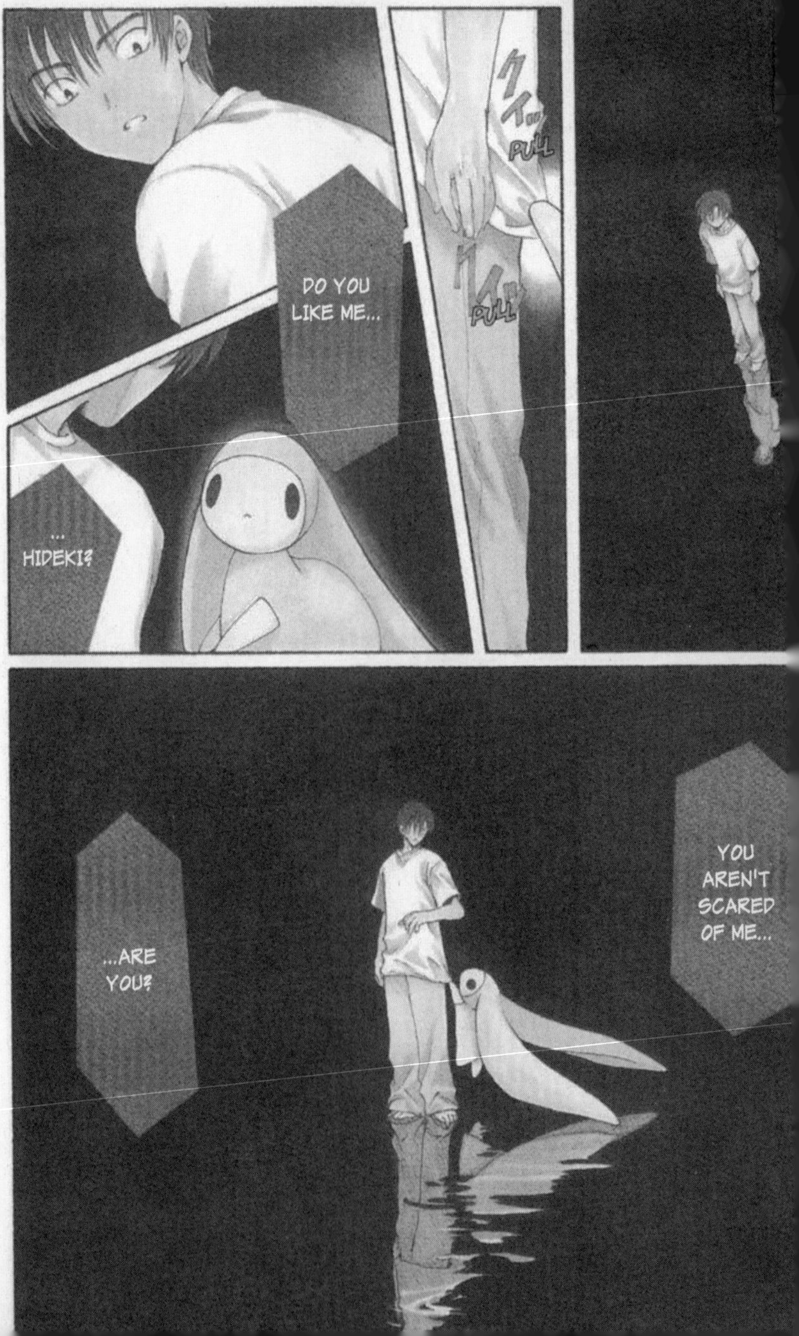
クイッ
PULL
クイッ
PULL
DO YOU LIKE ME...
...HIDEKI?
YOU AREN'T SCARED OF ME...
...ARE YOU?

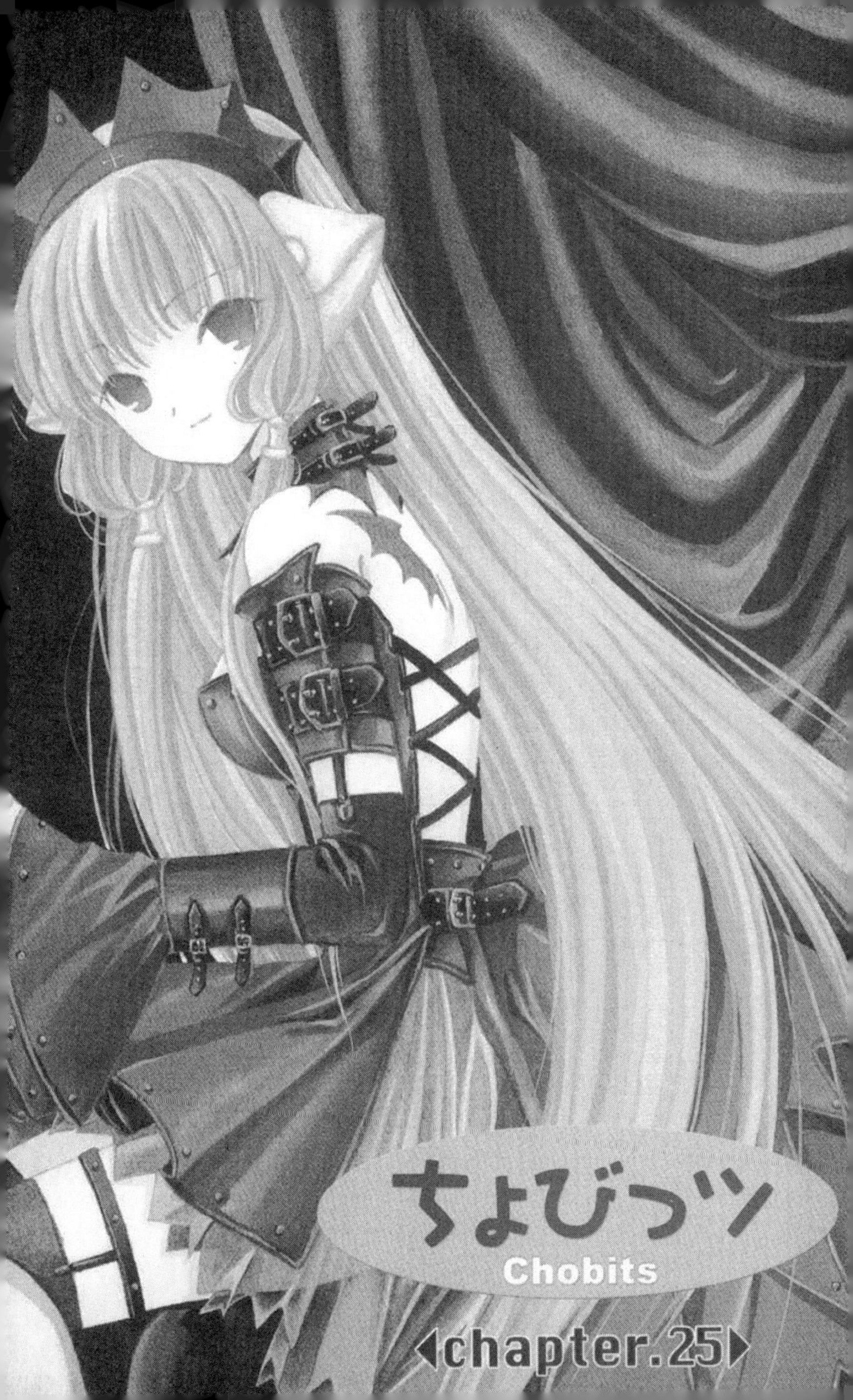
ちょびっツ
Chobits
chapter.25

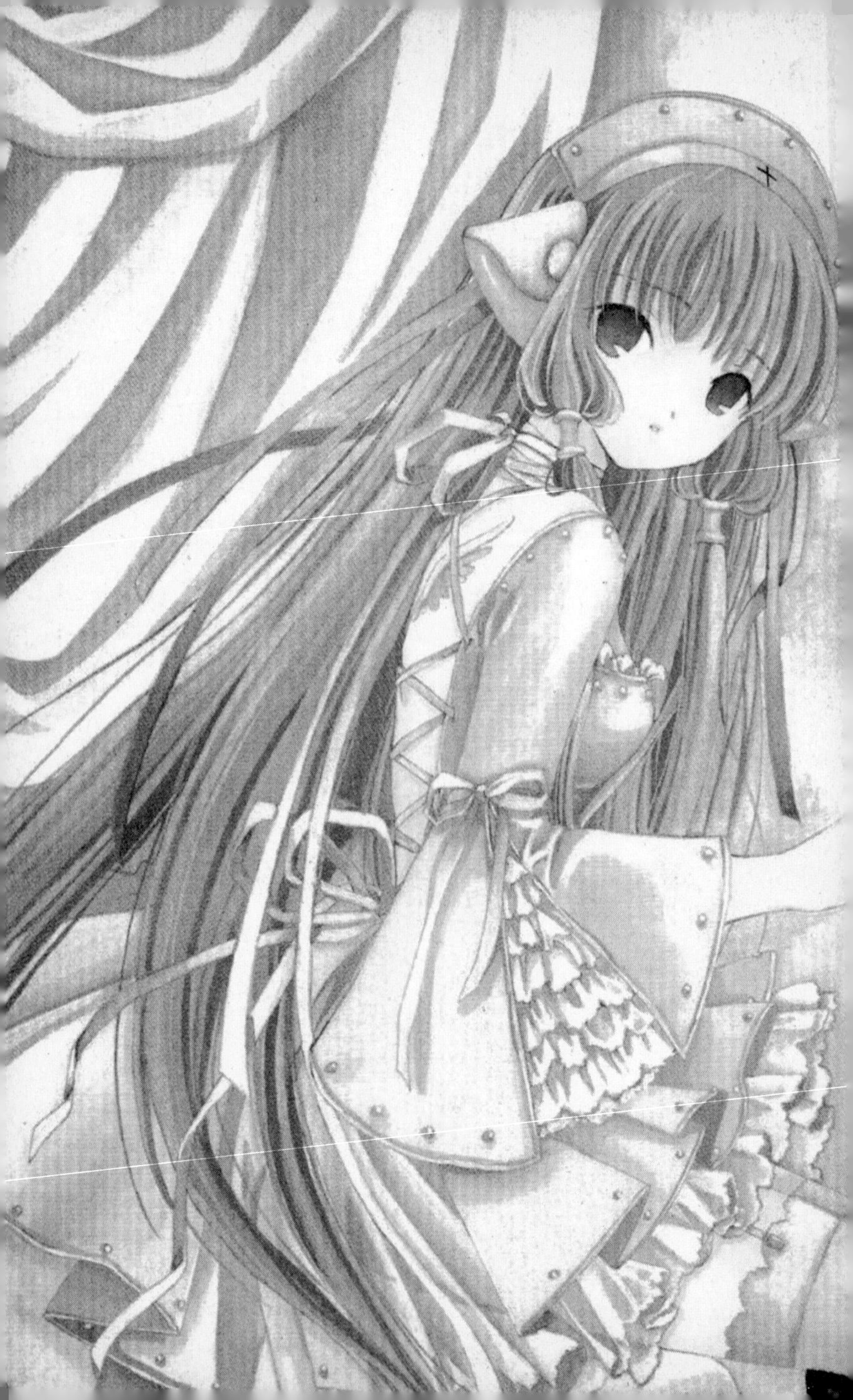

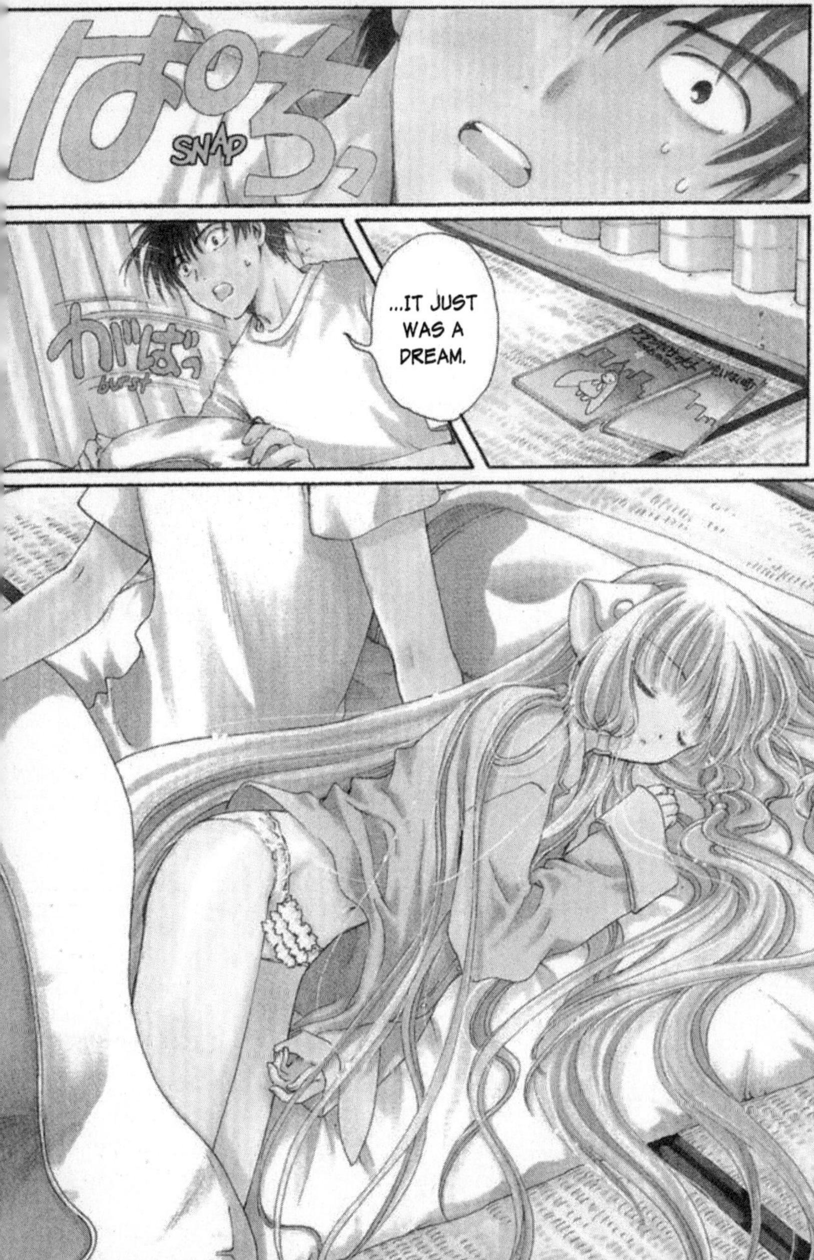
SNAP
...IT JUST WAS A DREAM.

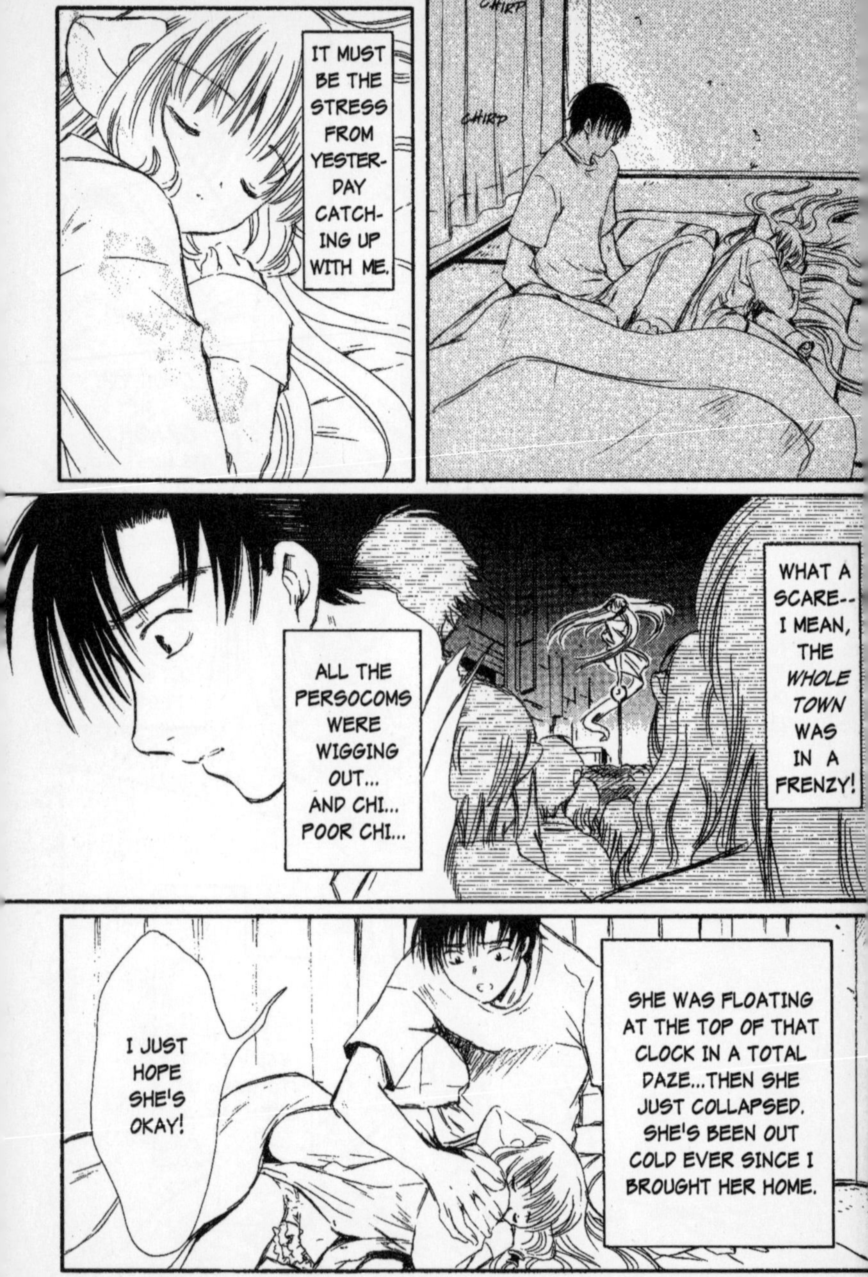
CHIRP
CHIRP
IT MUST BE THE STRESS FROM YESTER-DAY CATCH-ING UP WITH ME.
WHAT A SCARE-- I MEAN, THE *WHOLE TOWN* WAS IN A FRENZY!
ALL THE PERSOCOMS WERE WIGGING OUT... AND CHI... POOR CHI...
SHE WAS FLOATING AT THE TOP OF THAT CLOCK IN A TOTAL DAZE...THEN SHE JUST COLLAPSED. SHE'S BEEN OUT COLD EVER SINCE I BROUGHT HER HOME.
I JUST HOPE SHE'S OKAY!

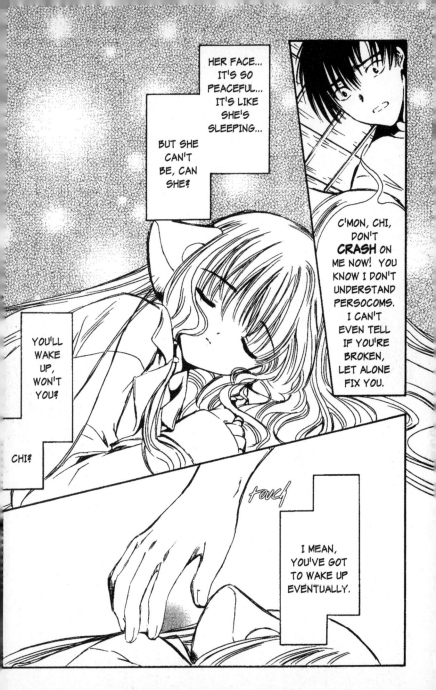

HER FACE... IT'S SO PEACEFUL... IT'S LIKE SHE'S SLEEPING...

BUT SHE CAN'T BE, CAN SHE?

C'MON, CHI, DON'T **CRASH** ON ME NOW! YOU KNOW I DON'T UNDERSTAND PERSOCOMS. I CAN'T EVEN TELL IF YOU'RE BROKEN, LET ALONE FIX YOU.

YOU'LL WAKE UP, WON'T YOU?

CHI?

touch

I MEAN, YOU'VE GOT TO WAKE UP EVENTUALLY.

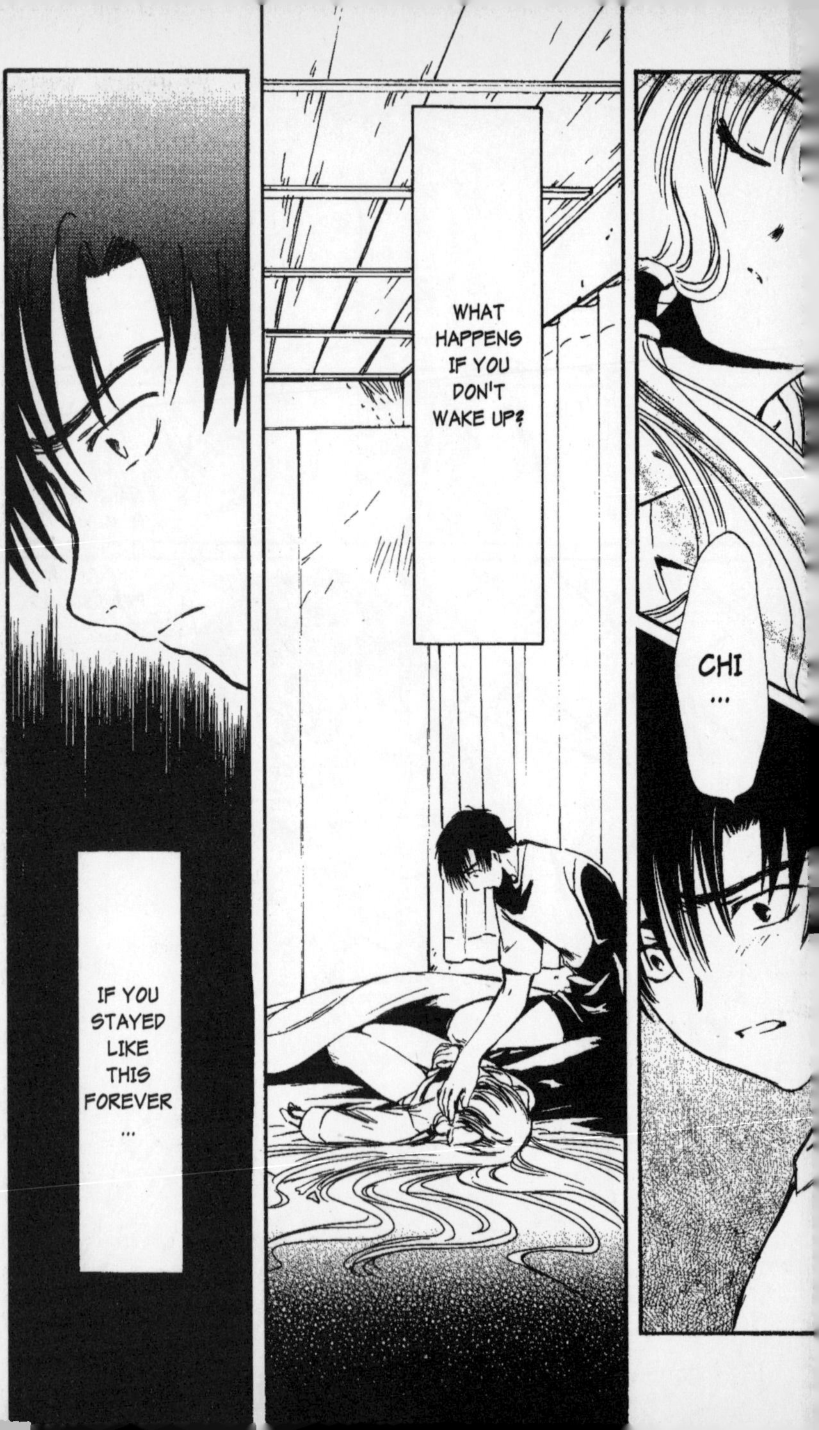
CHI ...
WHAT HAPPENS IF YOU DON'T WAKE UP?
IF YOU STAYED LIKE THIS FOREVER ...

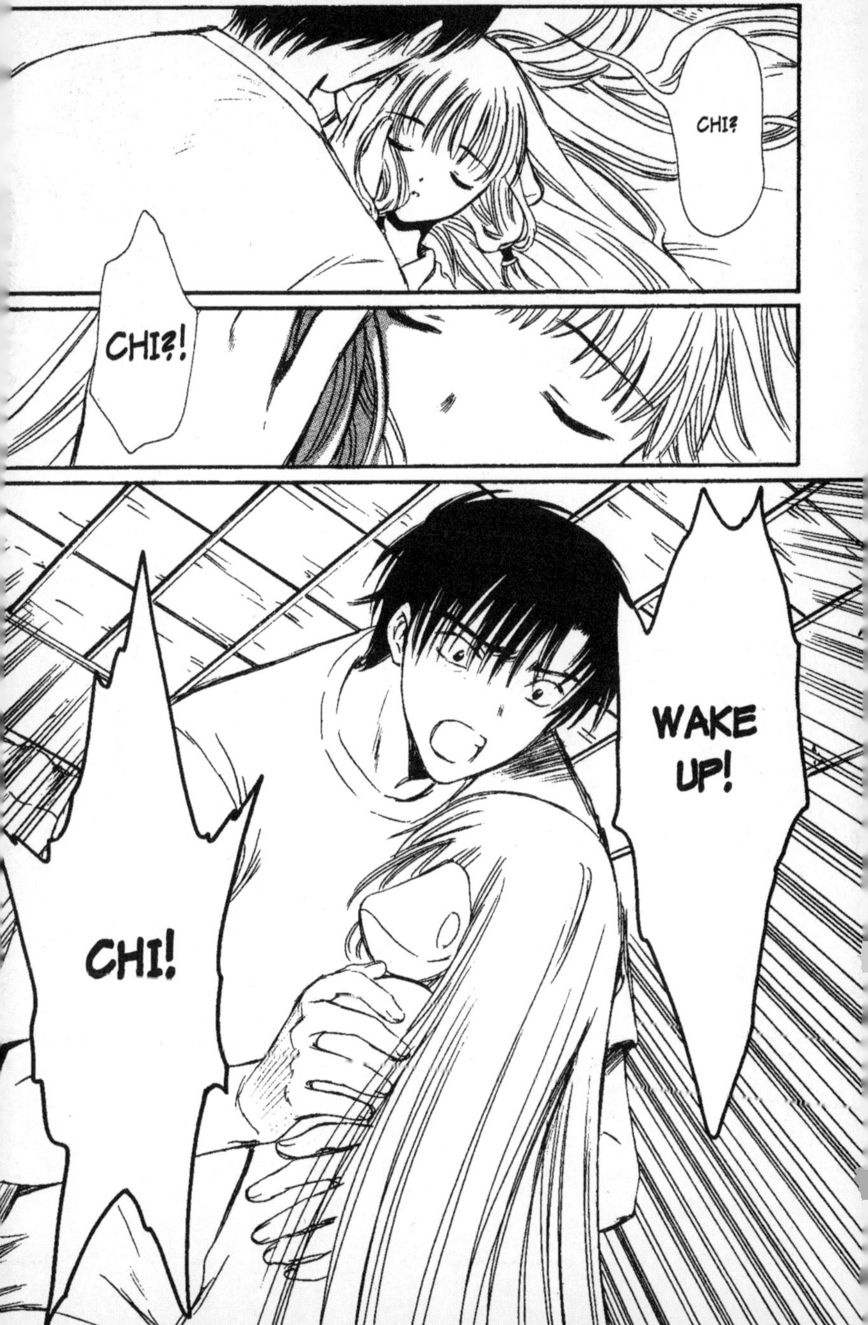
CHI?
CHI?!
WAKE UP!
CHI!

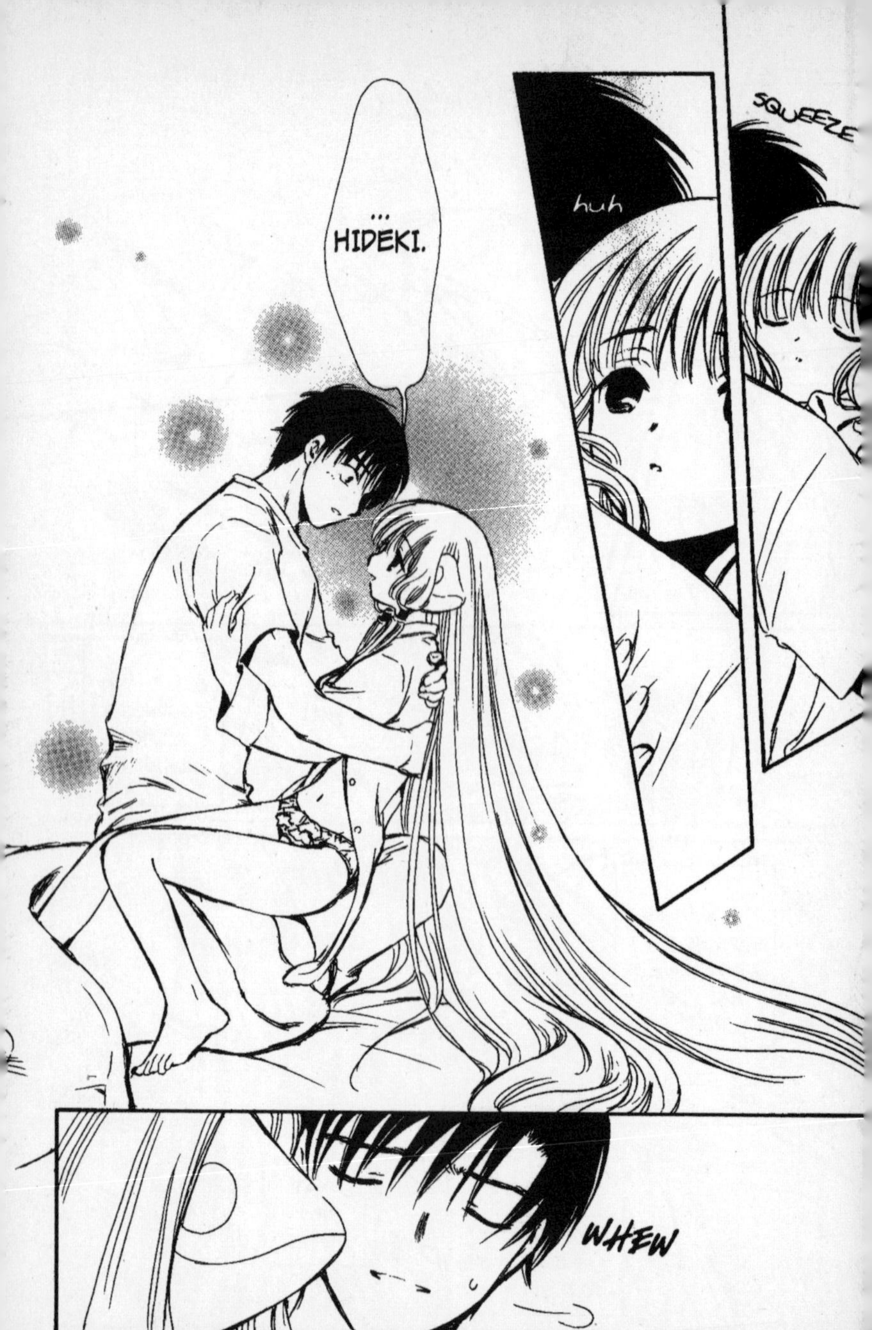
SQUEEZE
huh
... HIDEKI.
WHEW

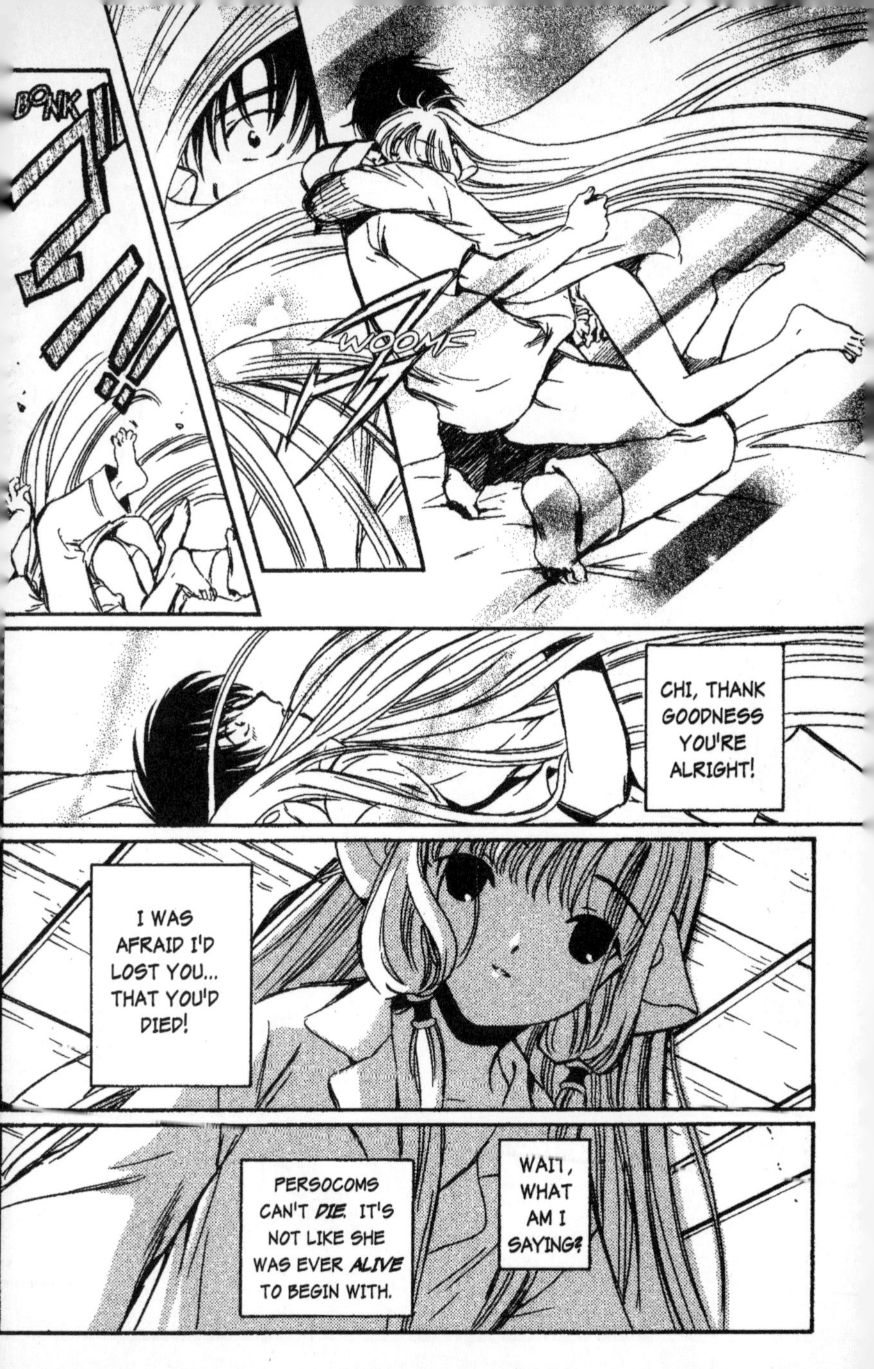
WOOMF
BONK
CHI, THANK GOODNESS YOU'RE ALRIGHT!
I WAS AFRAID I'D LOST YOU... THAT YOU'D DIED!
WAIT, WHAT AM I SAYING?
PERSOCOMS CAN'T *DIE*. IT'S NOT LIKE SHE WAS EVER *ALIVE* TO BEGIN WITH.

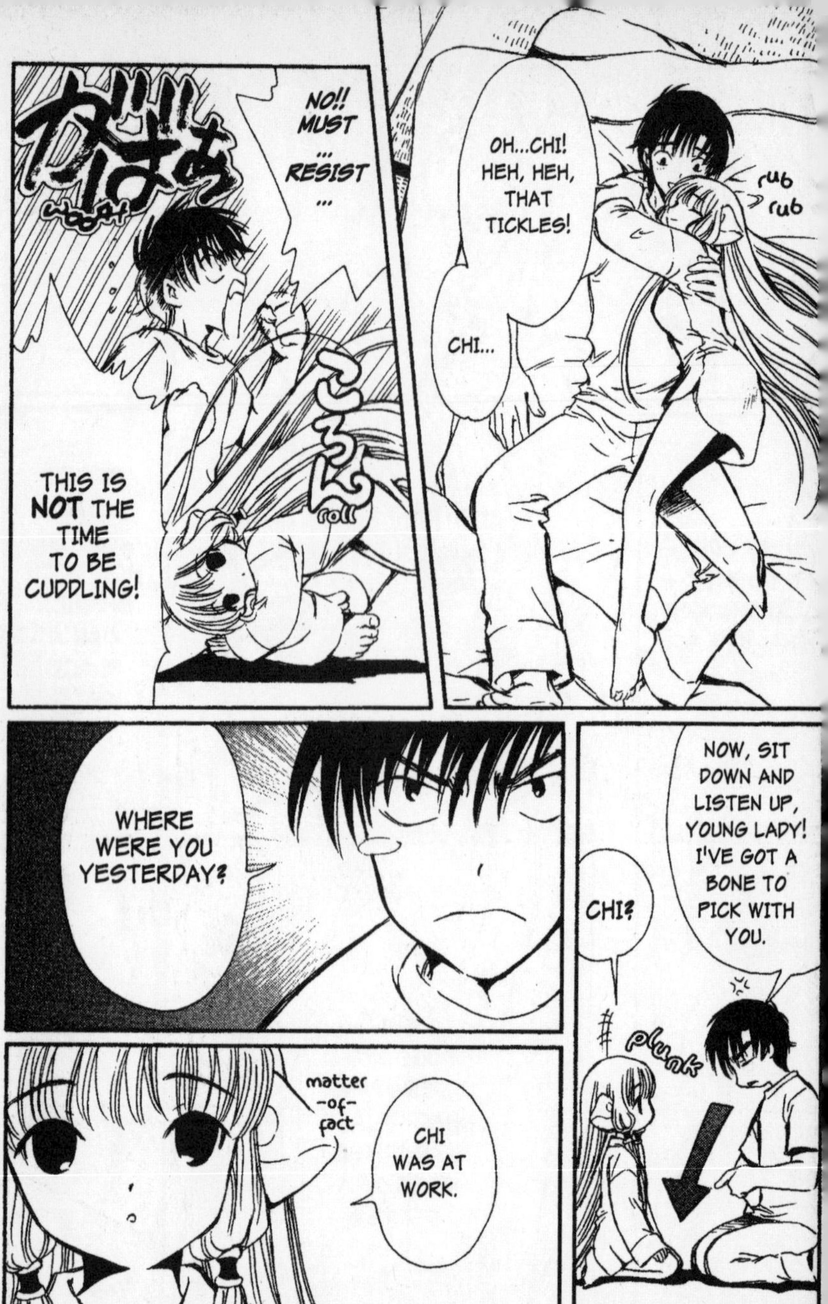
OH...CHI! HEH, HEH, THAT TICKLES!
rub rub
CHI...
NO!! MUST ... RESIST ...
がばぁ
THIS IS NOT THE TIME TO BE CUDDLING!
ころん
roll
NOW, SIT DOWN AND LISTEN UP, YOUNG LADY! I'VE GOT A BONE TO PICK WITH YOU.
CHI?
plunk
WHERE WERE YOU YESTERDAY?
matter-of-fact
CHI WAS AT WORK.

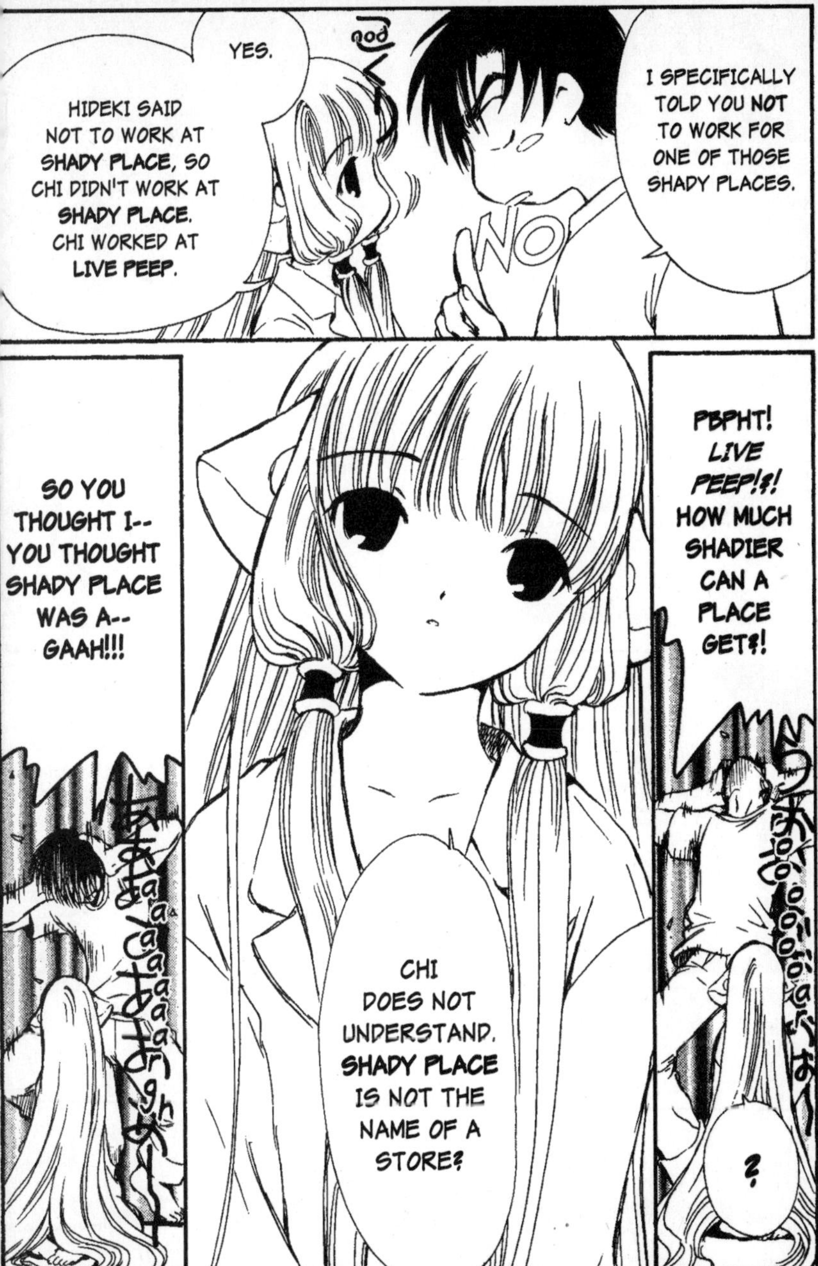
I SPECIFICALLY TOLD YOU NOT TO WORK FOR ONE OF THOSE SHADY PLACES.
NO
nod
YES.
HIDEKI SAID NOT TO WORK AT SHADY PLACE, SO CHI DIDN'T WORK AT SHADY PLACE. CHI WORKED AT LIVE PEEP.
PBPHT! LIVE PEEP!?! HOW MUCH SHADIER CAN A PLACE GET?!
?
CHI DOES NOT UNDERSTAND. SHADY PLACE IS NOT THE NAME OF A STORE?
SO YOU THOUGHT I-- YOU THOUGHT SHADY PLACE WAS A-- GAAH!!!

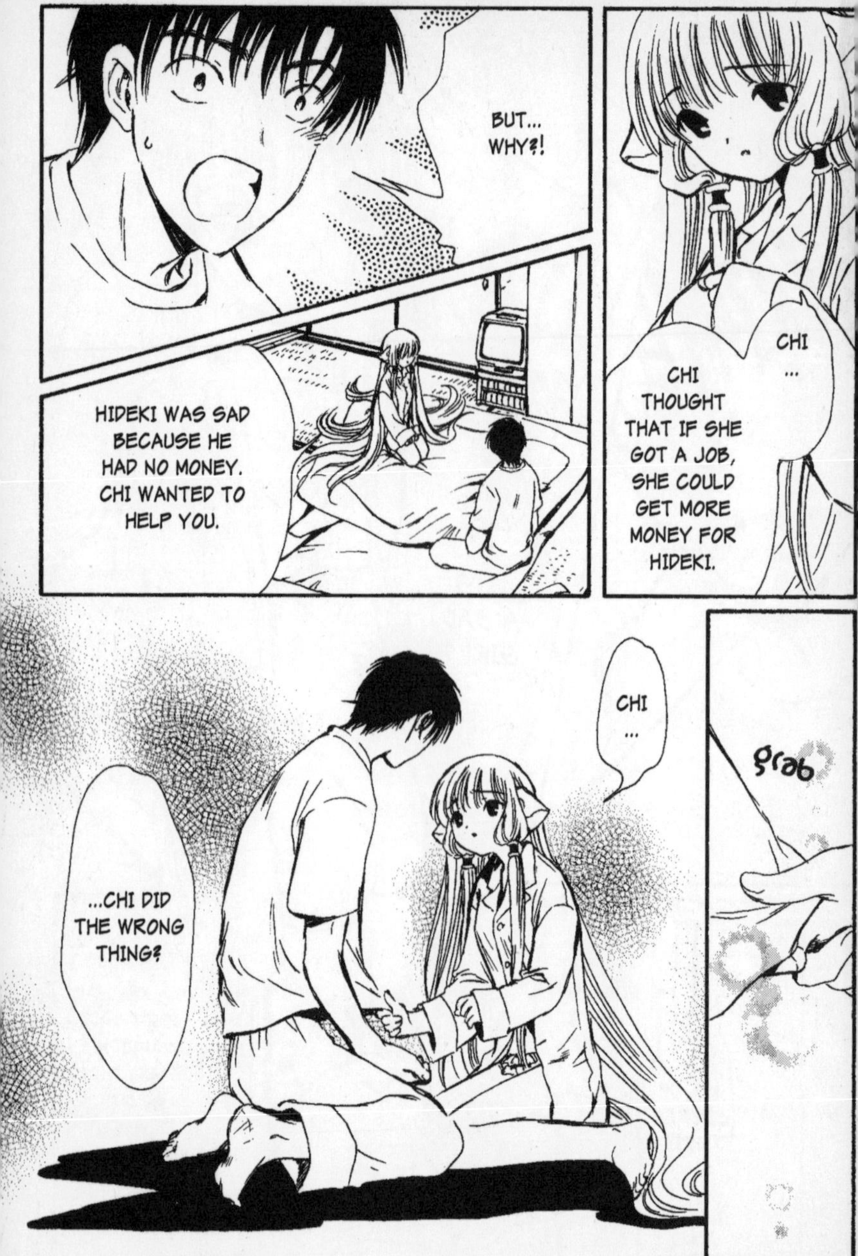
CHI ...
CHI THOUGHT THAT IF SHE GOT A JOB, SHE COULD GET MORE MONEY FOR HIDEKI.
BUT... WHY?!
HIDEKI WAS SAD BECAUSE HE HAD NO MONEY. CHI WANTED TO HELP YOU.
grab
CHI ...
...CHI DID THE WRONG THING?

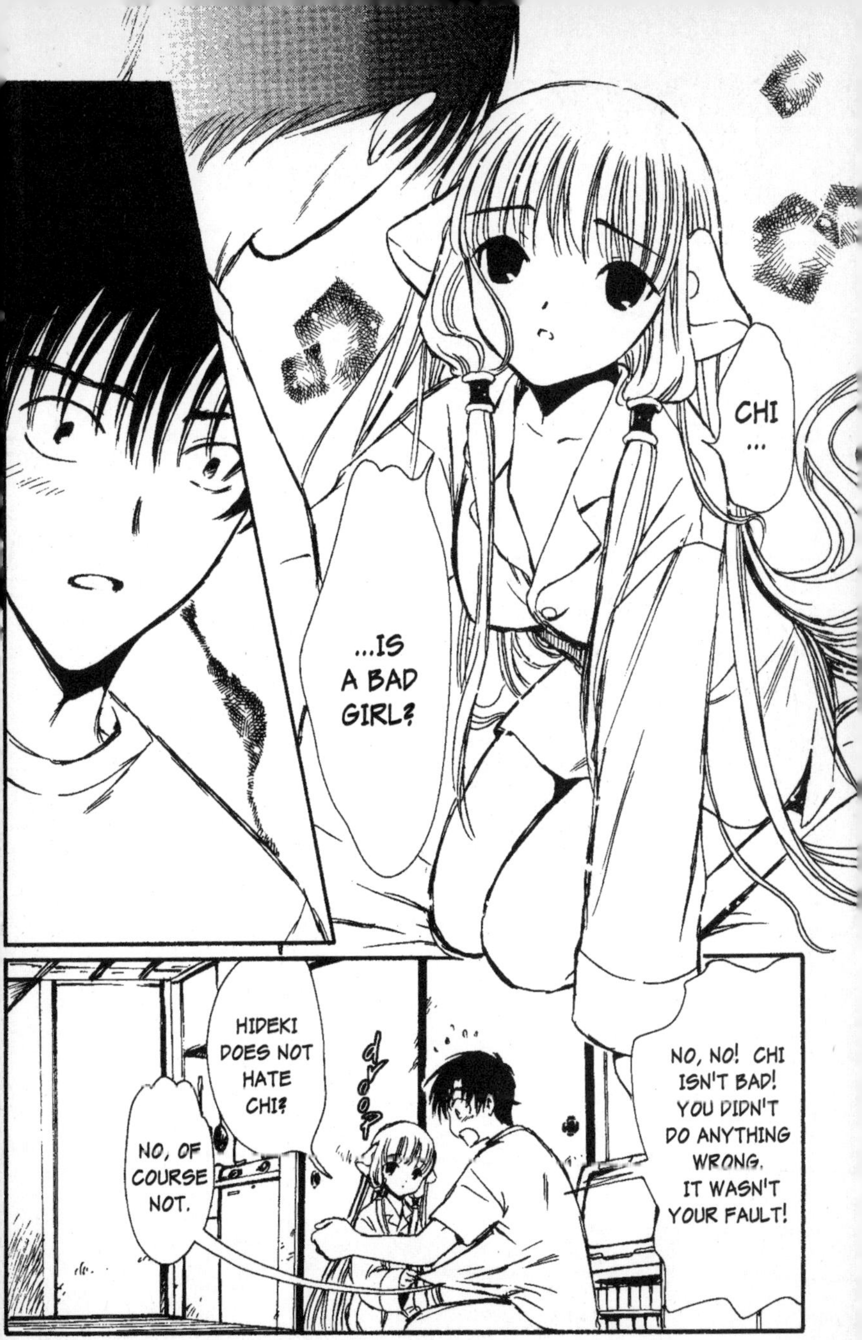
CHI ...
...IS A BAD GIRL?
NO, NO! CHI ISN'T BAD! YOU DIDN'T DO ANYTHING WRONG. IT WASN'T YOUR FAULT!
droop
HIDEKI DOES NOT HATE CHI?
NO, OF COURSE NOT.

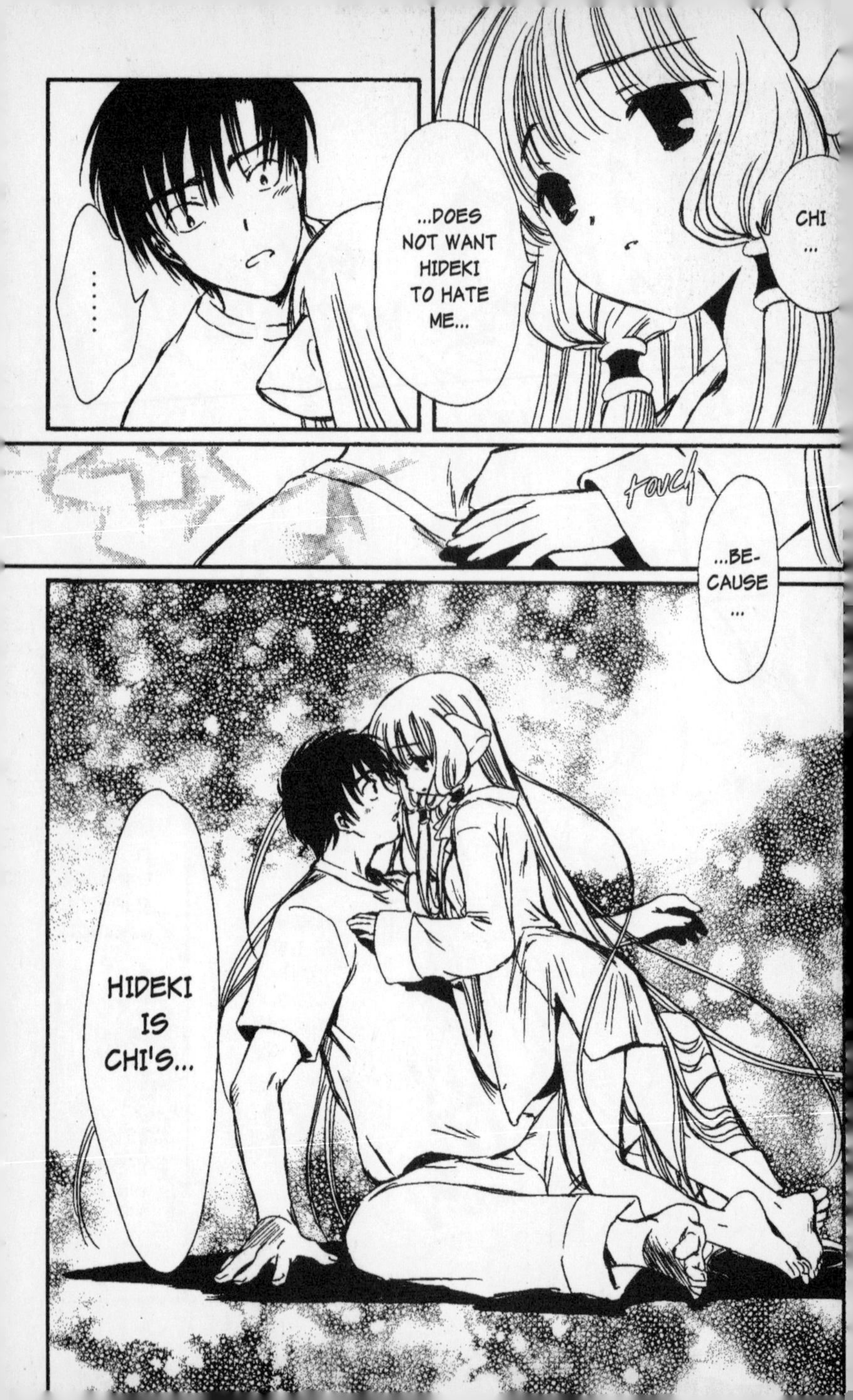
CHI ...
...DOES NOT WANT HIDEKI TO HATE ME...
......
touch
...BE-CAUSE ...
HIDEKI IS CHI'S...

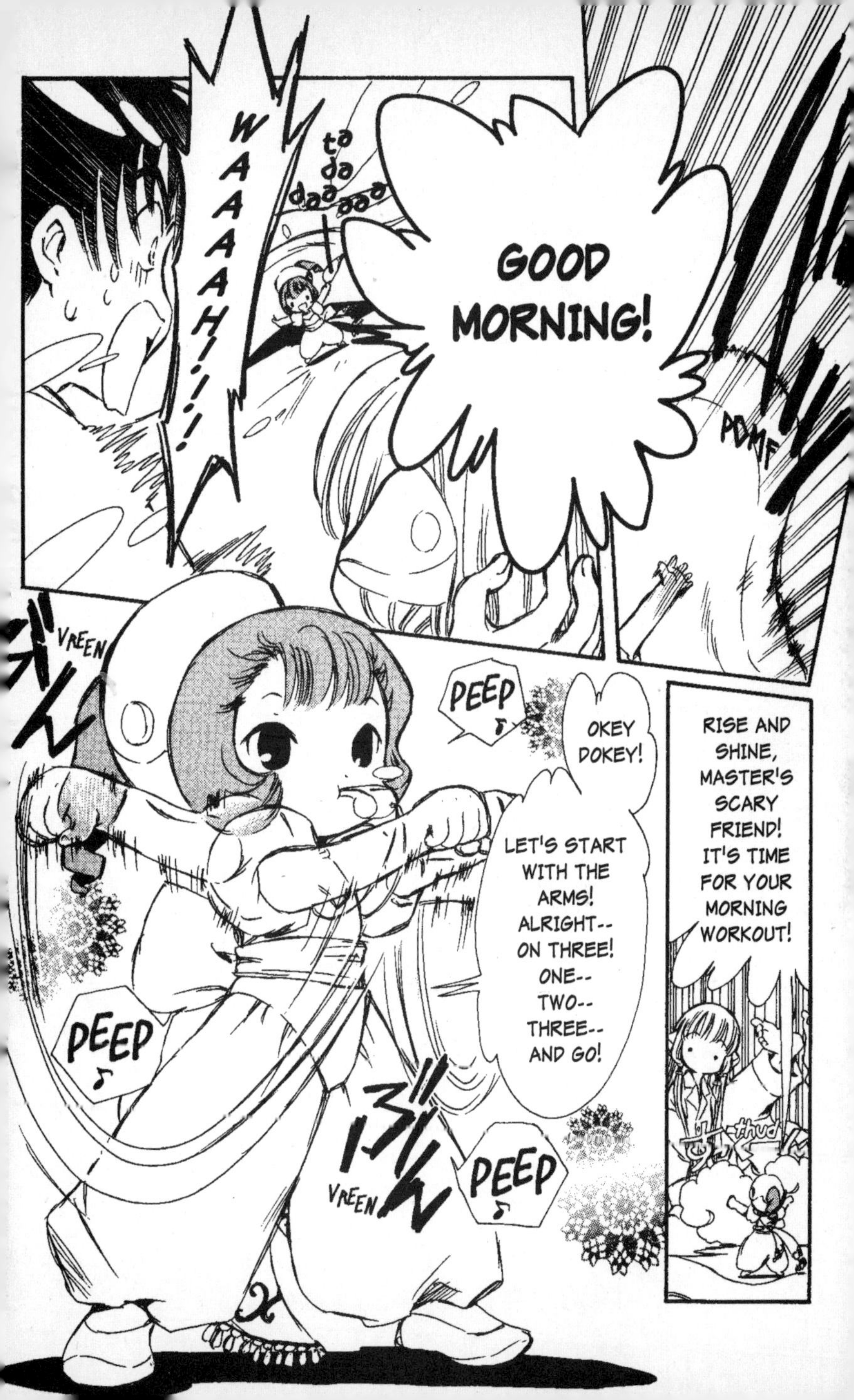
GOOD MORNING!
POMF
ta da da da da da
WAAAAAH!!!!!
RISE AND SHINE, MASTER'S SCARY FRIEND! IT'S TIME FOR YOUR MORNING WORKOUT!
thud
OKEY DOKEY!
PEEP
LET'S START WITH THE ARMS! ALRIGHT-- ON THREE! ONE-- TWO-- THREE-- AND GO!
VREEN
PEEP
PEEP
VREEN

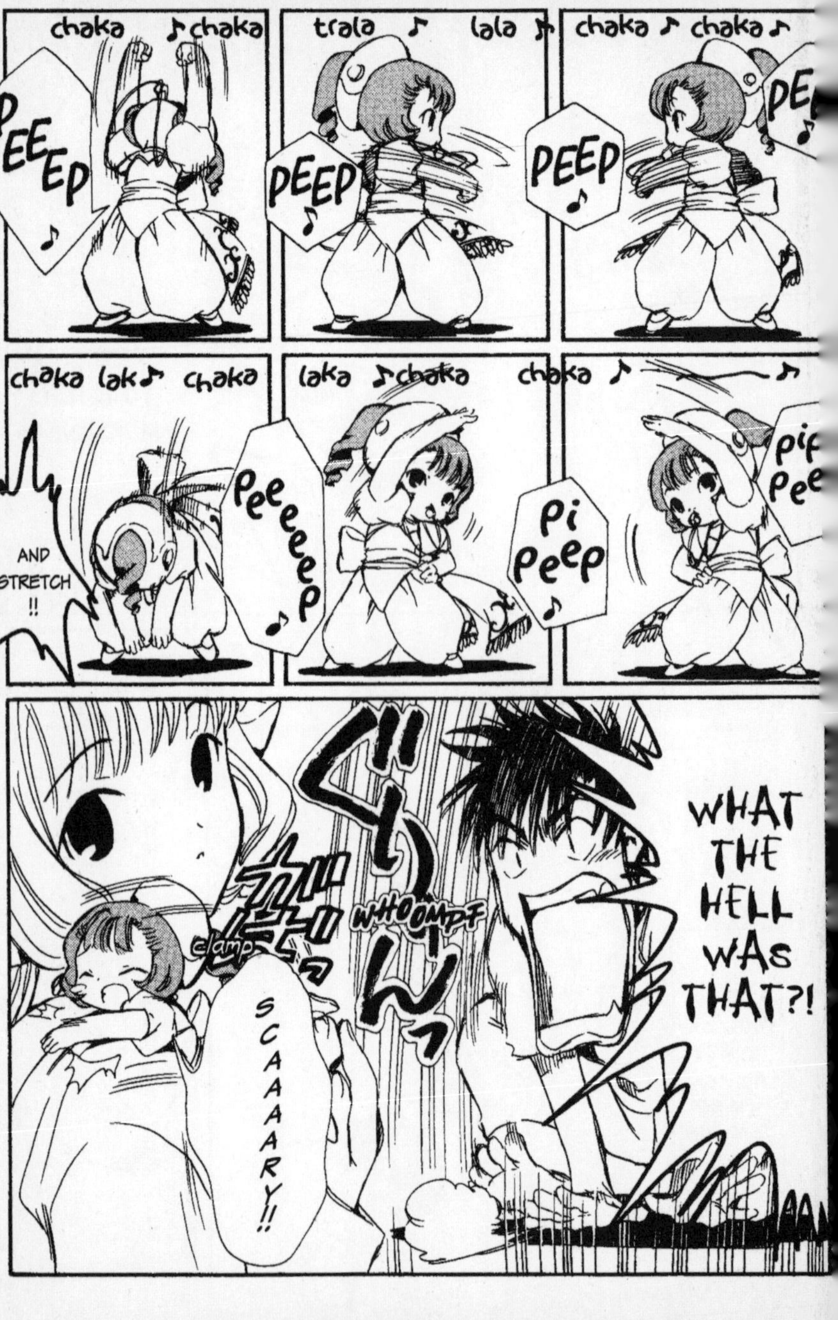
chaka ♪ chaka ♪
PE
PEEP ♪
trala ♪ lala ♪
PEEP ♪
chaka ♪chaka
PEEEP ♪
chaka ♪ ♪
pi pee
pi peep ♪
laka ♪chaka
Peeeeeep ♪
chaka lak♪ chaka
AND STRETCH !!
WHAT THE HELL WAS THAT?!
WHOOMPF
clamp
SCAAAARY!!

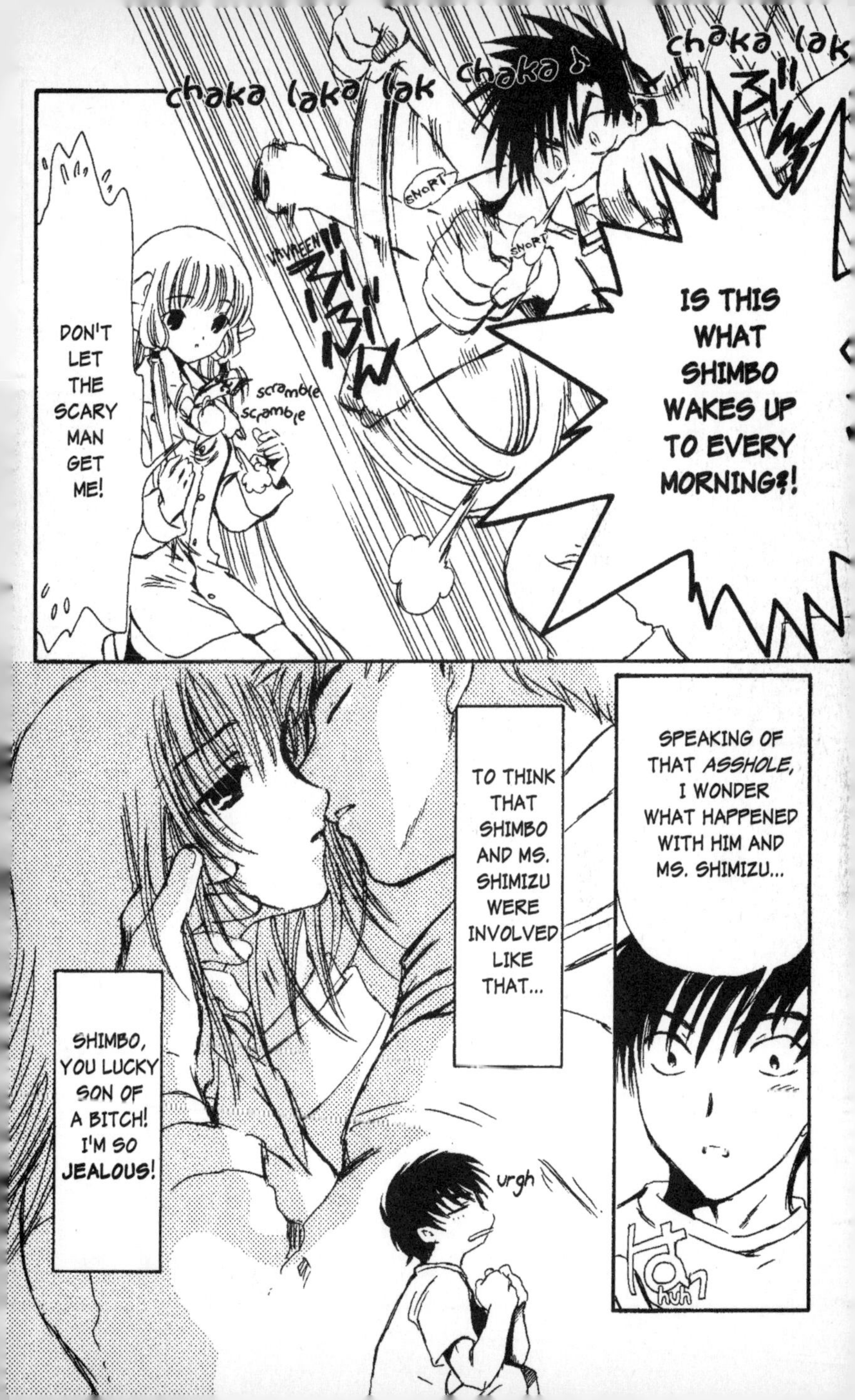
chaka lak
chaka laka lak chaka ♪
IS THIS WHAT SHIMBO WAKES UP TO EVERY MORNING?!
SNORT
SNORT
scramble scramble
DON'T LET THE SCARY MAN GET ME!
SPEAKING OF THAT *ASSHOLE*, I WONDER WHAT HAPPENED WITH HIM AND MS. SHIMIZU...
huh
TO THINK THAT SHIMBO AND MS. SHIMIZU WERE INVOLVED LIKE THAT...
urgh
SHIMBO, YOU LUCKY SON OF A BITCH! I'M SO **JEALOUS!**

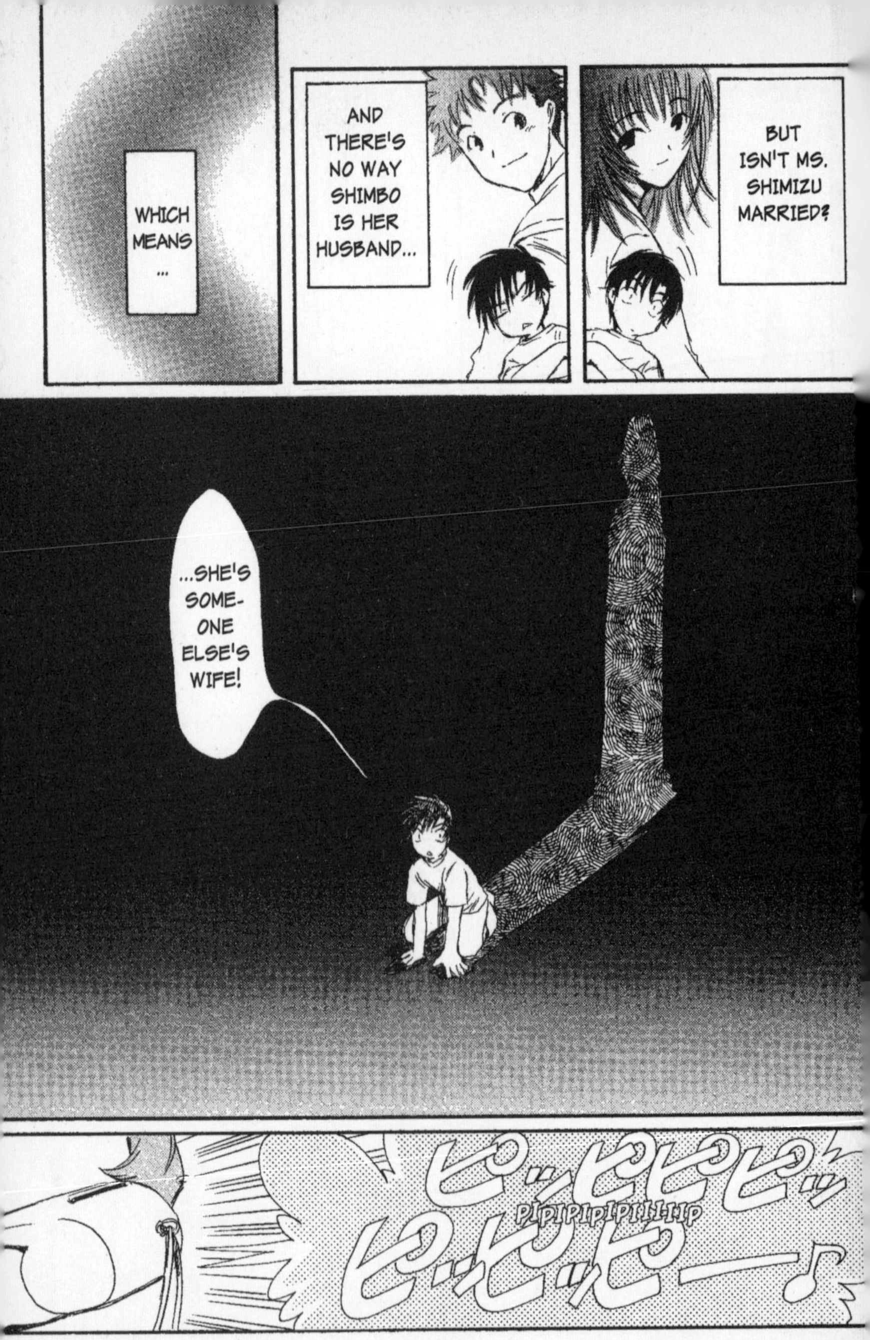
BUT ISN'T MS. SHIMIZU MARRIED?
AND THERE'S NO WAY SHIMBO IS HER HUSBAND...
WHICH MEANS ...
...SHE'S SOME-ONE ELSE'S WIFE!
ピッ、ピピピピッ
PIPIPIPIPIIIIIP
ピッピッピー♪

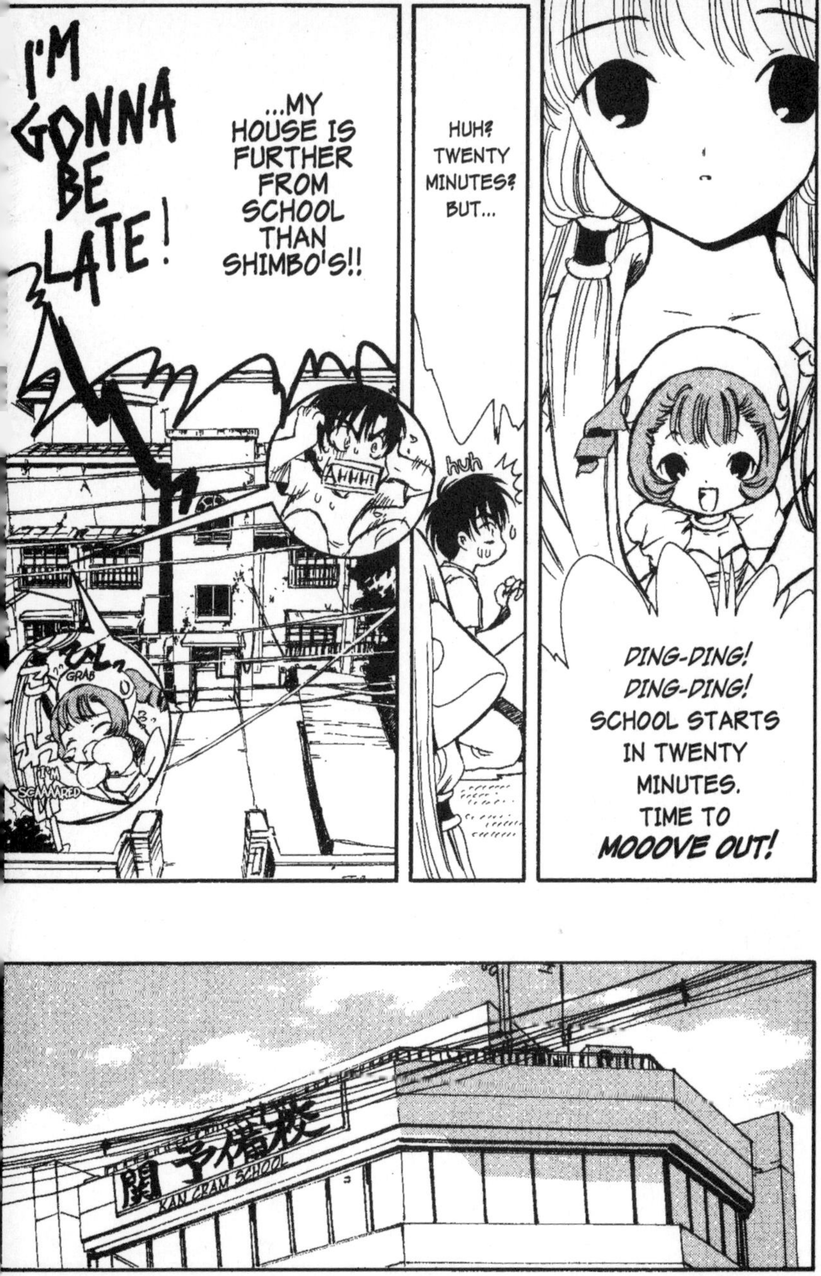
DING-DING! DING-DING! SCHOOL STARTS IN TWENTY MINUTES. TIME TO MOOOVE OUT!
HUH? TWENTY MINUTES? BUT...
huh
...MY HOUSE IS FURTHER FROM SCHOOL THAN SHIMBO'S!!
I'M GONNA BE LATE!
AHHH!
GRAB
I'M SCAAARED
KAN CRAM SCHOOL

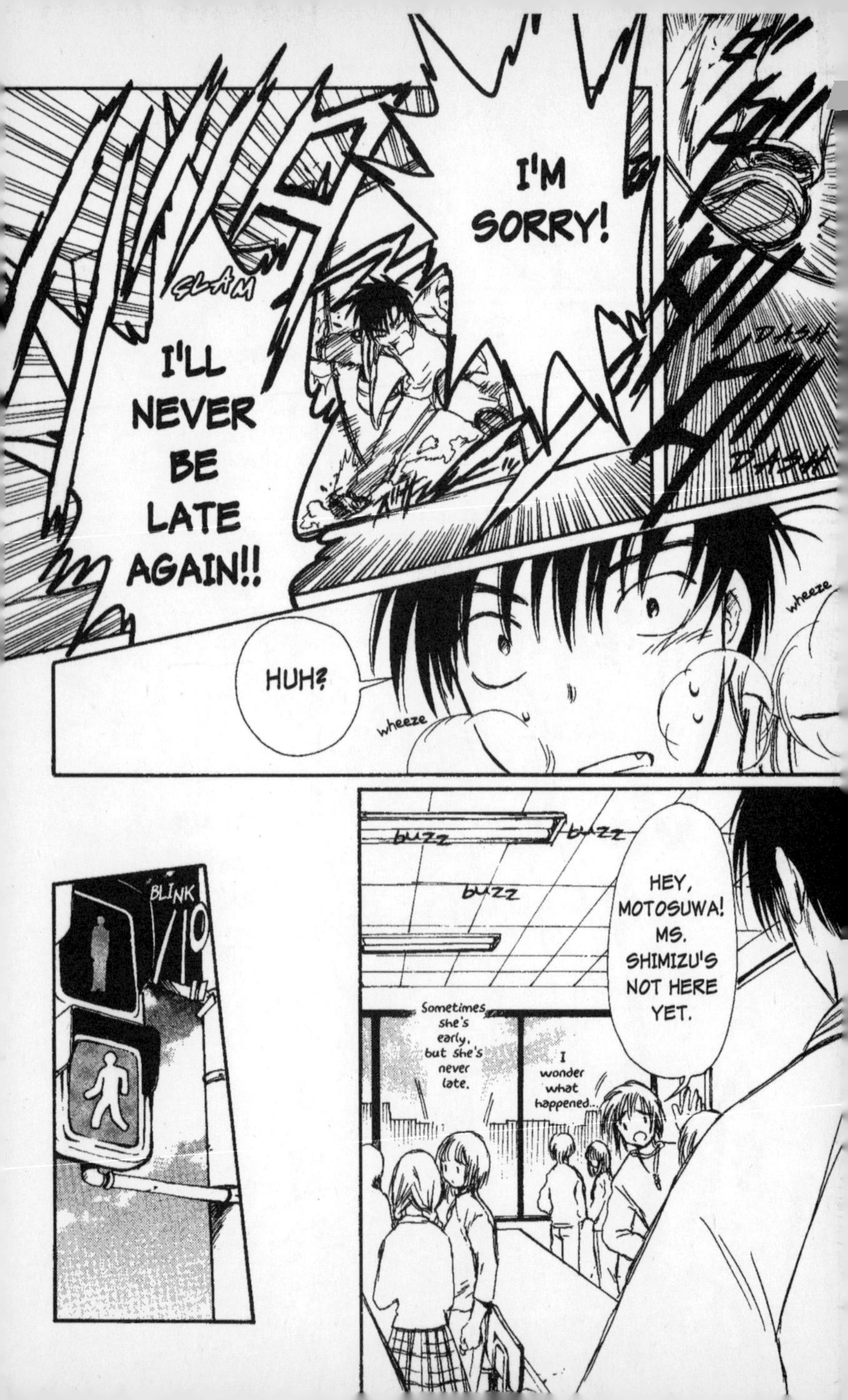
DASH
DASH
I'M SORRY!
SLAM
I'LL NEVER BE LATE AGAIN!!
wheeze
HUH?
wheeze
buzz
buzz
buzz
HEY, MOTOSUWA! MS. SHIMIZU'S NOT HERE YET.
I wonder what happened...
Sometimes she's early, but she's never late.
BLINK

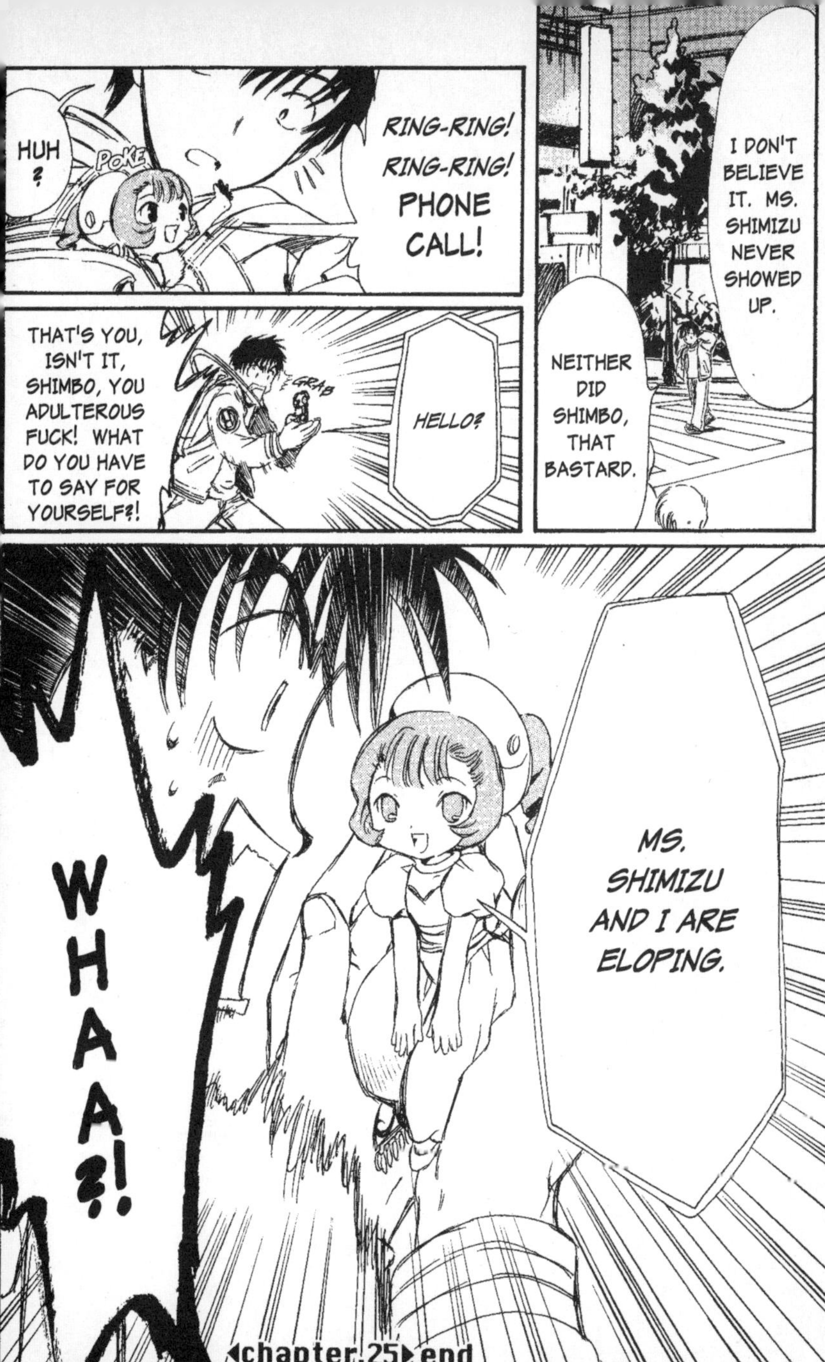
I DON'T BELIEVE IT. MS. SHIMIZU NEVER SHOWED UP.
NEITHER DID SHIMBO, THAT BASTARD.
RING-RING! RING-RING! PHONE CALL!
POKE
HUH?
HELLO?
GRAB
THAT'S YOU, ISN'T IT, SHIMBO, YOU ADULTEROUS FUCK! WHAT DO YOU HAVE TO SAY FOR YOURSELF?!
MS. SHIMIZU AND I ARE ELOPING.
WHAAA?!
◀chapter.25▶ end

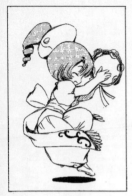
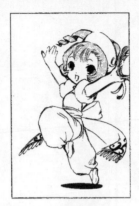
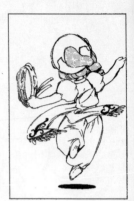
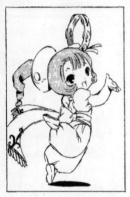
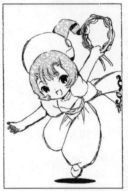
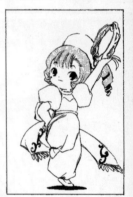

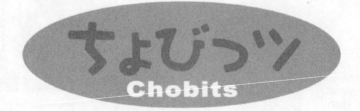

ちょびっツ
Chobits

◀chapter.26▶

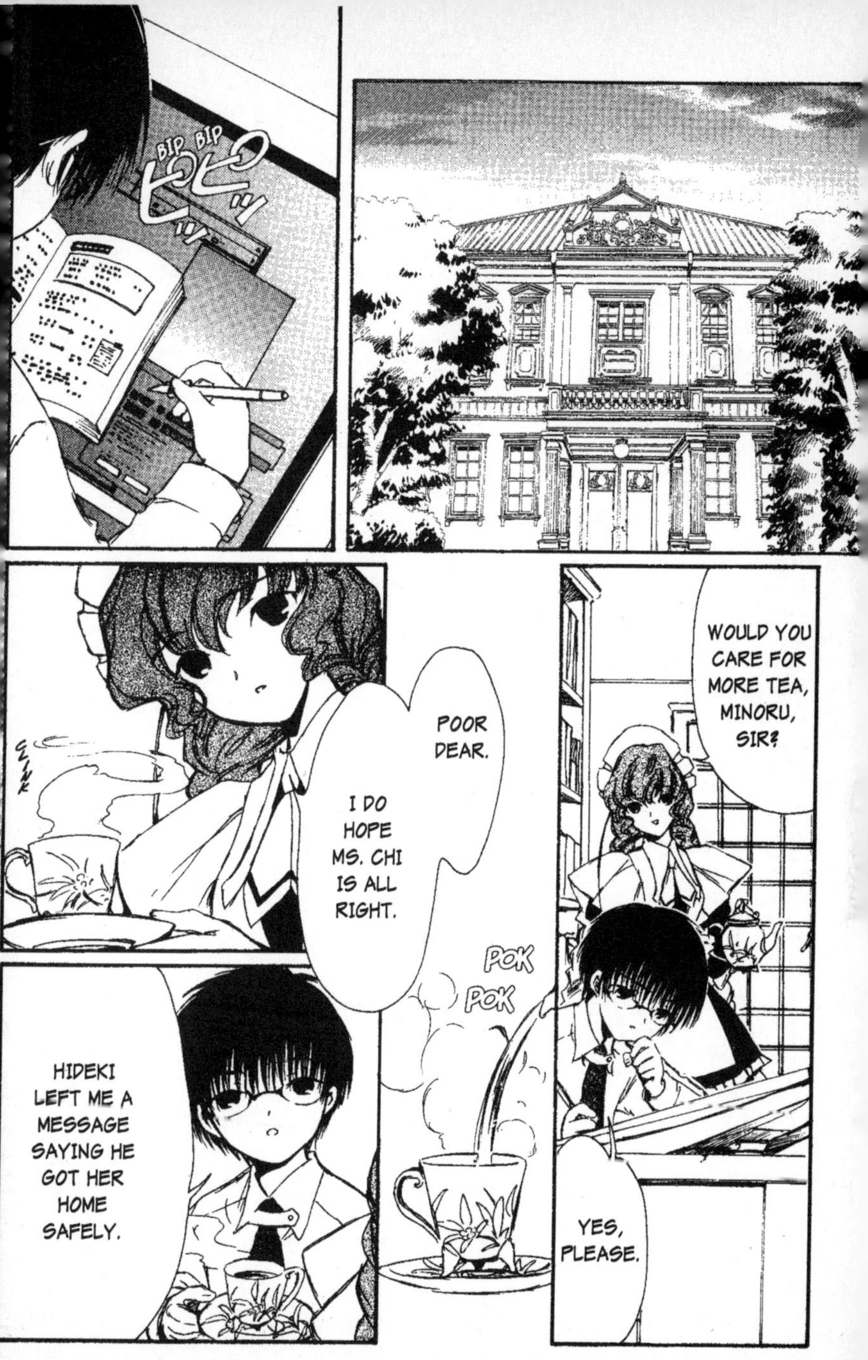
BIP BIP
WOULD YOU CARE FOR MORE TEA, MINORU, SIR?
POK POK
YES, PLEASE.
CLINK
POOR DEAR.
I DO HOPE MS. CHI IS ALL RIGHT.
HIDEKI LEFT ME A MESSAGE SAYING HE GOT HER HOME SAFELY.

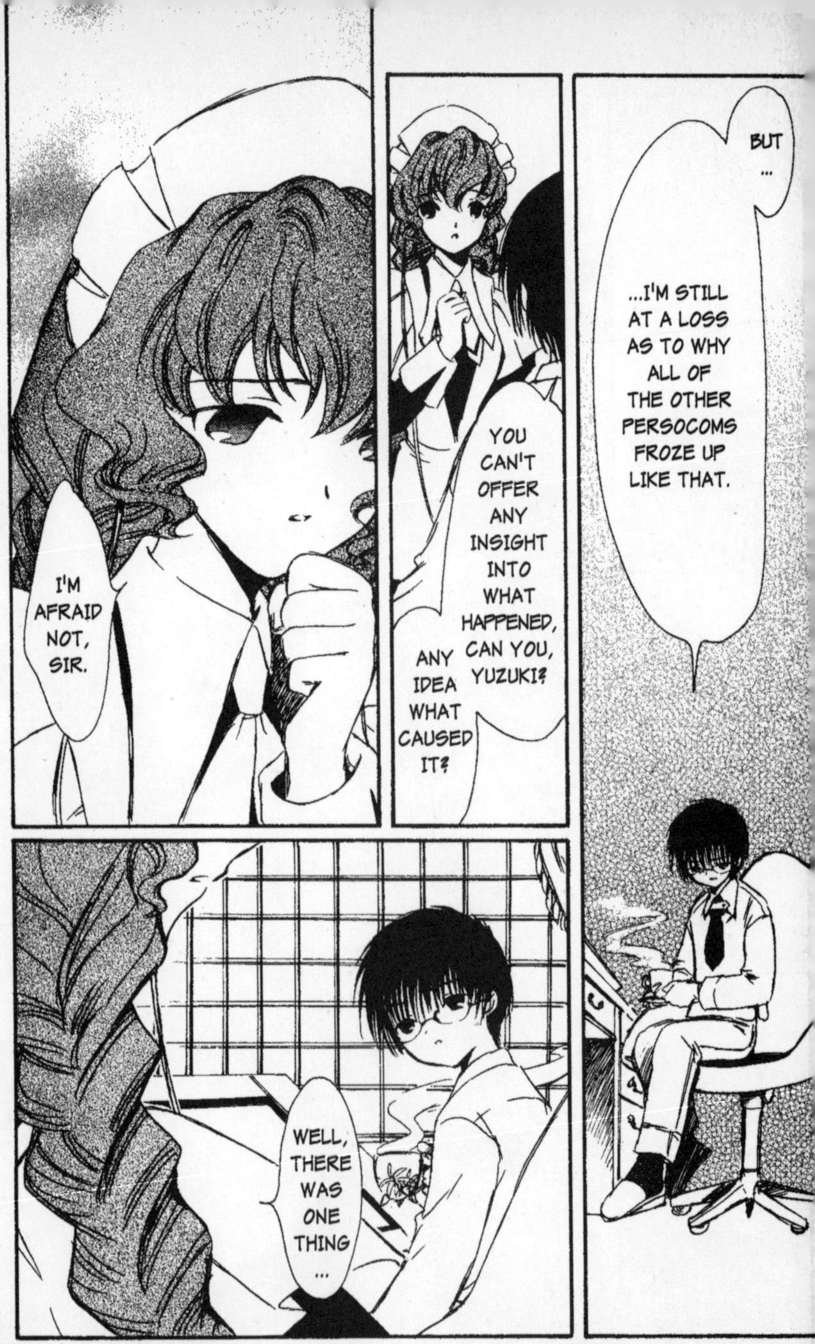
BUT ...
...I'M STILL AT A LOSS AS TO WHY ALL OF THE OTHER PERSOCOMS FROZE UP LIKE THAT.
YOU CAN'T OFFER ANY INSIGHT INTO WHAT HAPPENED, CAN YOU, YUZUKI?
ANY IDEA WHAT CAUSED IT?
I'M AFRAID NOT, SIR.
WELL, THERE WAS ONE THING ...

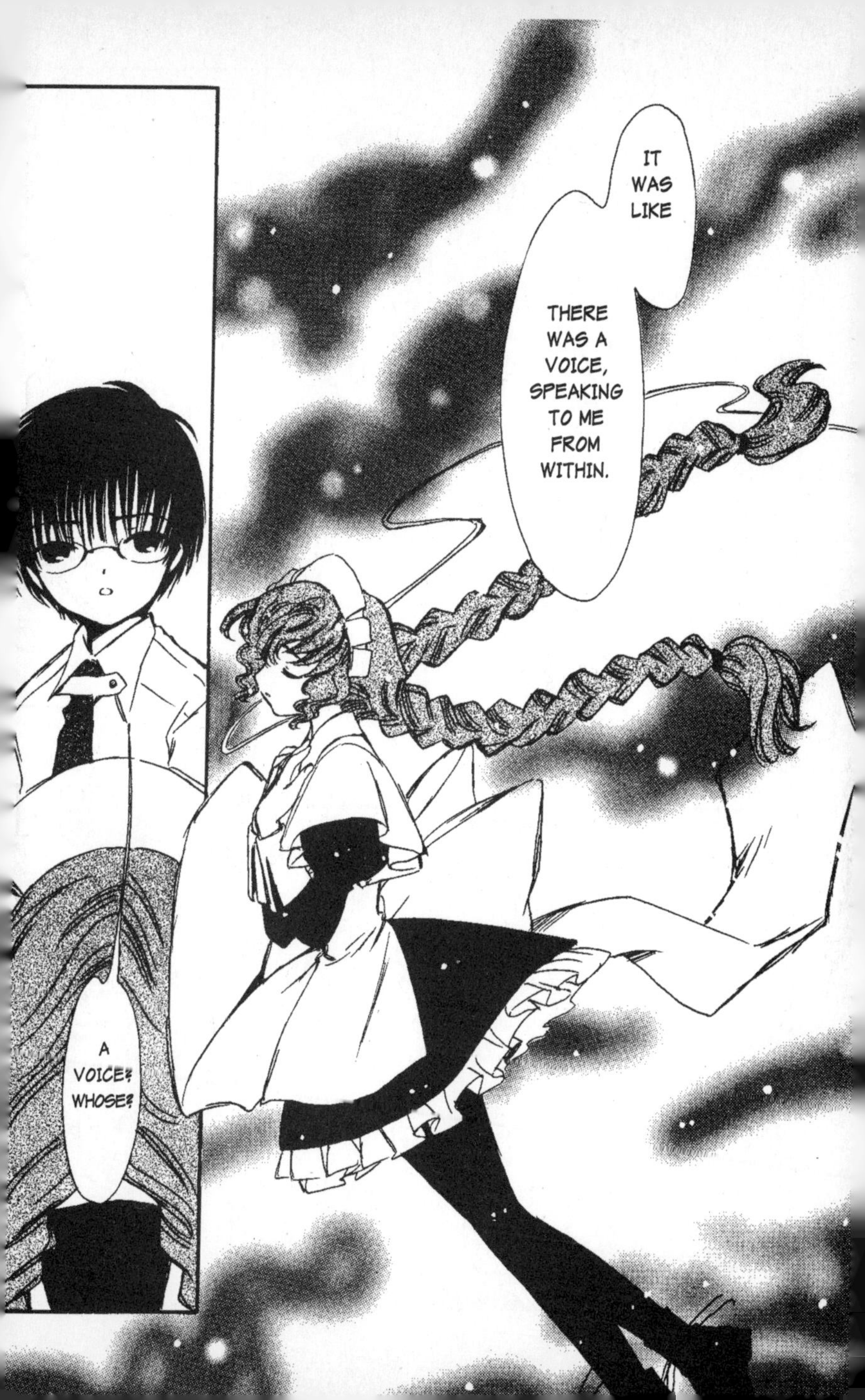
IT WAS LIKE THERE WAS A VOICE, SPEAKING TO ME FROM WITHIN.
A VOICE? WHOSE?

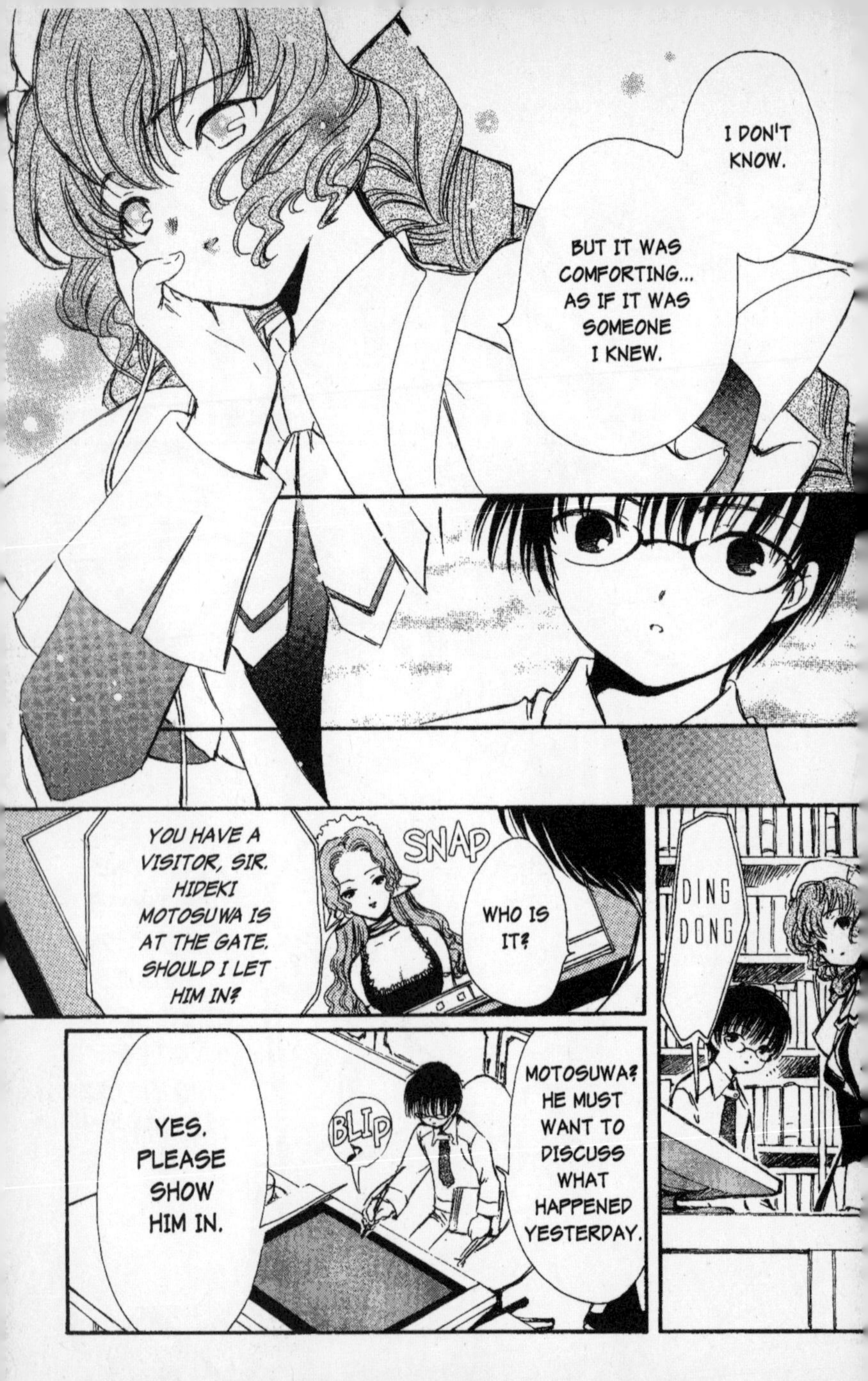
I DON'T KNOW.
BUT IT WAS COMFORTING... AS IF IT WAS SOMEONE I KNEW.
DING DONG
WHO IS IT?
SNAP
YOU HAVE A VISITOR, SIR. HIDEKI MOTOSUWA IS AT THE GATE. SHOULD I LET HIM IN?
MOTOSUWA? HE MUST WANT TO DISCUSS WHAT HAPPENED YESTERDAY.
BLIP
YES. PLEASE SHOW HIM IN.

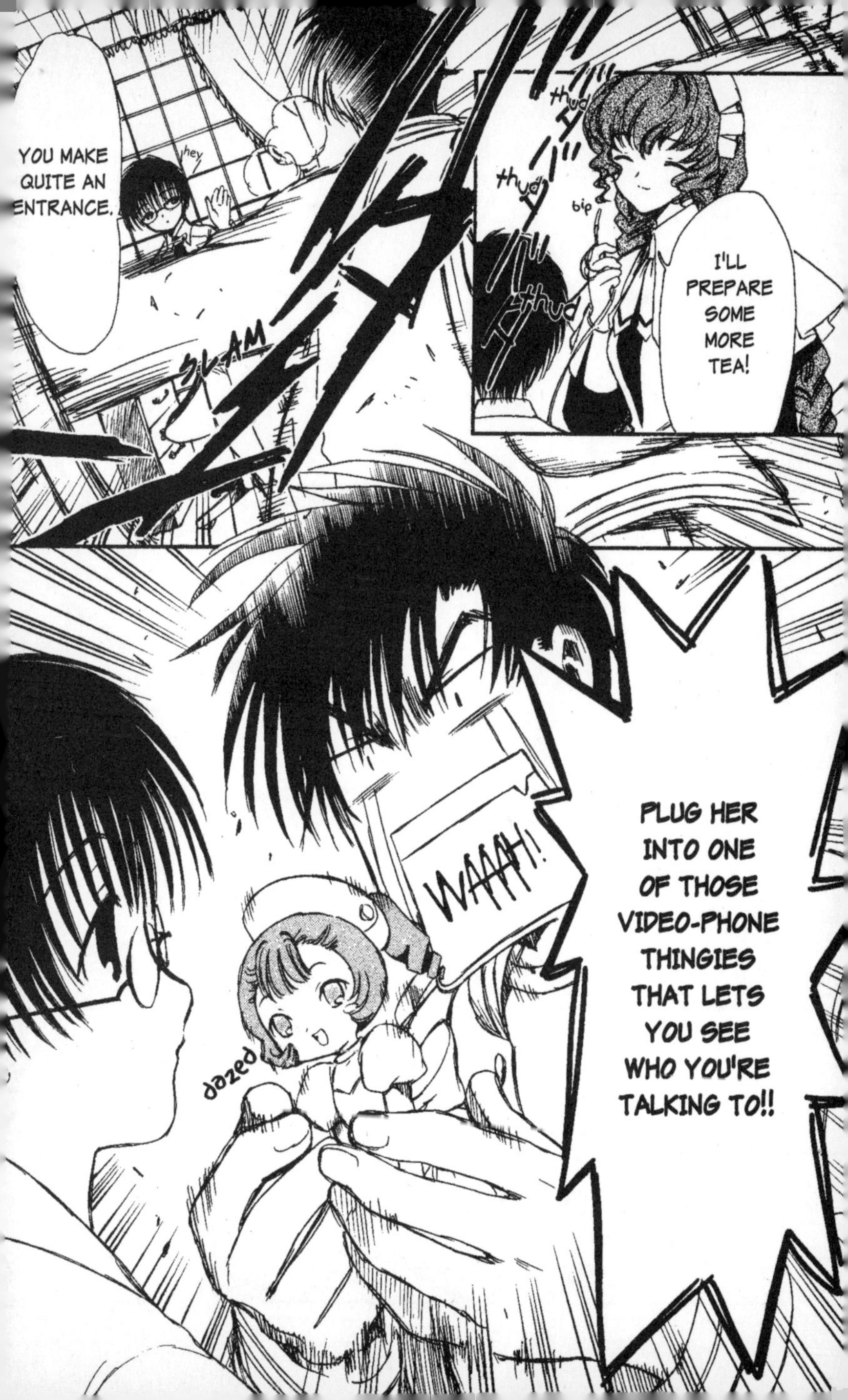
thud
thud
bip
thud
I'LL PREPARE SOME MORE TEA!
SLAM
hey
YOU MAKE QUITE AN ENTRANCE.
PLUG HER INTO ONE OF THOSE VIDEO-PHONE THINGIES THAT LETS YOU SEE WHO YOU'RE TALKING TO!!
WAAAH!
dazed

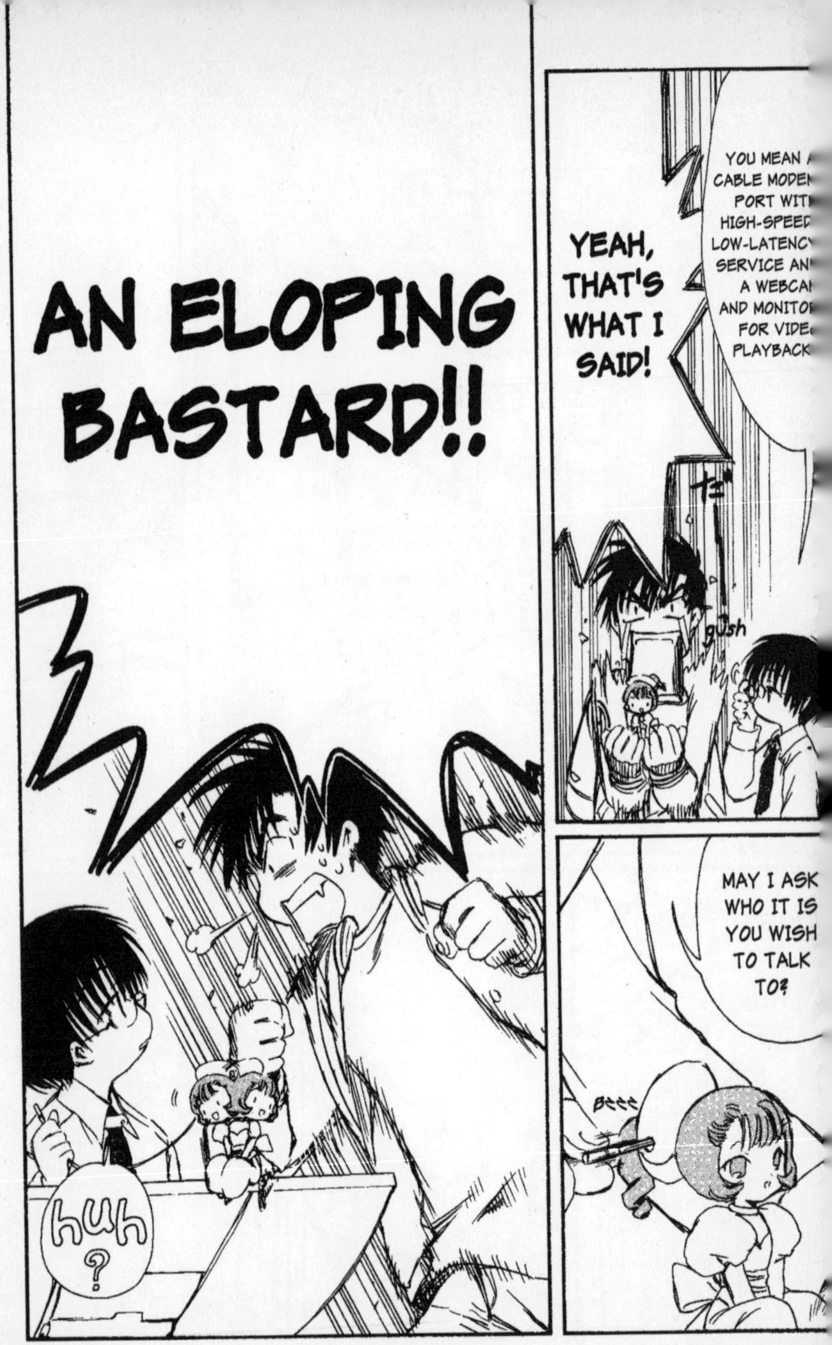
YOU MEAN
CABLE MODE
PORT WIT
HIGH-SPEED
LOW-LATENC
SERVICE AN
A WEBCA
AND MONITO
FOR VIDE
PLAYBACK
YEAH, THAT'S WHAT I SAID!
gush
MAY I ASK WHO IT IS YOU WISH TO TALK TO?
AN ELOPING BASTARD!!
huh?

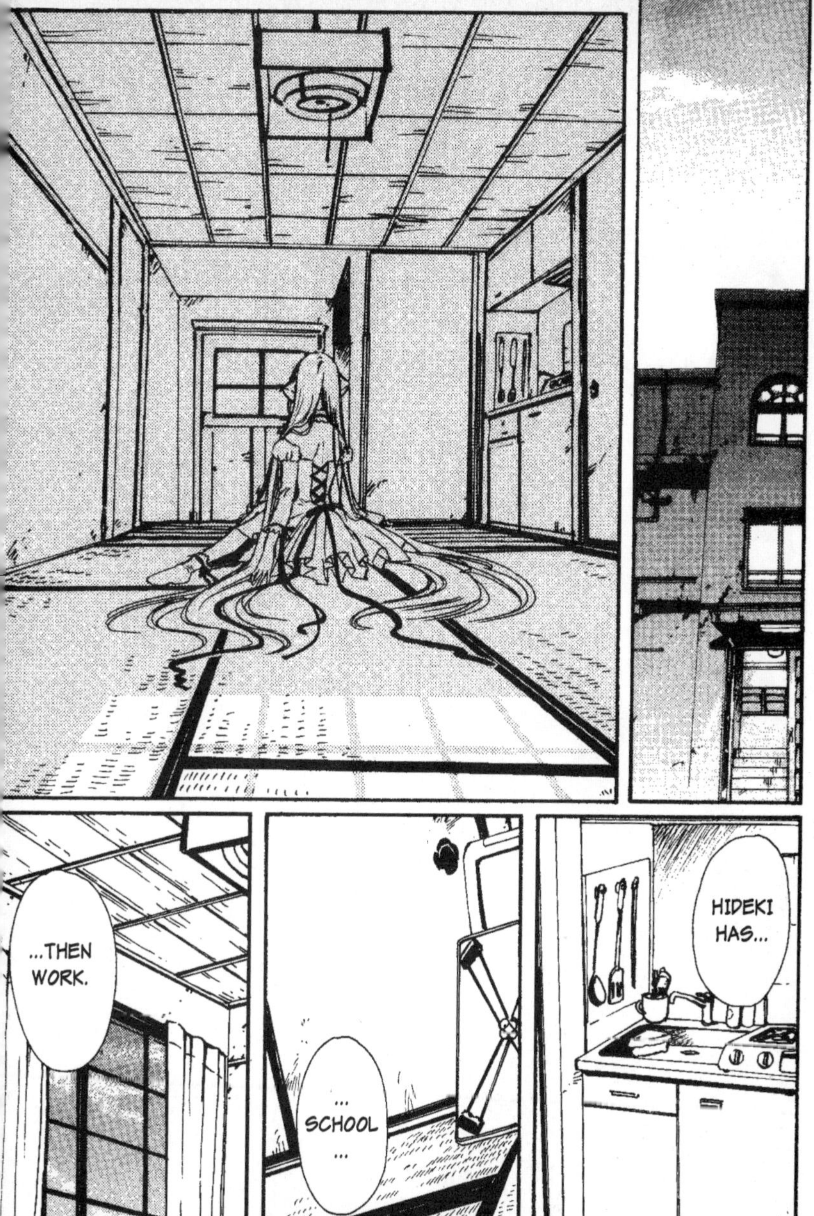
HIDEKI HAS...
... SCHOOL ...
...THEN WORK.

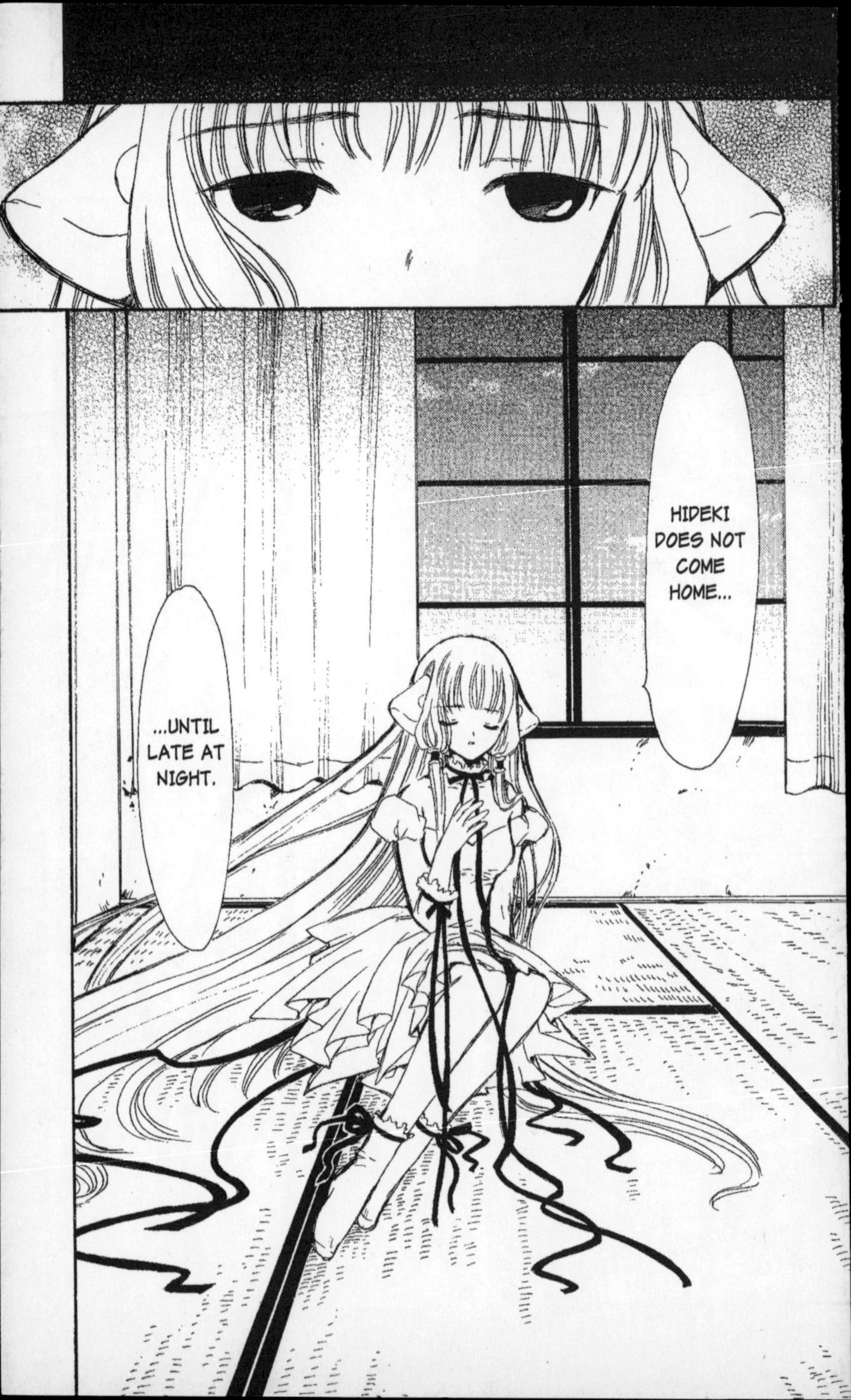
HIDEKI DOES NOT COME HOME...
...UNTIL LATE AT NIGHT.

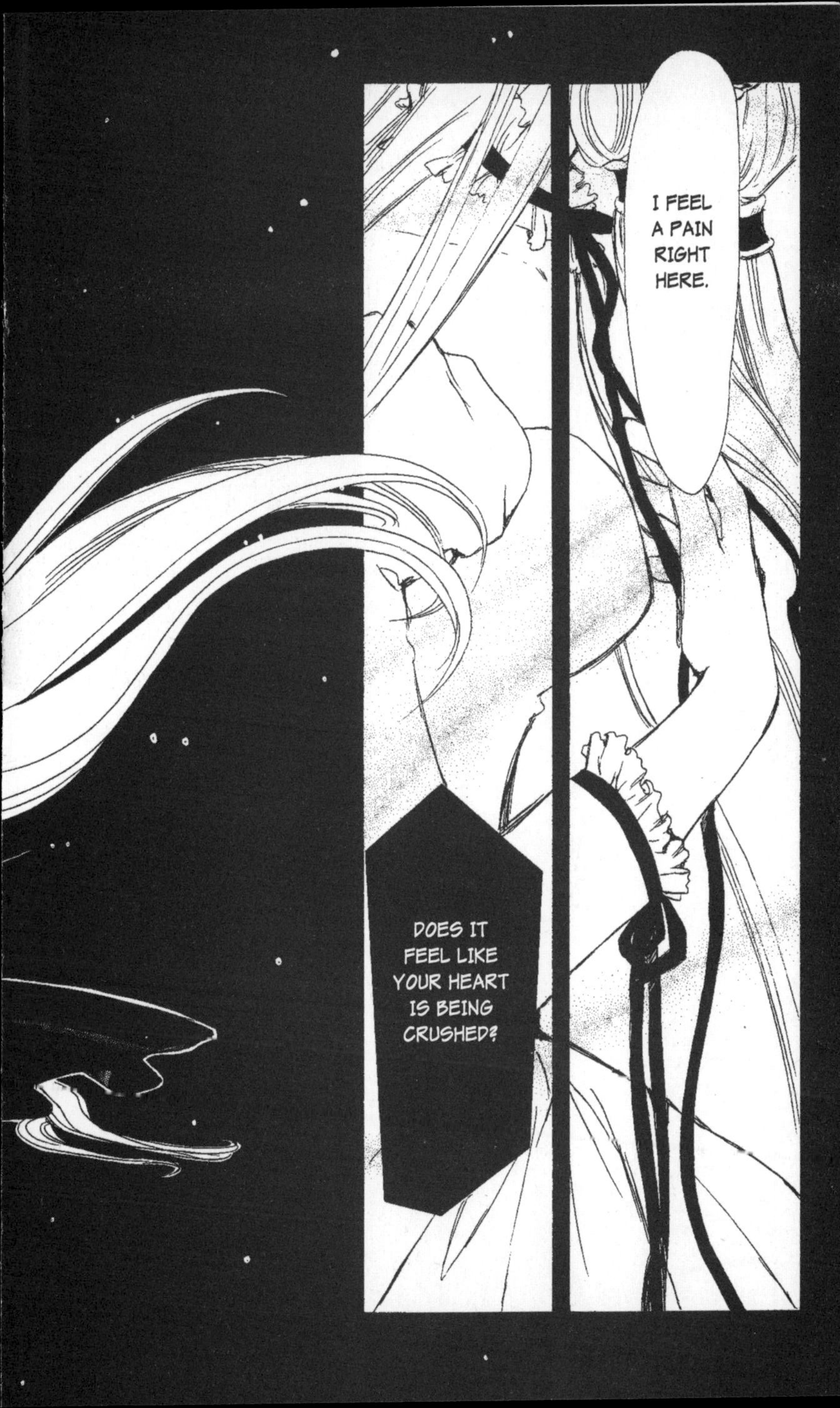
I FEEL A PAIN RIGHT HERE.
DOES IT FEEL LIKE YOUR HEART IS BEING CRUSHED?

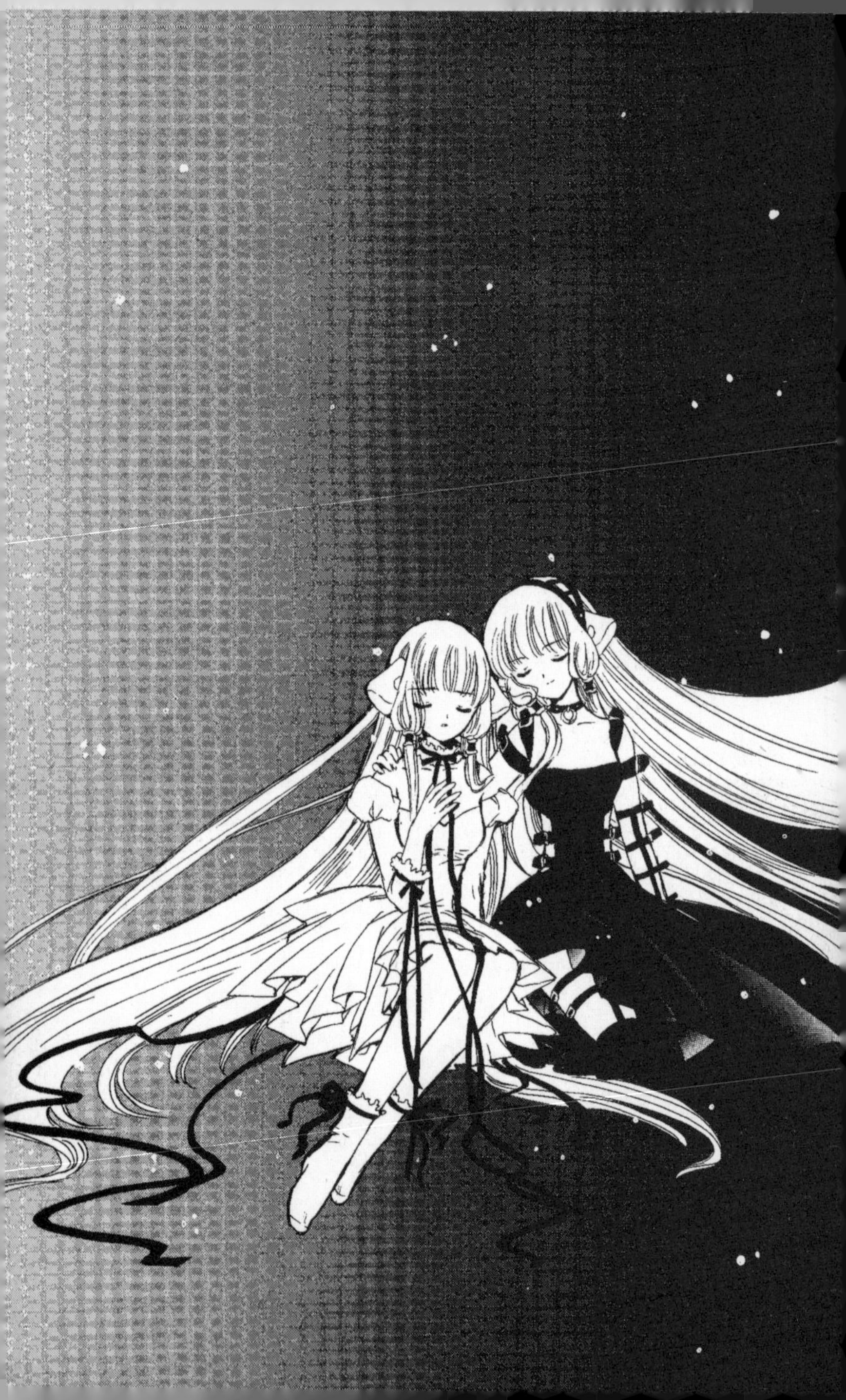

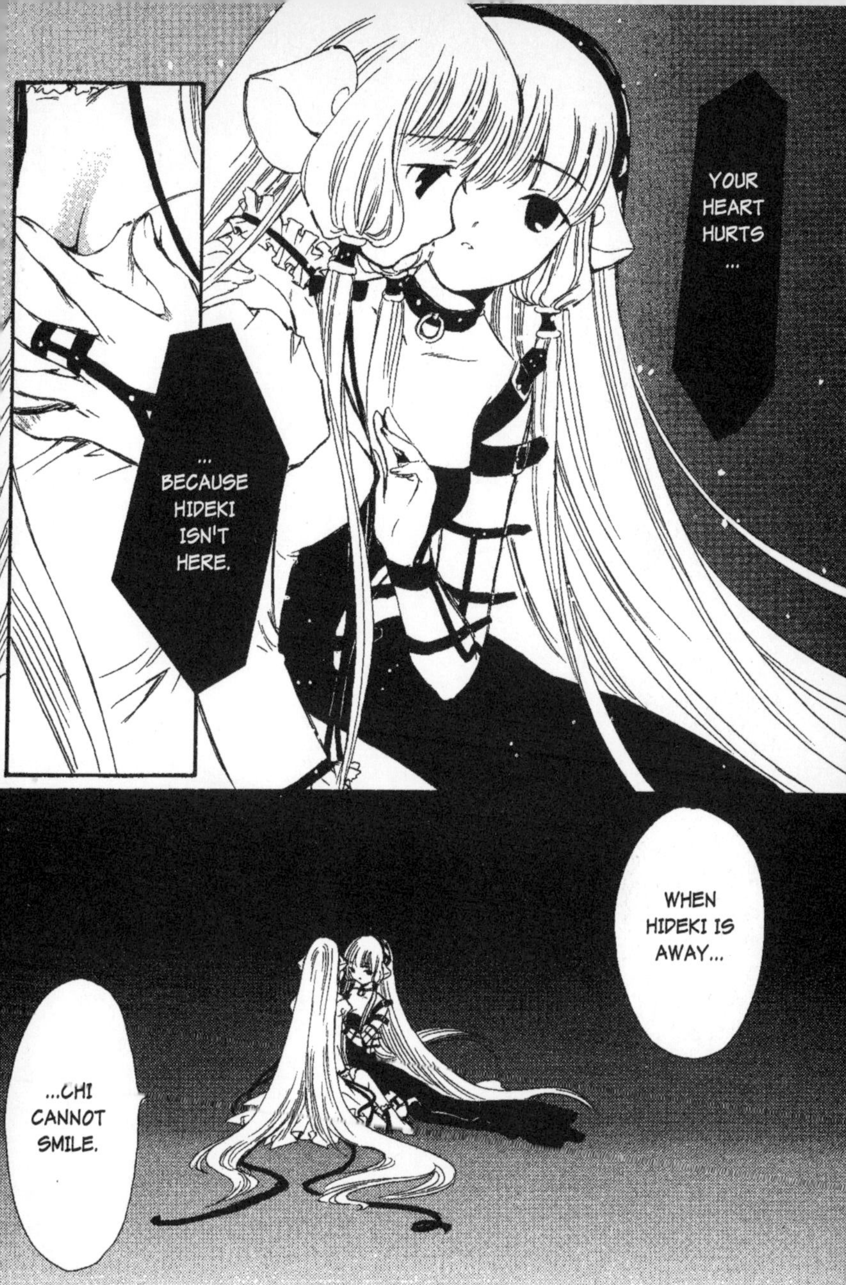
YOUR HEART HURTS ...
... BECAUSE HIDEKI ISN'T HERE.
WHEN HIDEKI IS AWAY...
...CHI CANNOT SMILE.

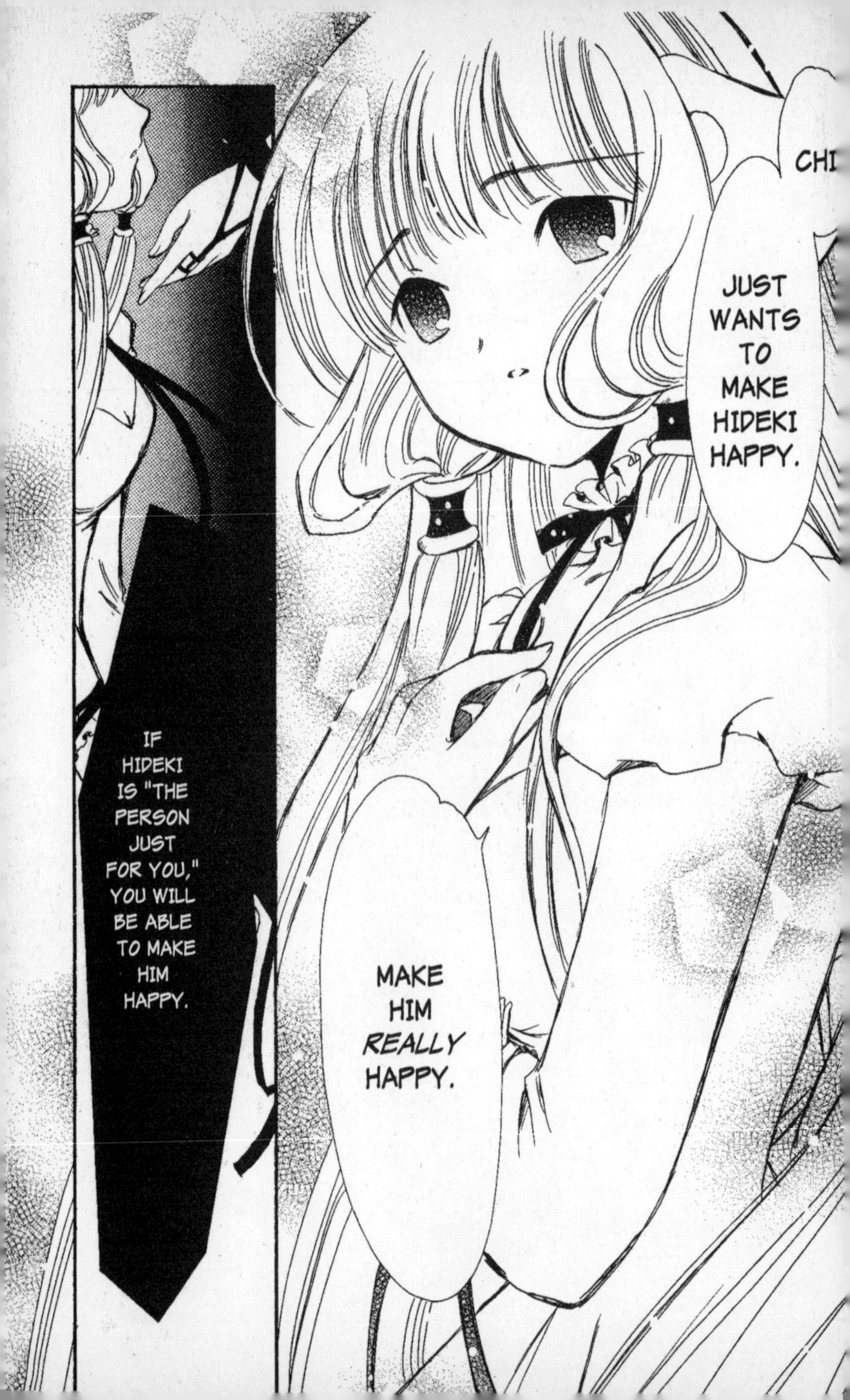
CHI
JUST WANTS TO MAKE HIDEKI HAPPY.
MAKE HIM REALLY HAPPY.
IF HIDEKI IS "THE PERSON JUST FOR YOU," YOU WILL BE ABLE TO MAKE HIM HAPPY.

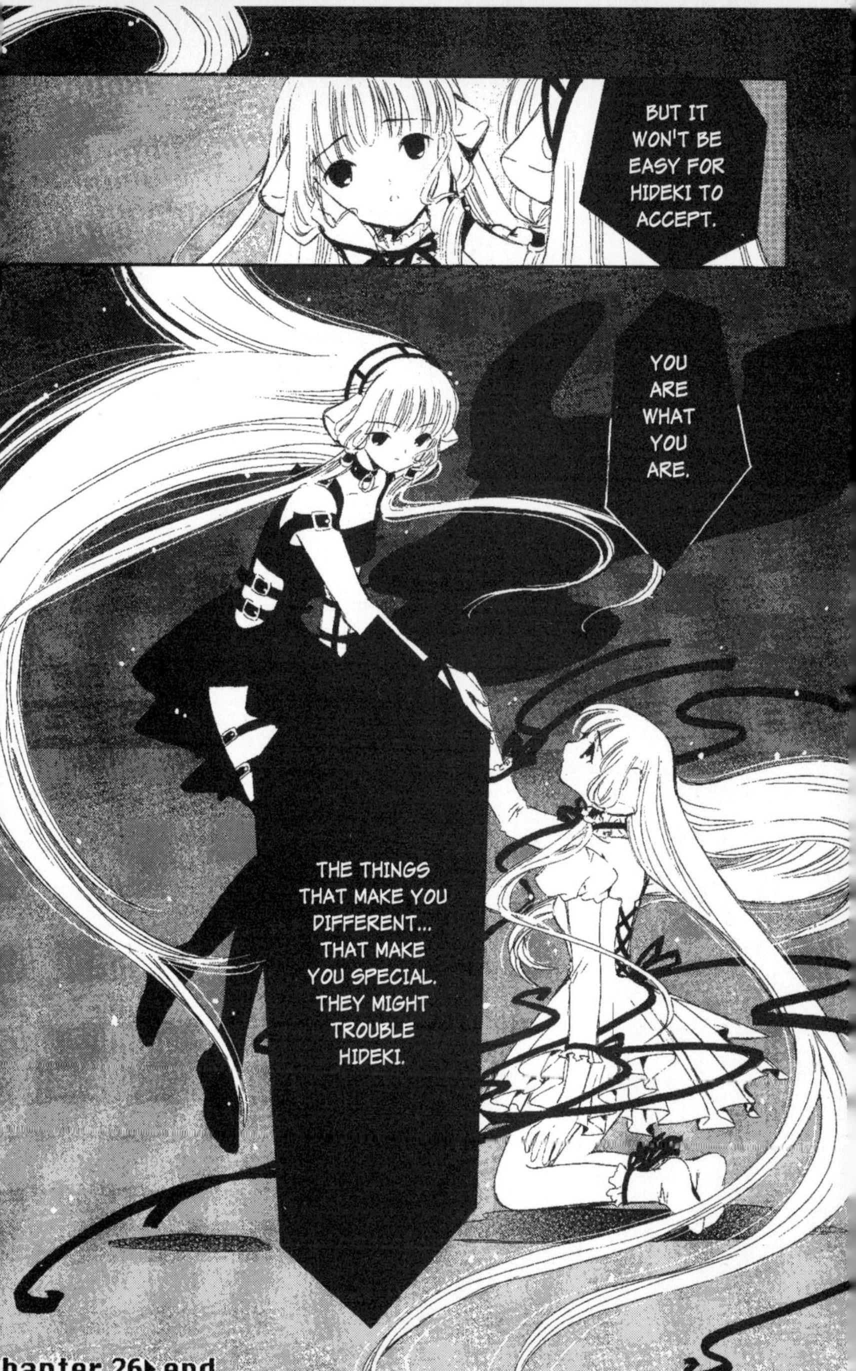
BUT IT WON'T BE EASY FOR HIDEKI TO ACCEPT.
YOU ARE WHAT YOU ARE.
THE THINGS THAT MAKE YOU DIFFERENT... THAT MAKE YOU SPECIAL. THEY MIGHT TROUBLE HIDEKI.

chapter.26 end

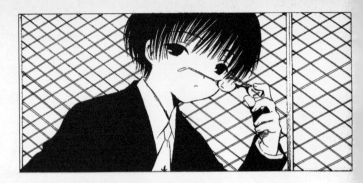

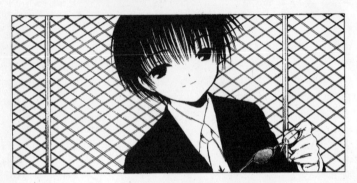

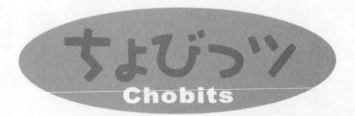

ちょびっツ
Chobits

◀chapter.27▶

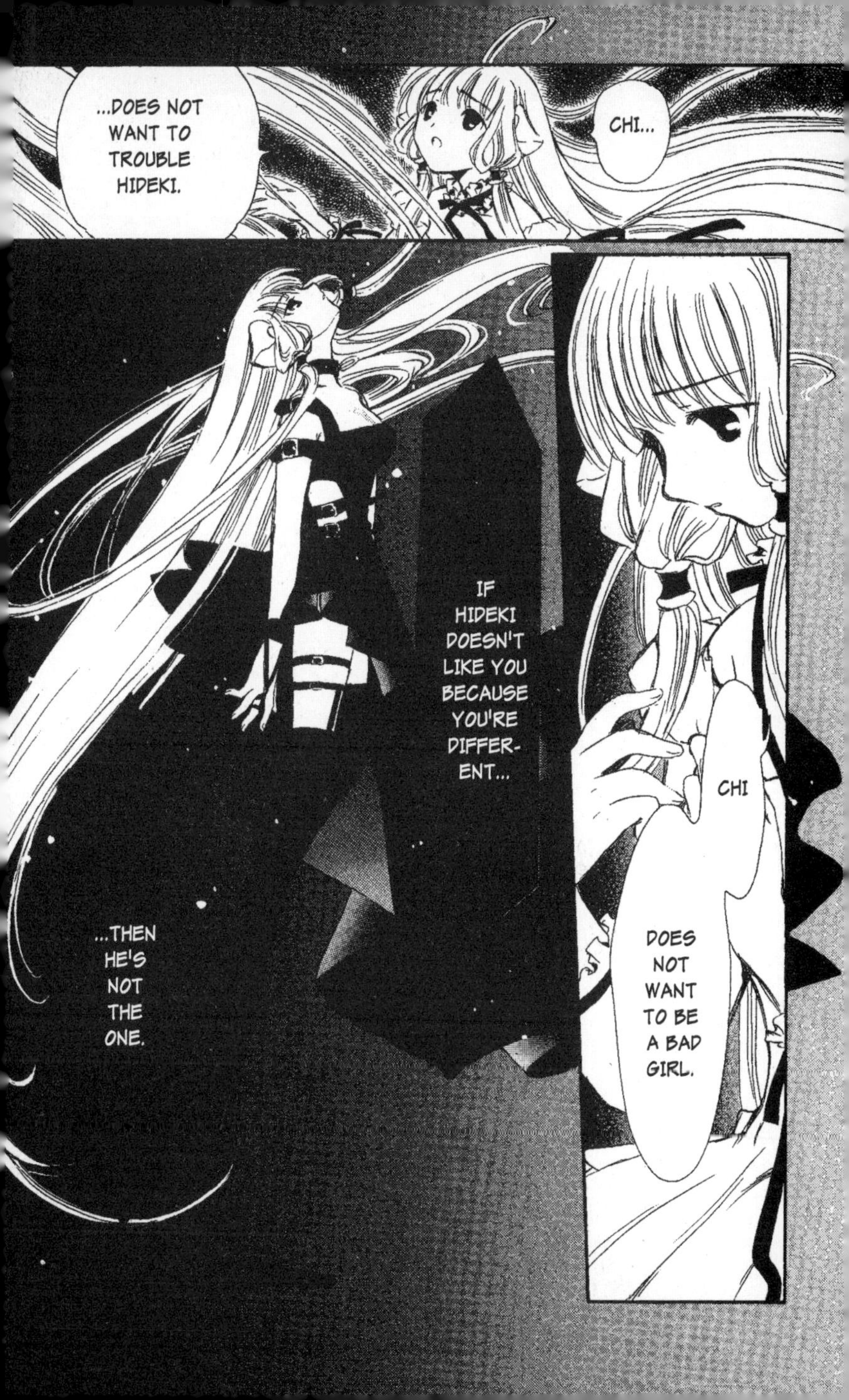
CHI...
...DOES NOT WANT TO TROUBLE HIDEKI.
CHI
DOES NOT WANT TO BE A BAD GIRL.
IF HIDEKI DOESN'T LIKE YOU BECAUSE YOU'RE DIFFER-ENT...
...THEN HE'S NOT THE ONE.

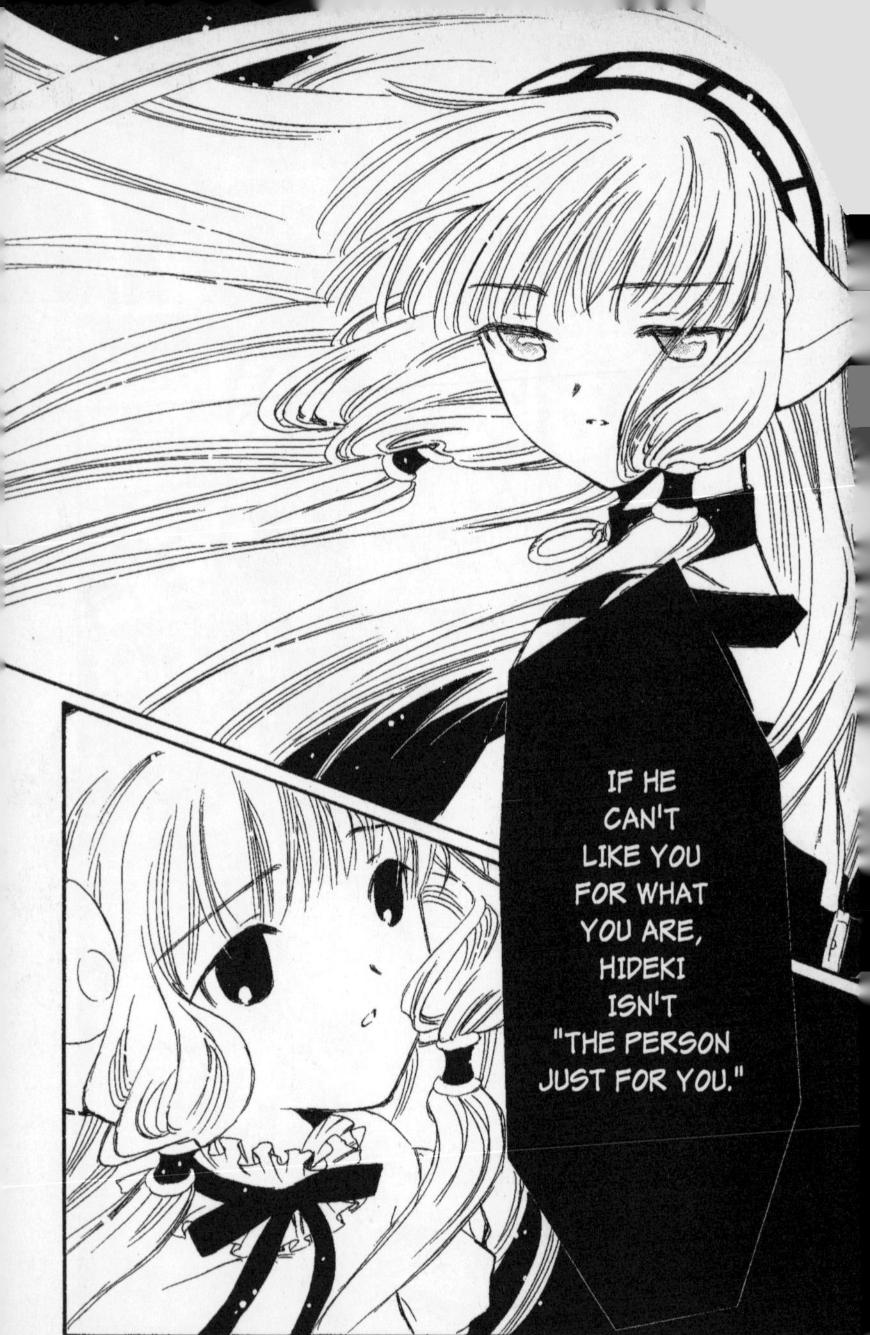
IF HE CAN'T LIKE YOU FOR WHAT YOU ARE, HIDEKI ISN'T "THE PERSON JUST FOR YOU."

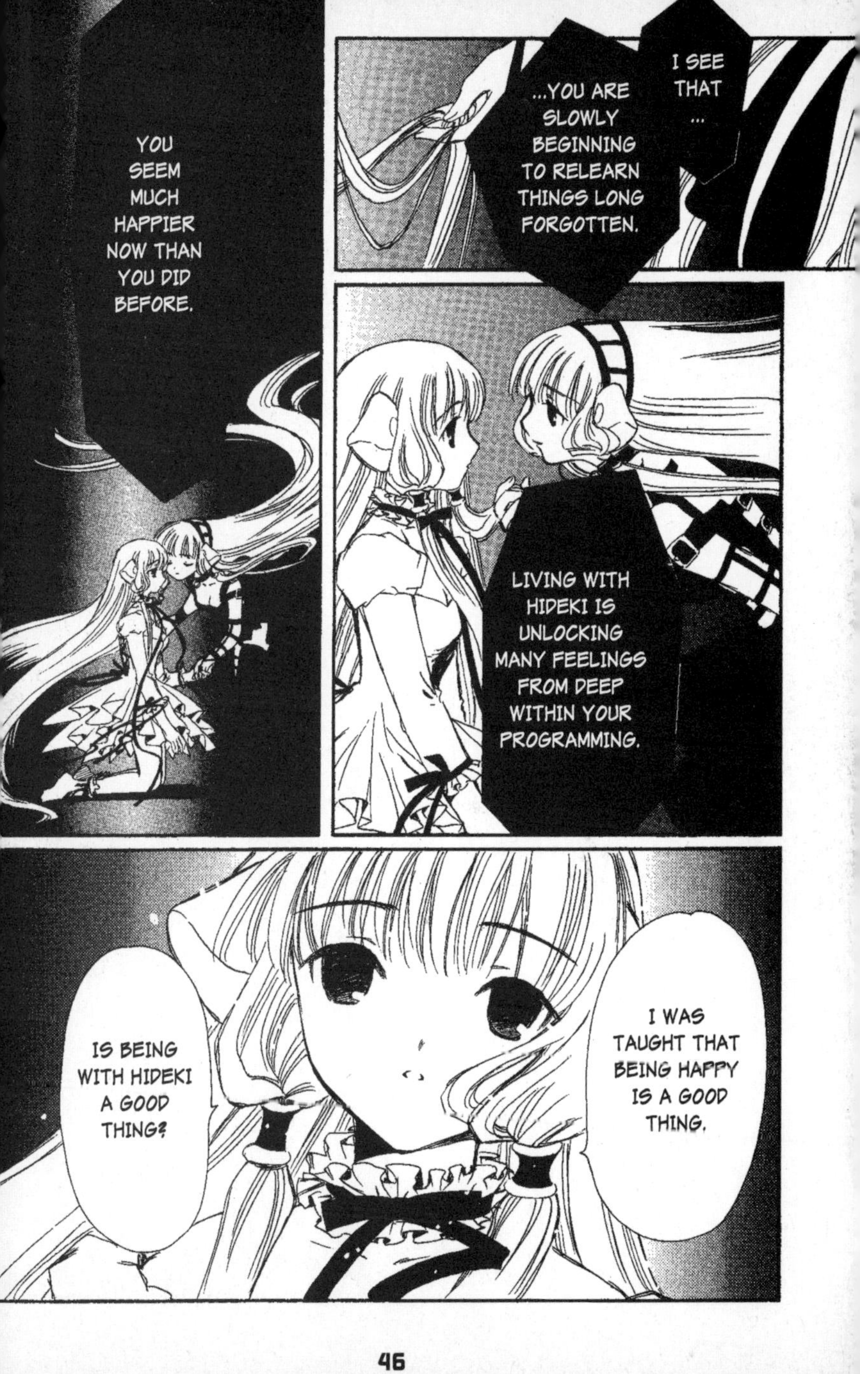
I SEE THAT ...
...YOU ARE SLOWLY BEGINNING TO RELEARN THINGS LONG FORGOTTEN.
LIVING WITH HIDEKI IS UNLOCKING MANY FEELINGS FROM DEEP WITHIN YOUR PROGRAMMING.
YOU SEEM MUCH HAPPIER NOW THAN YOU DID BEFORE.
I WAS TAUGHT THAT BEING HAPPY IS A GOOD THING.
IS BEING WITH HIDEKI A GOOD THING?

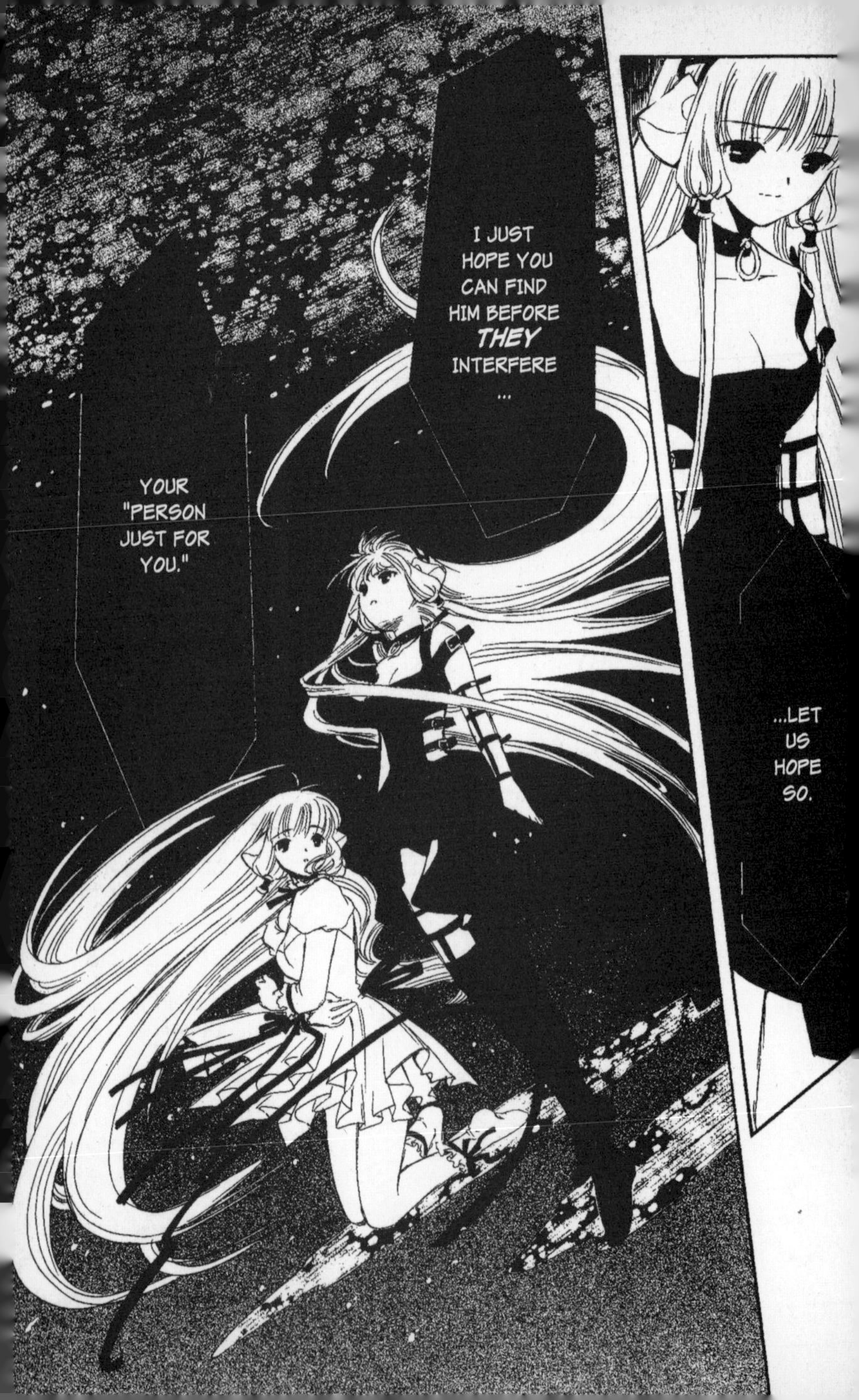
I JUST HOPE YOU CAN FIND HIM BEFORE *THEY* INTERFERE ...
YOUR "PERSON JUST FOR YOU."
...LET US HOPE SO.

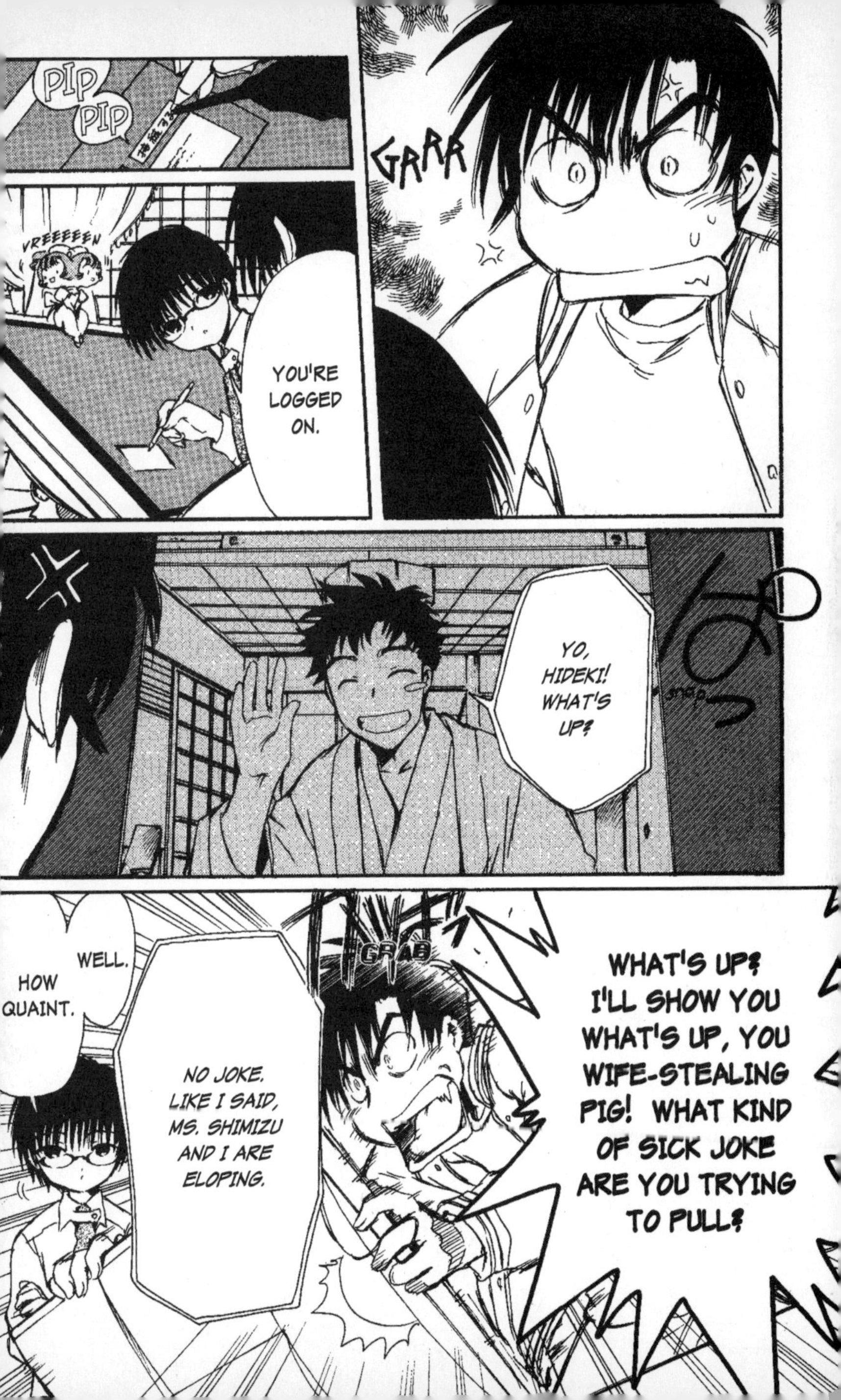
GRRR
PIP PIP
VREEEEEN
YOU'RE LOGGED ON.
snap
YO, HIDEKI! WHAT'S UP?
WHAT'S UP? I'LL SHOW YOU WHAT'S UP, YOU WIFE-STEALING PIG! WHAT KIND OF SICK JOKE ARE YOU TRYING TO PULL?
GRAB
NO JOKE. LIKE I SAID, MS. SHIMIZU AND I ARE ELOPING.
WELL. HOW QUAINT.

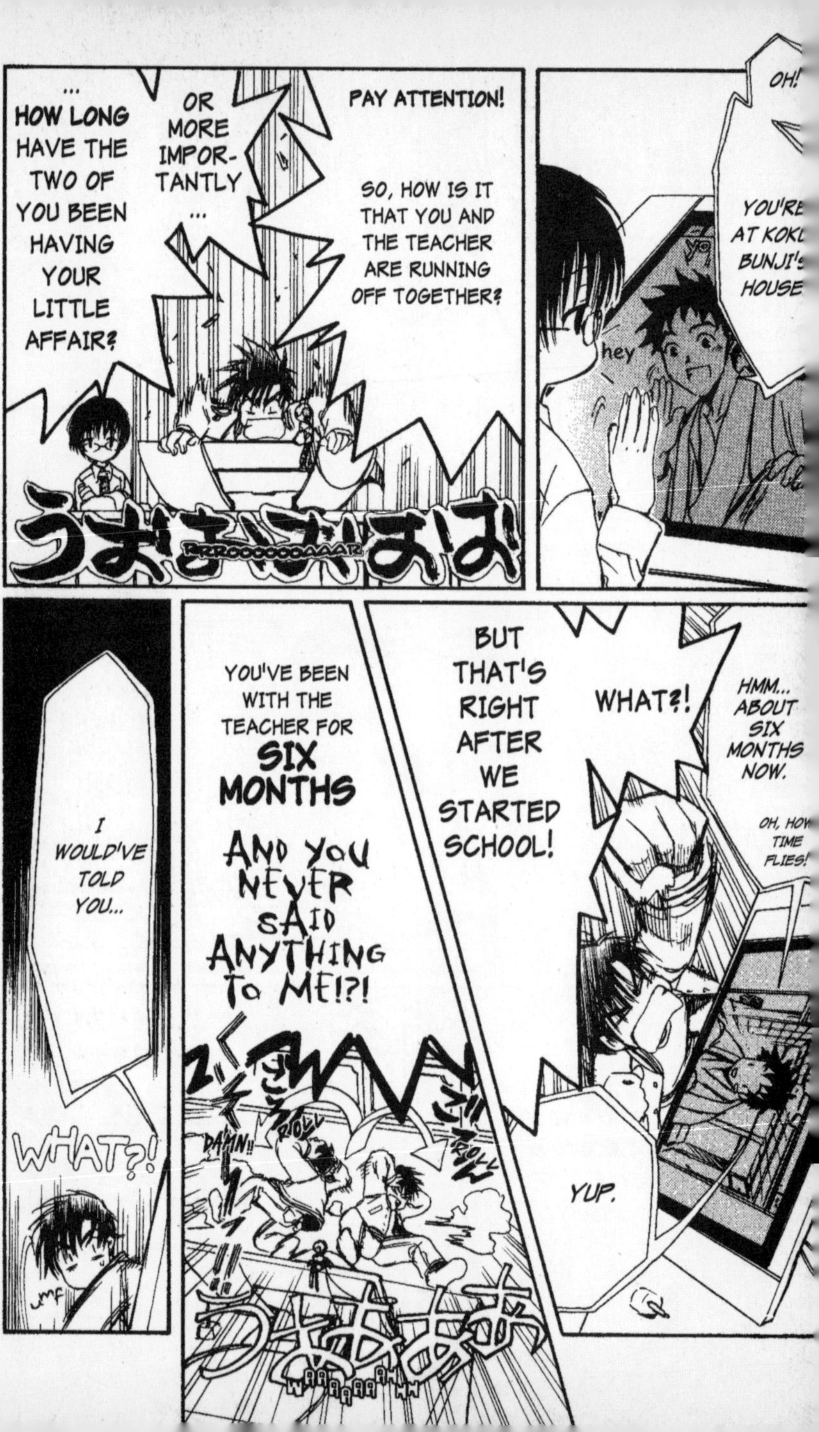
OH!
YOU'RE AT KOK BUNJI'S HOUSE
yo
hey
PAY ATTENTION!
SO, HOW IS IT THAT YOU AND THE TEACHER ARE RUNNING OFF TOGETHER?
OR MORE IMPORTANTLY ...
... HOW LONG HAVE THE TWO OF YOU BEEN HAVING YOUR LITTLE AFFAIR?
RRRROOOOOOOOAAAR
HMM... ABOUT SIX MONTHS NOW.
OH, HOW TIME FLIES!
YUP.
WHAT?!
BUT THAT'S RIGHT AFTER WE STARTED SCHOOL!
YOU'VE BEEN WITH THE TEACHER FOR SIX MONTHS
AND YOU NEVER SAID ANYTHING TO ME!?!
DAMN!!
ROLL
ROLL
WAAAAAAAHH
I WOULD'VE TOLD YOU...
WHAT?!
umf

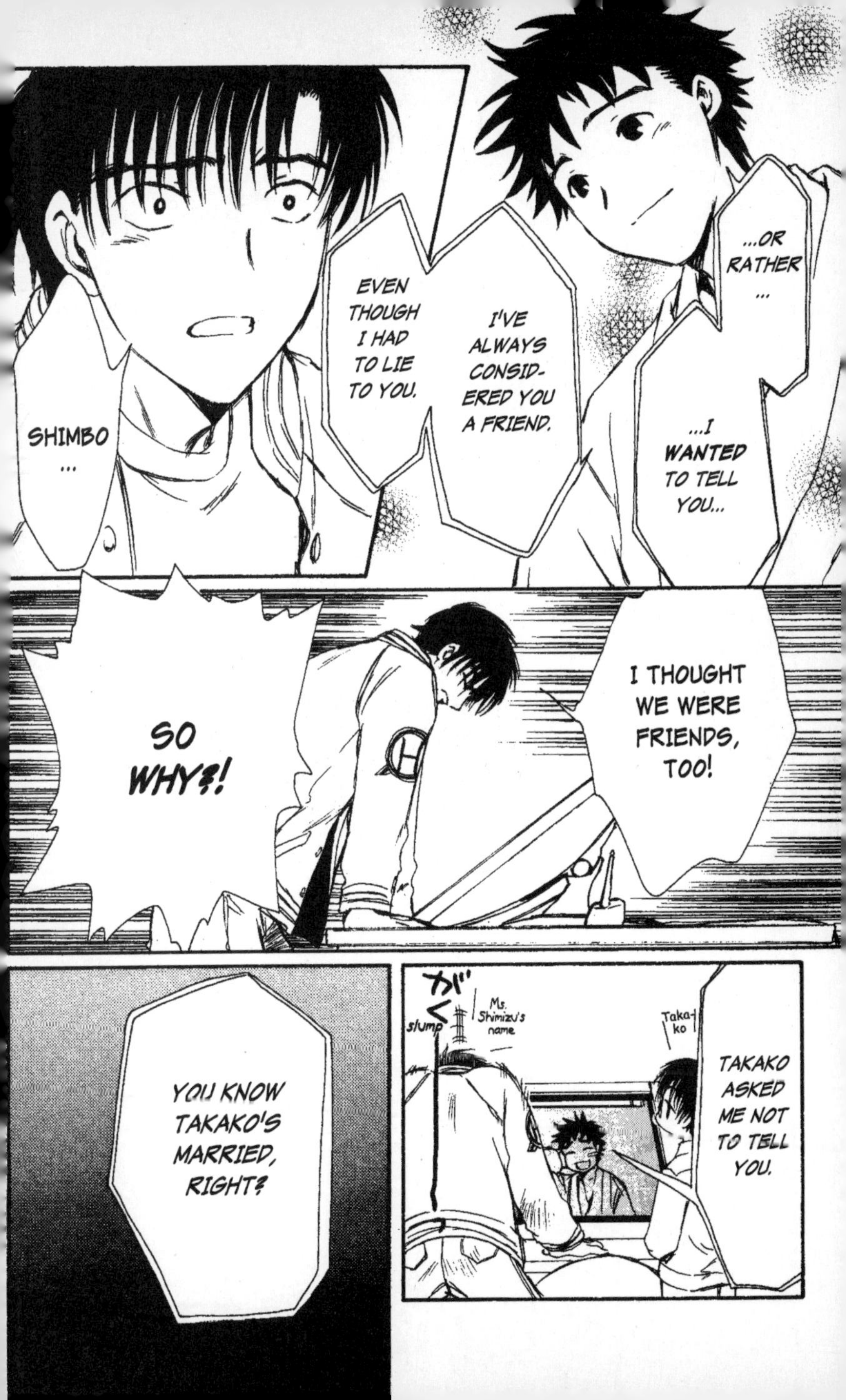
...OR RATHER ...
...I WANTED TO TELL YOU...
I'VE ALWAYS CONSIDERED YOU A FRIEND.
EVEN THOUGH I HAD TO LIE TO YOU.
SHIMBO ...
I THOUGHT WE WERE FRIENDS, TOO!
SO WHY?!
Taka-ko
TAKAKO ASKED ME NOT TO TELL YOU.
Ms. Shimizu's name
がく
slump
YOU KNOW TAKAKO'S MARRIED, RIGHT?

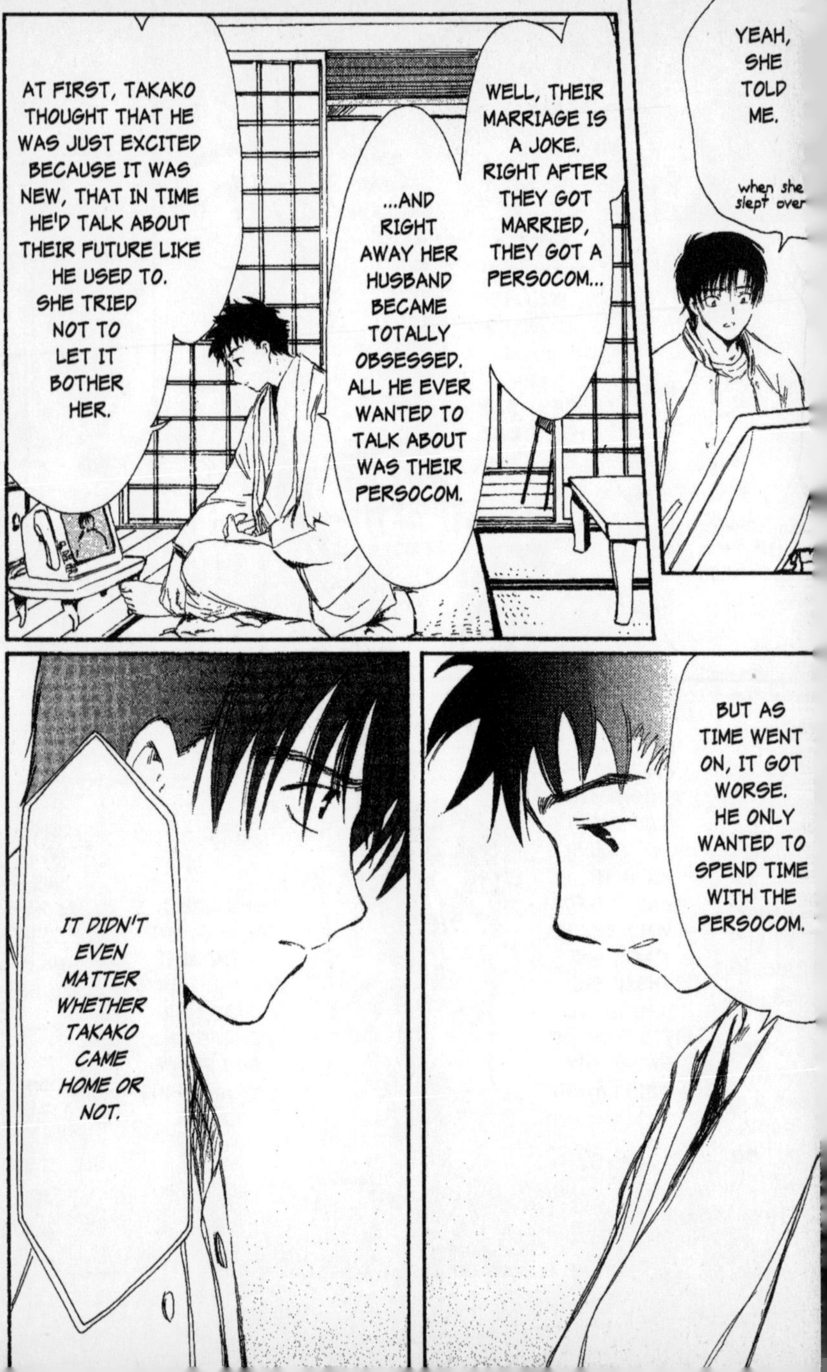
YEAH, SHE TOLD ME.
when she slept over
WELL, THEIR MARRIAGE IS A JOKE. RIGHT AFTER THEY GOT MARRIED, THEY GOT A PERSOCOM...
...AND RIGHT AWAY HER HUSBAND BECAME TOTALLY OBSESSED. ALL HE EVER WANTED TO TALK ABOUT WAS THEIR PERSOCOM.
AT FIRST, TAKAKO THOUGHT THAT HE WAS JUST EXCITED BECAUSE IT WAS NEW, THAT IN TIME HE'D TALK ABOUT THEIR FUTURE LIKE HE USED TO. SHE TRIED NOT TO LET IT BOTHER HER.
BUT AS TIME WENT ON, IT GOT WORSE. HE ONLY WANTED TO SPEND TIME WITH THE PERSOCOM.
IT DIDN'T EVEN MATTER WHETHER TAKAKO CAME HOME OR NOT.

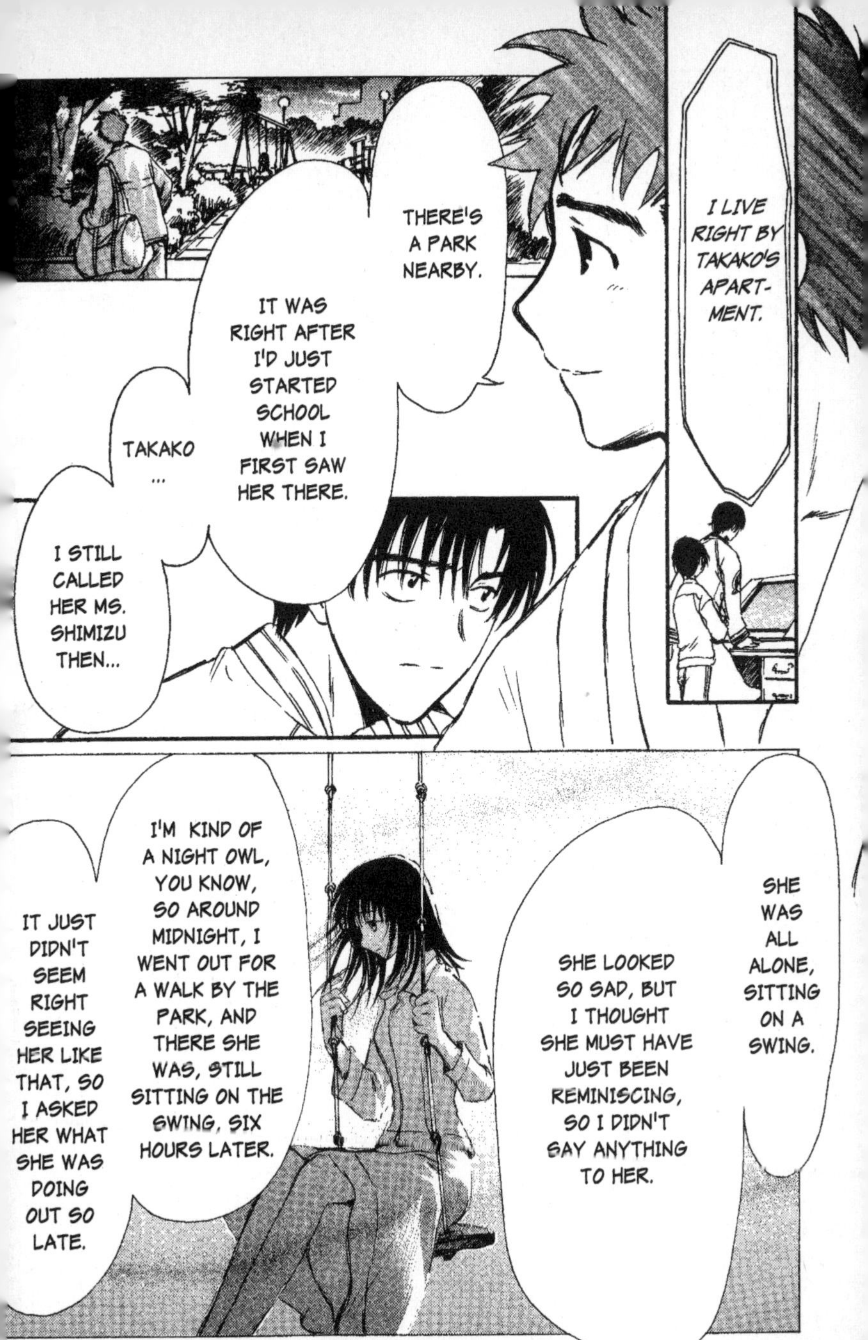
I LIVE RIGHT BY TAKAKO'S APARTMENT.
THERE'S A PARK NEARBY.
IT WAS RIGHT AFTER I'D JUST STARTED SCHOOL WHEN I FIRST SAW HER THERE.
TAKAKO ...
I STILL CALLED HER MS. SHIMIZU THEN...
SHE WAS ALL ALONE, SITTING ON A SWING.
SHE LOOKED SO SAD, BUT I THOUGHT SHE MUST HAVE JUST BEEN REMINISCING, SO I DIDN'T SAY ANYTHING TO HER.
I'M KIND OF A NIGHT OWL, YOU KNOW, SO AROUND MIDNIGHT, I WENT OUT FOR A WALK BY THE PARK, AND THERE SHE WAS, STILL SITTING ON THE SWING, SIX HOURS LATER.
IT JUST DIDN'T SEEM RIGHT SEEING HER LIKE THAT, SO I ASKED HER WHAT SHE WAS DOING OUT SO LATE.

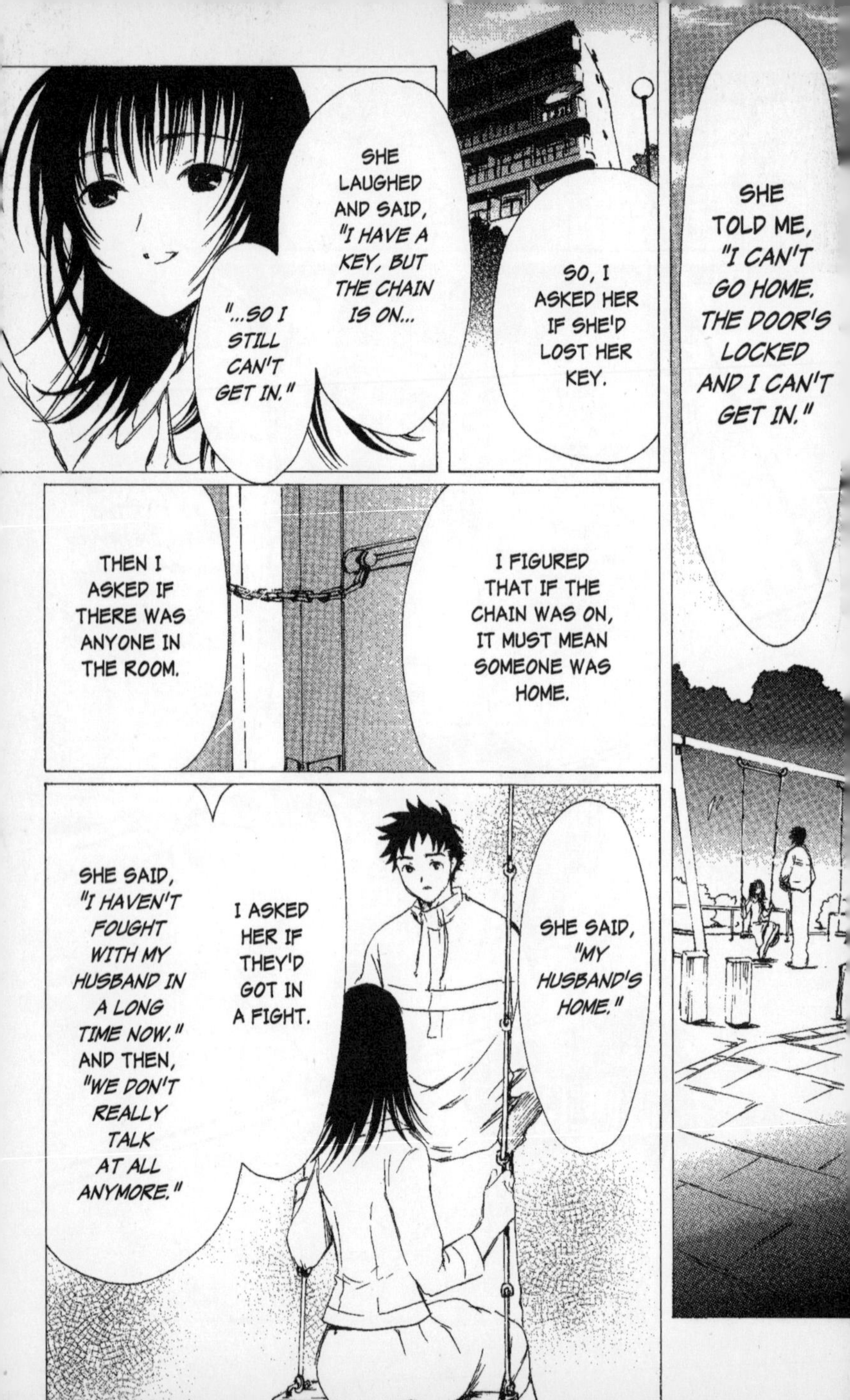
SHE TOLD ME, "I CAN'T GO HOME. THE DOOR'S LOCKED AND I CAN'T GET IN."
SO, I ASKED HER IF SHE'D LOST HER KEY.
SHE LAUGHED AND SAID, "I HAVE A KEY, BUT THE CHAIN IS ON...
"...SO I STILL CAN'T GET IN."
I FIGURED THAT IF THE CHAIN WAS ON, IT MUST MEAN SOMEONE WAS HOME.
THEN I ASKED IF THERE WAS ANYONE IN THE ROOM.
SHE SAID, "MY HUSBAND'S HOME."
I ASKED HER IF THEY'D GOT IN A FIGHT.
SHE SAID, "I HAVEN'T FOUGHT WITH MY HUSBAND IN A LONG TIME NOW." AND THEN, "WE DON'T REALLY TALK AT ALL ANYMORE."

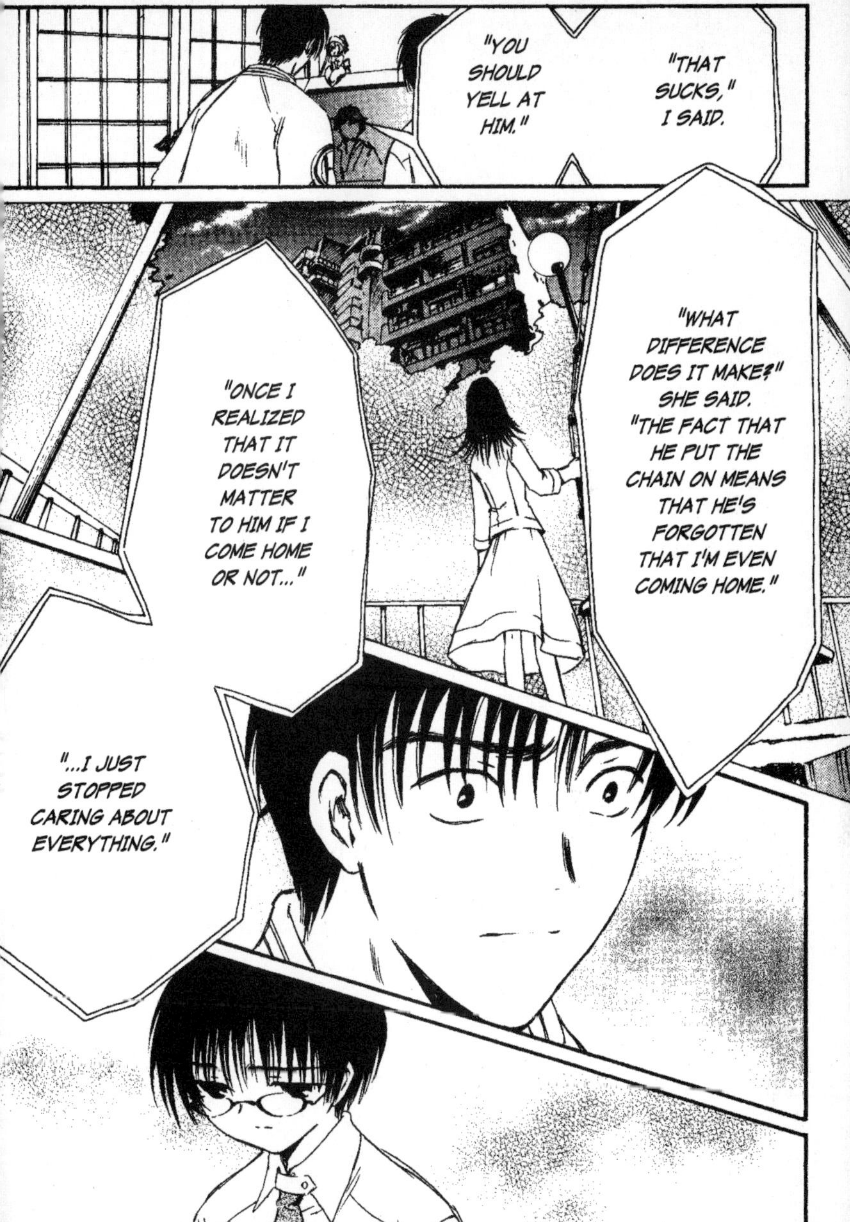
"THAT SUCKS," I SAID.
"YOU SHOULD YELL AT HIM."
"WHAT DIFFERENCE DOES IT MAKE?" SHE SAID. "THE FACT THAT HE PUT THE CHAIN ON MEANS THAT HE'S FORGOTTEN THAT I'M EVEN COMING HOME."
"ONCE I REALIZED THAT IT DOESN'T MATTER TO HIM IF I COME HOME OR NOT..."
"...I JUST STOPPED CARING ABOUT EVERYTHING."

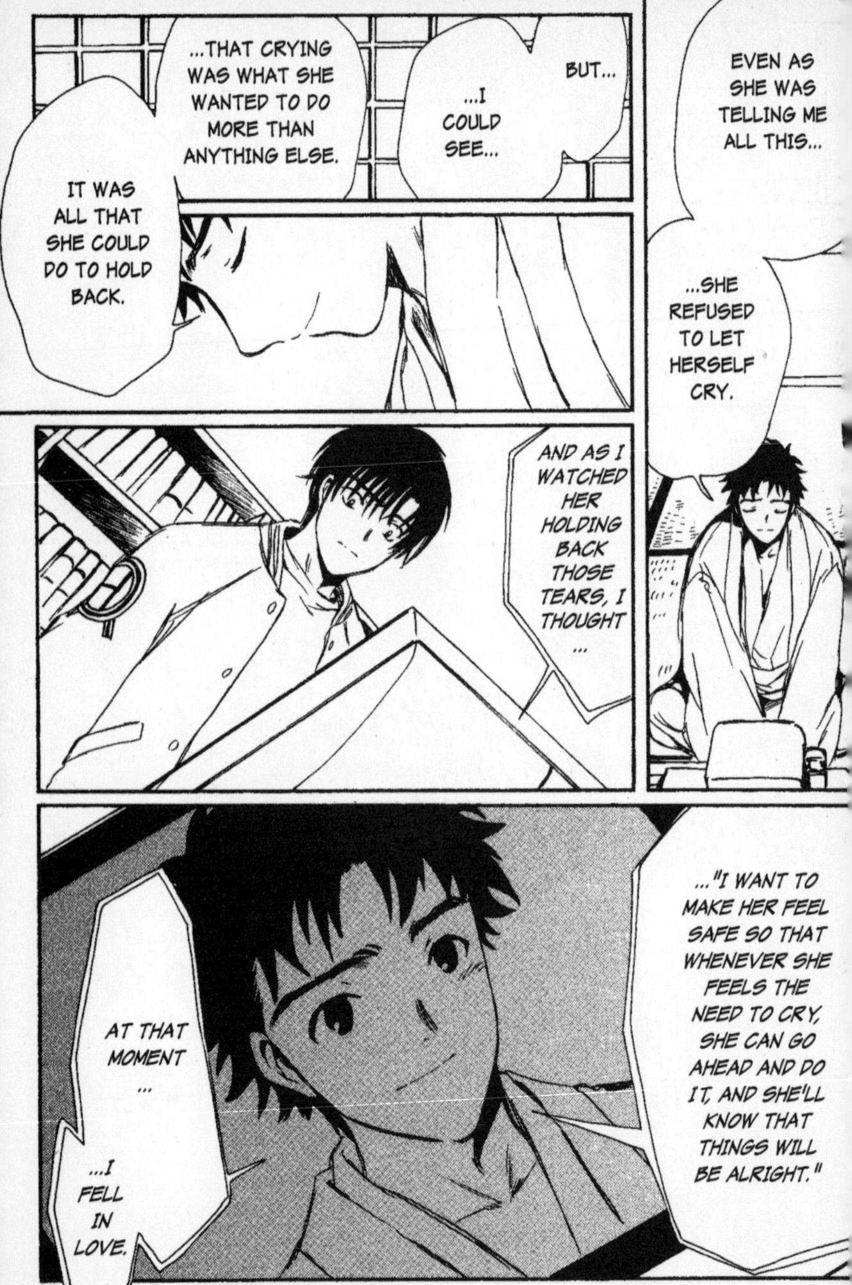
EVEN AS SHE WAS TELLING ME ALL THIS...
...SHE REFUSED TO LET HERSELF CRY.
BUT...
...I COULD SEE...
...THAT CRYING WAS WHAT SHE WANTED TO DO MORE THAN ANYTHING ELSE.
IT WAS ALL THAT SHE COULD DO TO HOLD BACK.
AND AS I WATCHED HER HOLDING BACK THOSE TEARS, I THOUGHT...
..."I WANT TO MAKE HER FEEL SAFE SO THAT WHENEVER SHE FEELS THE NEED TO CRY, SHE CAN GO AHEAD AND DO IT, AND SHE'LL KNOW THAT THINGS WILL BE ALRIGHT."
AT THAT MOMENT...
...I FELL IN LOVE.

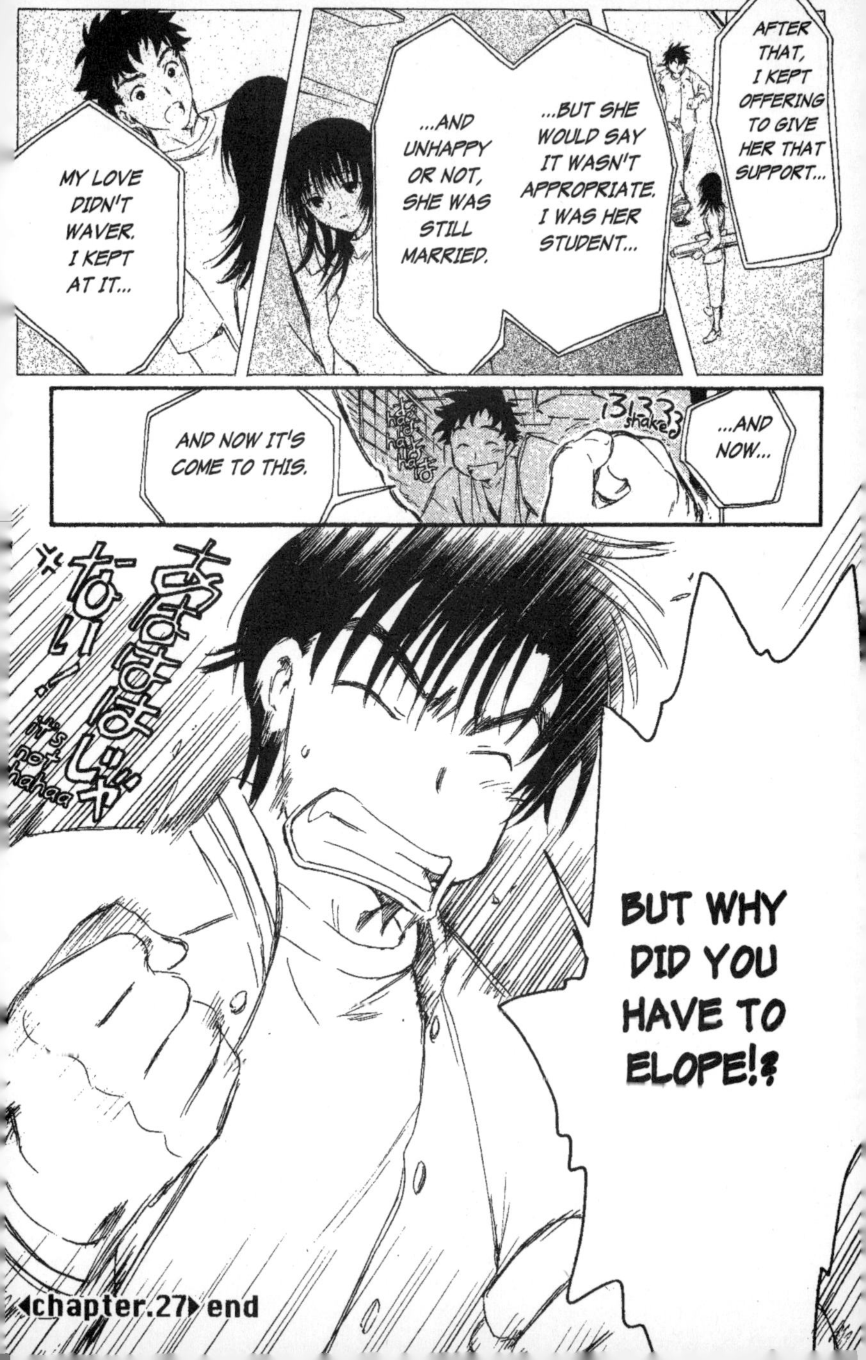
AFTER THAT, I KEPT OFFERING TO GIVE HER THAT SUPPORT...
...BUT SHE WOULD SAY IT WASN'T APPROPRIATE. I WAS HER STUDENT...
...AND UNHAPPY OR NOT, SHE WAS STILL MARRIED.
MY LOVE DIDN'T WAVER. I KEPT AT IT...
...AND NOW...
shake
haa haa haa
AND NOW IT'S COME TO THIS.
BUT WHY DID YOU HAVE TO ELOPE!?
it's not hahaa
chapter.27 end

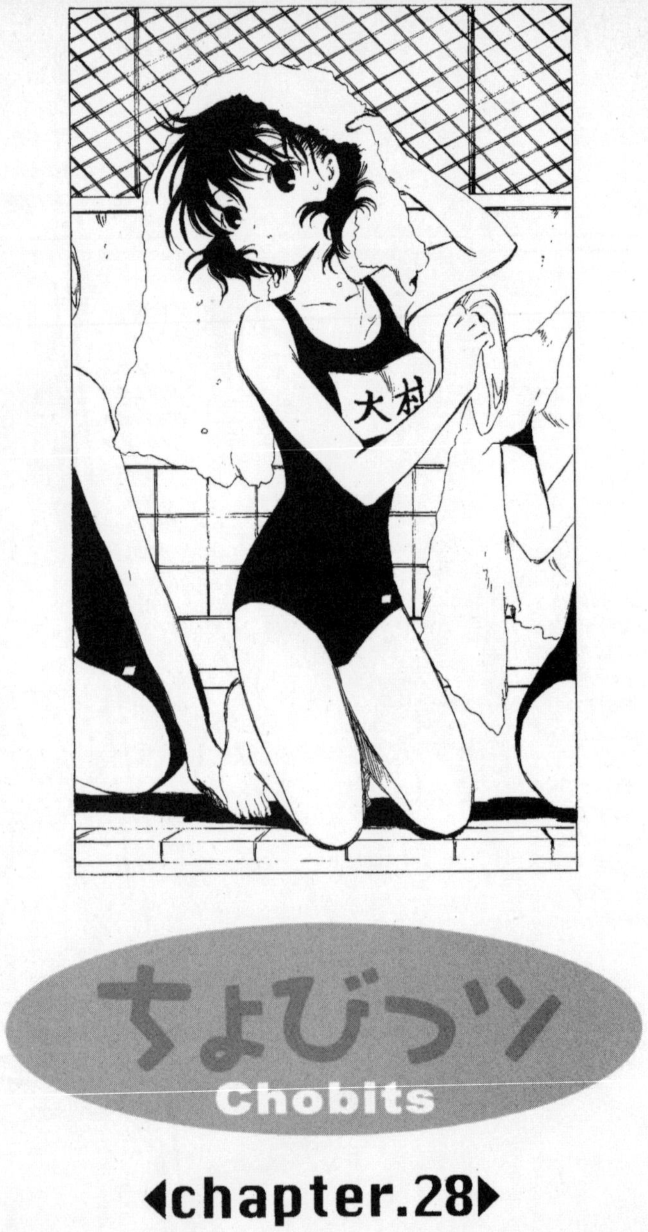
大村

ちょびっツ
Chobits

◀chapter.28▶

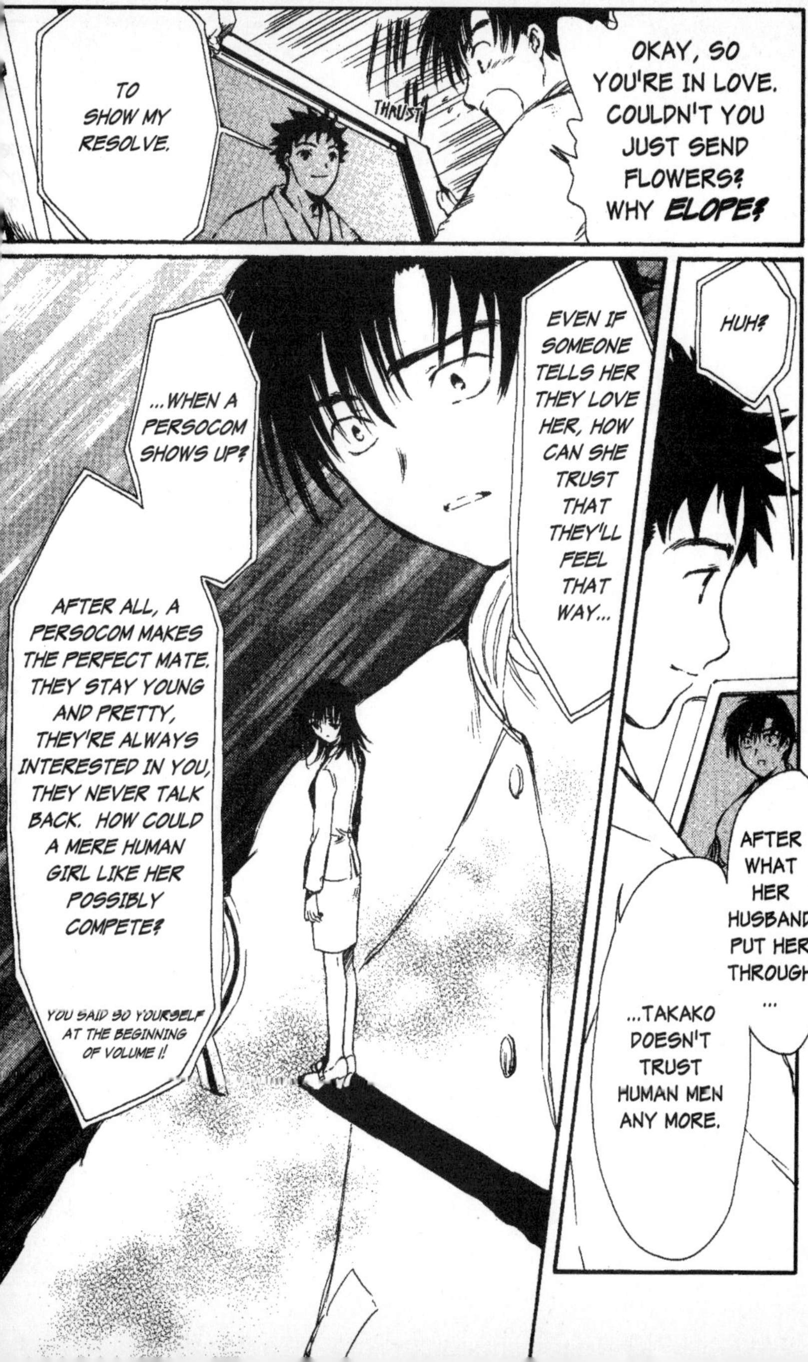
OKAY, SO YOU'RE IN LOVE. COULDN'T YOU JUST SEND FLOWERS? WHY ELOPE?
THRUST
TO SHOW MY RESOLVE.
HUH?
AFTER WHAT HER HUSBAND PUT HER THROUGH...
...TAKAKO DOESN'T TRUST HUMAN MEN ANY MORE.
EVEN IF SOMEONE TELLS HER THEY LOVE HER, HOW CAN SHE TRUST THAT THEY'LL FEEL THAT WAY...
...WHEN A PERSOCOM SHOWS UP?
AFTER ALL, A PERSOCOM MAKES THE PERFECT MATE. THEY STAY YOUNG AND PRETTY, THEY'RE ALWAYS INTERESTED IN YOU, THEY NEVER TALK BACK. HOW COULD A MERE HUMAN GIRL LIKE HER POSSIBLY COMPETE?
YOU SAID SO YOURSELF AT THE BEGINNING OF VOLUME 1!

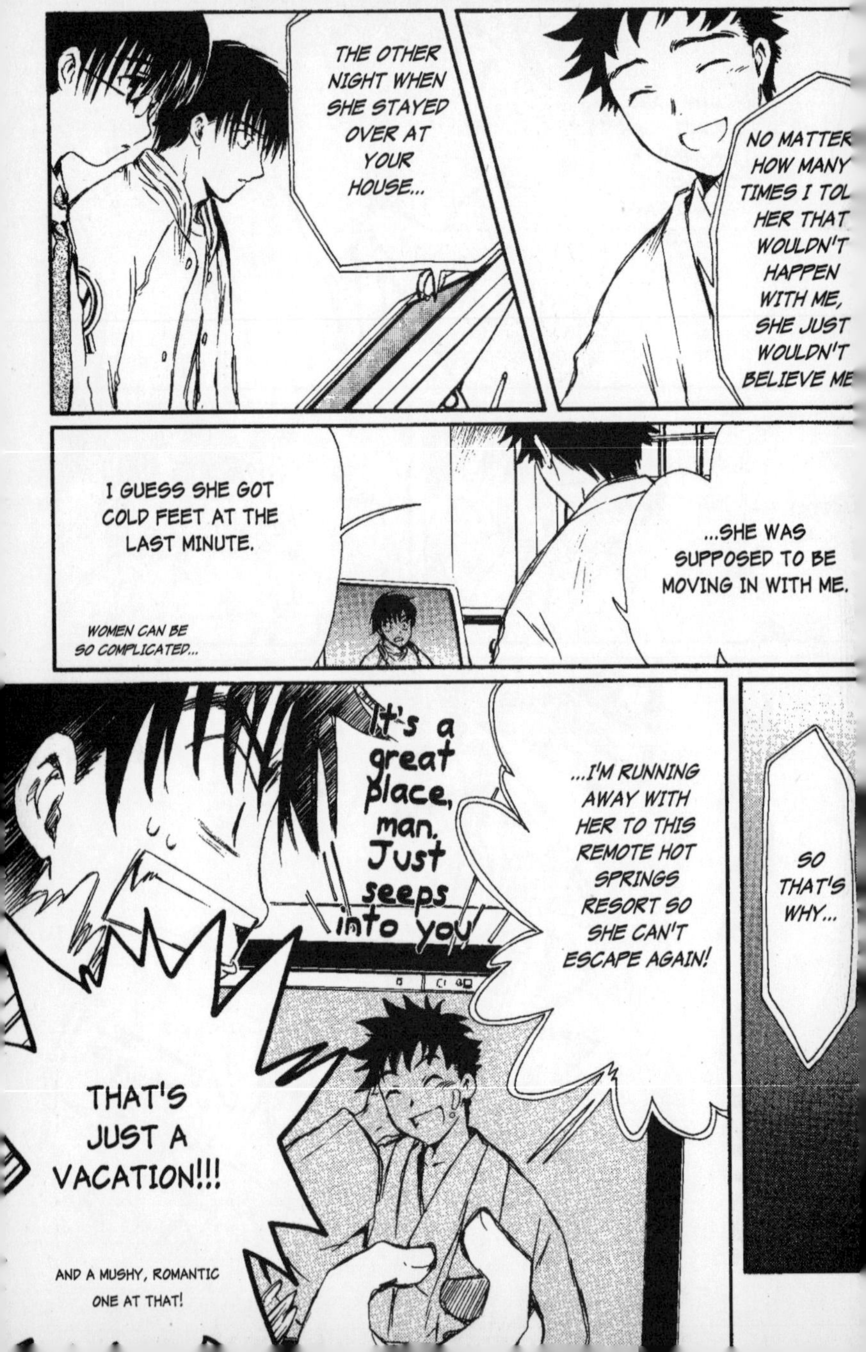
NO MATTER HOW MANY TIMES I TOL HER THAT WOULDN'T HAPPEN WITH ME, SHE JUST WOULDN'T BELIEVE ME
THE OTHER NIGHT WHEN SHE STAYED OVER AT YOUR HOUSE...
...SHE WAS SUPPOSED TO BE MOVING IN WITH ME.
I GUESS SHE GOT COLD FEET AT THE LAST MINUTE.
WOMEN CAN BE SO COMPLICATED...
SO THAT'S WHY...
...I'M RUNNING AWAY WITH HER TO THIS REMOTE HOT SPRINGS RESORT SO SHE CAN'T ESCAPE AGAIN!
It's a great place, man. Just seeps into you
THAT'S JUST A VACATION!!!
AND A MUSHY, ROMANTIC ONE AT THAT!

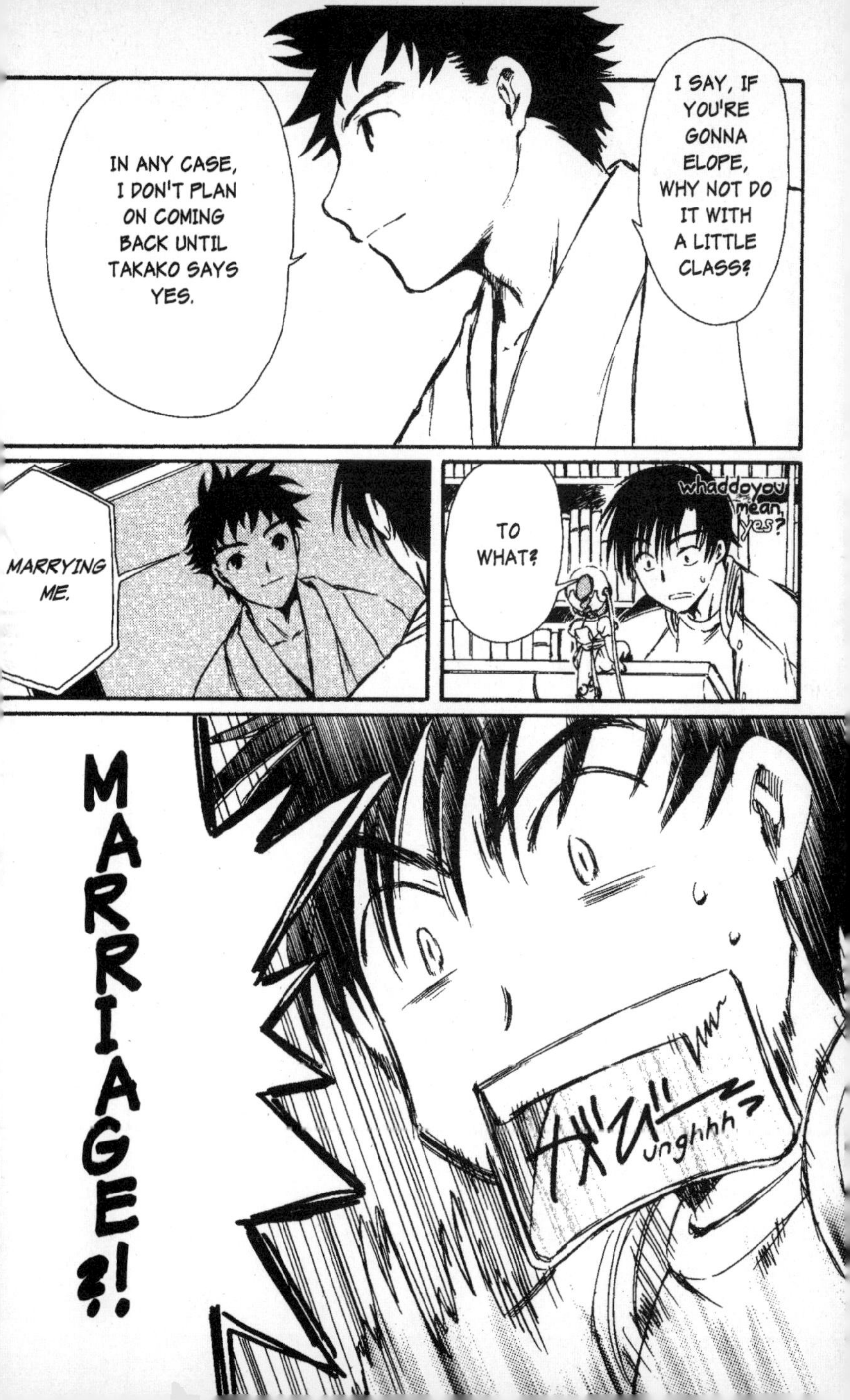
I SAY, IF YOU'RE GONNA ELOPE, WHY NOT DO IT WITH A LITTLE CLASS?
IN ANY CASE, I DON'T PLAN ON COMING BACK UNTIL TAKAKO SAYS YES.
whaddoyou mean, yes?
TO WHAT?
MARRYING ME.
MARRIAGE?!
unghhh

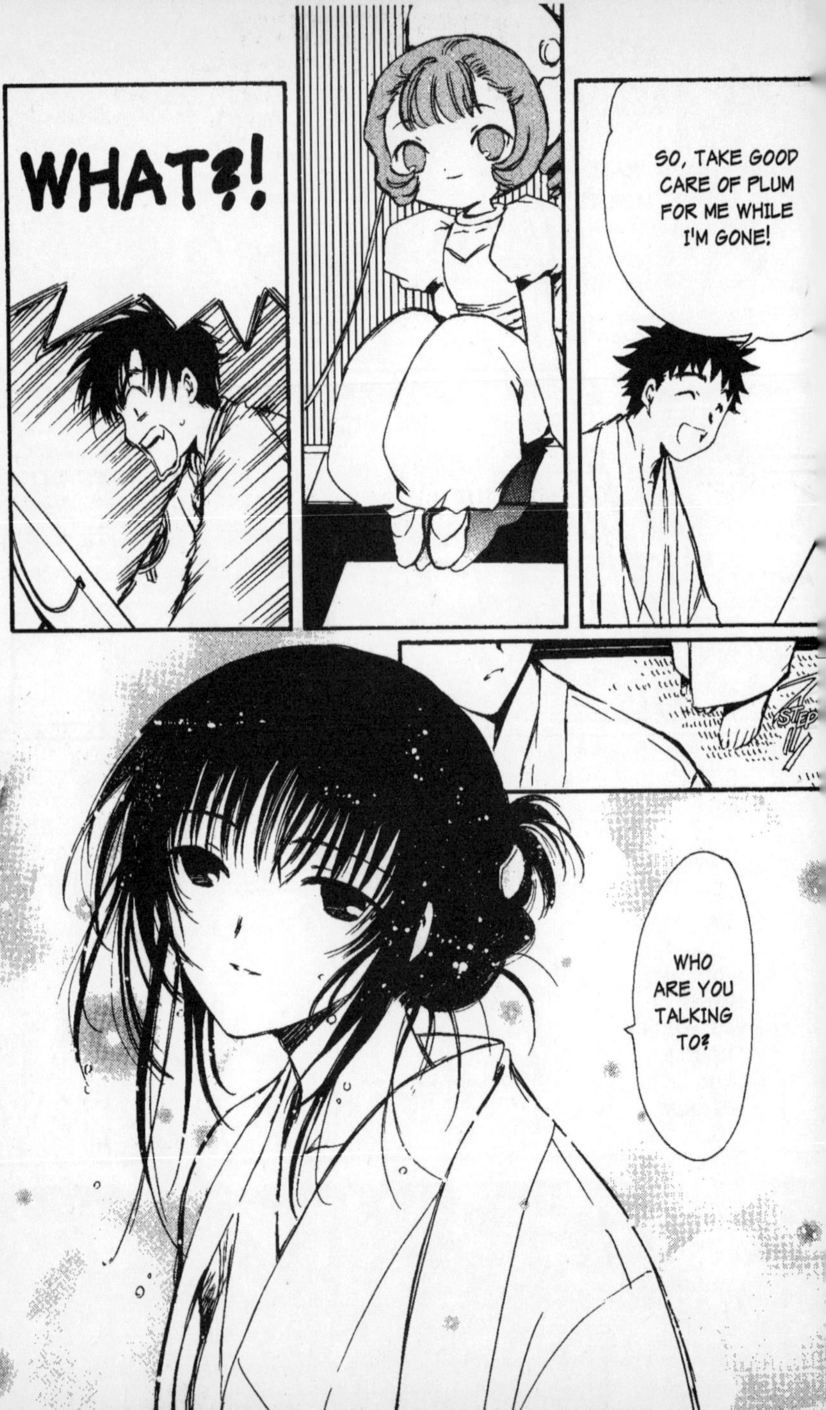
SO, TAKE GOOD CARE OF PLUM FOR ME WHILE I'M GONE!
WHAT?!
STEP
WHO ARE YOU TALKING TO?

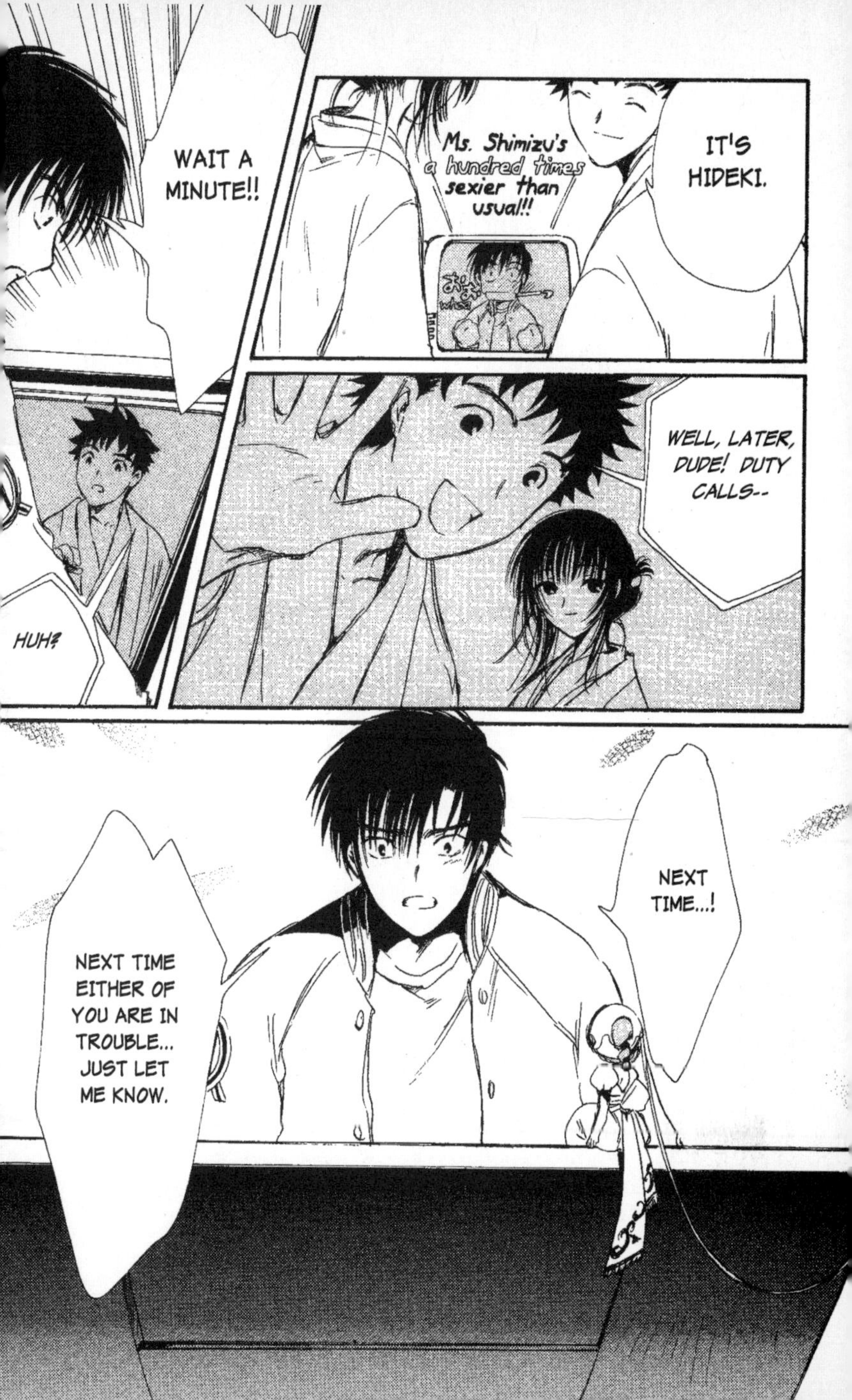
IT'S HIDEKI.
Ms. Shimizu's a hundred times sexier than usual!!
whoa
WAIT A MINUTE!!
WELL, LATER, DUDE! DUTY CALLS--
HUH?
NEXT TIME...!
NEXT TIME EITHER OF YOU ARE IN TROUBLE... JUST LET ME KNOW.

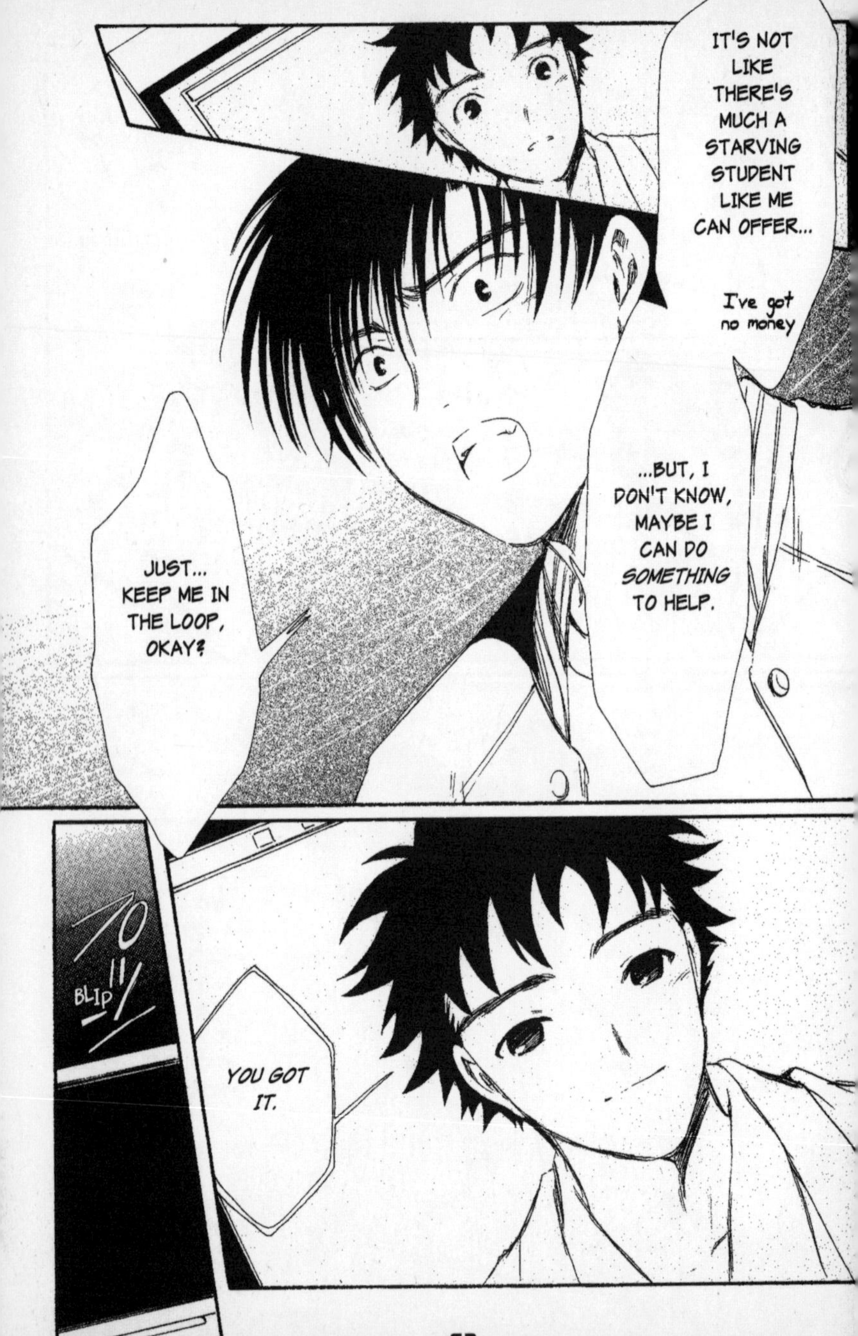
IT'S NOT LIKE THERE'S MUCH A STARVING STUDENT LIKE ME CAN OFFER...
I've got no money
...BUT, I DON'T KNOW, MAYBE I CAN DO SOMETHING TO HELP.
JUST... KEEP ME IN THE LOOP, OKAY?
BLIP
YOU GOT IT.

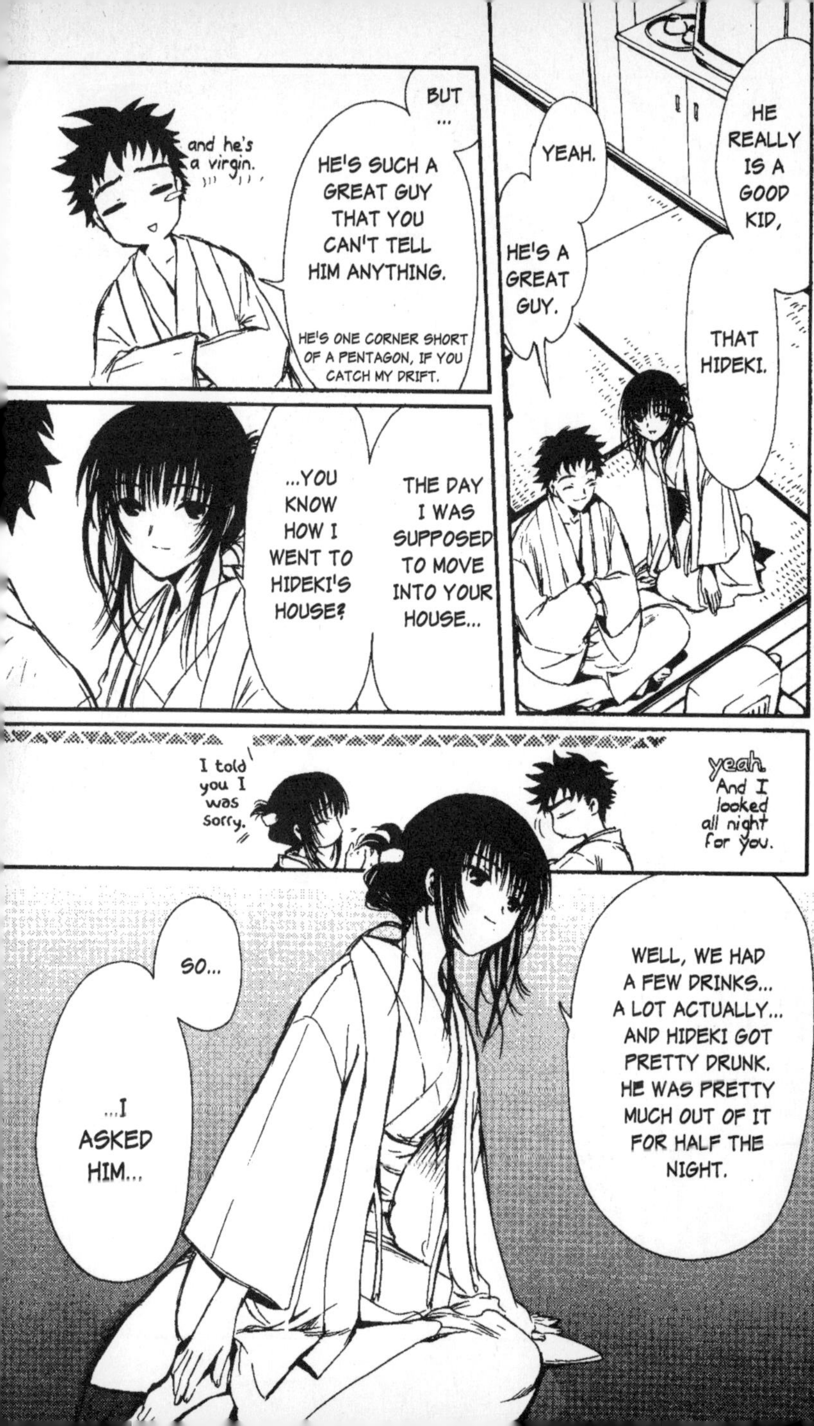
HE REALLY IS A GOOD KID,
THAT HIDEKI.
YEAH.
HE'S A GREAT GUY.
BUT ...
HE'S SUCH A GREAT GUY THAT YOU CAN'T TELL HIM ANYTHING.
HE'S ONE CORNER SHORT OF A PENTAGON, IF YOU CATCH MY DRIFT.
and he's a virgin.
THE DAY I WAS SUPPOSED TO MOVE INTO YOUR HOUSE...
...YOU KNOW HOW I WENT TO HIDEKI'S HOUSE?
yeah. And I looked all night for you.
I told you I was sorry.
WELL, WE HAD A FEW DRINKS... A LOT ACTUALLY... AND HIDEKI GOT PRETTY DRUNK. HE WAS PRETTY MUCH OUT OF IT FOR HALF THE NIGHT.
SO...
...I ASKED HIM...

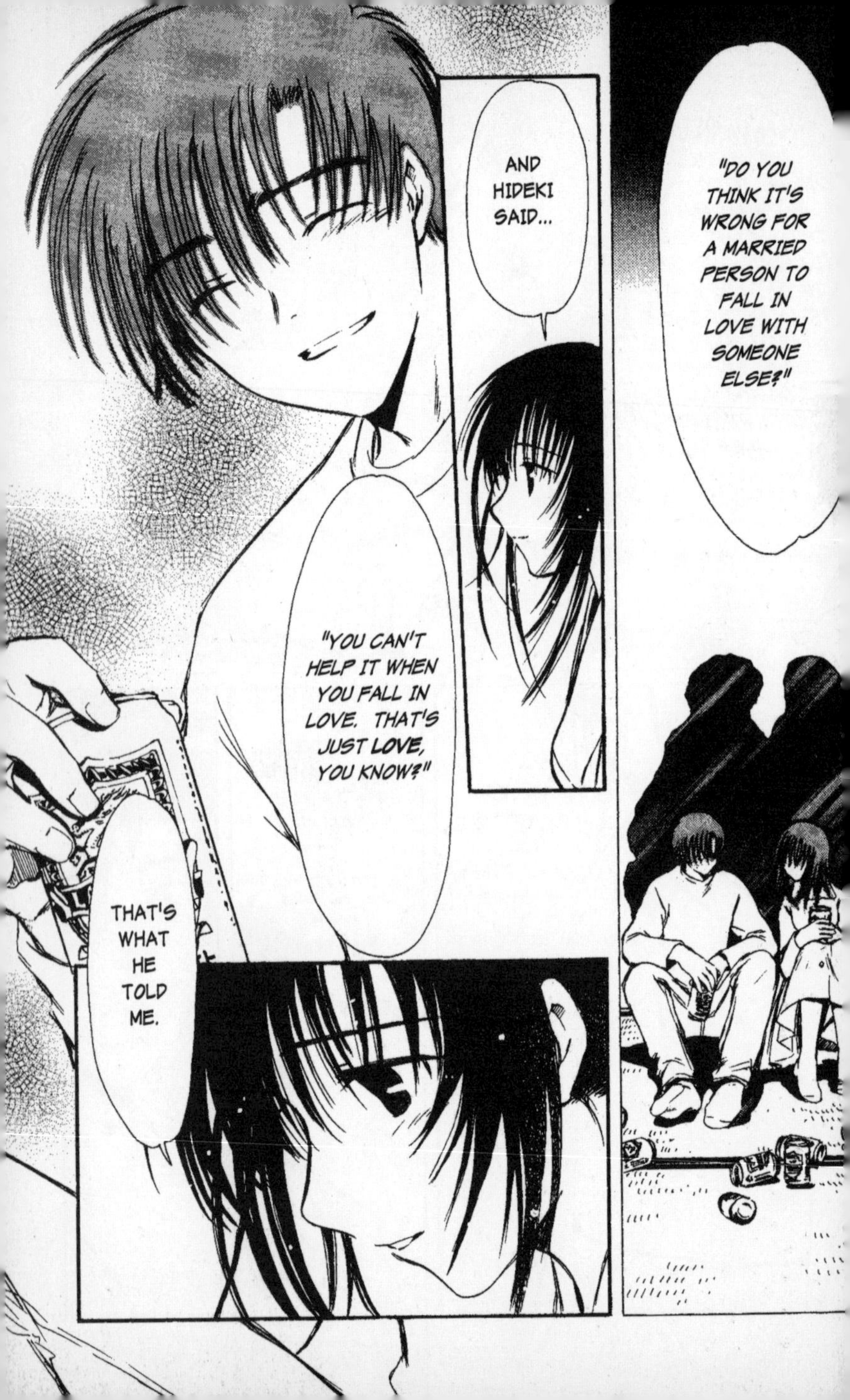
"DO YOU THINK IT'S WRONG FOR A MARRIED PERSON TO FALL IN LOVE WITH SOMEONE ELSE?"
AND HIDEKI SAID...
"YOU CAN'T HELP IT WHEN YOU FALL IN LOVE. THAT'S JUST LOVE, YOU KNOW?"
THAT'S WHAT HE TOLD ME.

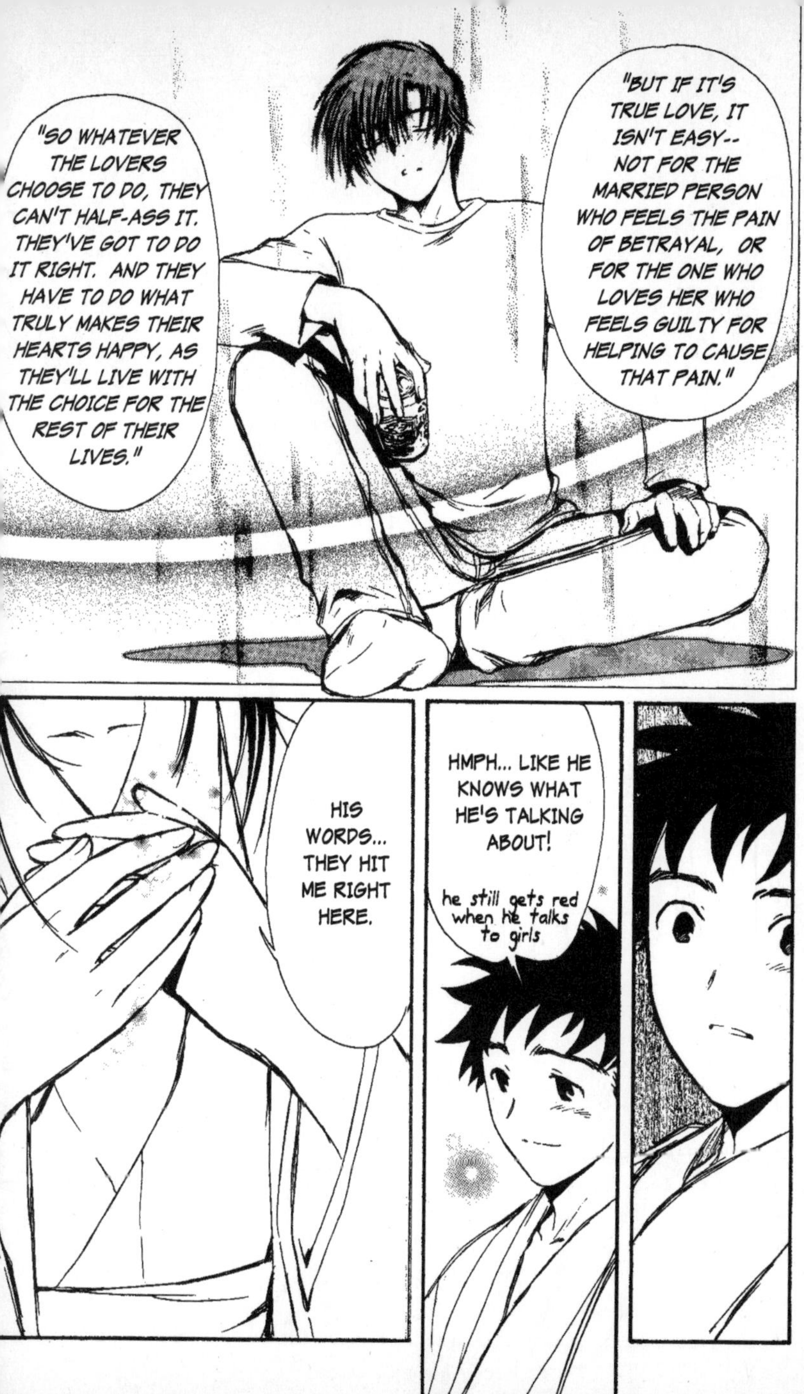
"BUT IF IT'S TRUE LOVE, IT ISN'T EASY-- NOT FOR THE MARRIED PERSON WHO FEELS THE PAIN OF BETRAYAL, OR FOR THE ONE WHO LOVES HER WHO FEELS GUILTY FOR HELPING TO CAUSE THAT PAIN."
"SO WHATEVER THE LOVERS CHOOSE TO DO, THEY CAN'T HALF-ASS IT. THEY'VE GOT TO DO IT RIGHT. AND THEY HAVE TO DO WHAT TRULY MAKES THEIR HEARTS HAPPY, AS THEY'LL LIVE WITH THE CHOICE FOR THE REST OF THEIR LIVES."
HMPH... LIKE HE KNOWS WHAT HE'S TALKING ABOUT!
he still gets red when he talks to girls
HIS WORDS... THEY HIT ME RIGHT HERE.

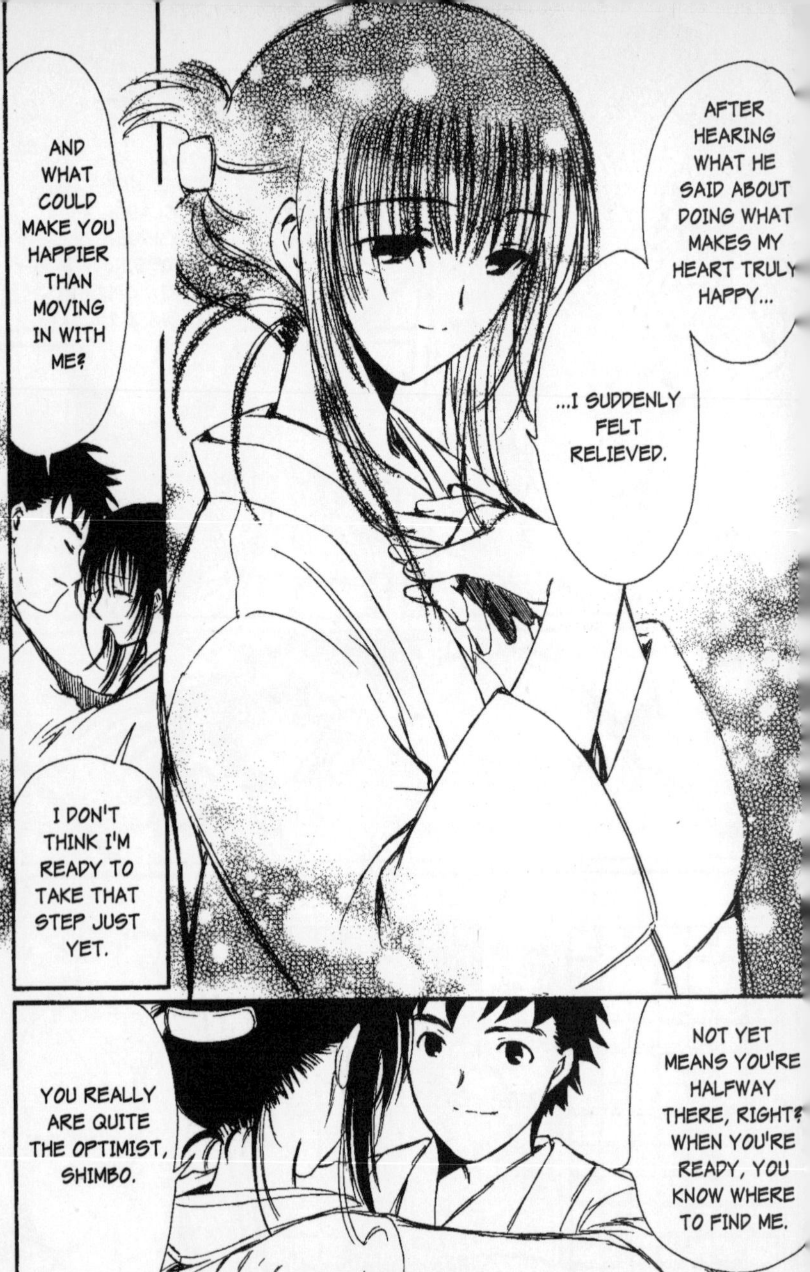
AFTER HEARING WHAT HE SAID ABOUT DOING WHAT MAKES MY HEART TRULY HAPPY...
...I SUDDENLY FELT RELIEVED.
AND WHAT COULD MAKE YOU HAPPIER THAN MOVING IN WITH ME?
I DON'T THINK I'M READY TO TAKE THAT STEP JUST YET.
NOT YET MEANS YOU'RE HALFWAY THERE, RIGHT? WHEN YOU'RE READY, YOU KNOW WHERE TO FIND ME.
YOU REALLY ARE QUITE THE OPTIMIST, SHIMBO.

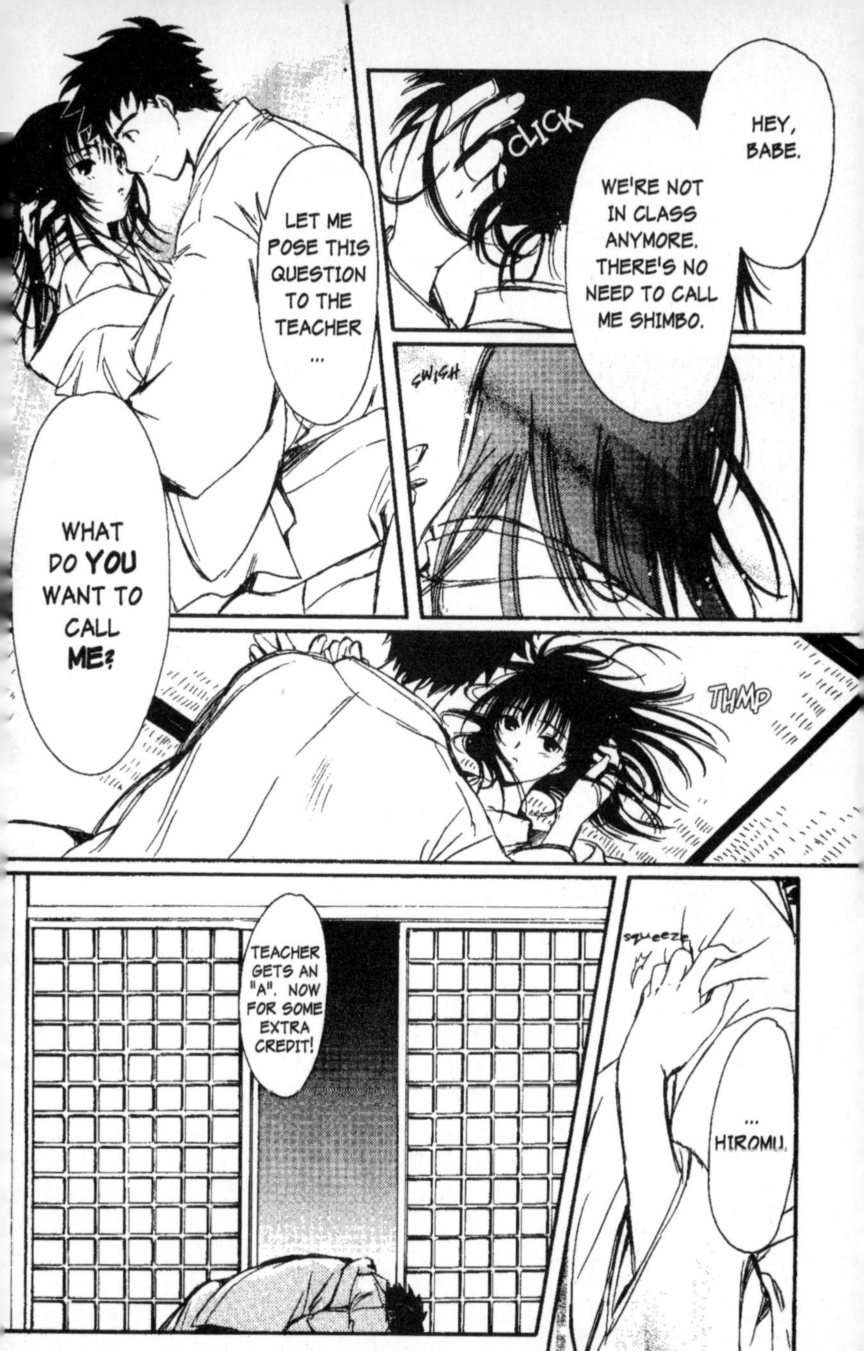
CLICK
HEY, BABE.
WE'RE NOT IN CLASS ANYMORE. THERE'S NO NEED TO CALL ME SHIMBO.
SWISH
LET ME POSE THIS QUESTION TO THE TEACHER ...
WHAT DO YOU WANT TO CALL ME?
THMP
squeeze
... HIROMU.
TEACHER GETS AN "A". NOW FOR SOME EXTRA CREDIT!

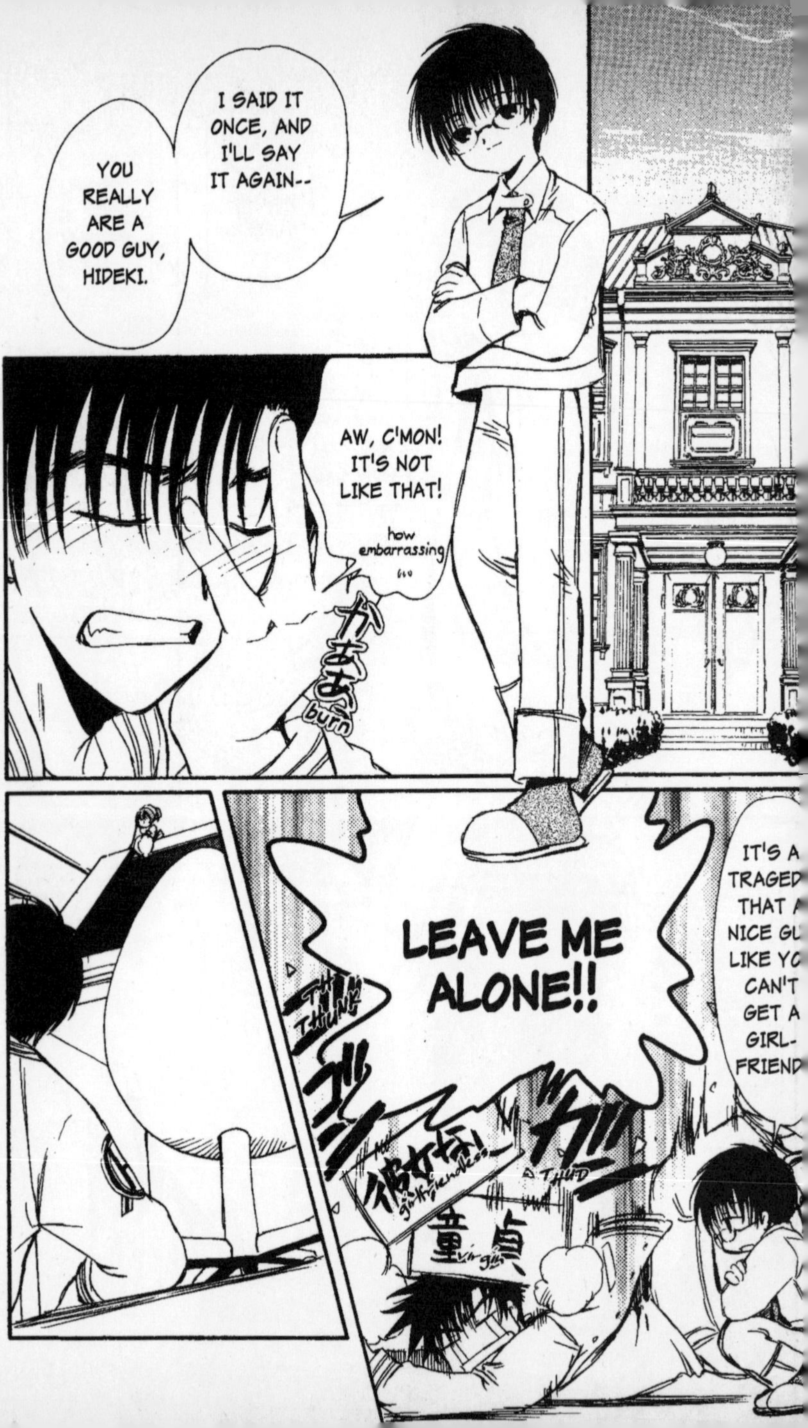
I SAID IT ONCE, AND I'LL SAY IT AGAIN--
YOU REALLY ARE A GOOD GUY, HIDEKI.
AW, C'MON! IT'S NOT LIKE THAT!
how embarrassing
かぁぁ
burn
IT'S A TRAGED THAT A NICE GU LIKE YO CAN'T GET A GIRL-FRIEND
LEAVE ME ALONE!!
THUNK
THUD
girlfriendless
童貞
virgin

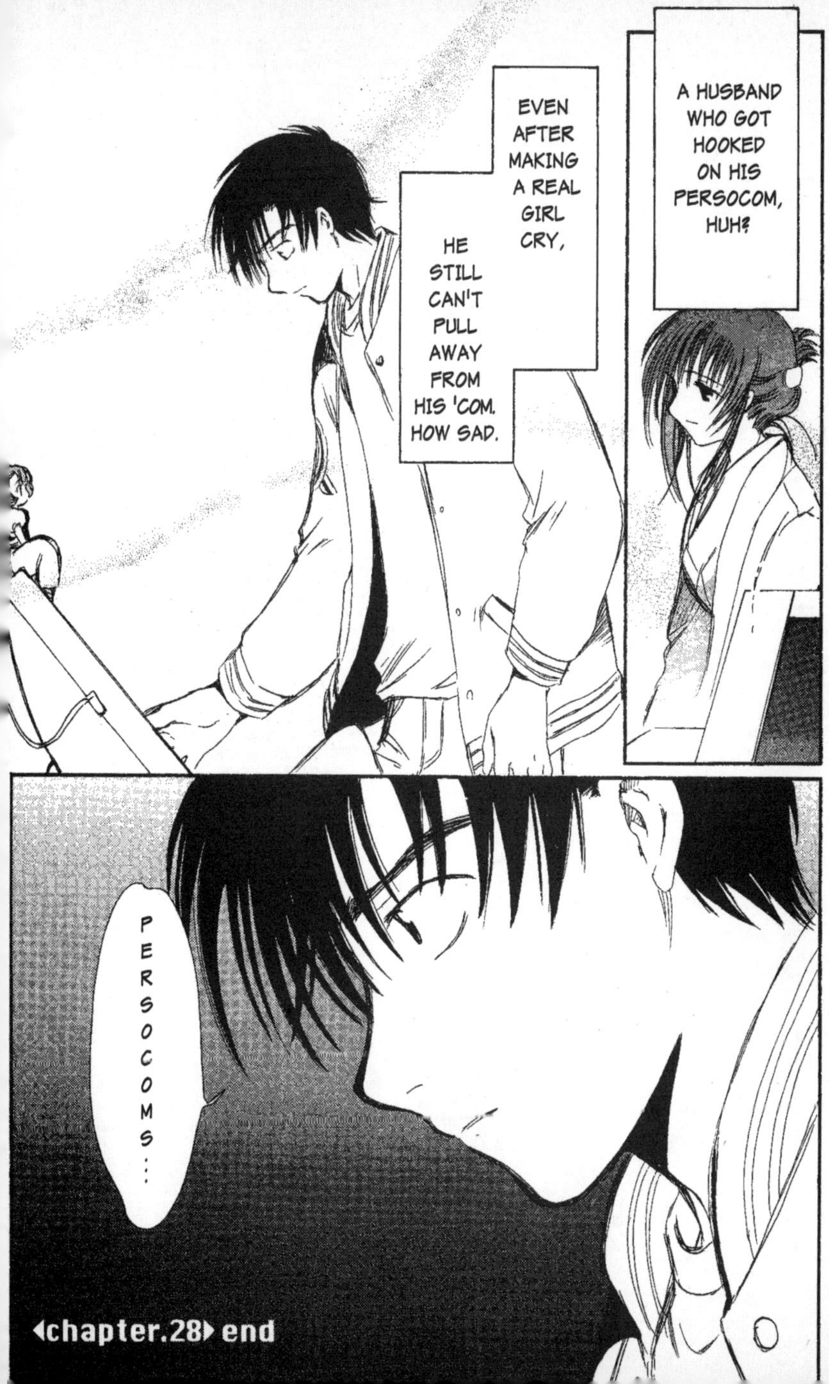
A HUSBAND WHO GOT HOOKED ON HIS PERSOCOM, HUH?
EVEN AFTER MAKING A REAL GIRL CRY,
HE STILL CAN'T PULL AWAY FROM HIS 'COM. HOW SAD.
PERSOCOMS...
‹chapter.28› end

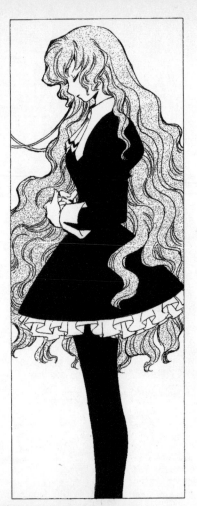

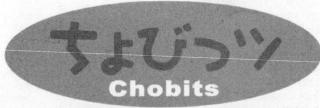

ちょびっツ
Chobits

◀chapter.29▶

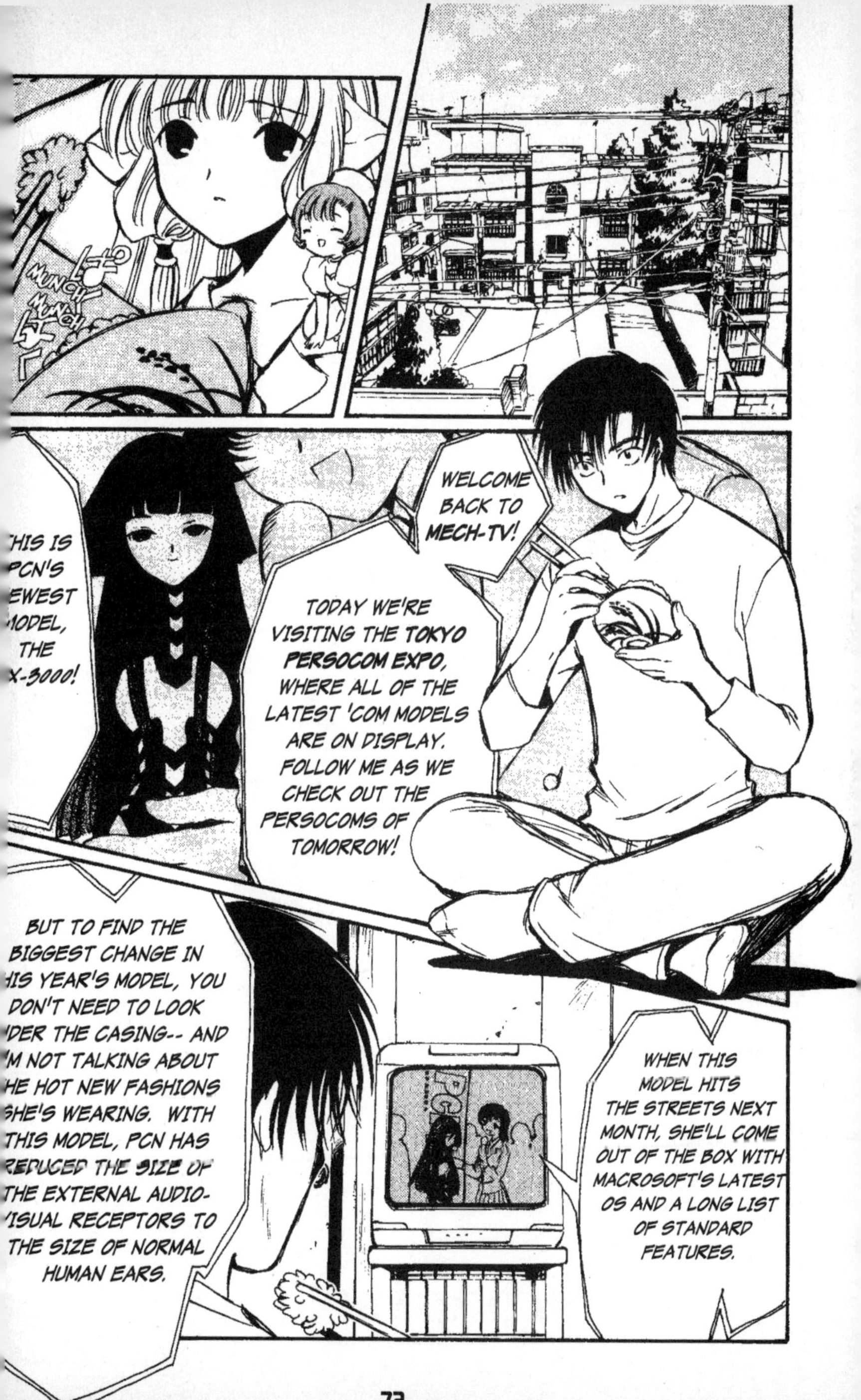
MUNCH
MUNCH
WELCOME BACK TO MECH-TV!
TODAY WE'RE VISITING THE TOKYO PERSOCOM EXPO, WHERE ALL OF THE LATEST 'COM MODELS ARE ON DISPLAY. FOLLOW ME AS WE CHECK OUT THE PERSOCOMS OF TOMORROW!
HIS IS PCN'S EWEST ODEL, THE X-3000!
WHEN THIS MODEL HITS THE STREETS NEXT MONTH, SHE'LL COME OUT OF THE BOX WITH MACROSOFT'S LATEST OS AND A LONG LIST OF STANDARD FEATURES.
BUT TO FIND THE BIGGEST CHANGE IN HIS YEAR'S MODEL, YOU DON'T NEED TO LOOK DER THE CASING-- AND M NOT TALKING ABOUT HE HOT NEW FASHIONS SHE'S WEARING. WITH THIS MODEL, PCN HAS REDUCED THE SIZE OF THE EXTERNAL AUDIO-ISUAL RECEPTORS TO THE SIZE OF NORMAL HUMAN EARS.

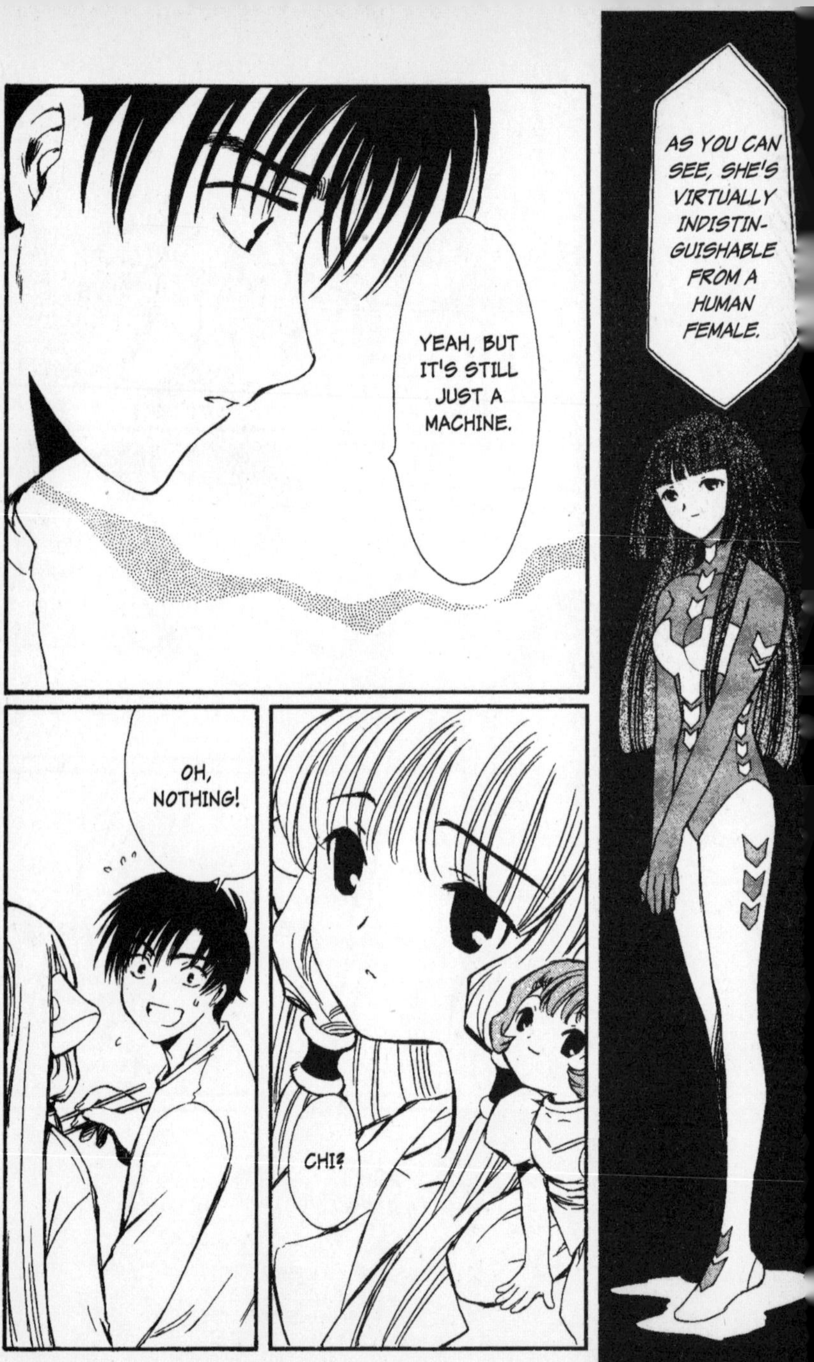
AS YOU CAN SEE, SHE'S VIRTUALLY INDISTIN-GUISHABLE FROM A HUMAN FEMALE.
YEAH, BUT IT'S STILL JUST A MACHINE.
CHI?
OH, NOTHING!

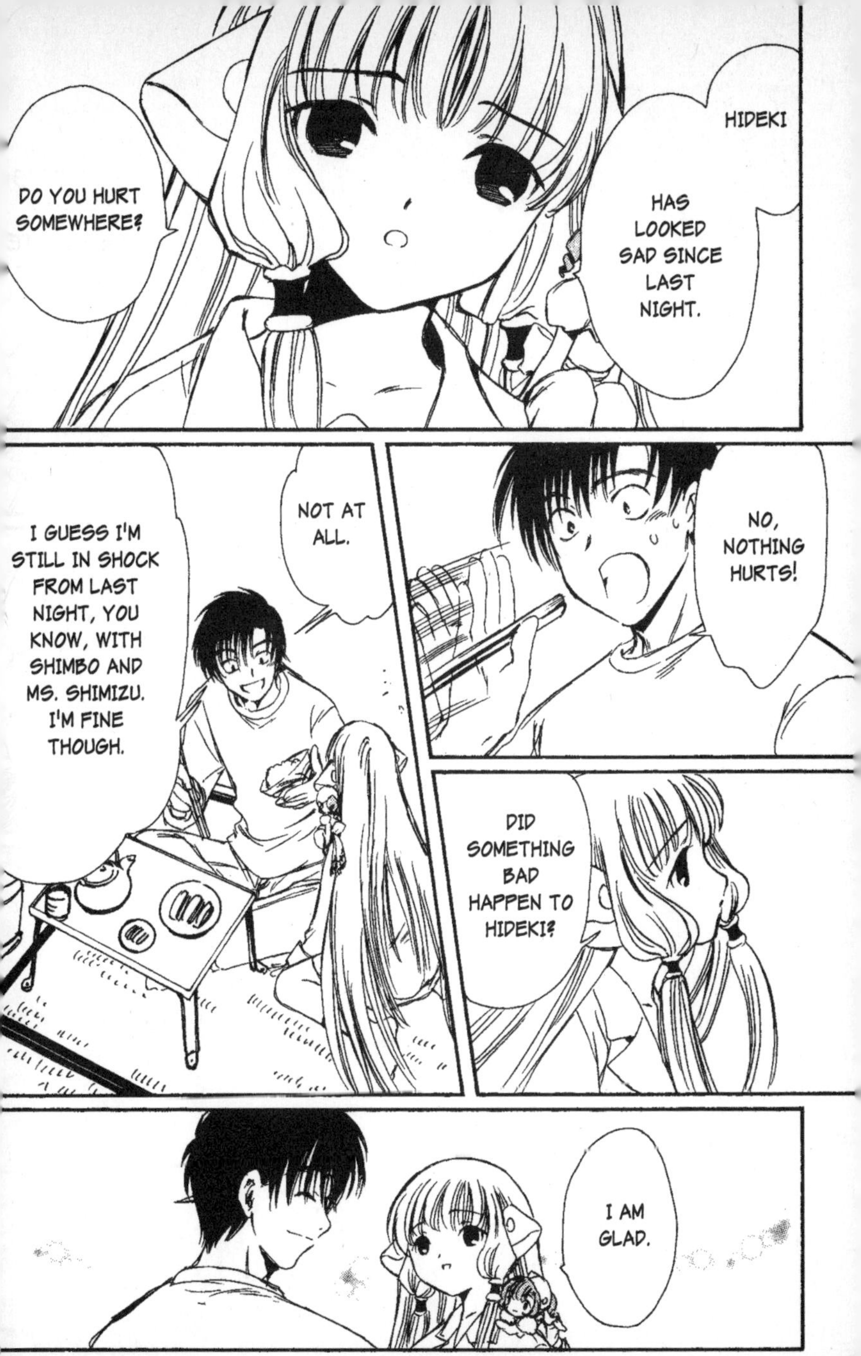
HIDEKI HAS LOOKED SAD SINCE LAST NIGHT.
DO YOU HURT SOMEWHERE?
NO, NOTHING HURTS!
DID SOMETHING BAD HAPPEN TO HIDEKI?
NOT AT ALL.
I GUESS I'M STILL IN SHOCK FROM LAST NIGHT, YOU KNOW, WITH SHIMBO AND MS. SHIMIZU. I'M FINE THOUGH.
I AM GLAD.

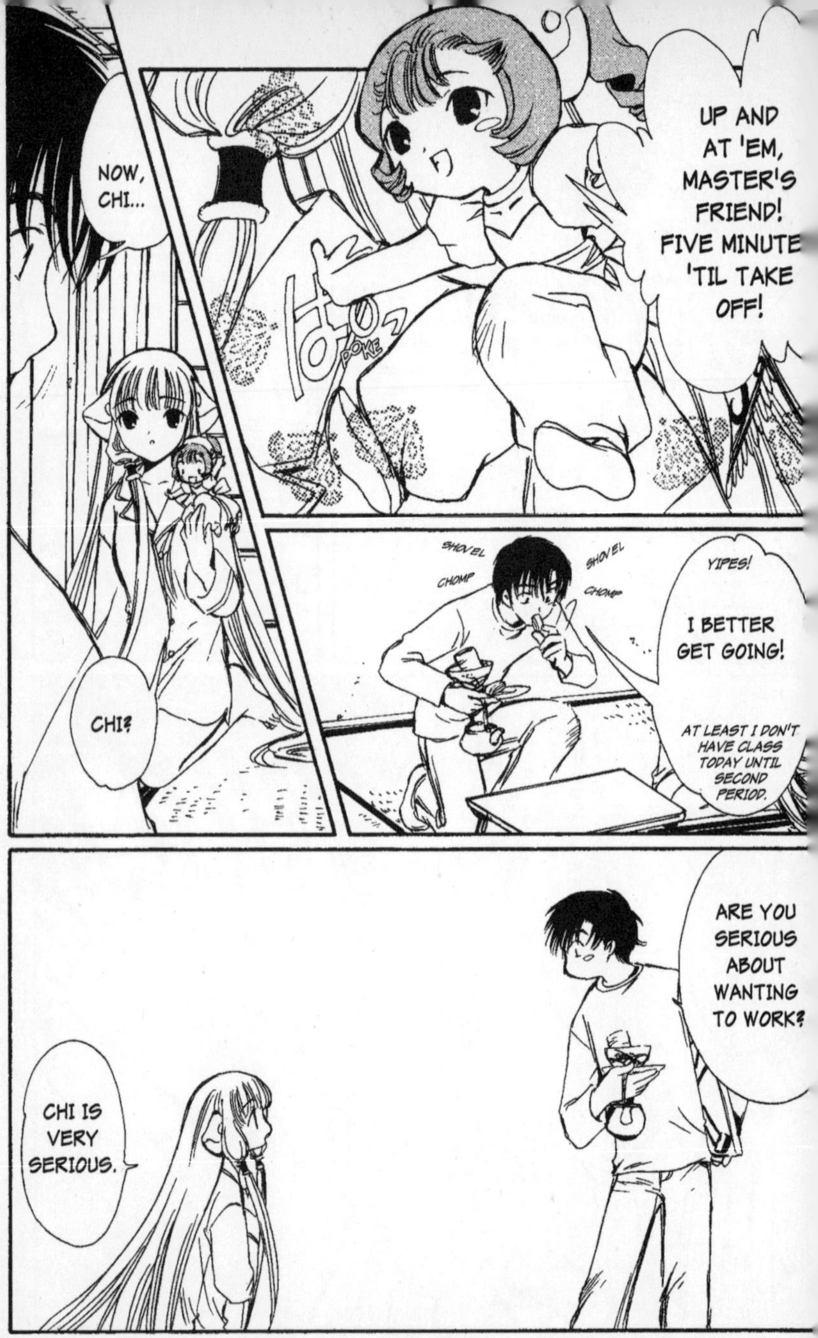
UP AND AT 'EM, MASTER'S FRIEND! FIVE MINUTE 'TIL TAKE OFF!
POKE
SHOVEL
SHOVEL
CHOMP
CHOMP
YIPES!
I BETTER GET GOING!
AT LEAST I DON'T HAVE CLASS TODAY UNTIL SECOND PERIOD.
NOW, CHI...
CHI?
ARE YOU SERIOUS ABOUT WANTING TO WORK?
CHI IS VERY SERIOUS.

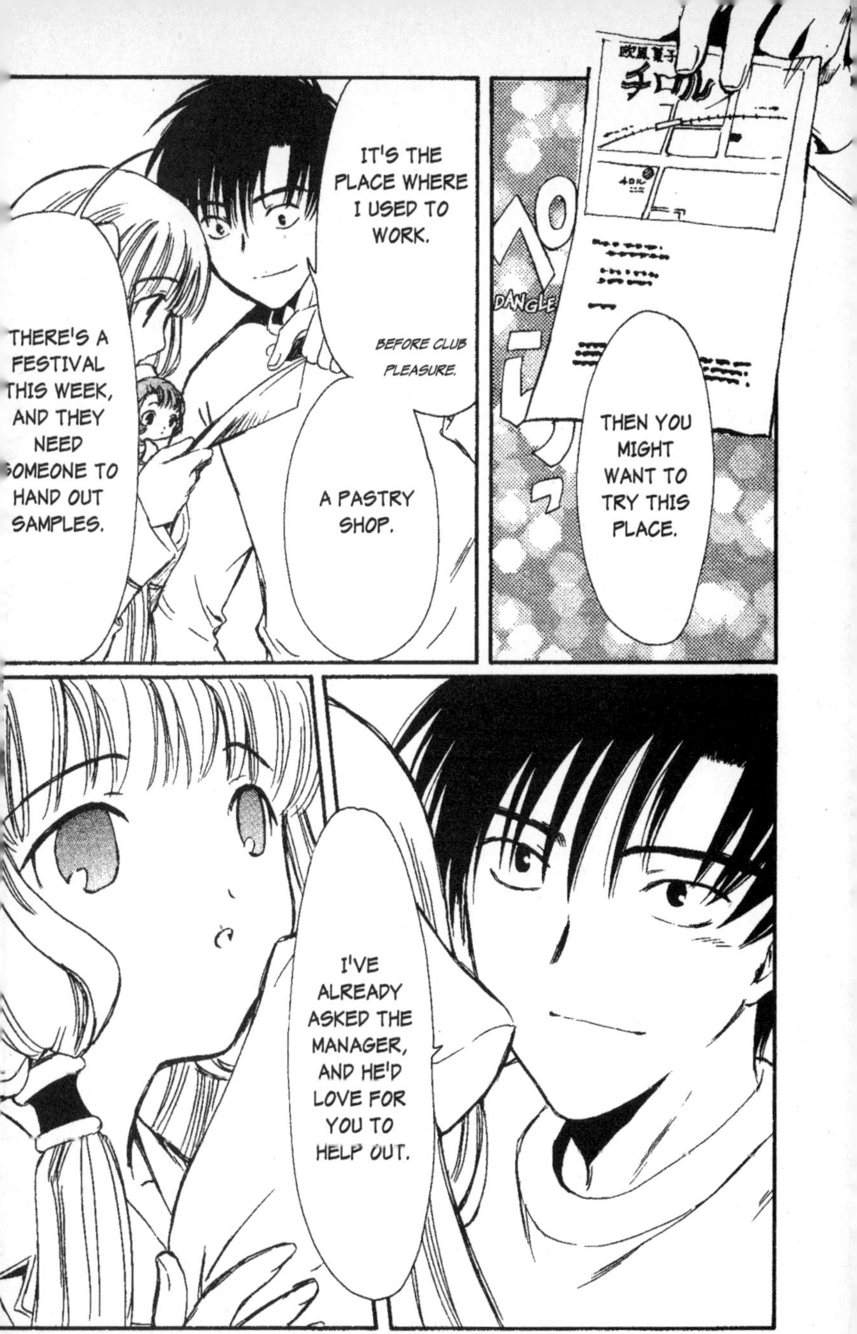
欧風菓子
チロル
DANGLE
THEN YOU MIGHT WANT TO TRY THIS PLACE.
IT'S THE PLACE WHERE I USED TO WORK.
BEFORE CLUB PLEASURE.
A PASTRY SHOP.
THERE'S A FESTIVAL THIS WEEK, AND THEY NEED SOMEONE TO HAND OUT SAMPLES.
I'VE ALREADY ASKED THE MANAGER, AND HE'D LOVE FOR YOU TO HELP OUT.

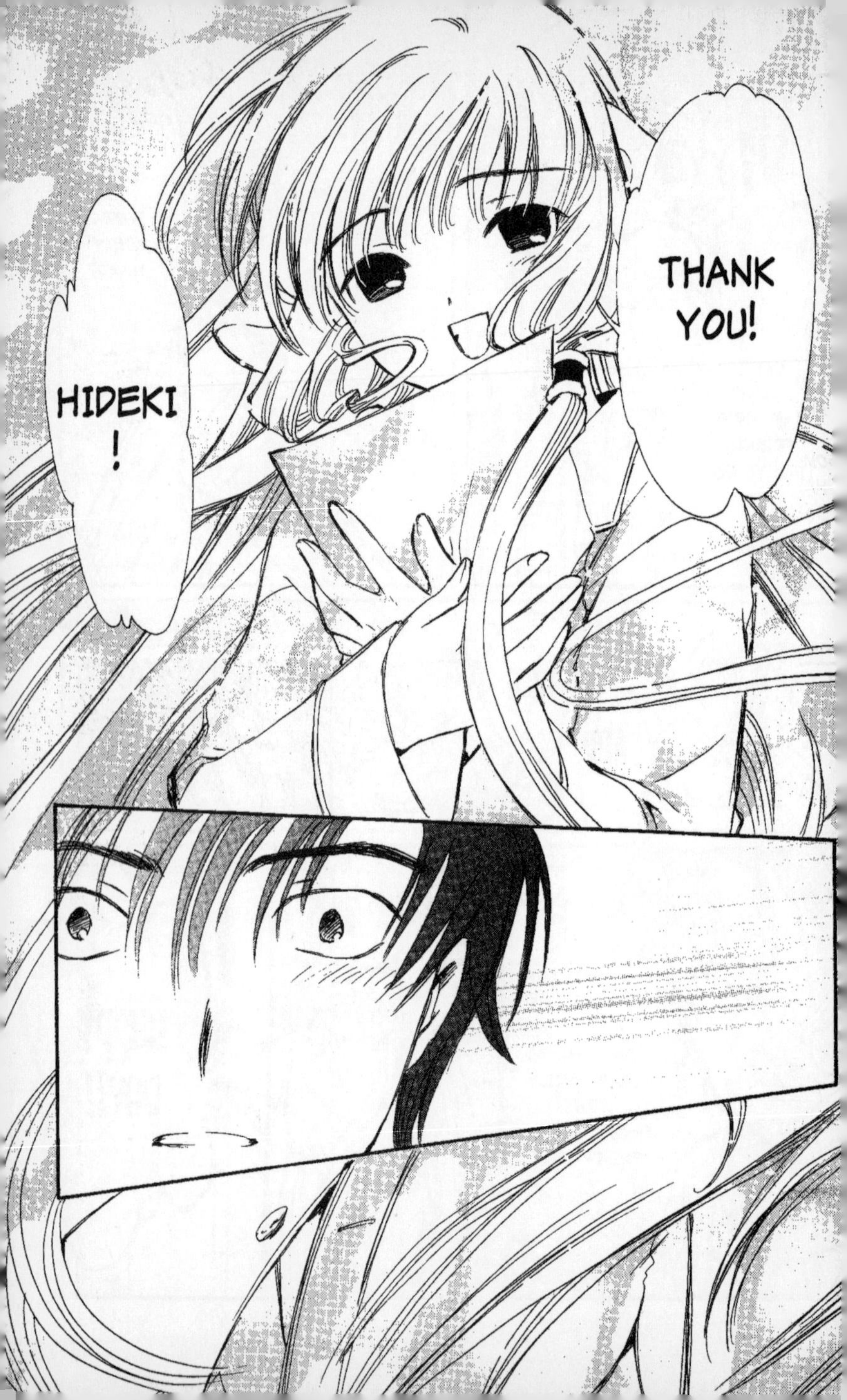
THANK YOU!
HIDEKI !

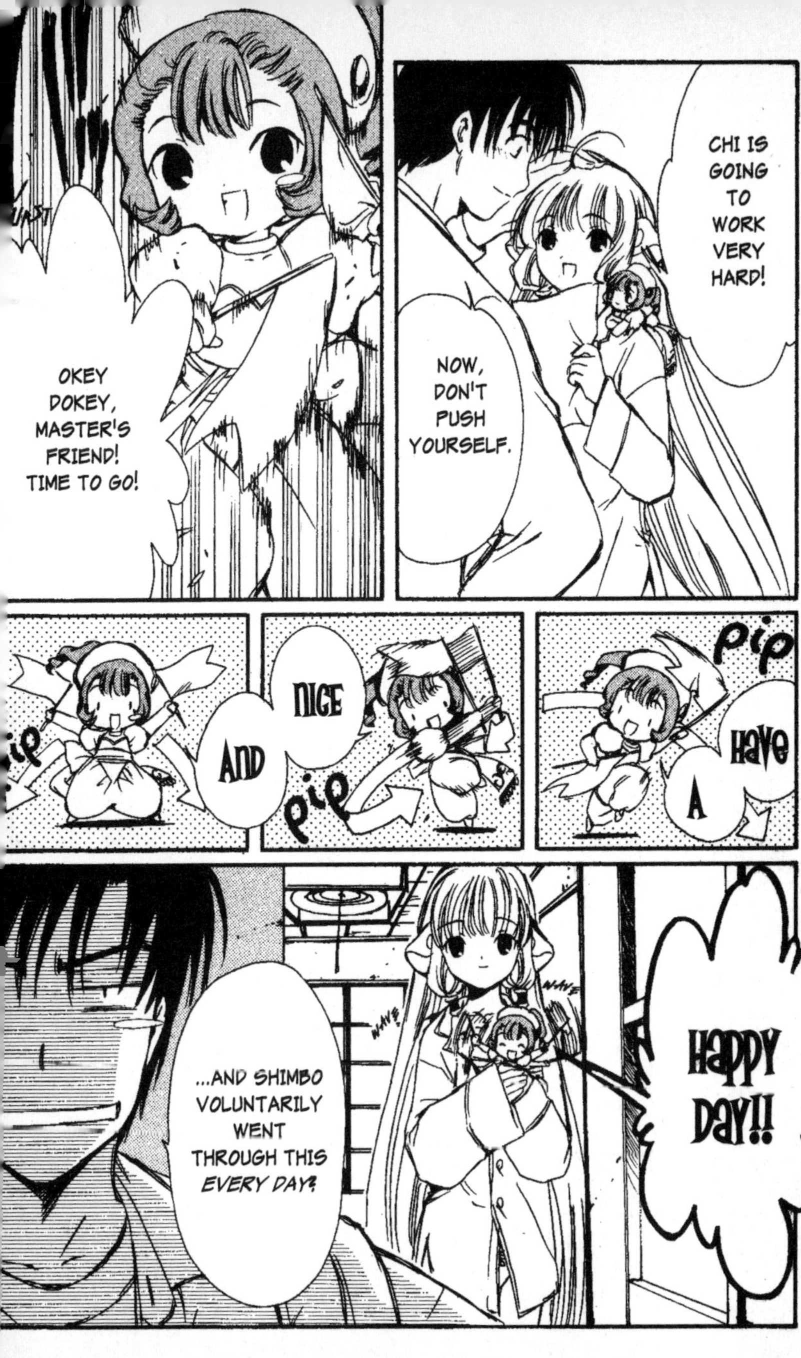
CHI IS GOING TO WORK VERY HARD!
NOW, DON'T PUSH YOURSELF.
OKEY DOKEY, MASTER'S FRIEND! TIME TO GO!
pip
HAVE
A
NICE
pip
AND
WAVE
WAVE
HAPPY DAY!!
...AND SHIMBO VOLUNTARILY WENT THROUGH THIS *EVERY DAY?*

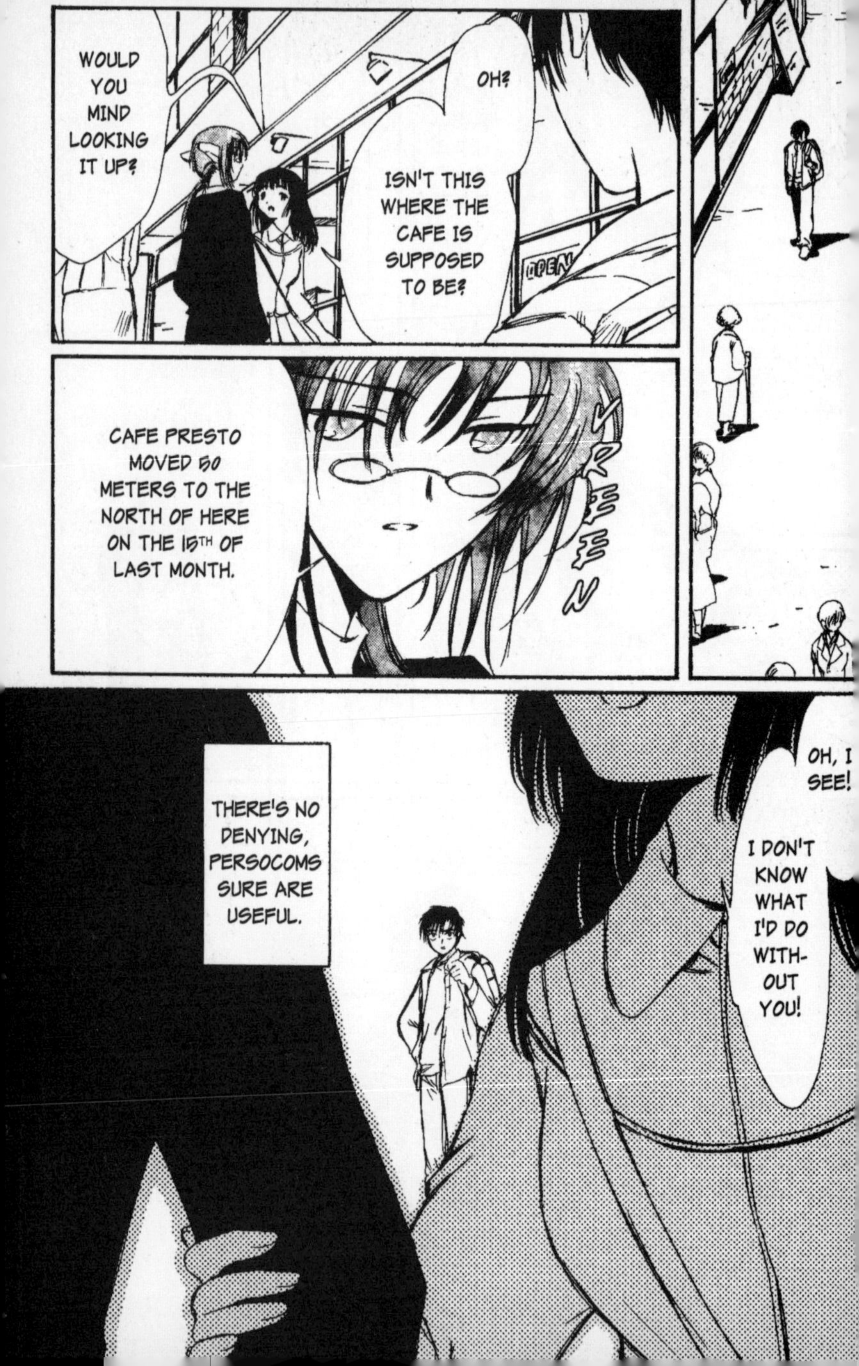
OH?
ISN'T THIS WHERE THE CAFE IS SUPPOSED TO BE?
OPEN
WOULD YOU MIND LOOKING IT UP?
VREEEN
CAFE PRESTO MOVED 50 METERS TO THE NORTH OF HERE ON THE 15TH OF LAST MONTH.
OH, I SEE!
I DON'T KNOW WHAT I'D DO WITH-OUT YOU!
THERE'S NO DENYING, PERSOCOMS SURE ARE USEFUL.

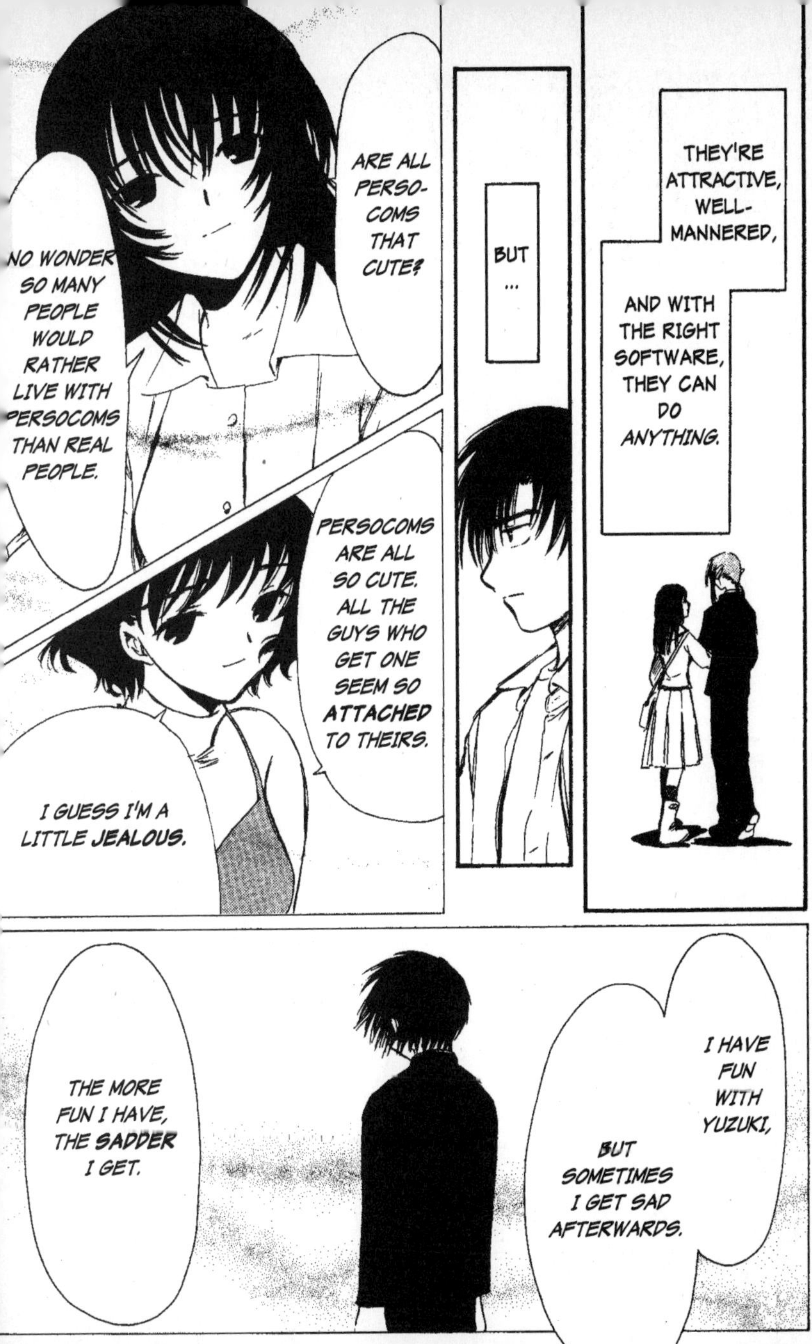
THEY'RE ATTRACTIVE, WELL-MANNERED,
AND WITH THE RIGHT SOFTWARE, THEY CAN DO ANYTHING.
BUT ...
ARE ALL PERSOCOMS THAT CUTE?
NO WONDER SO MANY PEOPLE WOULD RATHER LIVE WITH PERSOCOMS THAN REAL PEOPLE.
PERSOCOMS ARE ALL SO CUTE. ALL THE GUYS WHO GET ONE SEEM SO **ATTACHED** TO THEIRS.
I GUESS I'M A LITTLE **JEALOUS.**
I HAVE FUN WITH YUZUKI,
BUT SOMETIMES I GET SAD AFTERWARDS.
THE MORE FUN I HAVE, THE **SADDER** I GET.

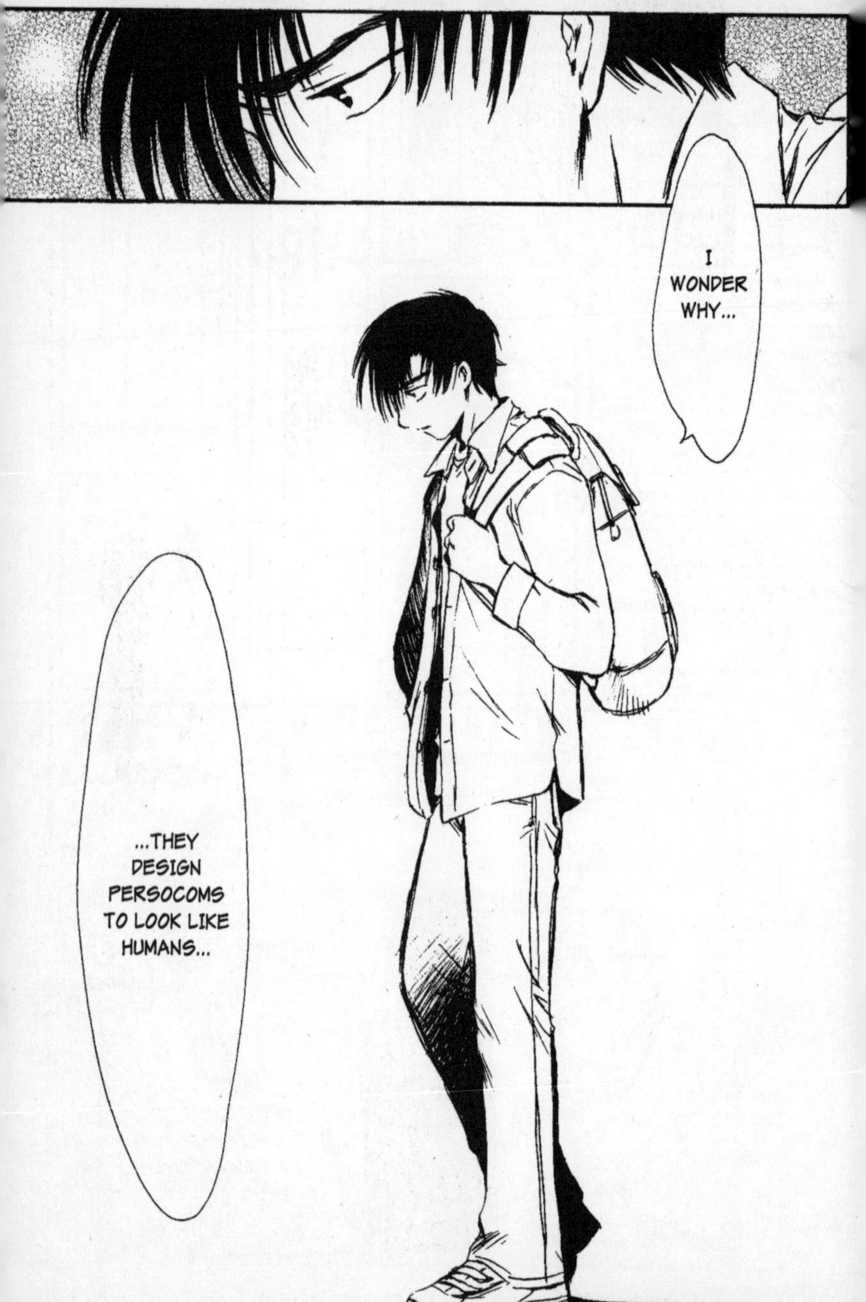
I WONDER WHY...
...THEY DESIGN PERSOCOMS TO LOOK LIKE HUMANS...

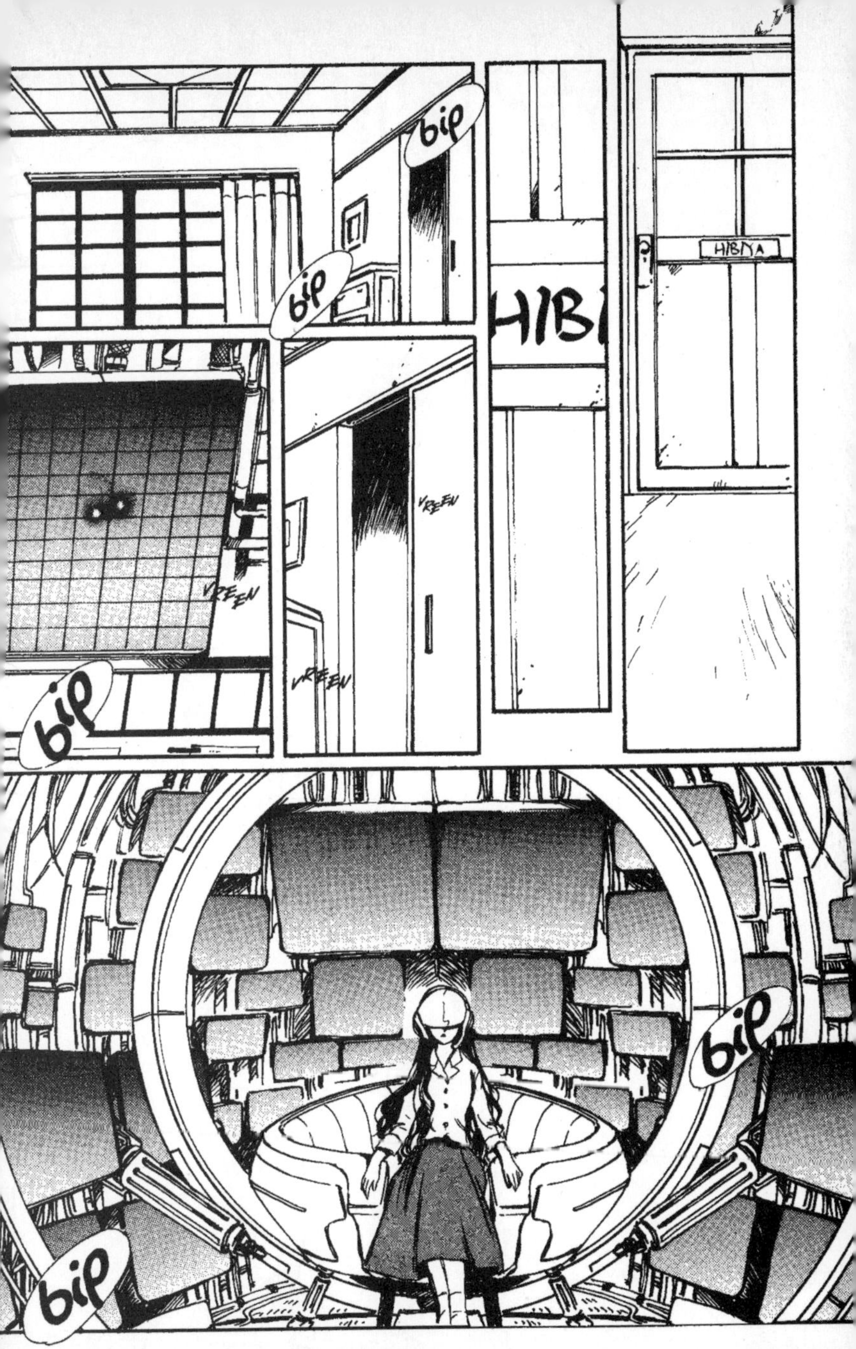
HIBIYA
HIBI
bip
bip
VREEN
VREEN
bip
VREEN
bip
bip
bip

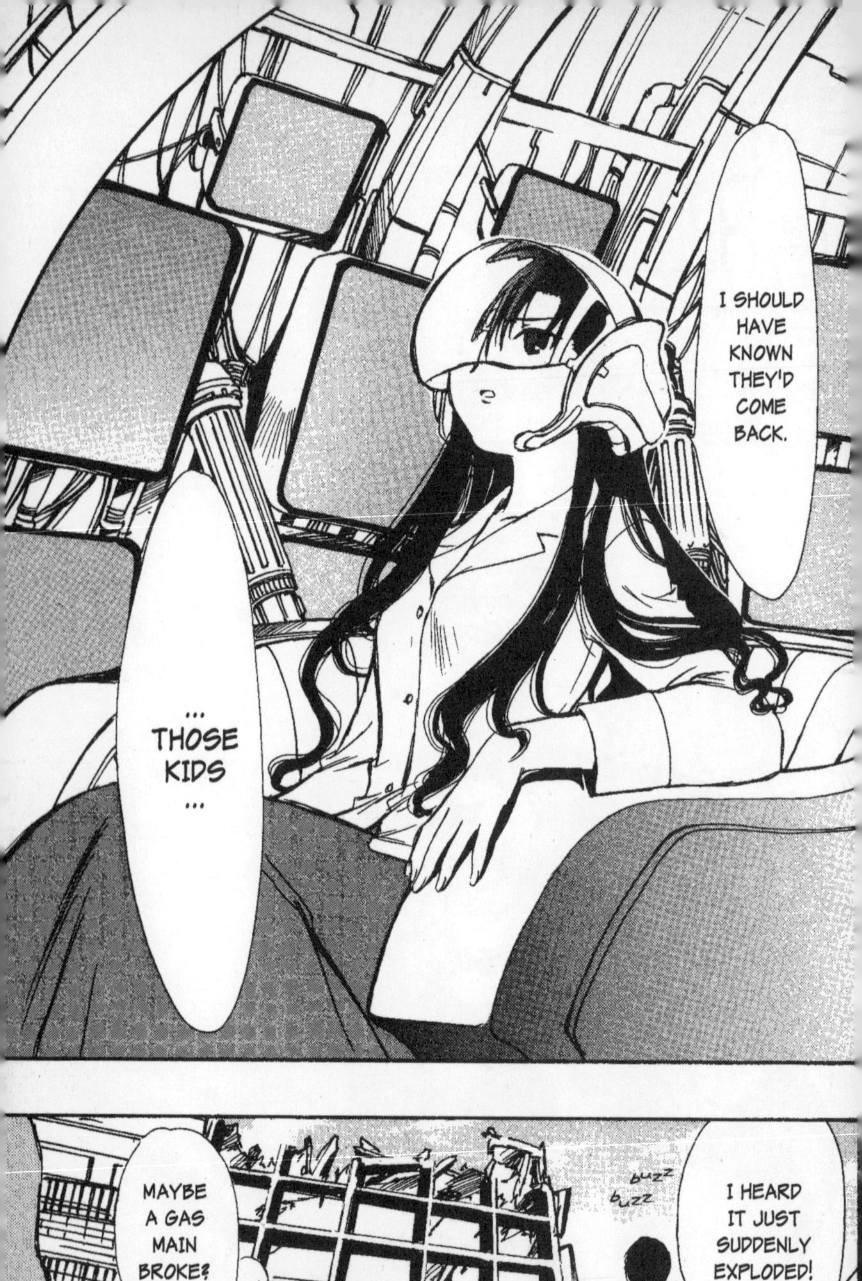
I SHOULD HAVE KNOWN THEY'D COME BACK.
... THOSE KIDS ...
I HEARD IT JUST SUDDENLY EXPLODED!
buzz buzz
MAYBE A GAS MAIN BROKE?

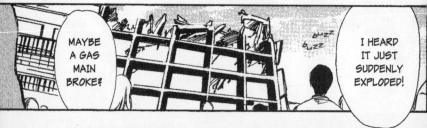

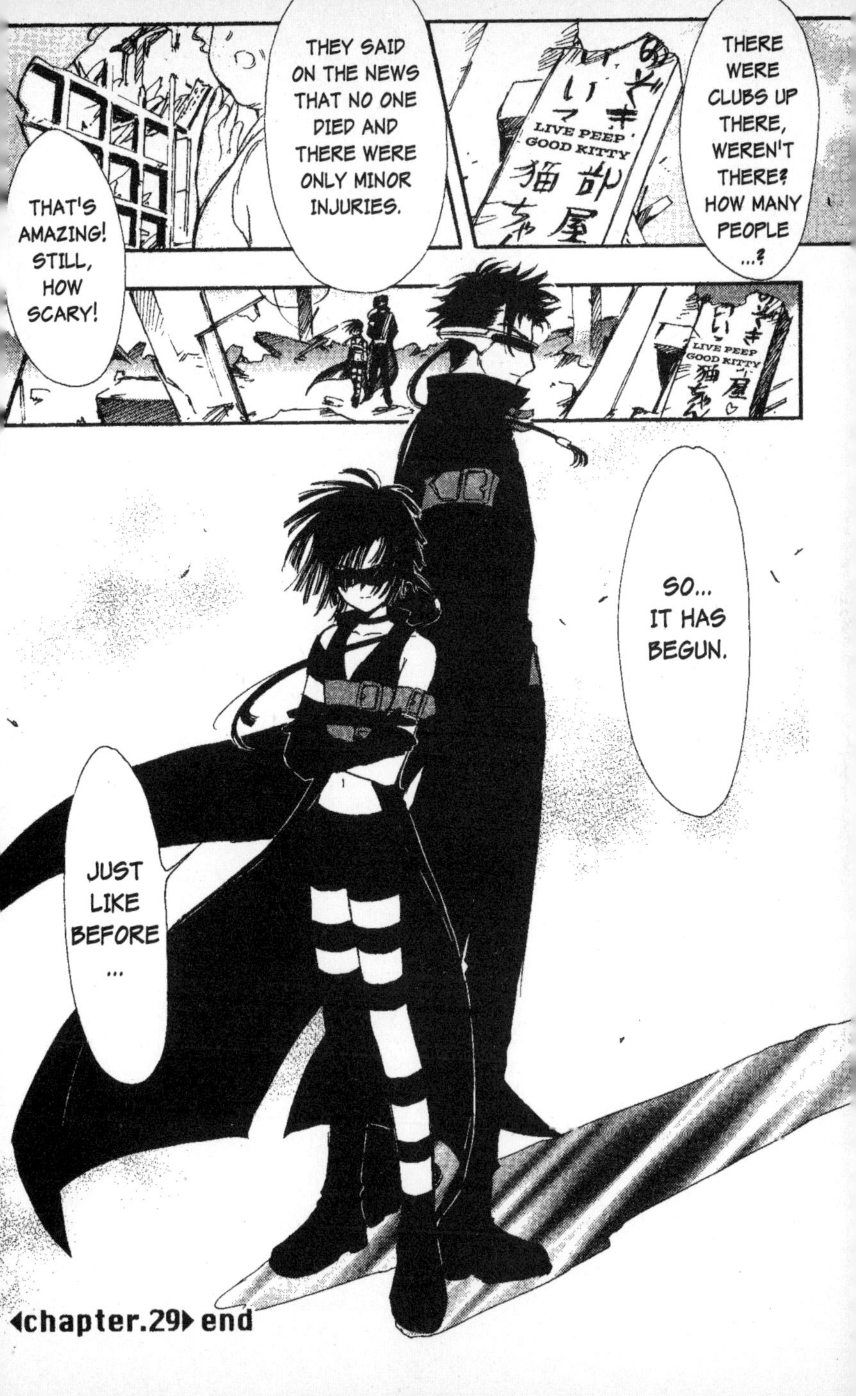
THERE WERE CLUBS UP THERE, WEREN'T THERE? HOW MANY PEOPLE ...?
LIVE PEEP GOOD KITTY
THEY SAID ON THE NEWS THAT NO ONE DIED AND THERE WERE ONLY MINOR INJURIES.
THAT'S AMAZING! STILL, HOW SCARY!
LIVE PEEP GOOD KITTY
SO... IT HAS BEGUN.
JUST LIKE BEFORE ...
◀chapter.29▶ end

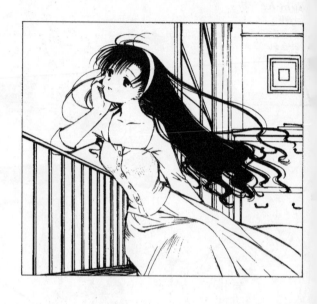

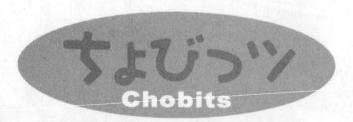

ちょびっツ
Chobits

◀chapter.30▶

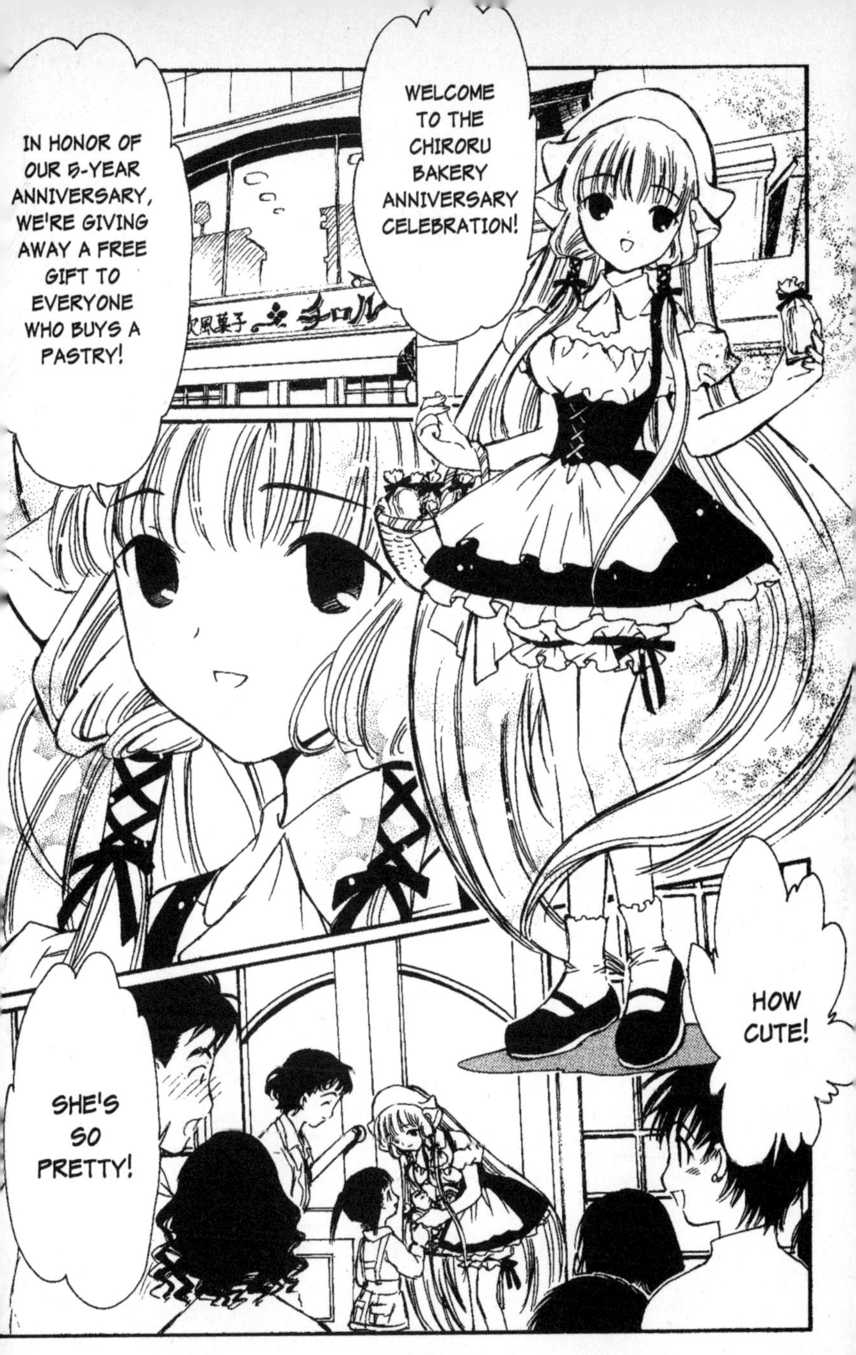
WELCOME TO THE CHIRORU BAKERY ANNIVERSARY CELEBRATION!
IN HONOR OF OUR 5-YEAR ANNIVERSARY, WE'RE GIVING AWAY A FREE GIFT TO EVERYONE WHO BUYS A PASTRY!
HOW CUTE!
SHE'S SO PRETTY!

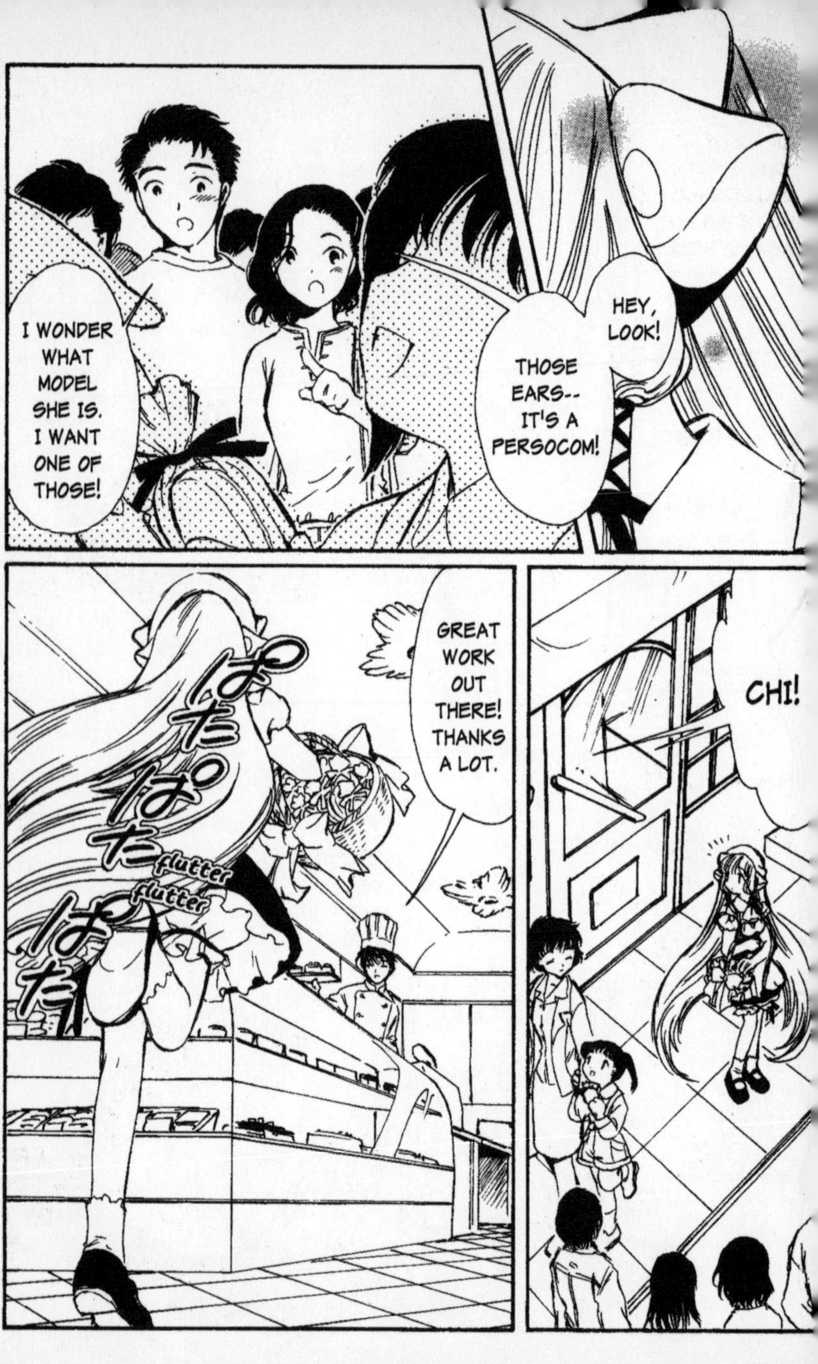
HEY, LOOK!
THOSE EARS-- IT'S A PERSOCOM!
I WONDER WHAT MODEL SHE IS. I WANT ONE OF THOSE!
CHI!
GREAT WORK OUT THERE! THANKS A LOT.
ぱたっぱたぱた
flutter flutter

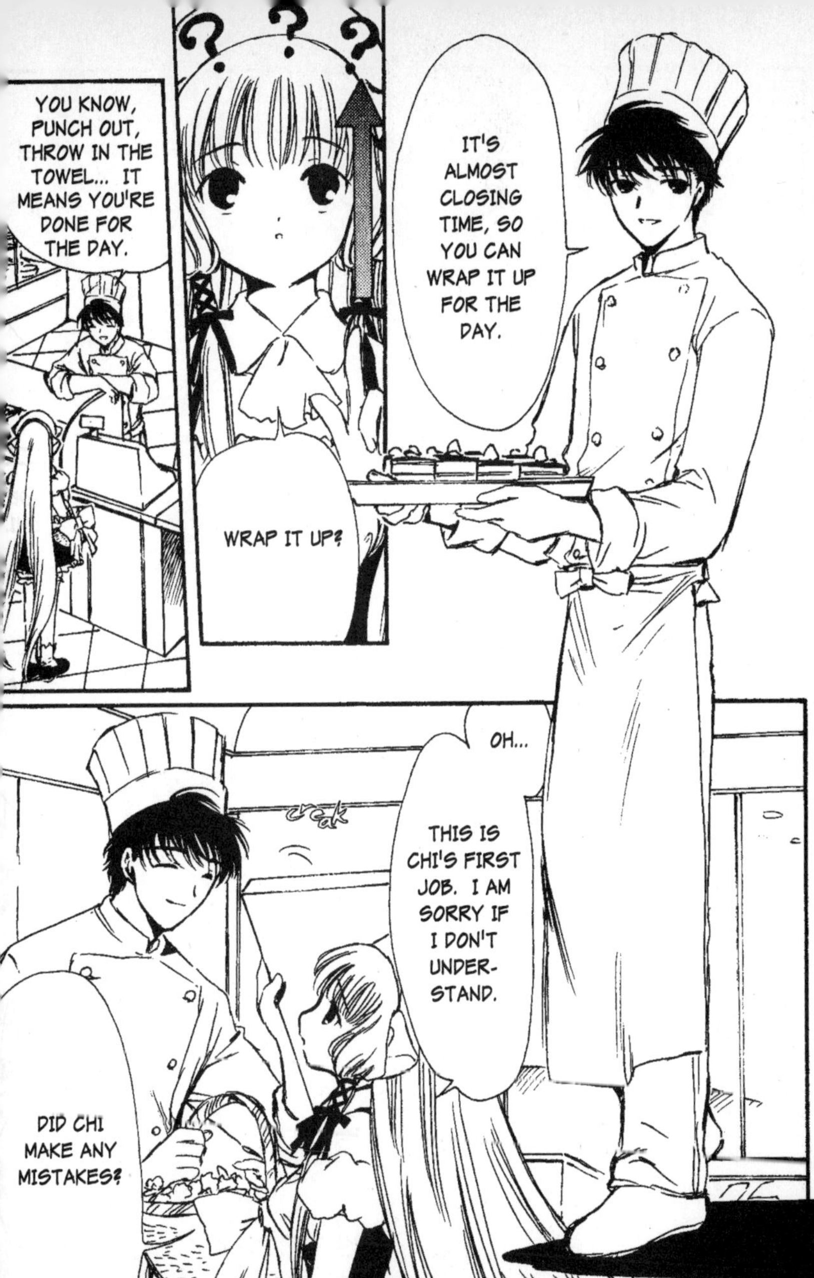
???
IT'S ALMOST CLOSING TIME, SO YOU CAN WRAP IT UP FOR THE DAY.
WRAP IT UP?
YOU KNOW, PUNCH OUT, THROW IN THE TOWEL... IT MEANS YOU'RE DONE FOR THE DAY.
OH...
THIS IS CHI'S FIRST JOB. I AM SORRY IF I DON'T UNDER-STAND.
creak
DID CHI MAKE ANY MISTAKES?

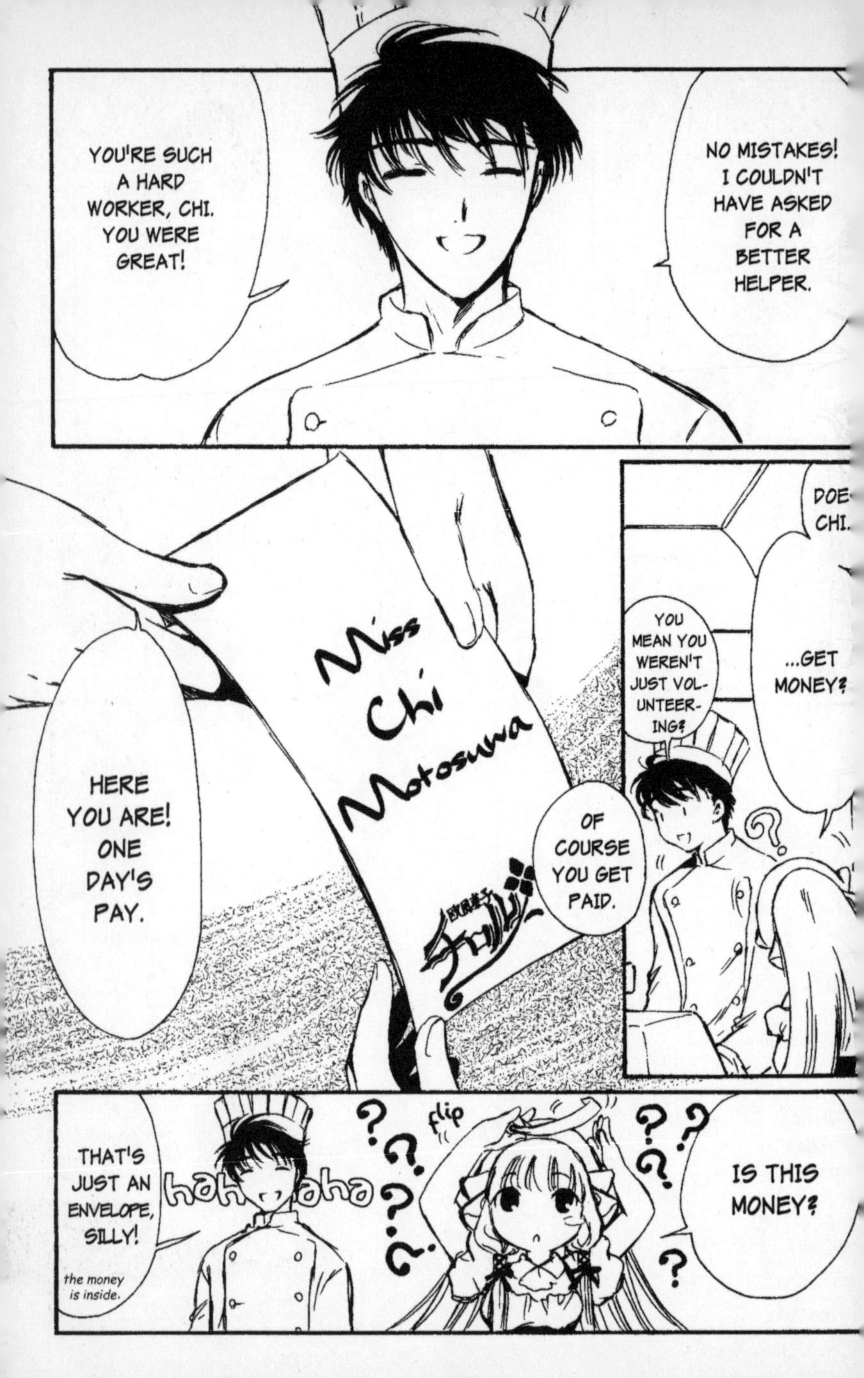
NO MISTAKES! I COULDN'T HAVE ASKED FOR A BETTER HELPER.
YOU'RE SUCH A HARD WORKER, CHI. YOU WERE GREAT!
DOE-CHI.
...GET MONEY?
YOU MEAN YOU WEREN'T JUST VOL-UNTEER-ING?
Miss Chi Motosuwa
OF COURSE YOU GET PAID.
HERE YOU ARE! ONE DAY'S PAY.
IS THIS MONEY?
flip
hahahaha
THAT'S JUST AN ENVELOPE, SILLY!
the money is inside.

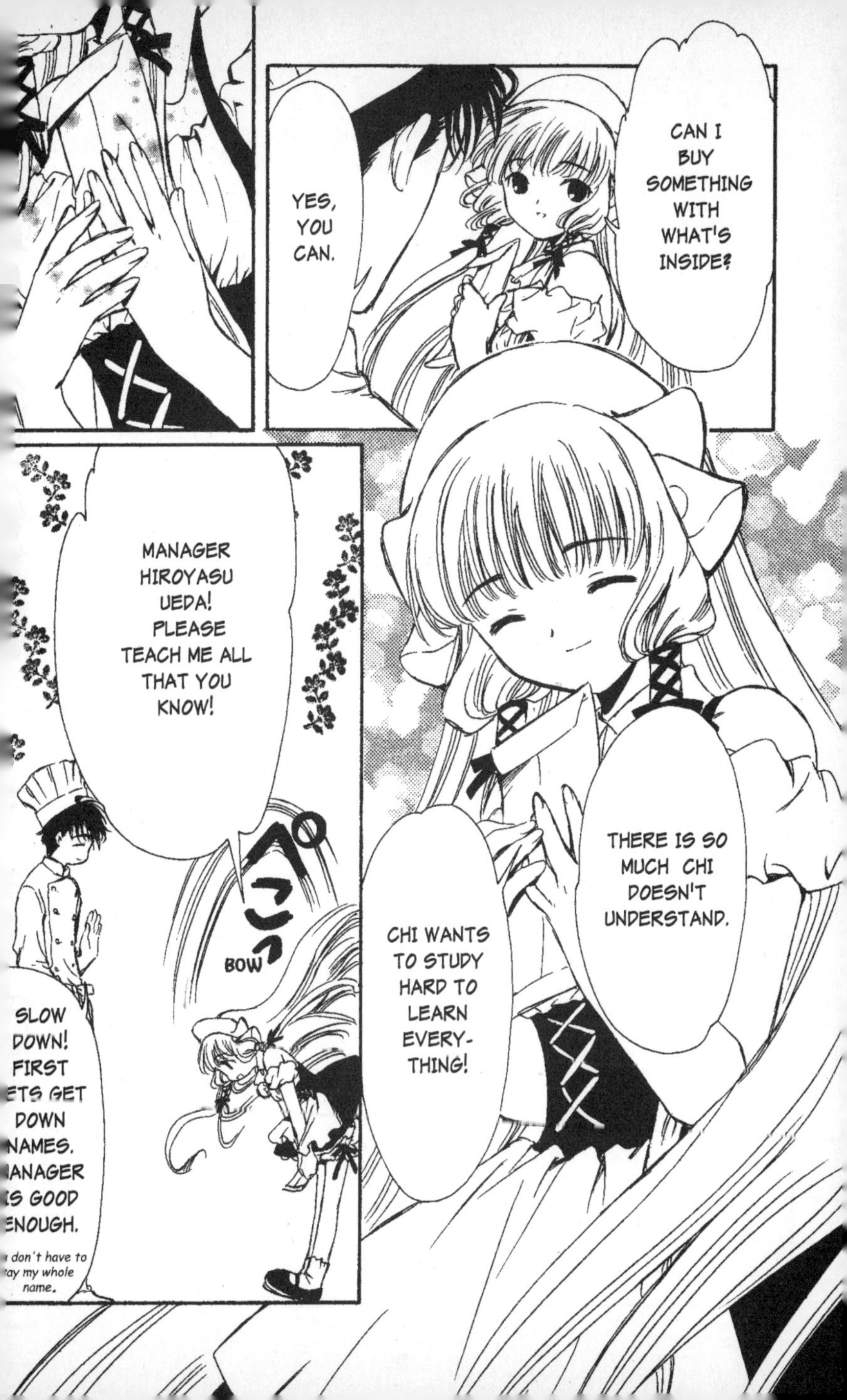
CAN I BUY SOMETHING WITH WHAT'S INSIDE?
YES, YOU CAN.
THERE IS SO MUCH CHI DOESN'T UNDERSTAND.
CHI WANTS TO STUDY HARD TO LEARN EVERY-THING!
MANAGER HIROYASU UEDA! PLEASE TEACH ME ALL THAT YOU KNOW!
BOW
SLOW DOWN! FIRST ETS GET DOWN NAMES. ANAGER S GOOD ENOUGH.
don't have to ay my whole name.

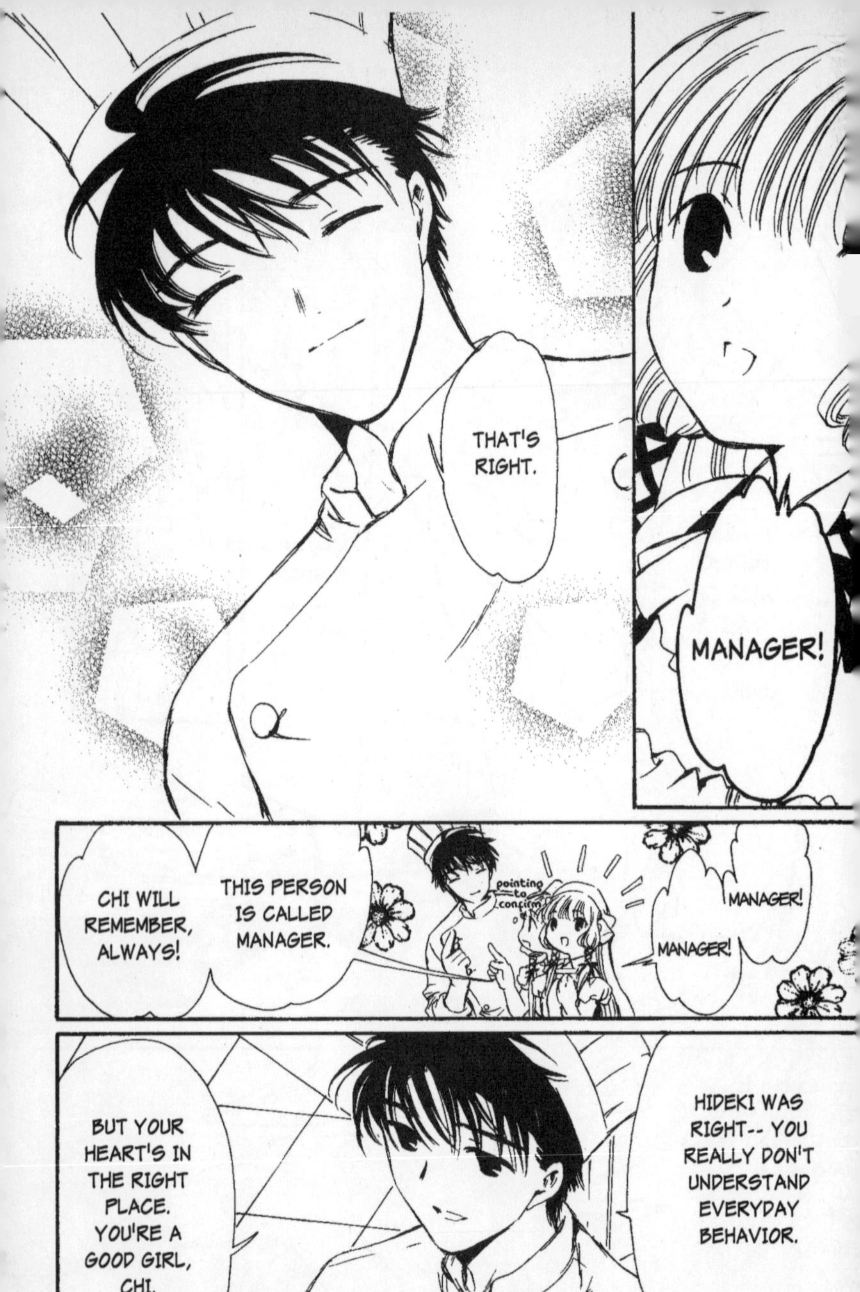
MANAGER!
THAT'S RIGHT.
MANAGER!
MANAGER!
pointing to confirm
THIS PERSON IS CALLED MANAGER.
CHI WILL REMEMBER, ALWAYS!
HIDEKI WAS RIGHT-- YOU REALLY DON'T UNDERSTAND EVERYDAY BEHAVIOR.
BUT YOUR HEART'S IN THE RIGHT PLACE. YOU'RE A GOOD GIRL, CHI.

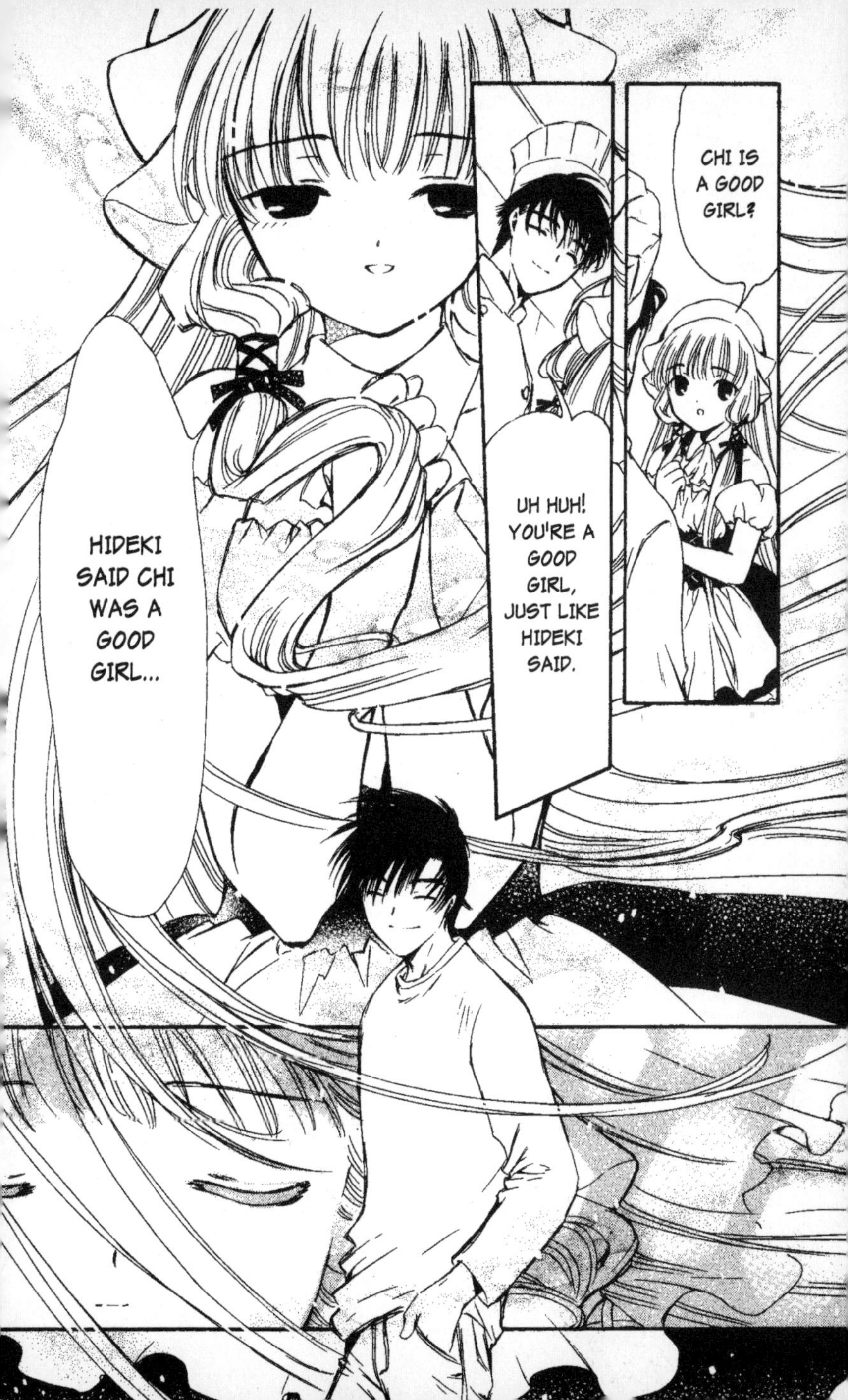
CHI IS A GOOD GIRL?
UH HUH! YOU'RE A GOOD GIRL, JUST LIKE HIDEKI SAID.
HIDEKI SAID CHI WAS A GOOD GIRL...

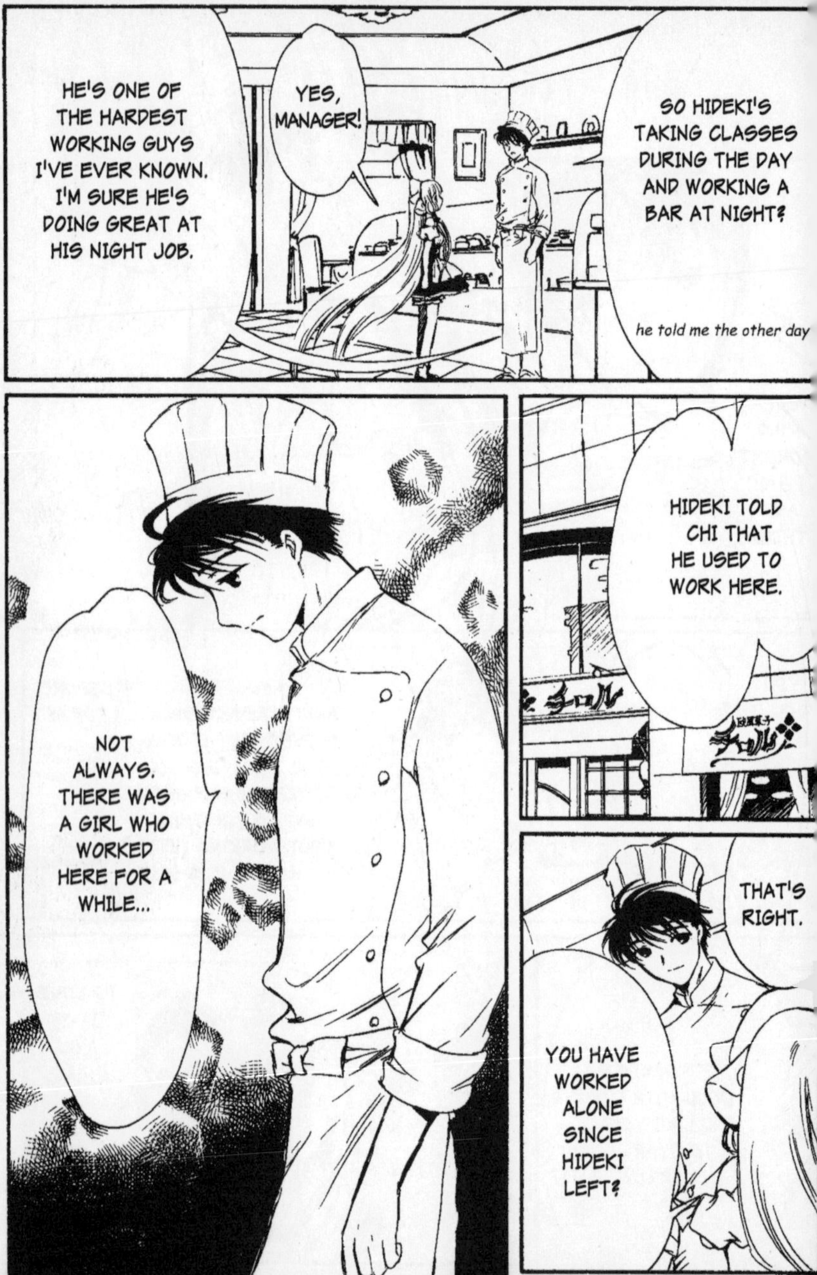
SO HIDEKI'S TAKING CLASSES DURING THE DAY AND WORKING A BAR AT NIGHT?
he told me the other day
YES, MANAGER!
HE'S ONE OF THE HARDEST WORKING GUYS I'VE EVER KNOWN. I'M SURE HE'S DOING GREAT AT HIS NIGHT JOB.
HIDEKI TOLD CHI THAT HE USED TO WORK HERE.
THAT'S RIGHT.
YOU HAVE WORKED ALONE SINCE HIDEKI LEFT?
NOT ALWAYS. THERE WAS A GIRL WHO WORKED HERE FOR A WHILE...

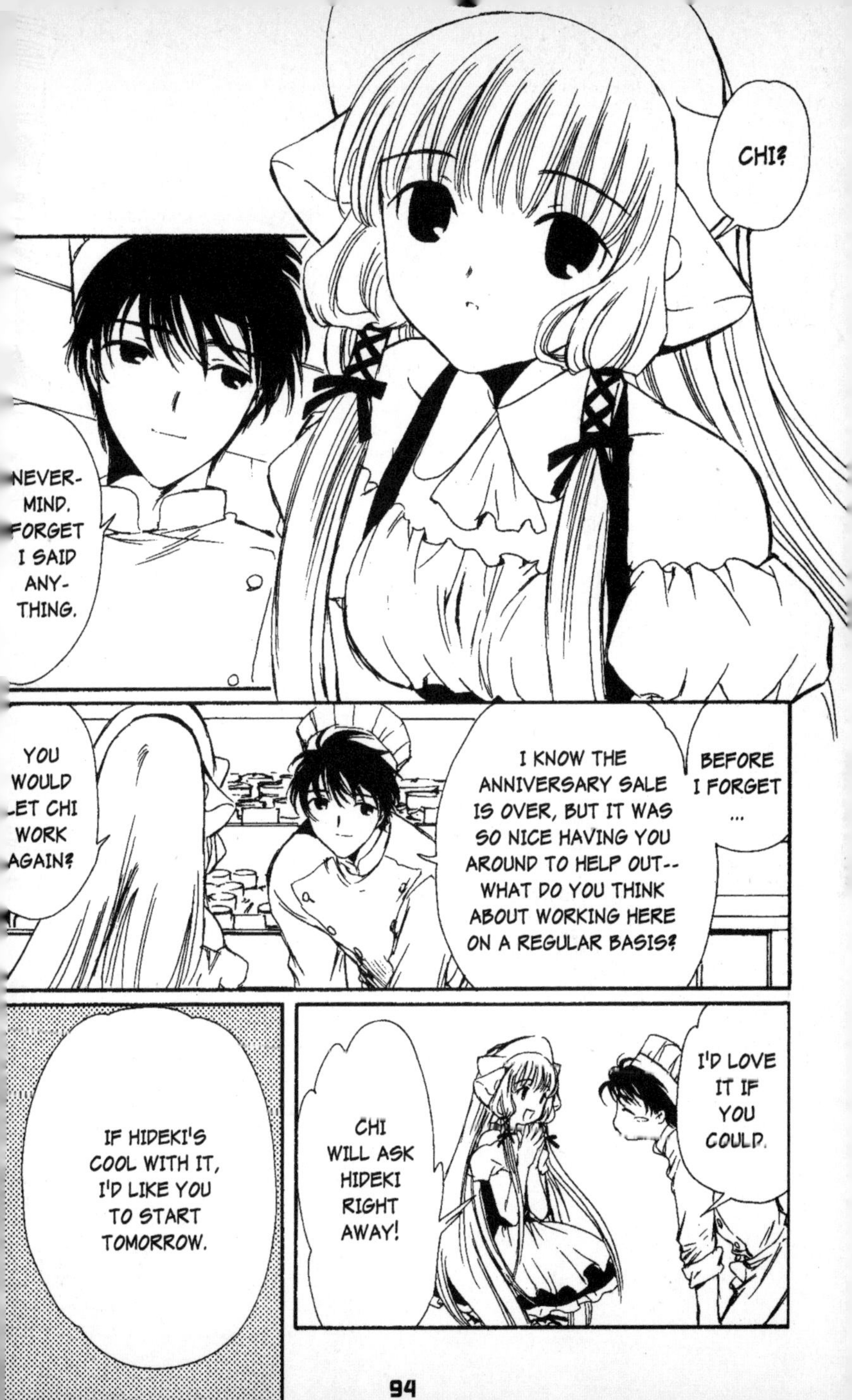
CHI?
NEVER-MIND. FORGET I SAID ANY-THING.
BEFORE I FORGET ...
I KNOW THE ANNIVERSARY SALE IS OVER, BUT IT WAS SO NICE HAVING YOU AROUND TO HELP OUT-- WHAT DO YOU THINK ABOUT WORKING HERE ON A REGULAR BASIS?
YOU WOULD LET CHI WORK AGAIN?
I'D LOVE IT IF YOU COULD.
CHI WILL ASK HIDEKI RIGHT AWAY!
IF HIDEKI'S COOL WITH IT, I'D LIKE YOU TO START TOMORROW.

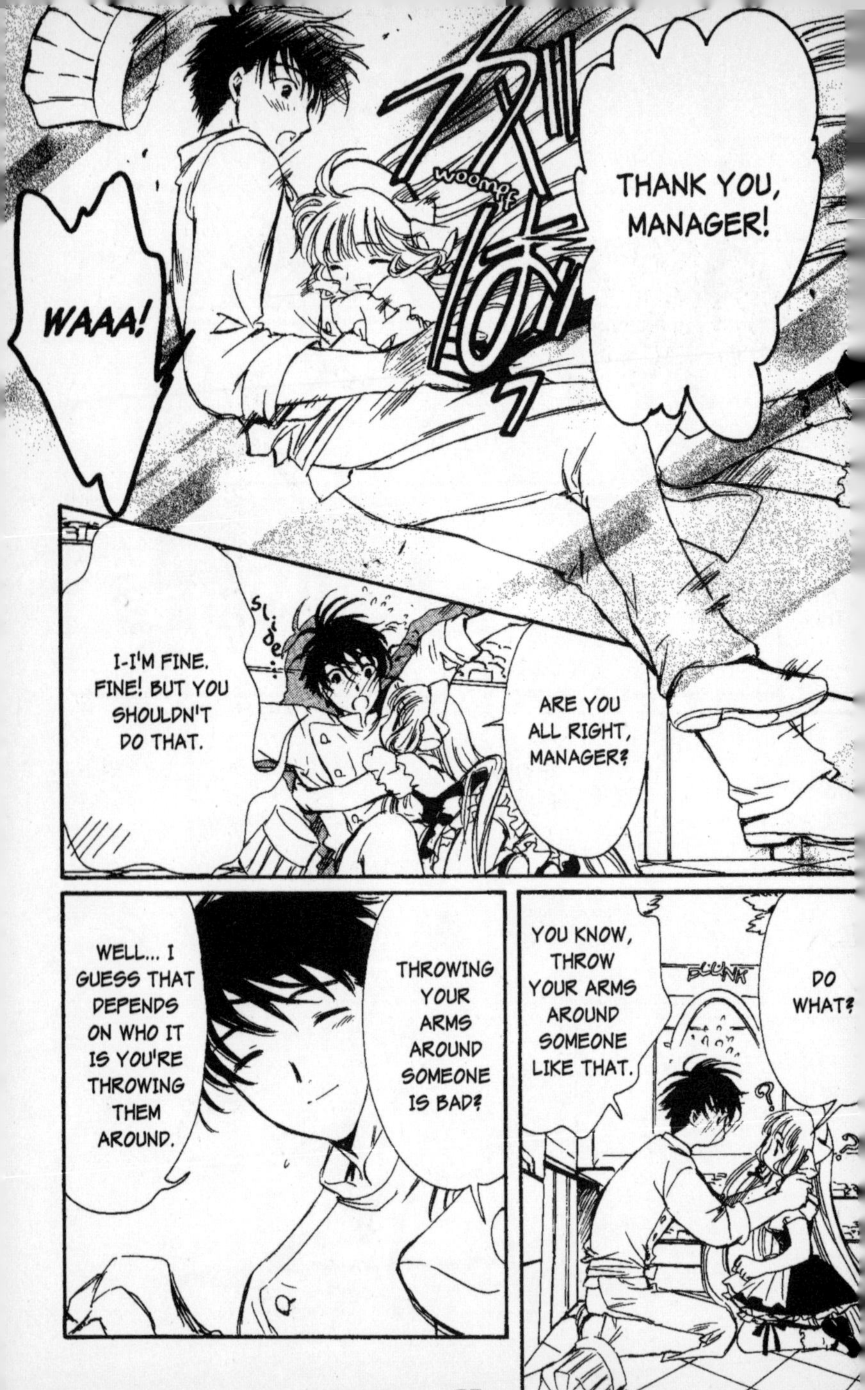
THANK YOU, MANAGER!
woompf
WAAA!
ARE YOU ALL RIGHT, MANAGER?
slide
I-I'M FINE. FINE! BUT YOU SHOULDN'T DO THAT.
DO WHAT?
YOU KNOW, THROW YOUR ARMS AROUND SOMEONE LIKE THAT.
BLUNK
THROWING YOUR ARMS AROUND SOMEONE IS BAD?
WELL... I GUESS THAT DEPENDS ON WHO IT IS YOU'RE THROWING THEM AROUND.

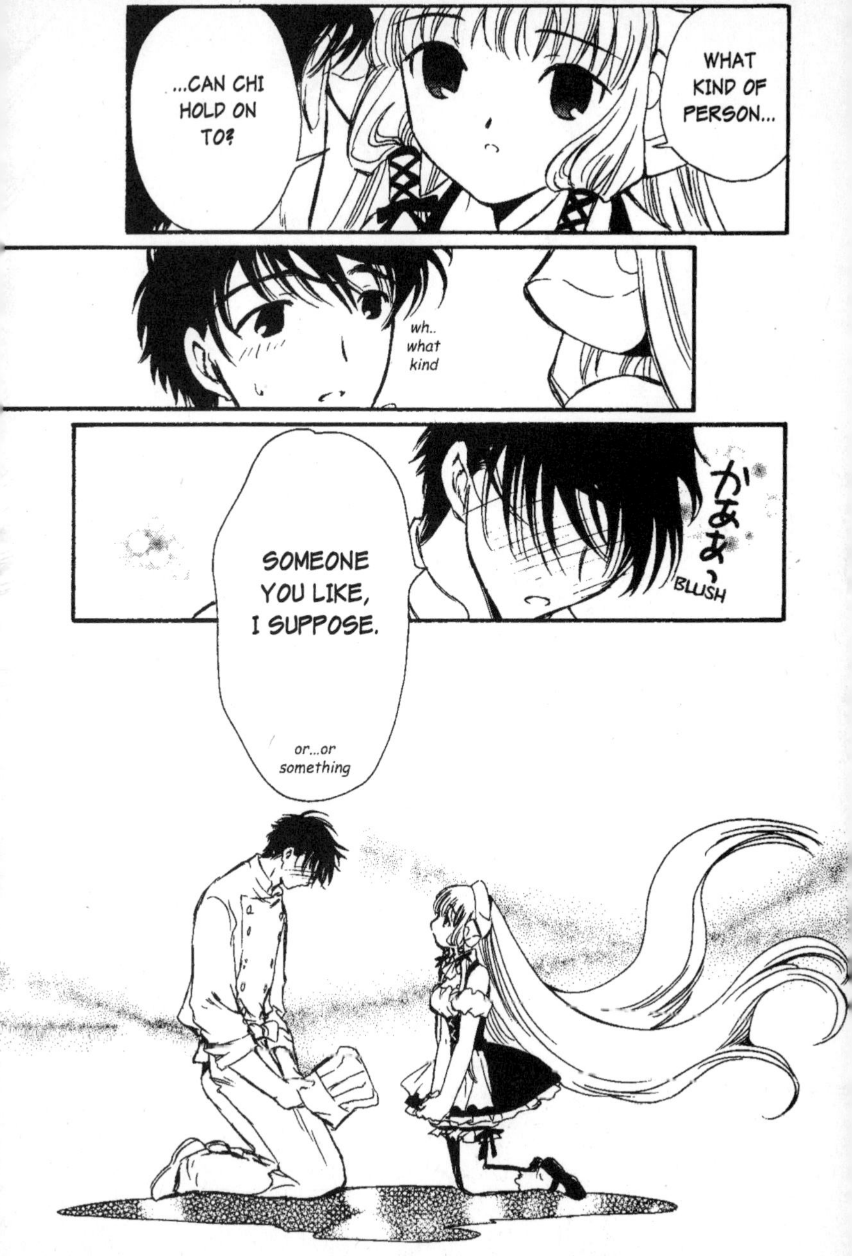
WHAT KIND OF PERSON...
...CAN CHI HOLD ON TO?
wh.. what kind
かあぁ
BLUSH
SOMEONE YOU LIKE, I SUPPOSE.
or...or something

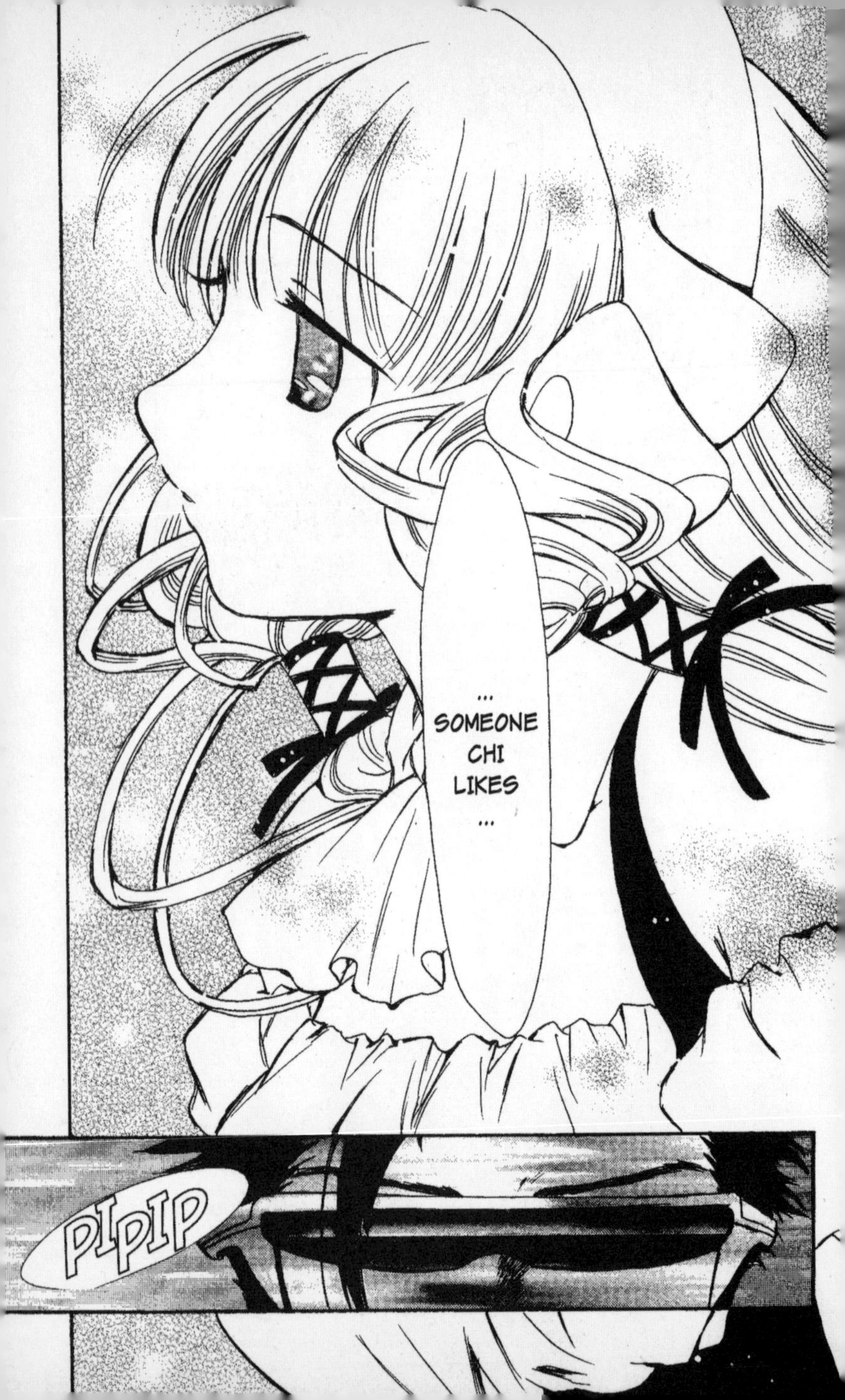
... SOMEONE CHI LIKES ...
PIPIP

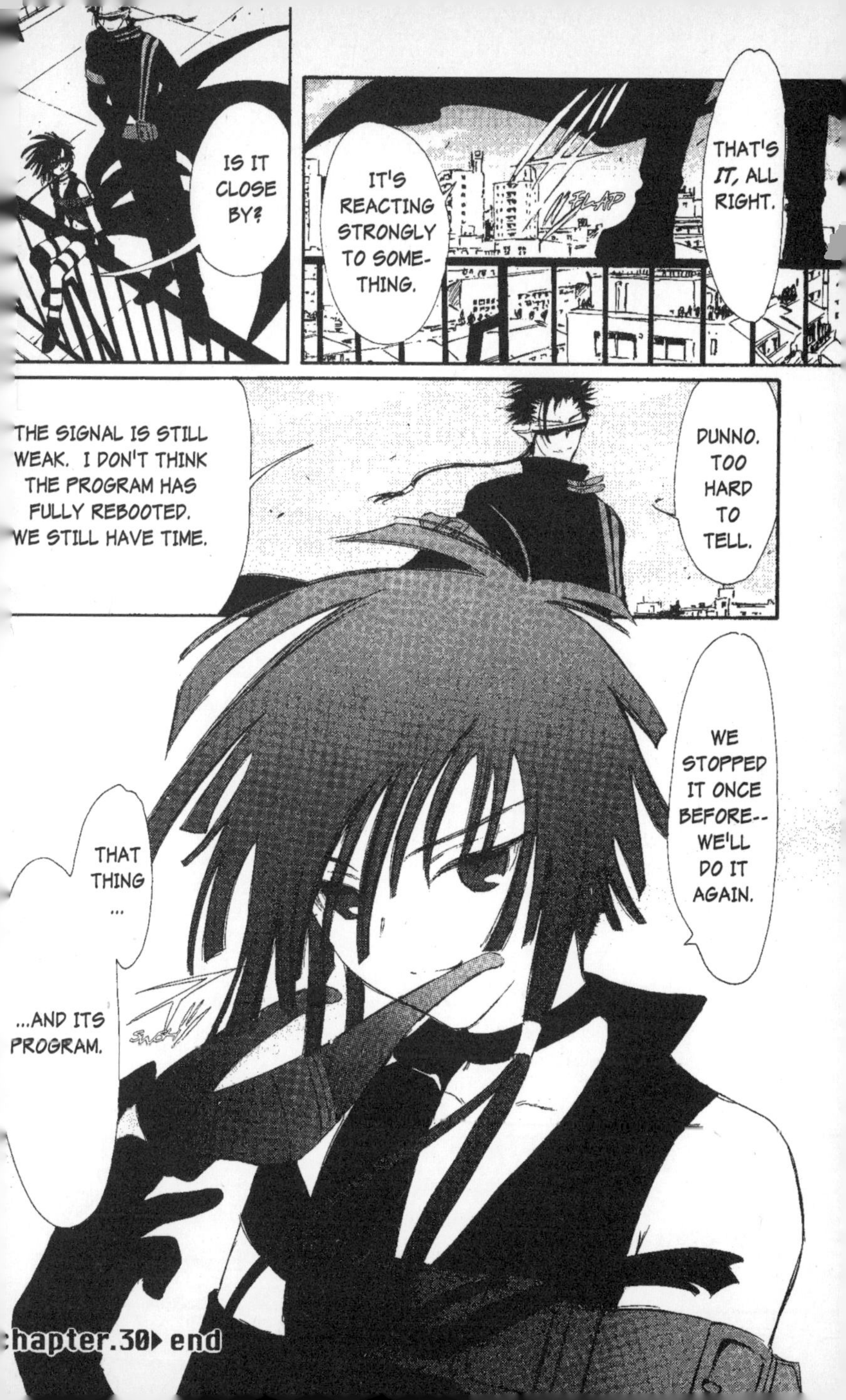
THAT'S *IT*, ALL RIGHT.
IT'S REACTING STRONGLY TO SOME-THING.
IS IT CLOSE BY?
DUNNO. TOO HARD TO TELL.
THE SIGNAL IS STILL WEAK. I DON'T THINK THE PROGRAM HAS FULLY REBOOTED. WE STILL HAVE TIME.
WE STOPPED IT ONCE BEFORE-- WE'LL DO IT AGAIN.
THAT THING ...
...AND ITS PROGRAM.
hapter.30 end

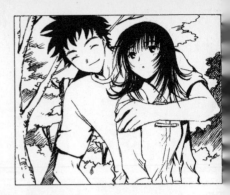

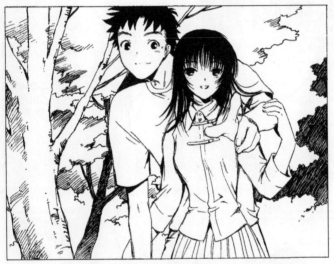

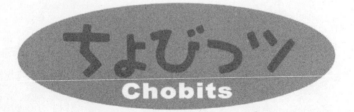

ちょびっツ
Chobits

◀chapter.31▶

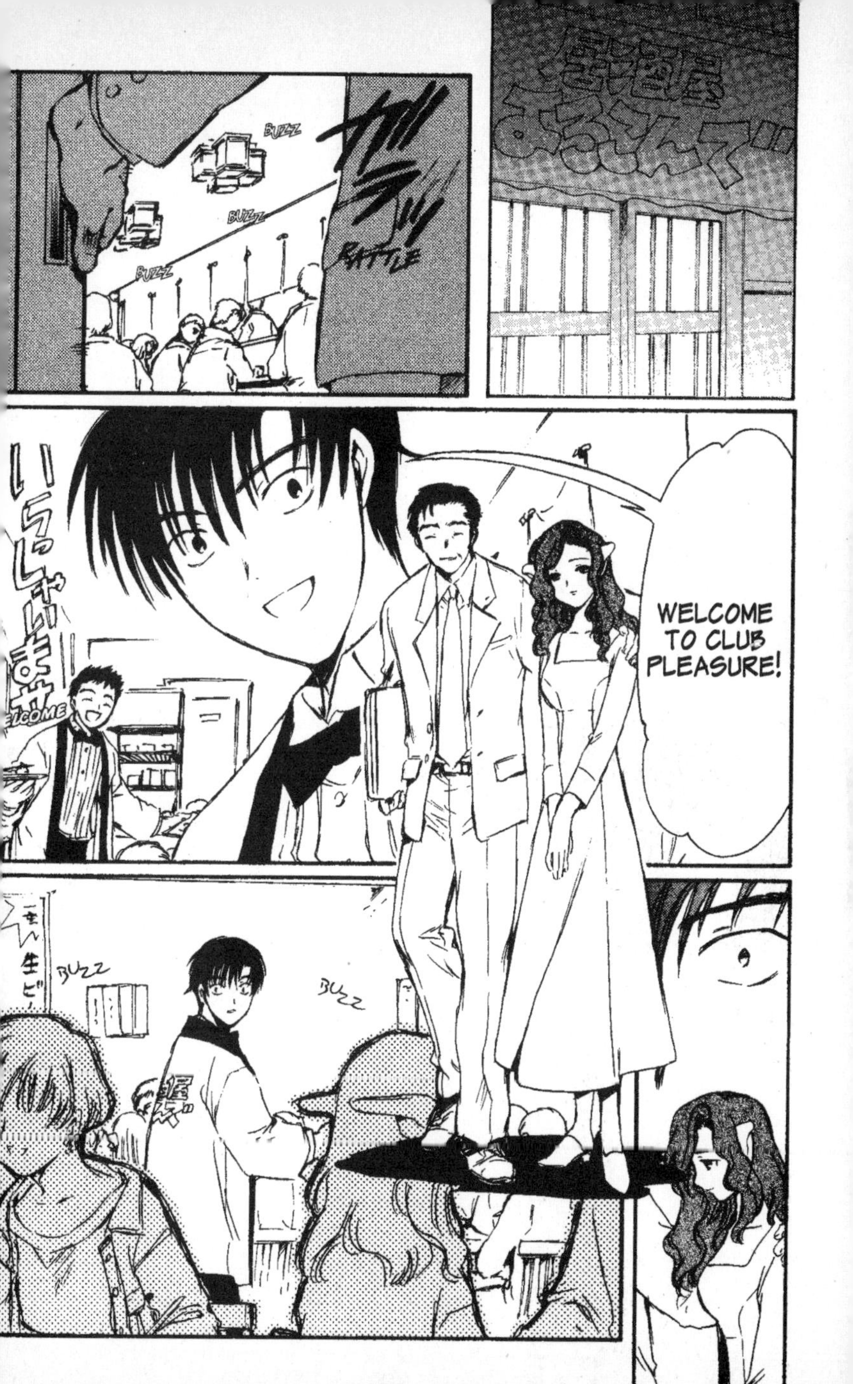
BUZZ
BUZZ
BUZZ
RATTLE
WELCOME TO CLUB PLEASURE!
いらっしゃいませ
WELCOME
BUZZ
BUZZ

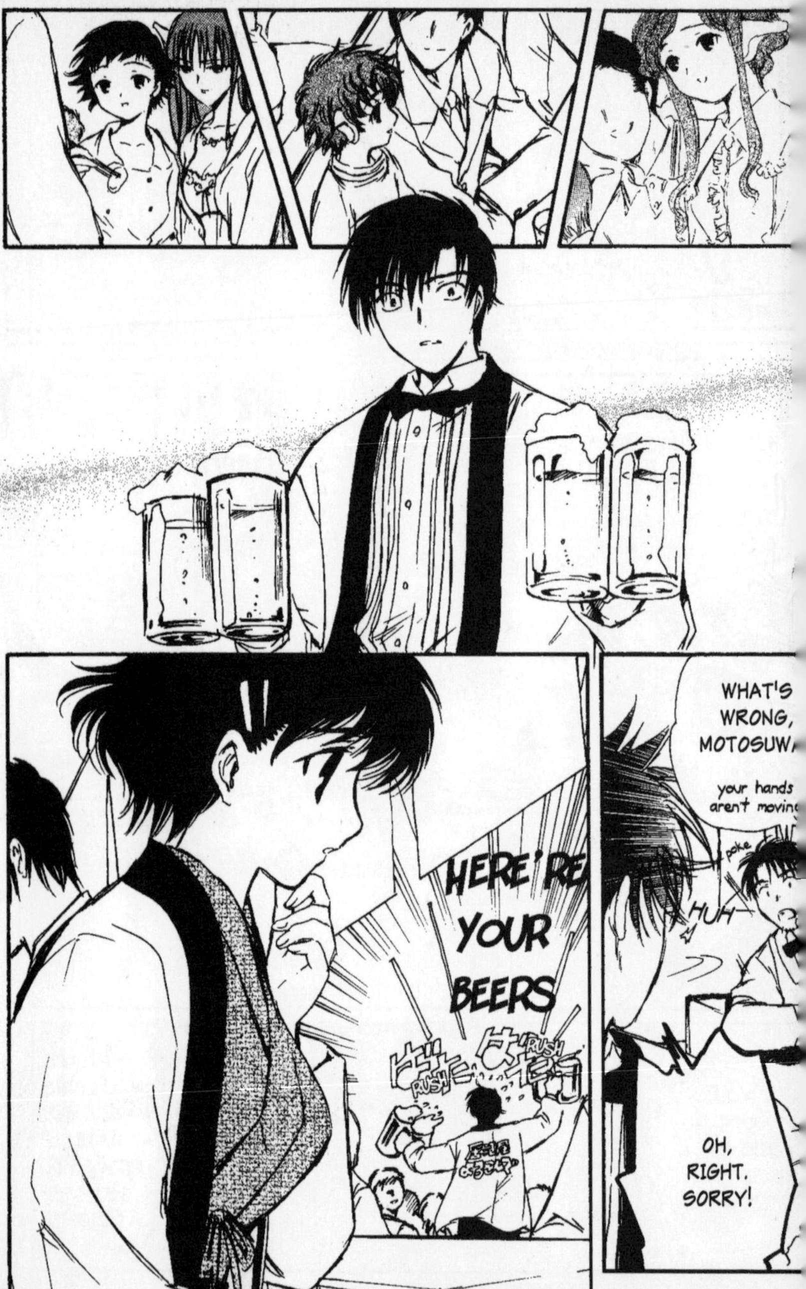
WHAT'S WRONG, MOTOSUW
your hands aren't movin
poke
HUH
OH, RIGHT. SORRY!
HERE'RE YOUR BEERS
RUSH
RUSH

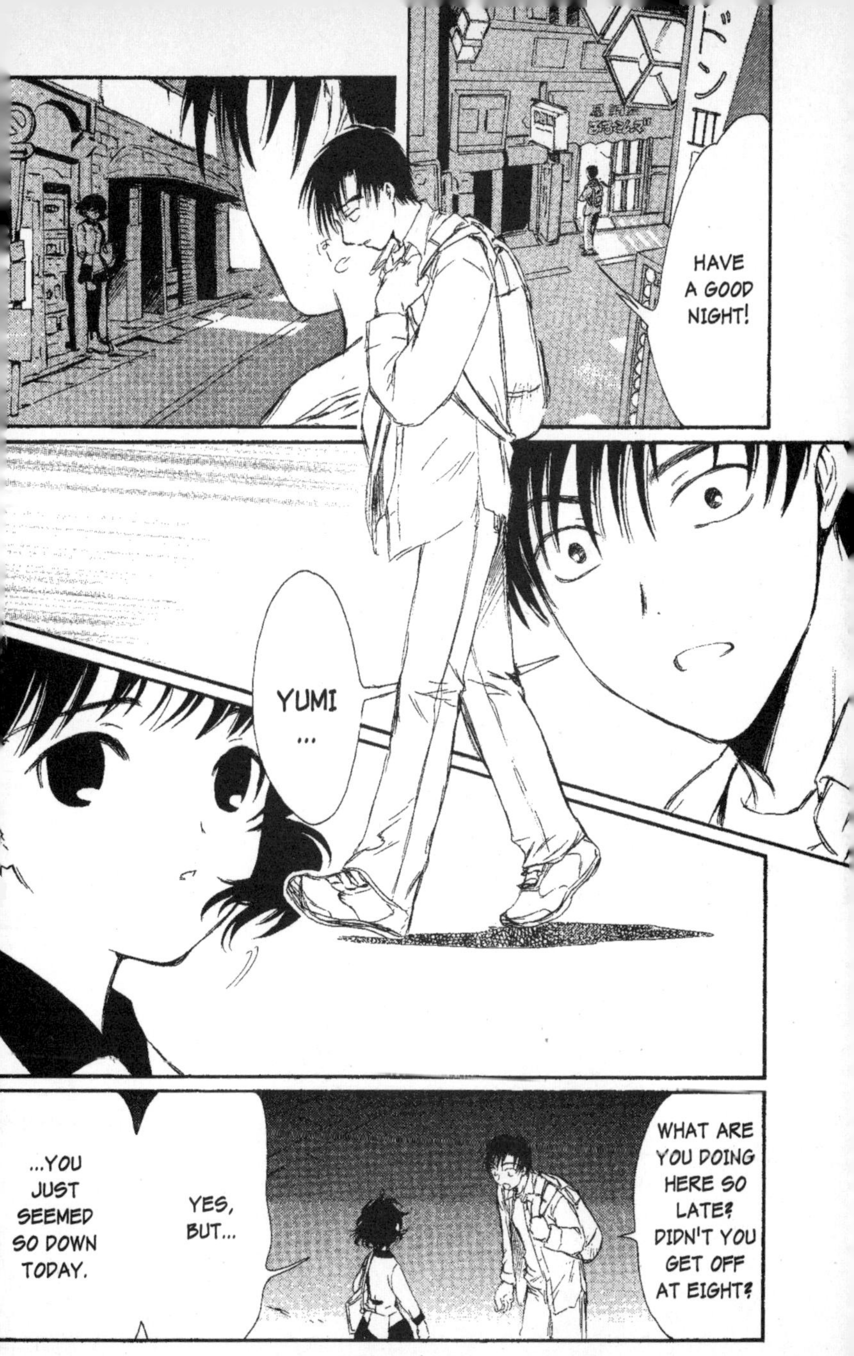
HAVE A GOOD NIGHT!
YUMI ...
WHAT ARE YOU DOING HERE SO LATE? DIDN'T YOU GET OFF AT EIGHT?
YES, BUT...
...YOU JUST SEEMED SO DOWN TODAY.

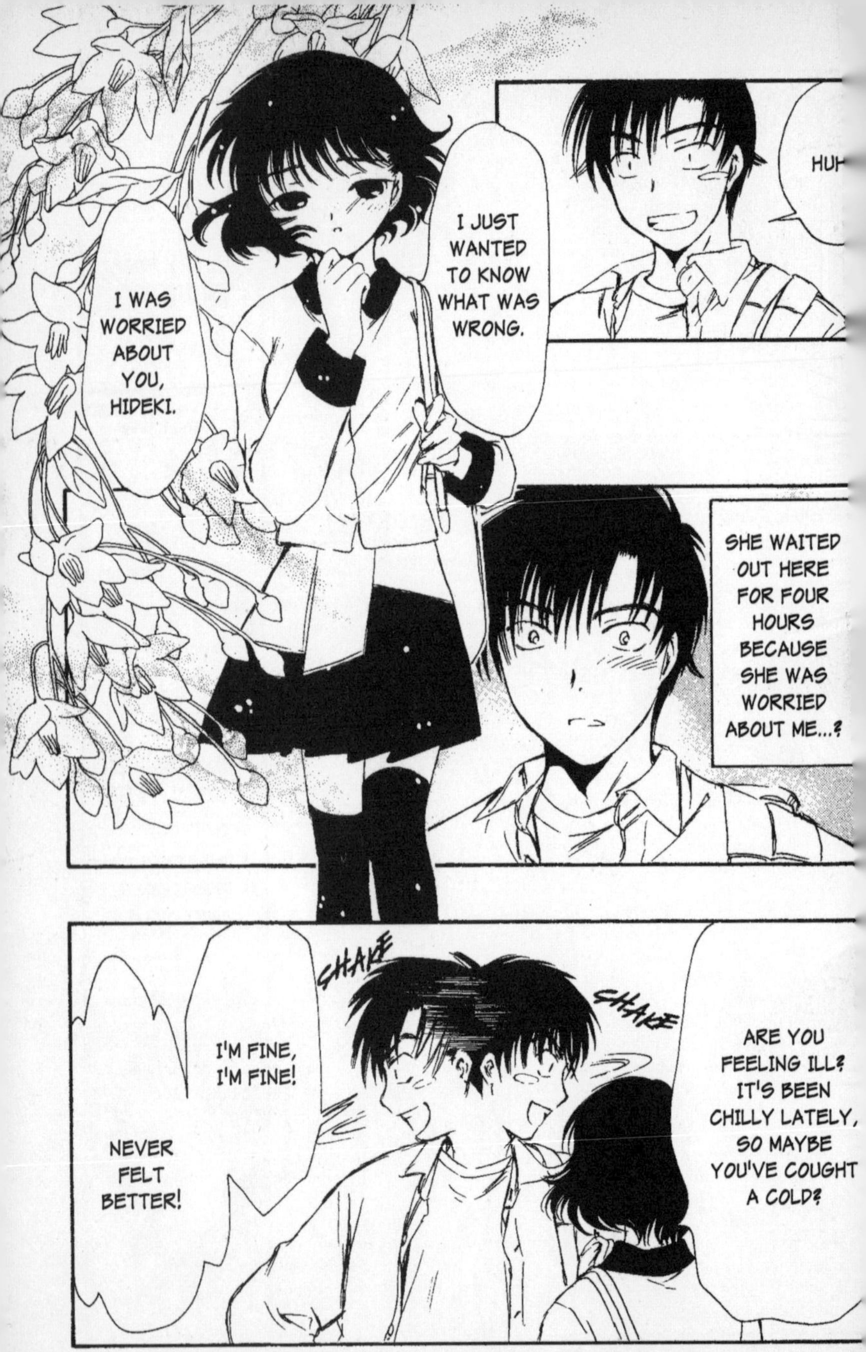
HUH
I JUST WANTED TO KNOW WHAT WAS WRONG.
I WAS WORRIED ABOUT YOU, HIDEKI.
SHE WAITED OUT HERE FOR FOUR HOURS BECAUSE SHE WAS WORRIED ABOUT ME...?
ARE YOU FEELING ILL? IT'S BEEN CHILLY LATELY, SO MAYBE YOU'VE COUGHT A COLD?
SHAKE
SHAKE
I'M FINE, I'M FINE!
NEVER FELT BETTER!

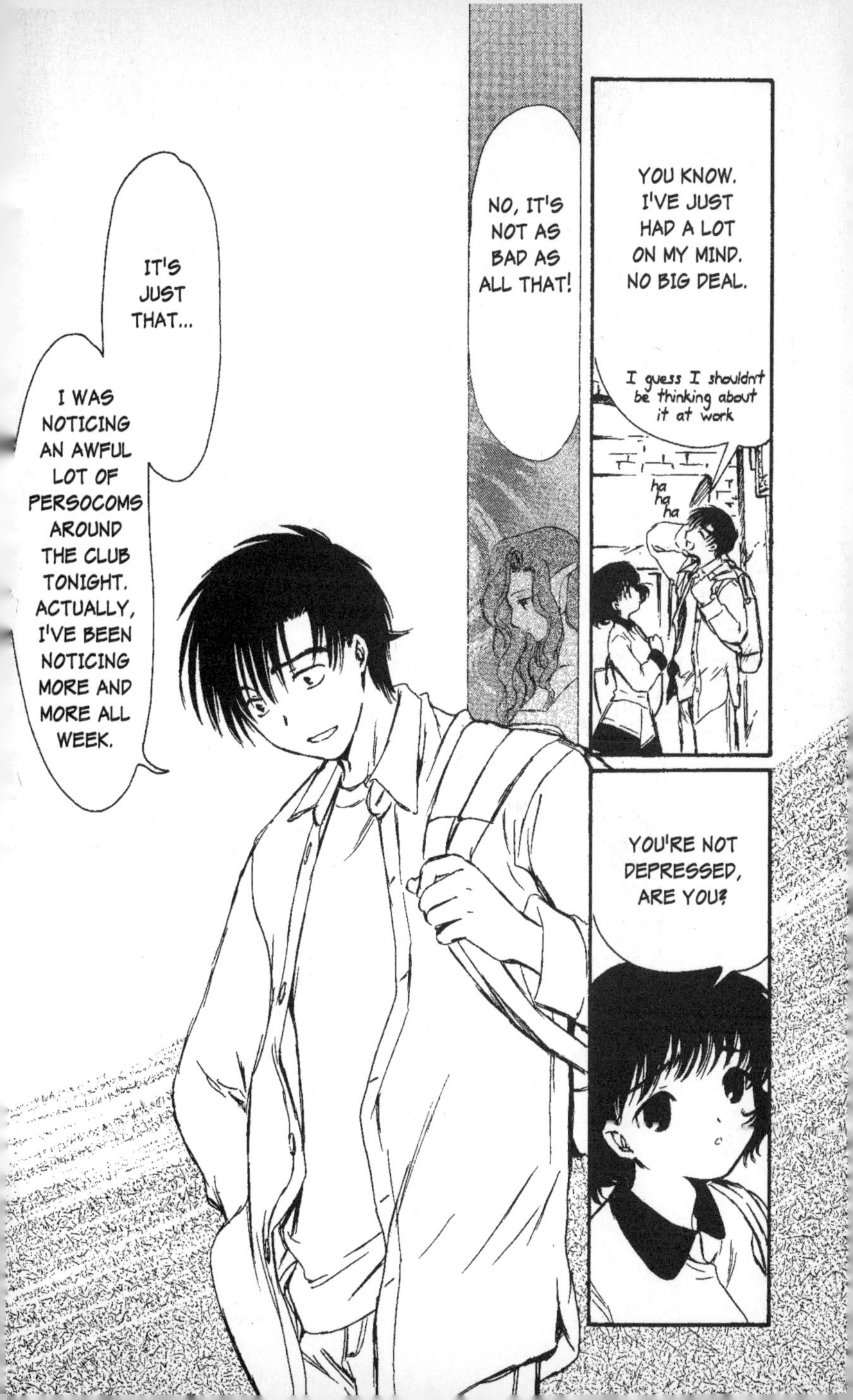

YOU KNOW. I'VE JUST HAD A LOT ON MY MIND. NO BIG DEAL.
I guess I shouldn't be thinking about it at work
ha ha ha
YOU'RE NOT DEPRESSED, ARE YOU?
NO, IT'S NOT AS BAD AS ALL THAT!
IT'S JUST THAT...
I WAS NOTICING AN AWFUL LOT OF PERSOCOMS AROUND THE CLUB TONIGHT. ACTUALLY, I'VE BEEN NOTICING MORE AND MORE ALL WEEK.

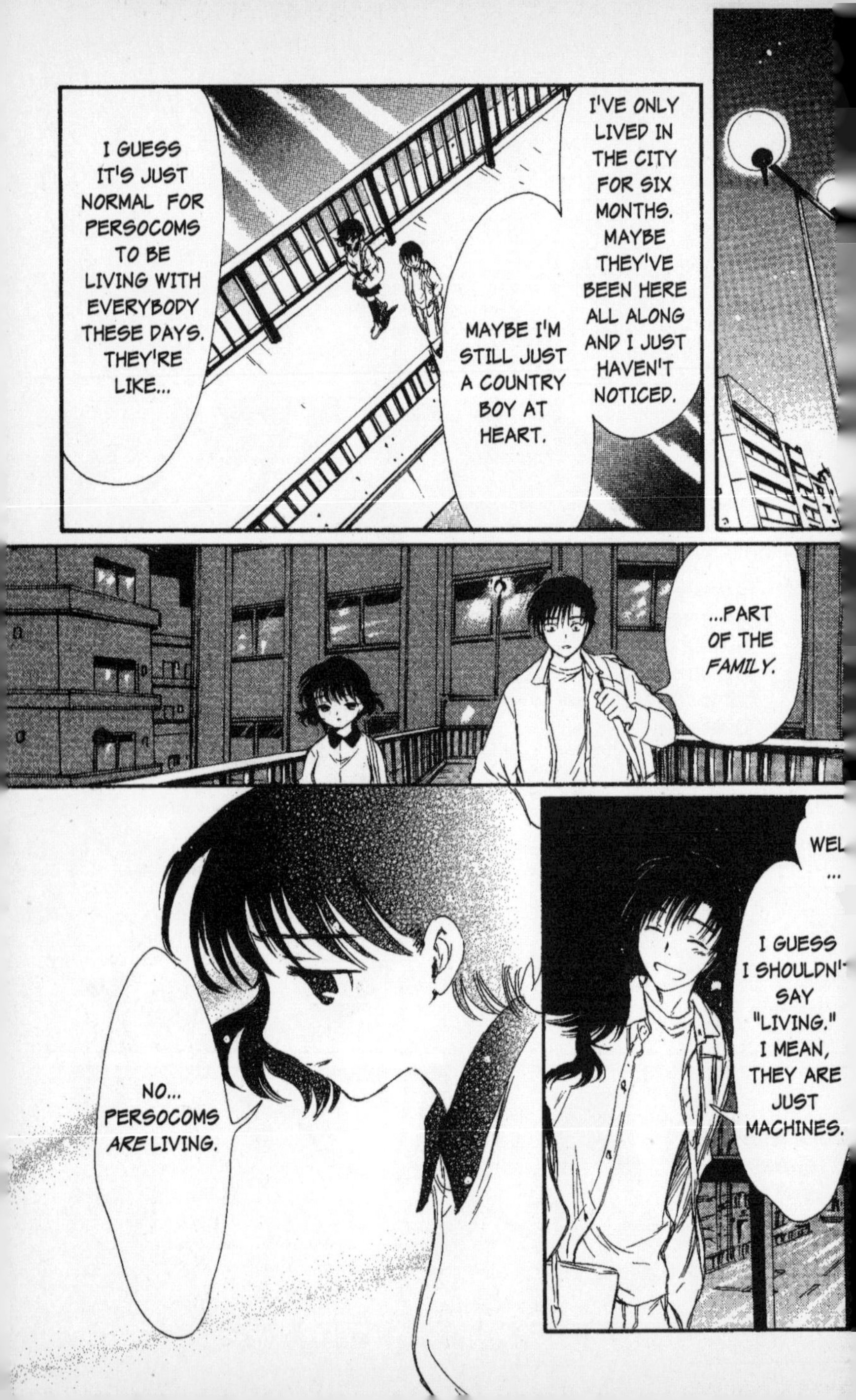
I'VE ONLY LIVED IN THE CITY FOR SIX MONTHS. MAYBE THEY'VE BEEN HERE ALL ALONG AND I JUST HAVEN'T NOTICED.
MAYBE I'M STILL JUST A COUNTRY BOY AT HEART.
I GUESS IT'S JUST NORMAL FOR PERSOCOMS TO BE LIVING WITH EVERYBODY THESE DAYS. THEY'RE LIKE...
...PART OF THE *FAMILY.*
WEL...
I GUESS I SHOULDN' SAY "LIVING." I MEAN, THEY ARE JUST MACHINES.
NO... PERSOCOMS *ARE* LIVING.

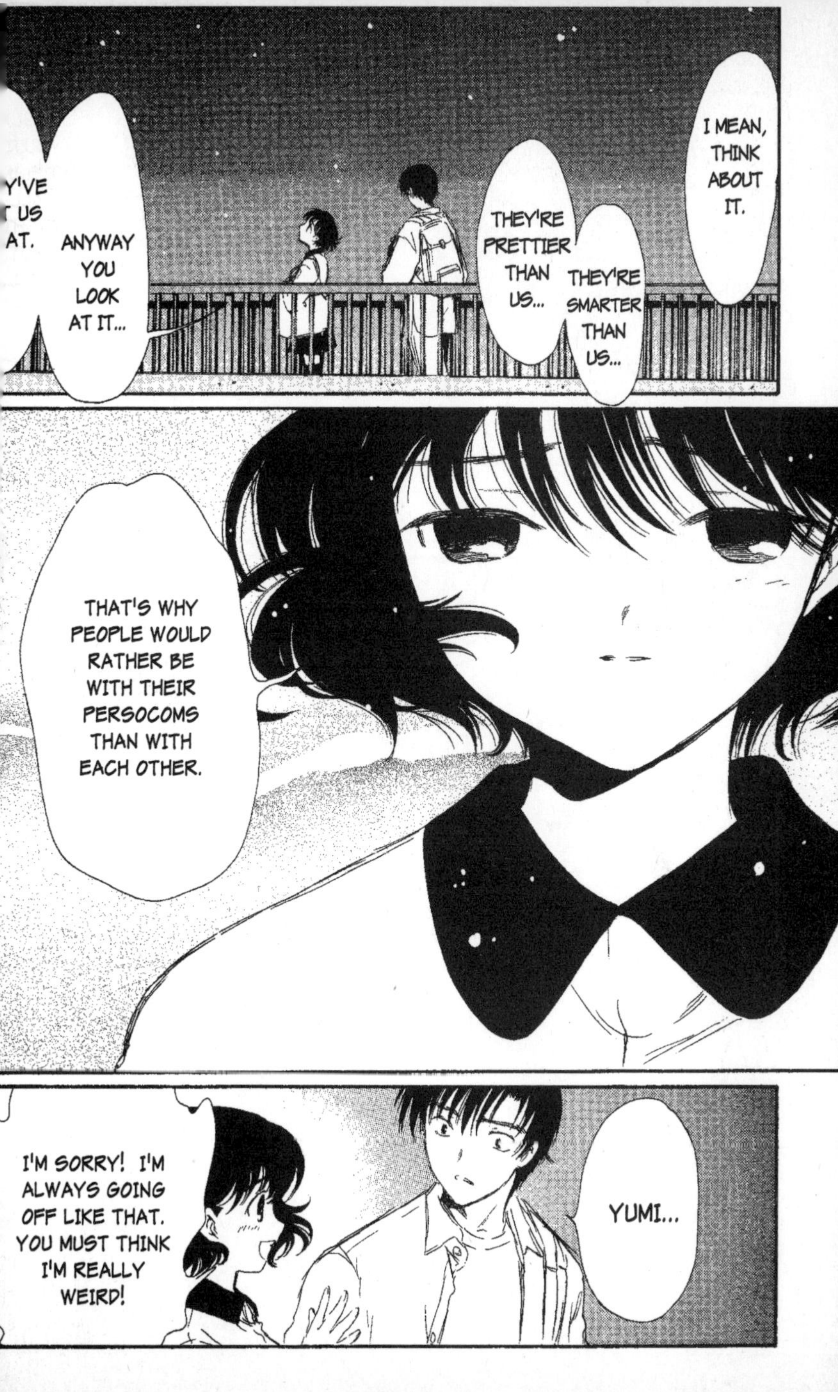
I MEAN, THINK ABOUT IT.
THEY'RE PRETTIER THAN US...
THEY'RE SMARTER THAN US...
ANYWAY YOU LOOK AT IT...
THAT'S WHY PEOPLE WOULD RATHER BE WITH THEIR PERSOCOMS THAN WITH EACH OTHER.
YUMI...
I'M SORRY! I'M ALWAYS GOING OFF LIKE THAT. YOU MUST THINK I'M REALLY WEIRD!

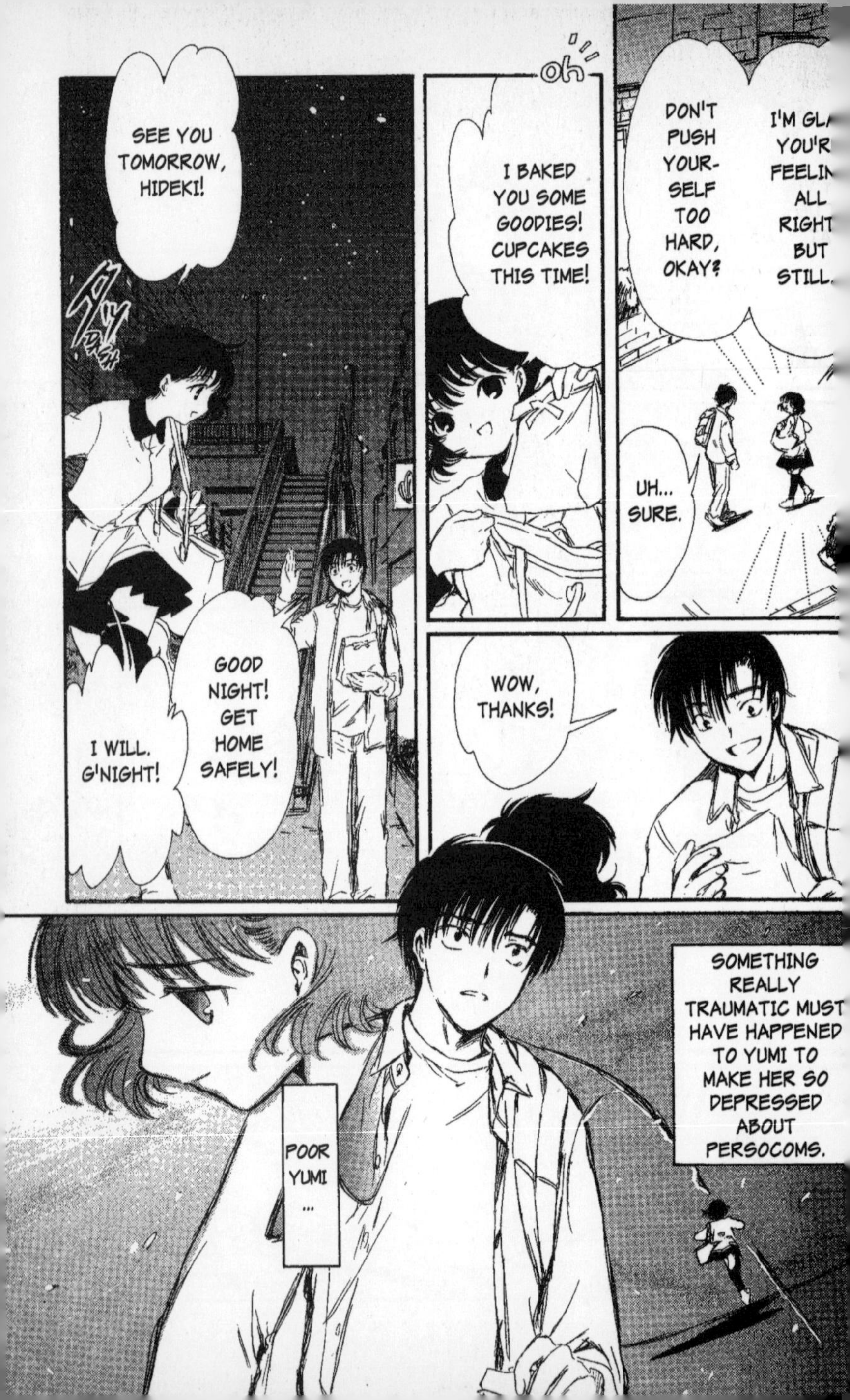
I'M GLA YOU'R FEELIN ALL RIGHT BUT STILL.
DON'T PUSH YOURSELF TOO HARD, OKAY?
UH... SURE.
oh
I BAKED YOU SOME GOODIES! CUPCAKES THIS TIME!
WOW, THANKS!
SEE YOU TOMORROW, HIDEKI!
GOOD NIGHT! GET HOME SAFELY!
I WILL. G'NIGHT!
SOMETHING REALLY TRAUMATIC MUST HAVE HAPPENED TO YUMI TO MAKE HER SO DEPRESSED ABOUT PERSOCOMS.
POOR YUMI ...

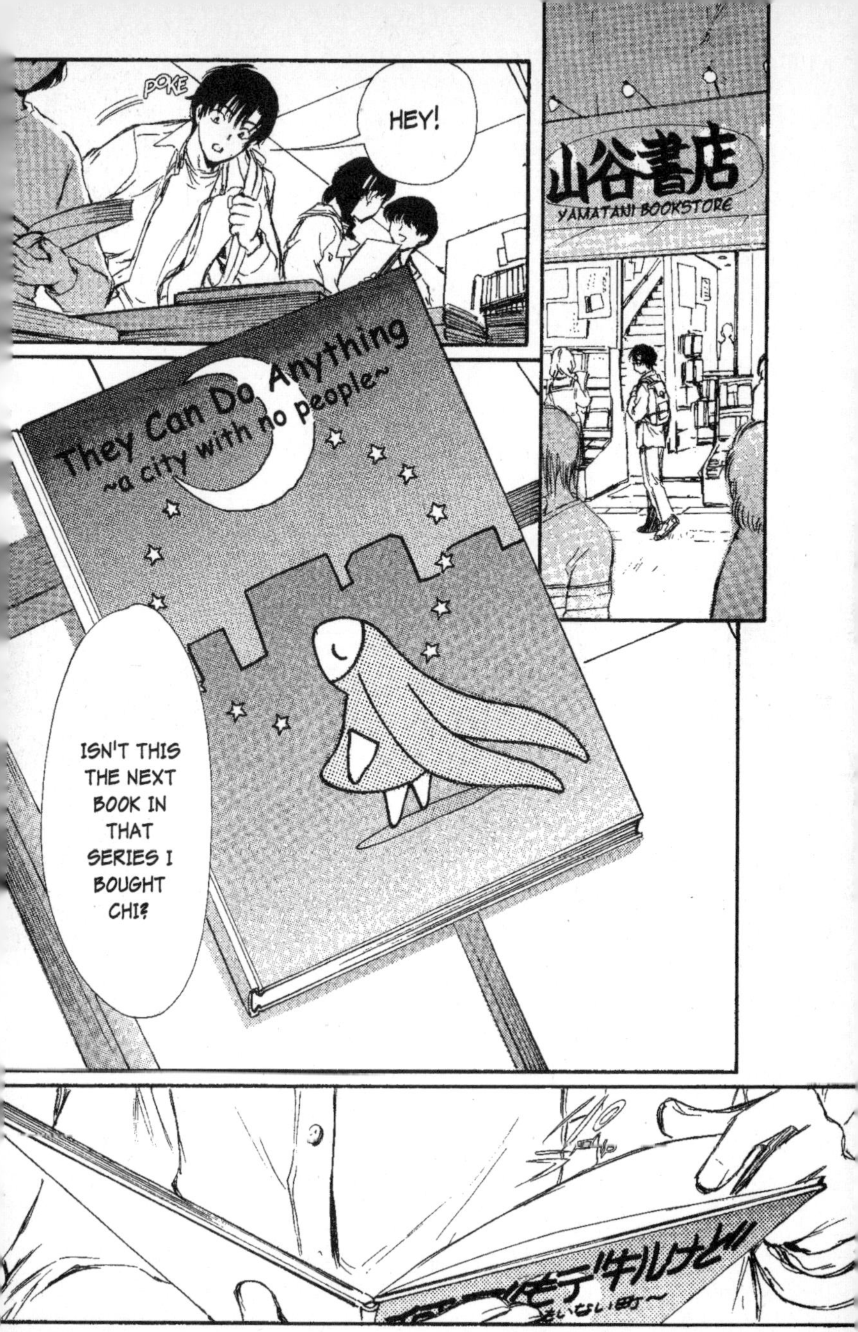

山谷書店
YAMATANI BOOKSTORE
POKE
HEY!
They Can Do Anything
~a city with no people~
ISN'T THIS THE NEXT BOOK IN THAT SERIES I BOUGHT CHI?

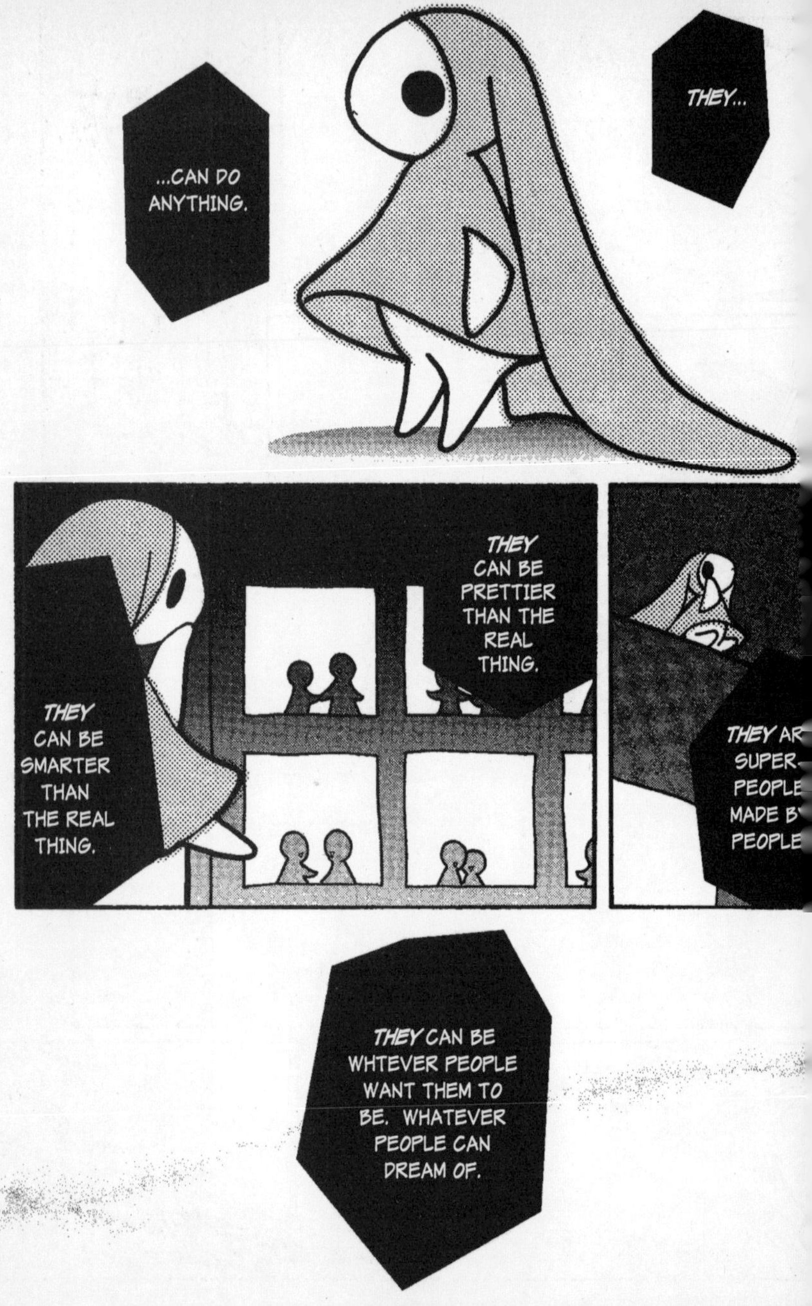
THEY...
...CAN DO ANYTHING.
THEY AR SUPER-PEOPLE MADE B PEOPLE
THEY CAN BE PRETTIER THAN THE REAL THING.
THEY CAN BE SMARTER THAN THE REAL THING.
THEY CAN BE WHTEVER PEOPLE WANT THEM TO BE. WHATEVER PEOPLE CAN DREAM OF.

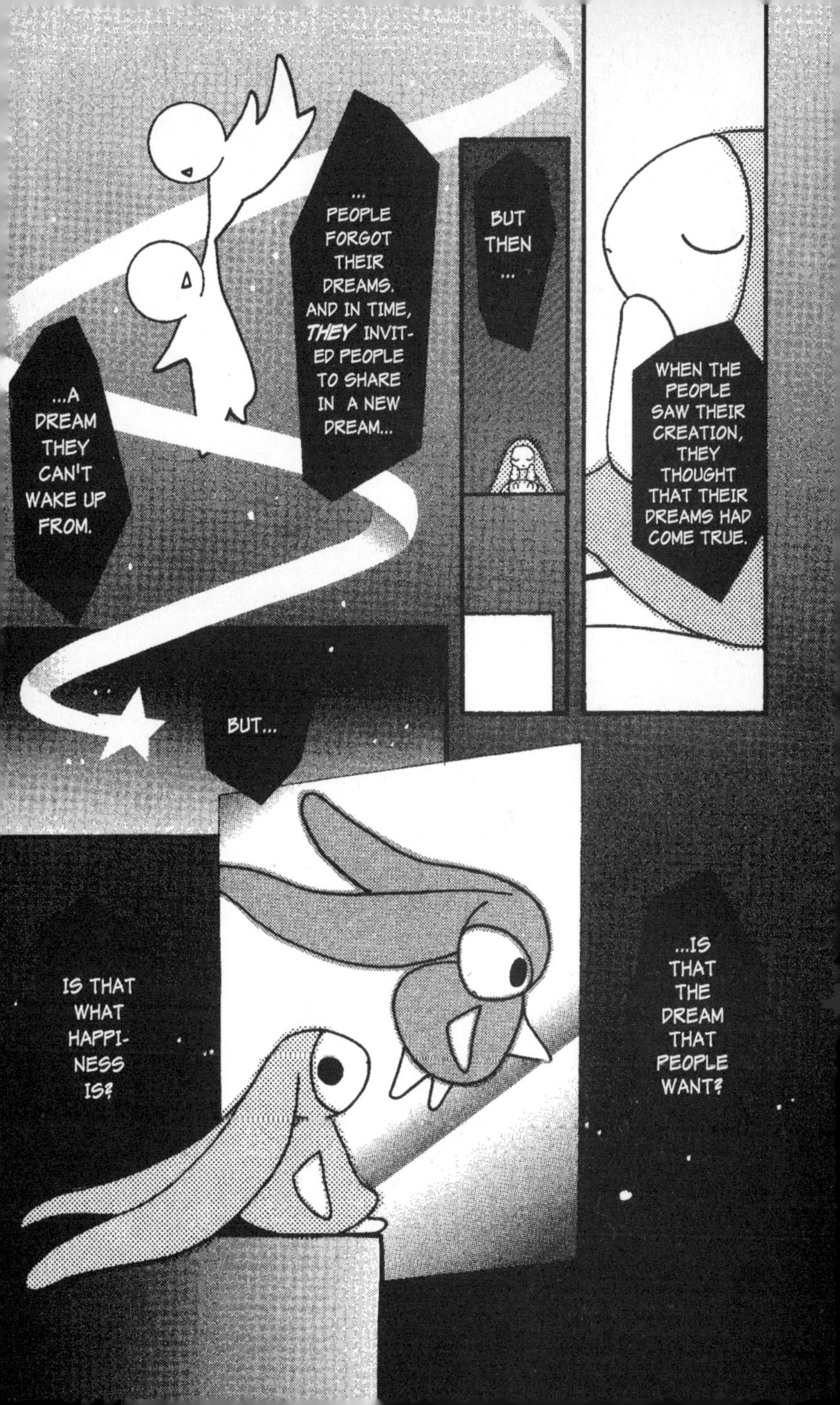
WHEN THE PEOPLE SAW THEIR CREATION, THEY THOUGHT THAT THEIR DREAMS HAD COME TRUE.
BUT THEN ...
... PEOPLE FORGOT THEIR DREAMS. AND IN TIME, *THEY* INVITED PEOPLE TO SHARE IN A NEW DREAM...
...A DREAM THEY CAN'T WAKE UP FROM.
BUT...
...IS THAT THE DREAM THAT PEOPLE WANT?
IS THAT WHAT HAPPINESS IS?

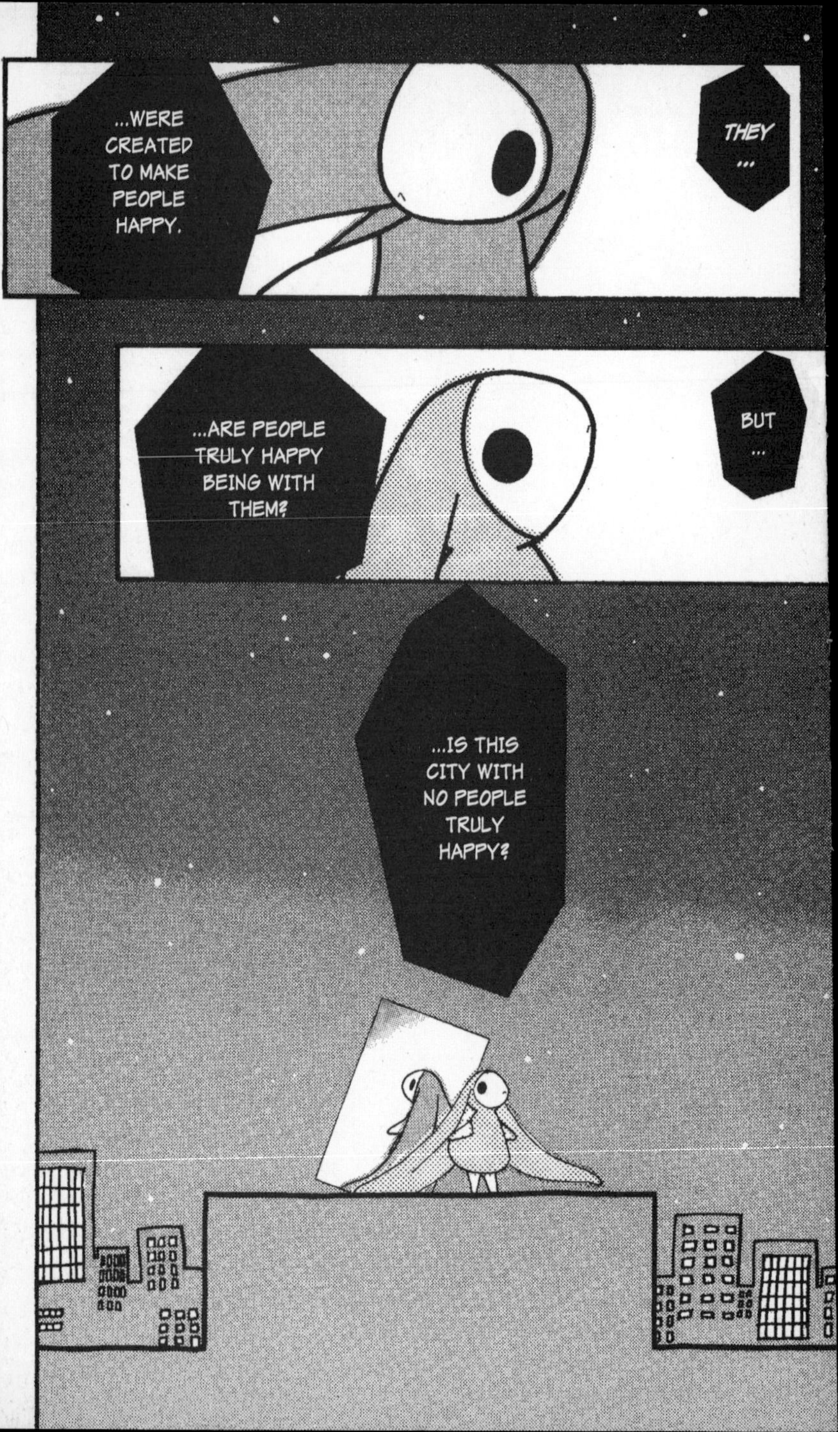
THEY ...
...WERE CREATED TO MAKE PEOPLE HAPPY.
BUT ...
...ARE PEOPLE TRULY HAPPY BEING WITH THEM?
...IS THIS CITY WITH NO PEOPLE TRULY HAPPY?

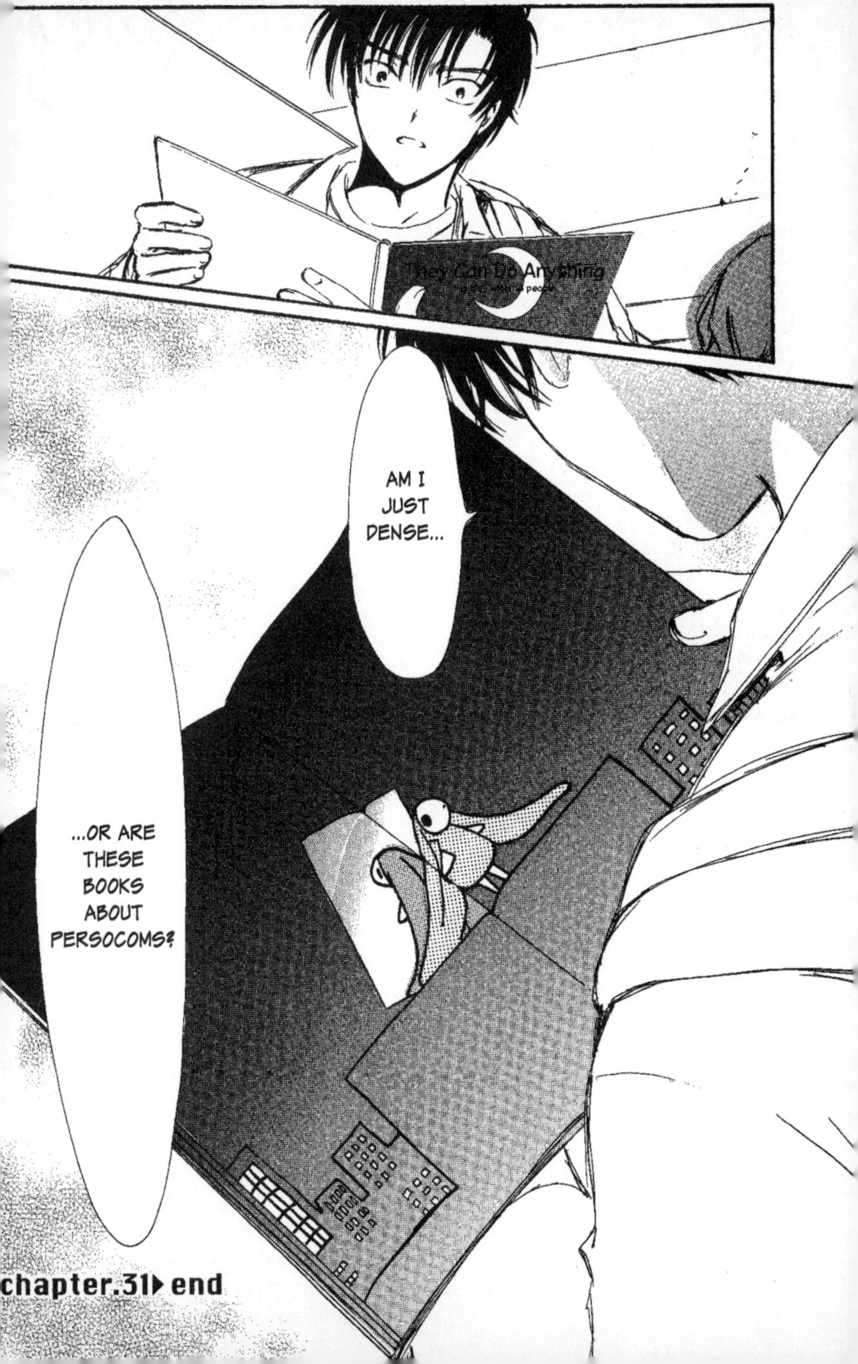
They Can Do Anything
AM I JUST DENSE...
...OR ARE THESE BOOKS ABOUT PERSOCOMS?
chapter.31▸ end

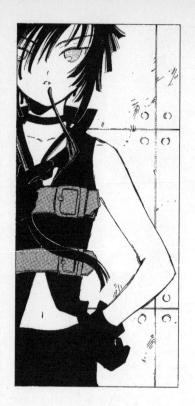
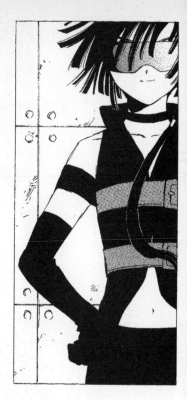

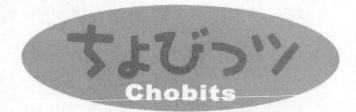

ちょびっツ
Chobits

◀chapter.32▶

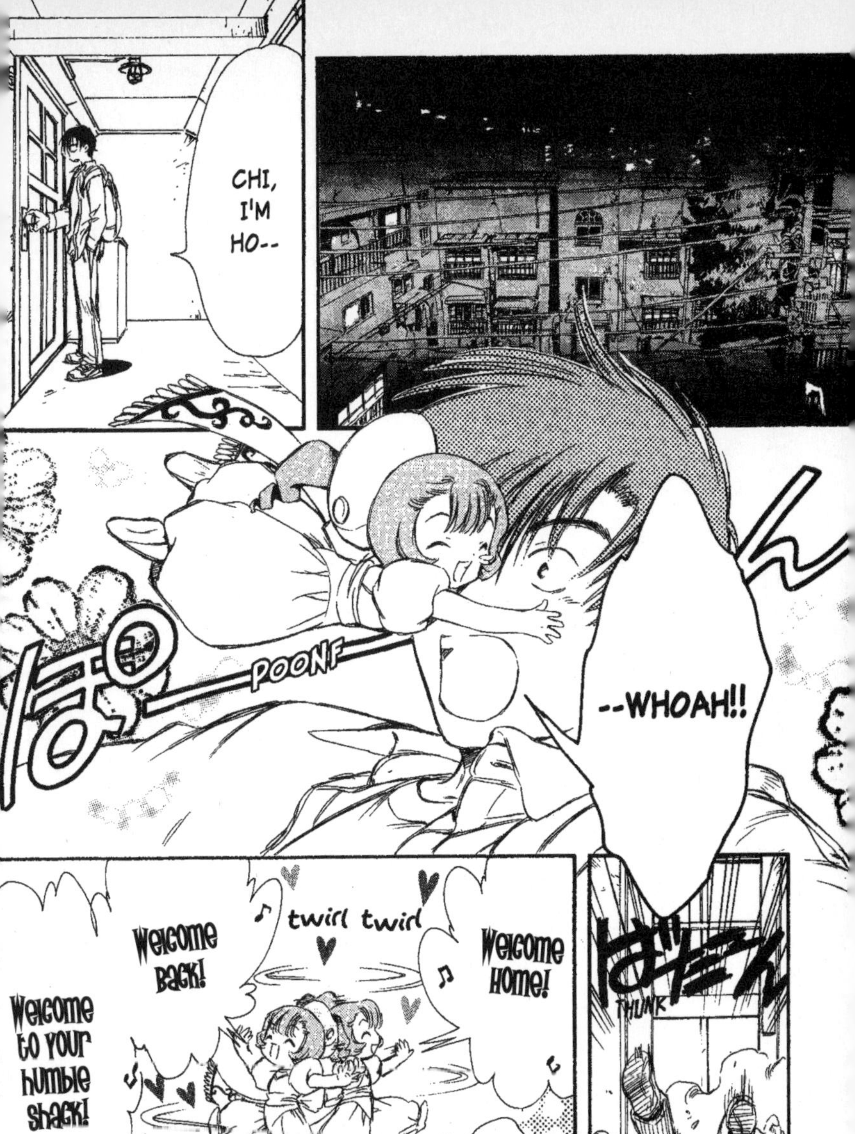
CHI, I'M HO--
POONF
--WHOAH!!
THUNK
Welcome Home!
twirl twirl
Welcome Back!
Welcome to your humble shack!
......

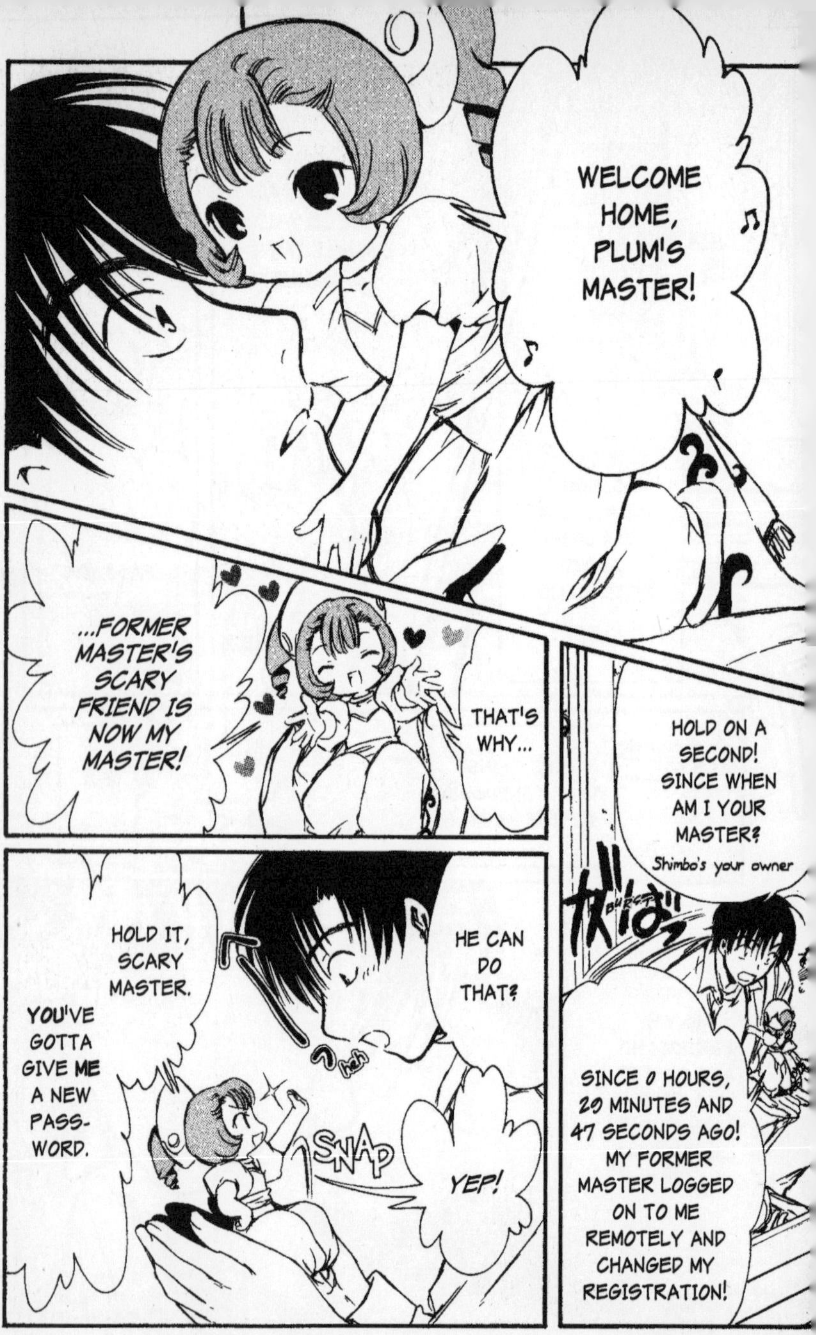
WELCOME HOME, PLUM'S MASTER!
HOLD ON A SECOND! SINCE WHEN AM I YOUR MASTER?
Shimbo's your owner
SINCE 0 HOURS, 29 MINUTES AND 47 SECONDS AGO! MY FORMER MASTER LOGGED ON TO ME REMOTELY AND CHANGED MY REGISTRATION!
THAT'S WHY...
...FORMER MASTER'S SCARY FRIEND IS NOW MY MASTER!
HE CAN DO THAT?
HOLD IT, SCARY MASTER.
YOU'VE GOTTA GIVE ME A NEW PASS-WORD.
heh
SNAP
YEP!

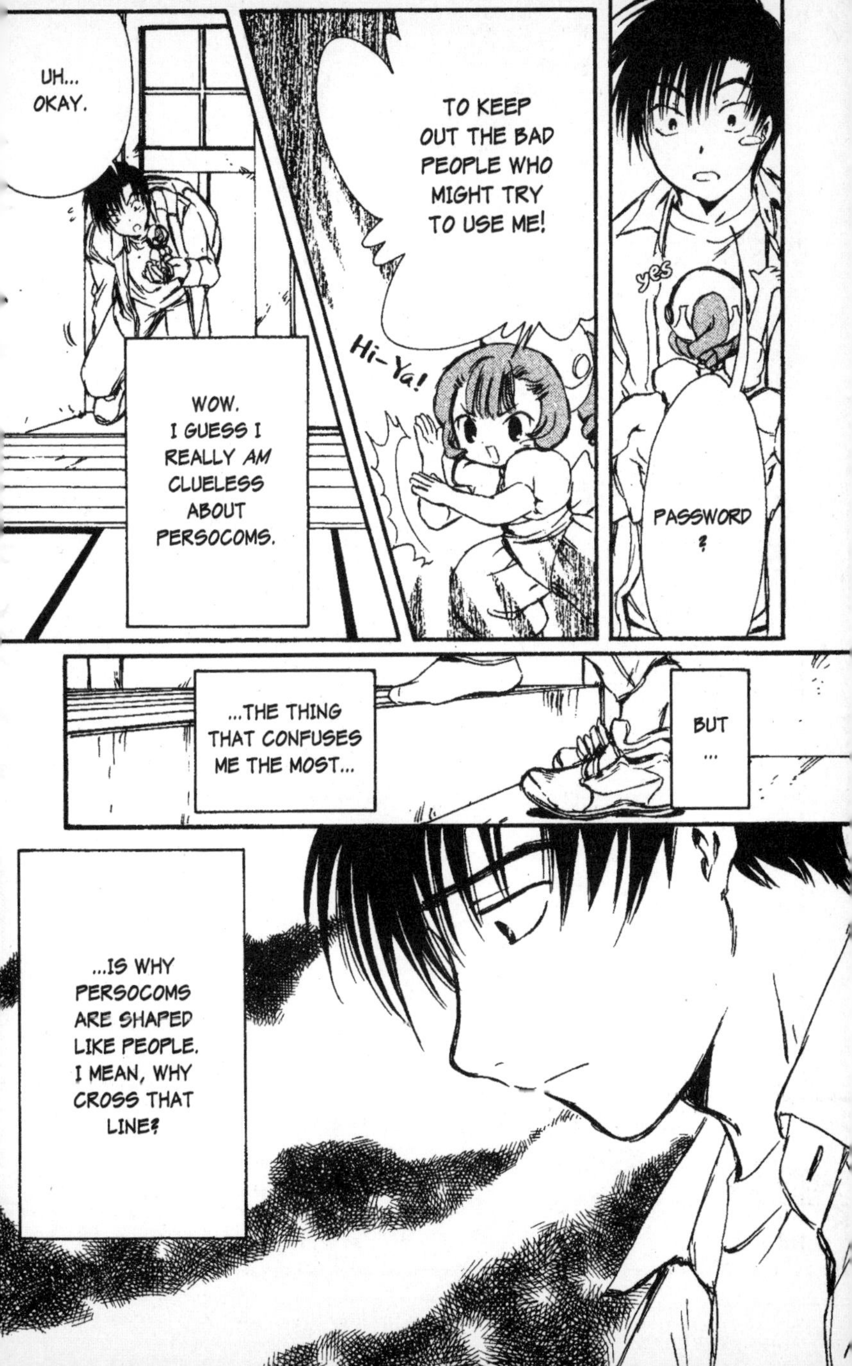
PASSWORD?
TO KEEP OUT THE BAD PEOPLE WHO MIGHT TRY TO USE ME!
Hi-Ya!
UH... OKAY.
WOW. I GUESS I REALLY *AM* CLUELESS ABOUT PERSOCOMS.
BUT ...
...THE THING THAT CONFUSES ME THE MOST...
...IS WHY PERSOCOMS ARE SHAPED LIKE PEOPLE. I MEAN, WHY CROSS THAT LINE?

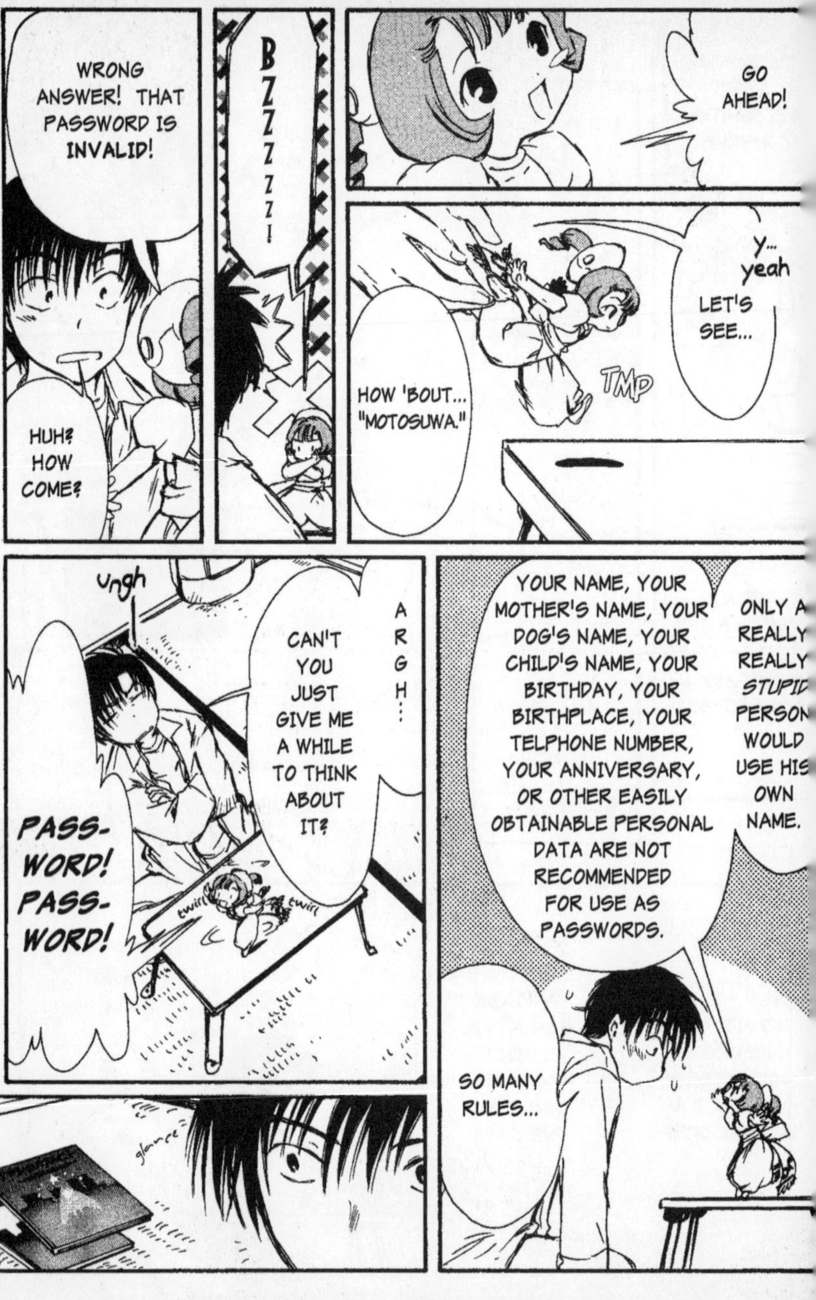
GO AHEAD!
Y... yeah
LET'S SEE...
TMP
HOW 'BOUT... "MOTOSUWA."
BZZZZZ!
WRONG ANSWER! THAT PASSWORD IS INVALID!
HUH? HOW COME?
ONLY A REALLY REALLY STUPID PERSON WOULD USE HIS OWN NAME.
YOUR NAME, YOUR MOTHER'S NAME, YOUR DOG'S NAME, YOUR CHILD'S NAME, YOUR BIRTHDAY, YOUR BIRTHPLACE, YOUR TELPHONE NUMBER, YOUR ANNIVERSARY, OR OTHER EASILY OBTAINABLE PERSONAL DATA ARE NOT RECOMMENDED FOR USE AS PASSWORDS.
SO MANY RULES...
ungh
ARGH...
CAN'T YOU JUST GIVE ME A WHILE TO THINK ABOUT IT?
PASS-WORD! PASS-WORD!
twirl
twirl
glance

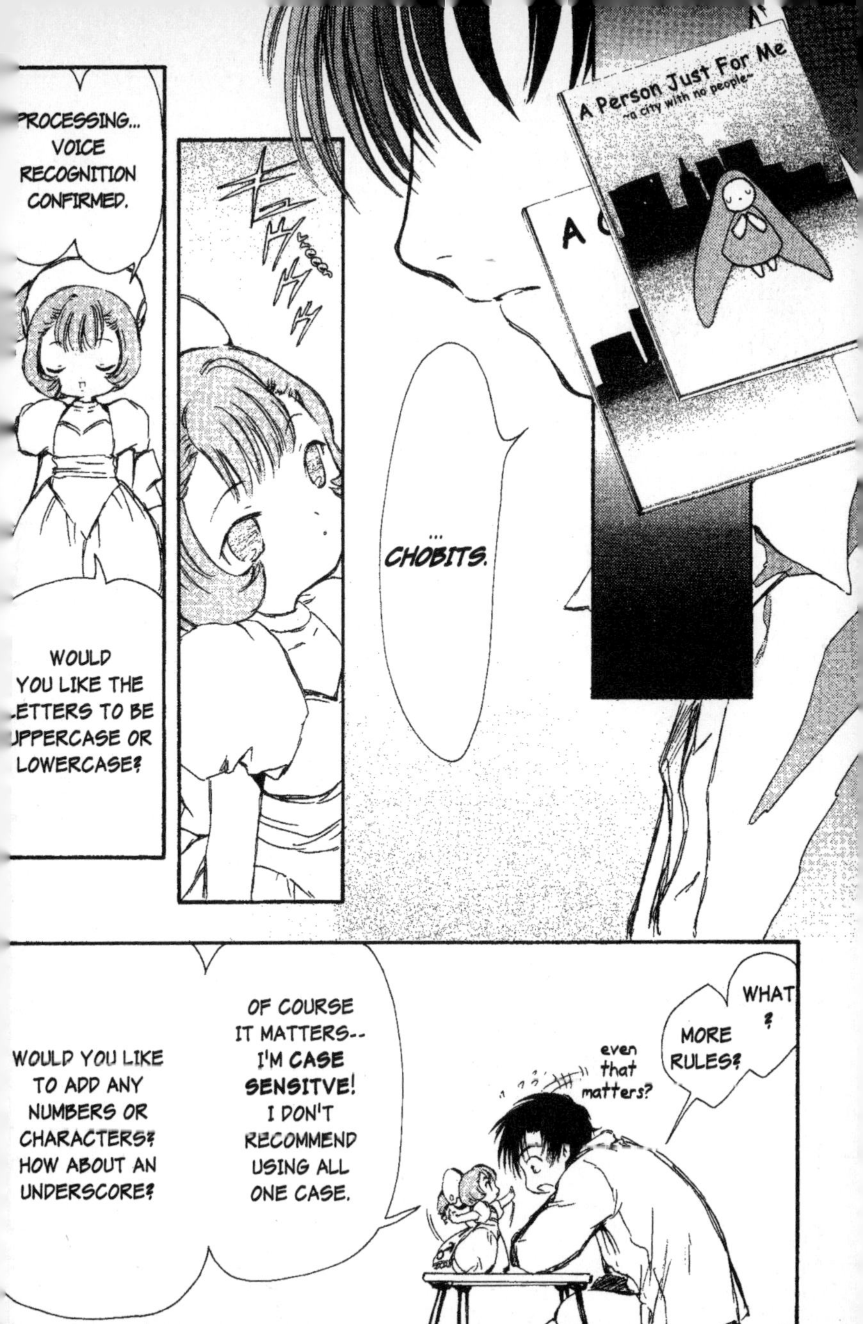
A Person Just For Me
~a city with no people~
A C
...CHOBITS.
PROCESSING... VOICE RECOGNITION CONFIRMED.
WOULD YOU LIKE THE LETTERS TO BE UPPERCASE OR LOWERCASE?
WHAT? MORE RULES?
even that matters?
OF COURSE IT MATTERS-- I'M CASE SENSITVE! I DON'T RECOMMEND USING ALL ONE CASE.
WOULD YOU LIKE TO ADD ANY NUMBERS OR CHARACTERS? HOW ABOUT AN UNDERSCORE?

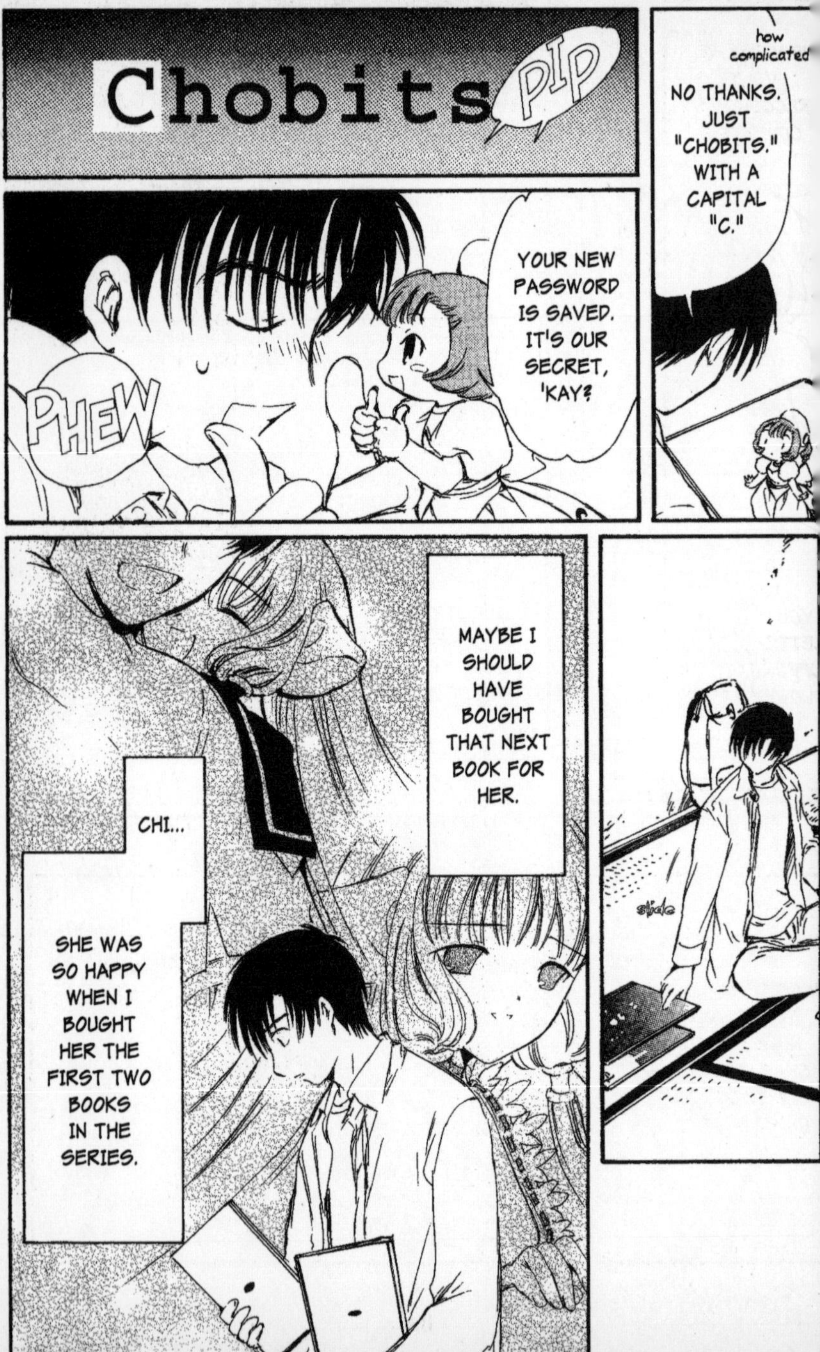
how complicated
NO THANKS. JUST "CHOBITS." WITH A CAPITAL "C."
Chobits
PIP
YOUR NEW PASSWORD IS SAVED. IT'S OUR SECRET, 'KAY?
PHEW
slide
MAYBE I SHOULD HAVE BOUGHT THAT NEXT BOOK FOR HER.
CHI...
SHE WAS SO HAPPY WHEN I BOUGHT HER THE FIRST TWO BOOKS IN THE SERIES.

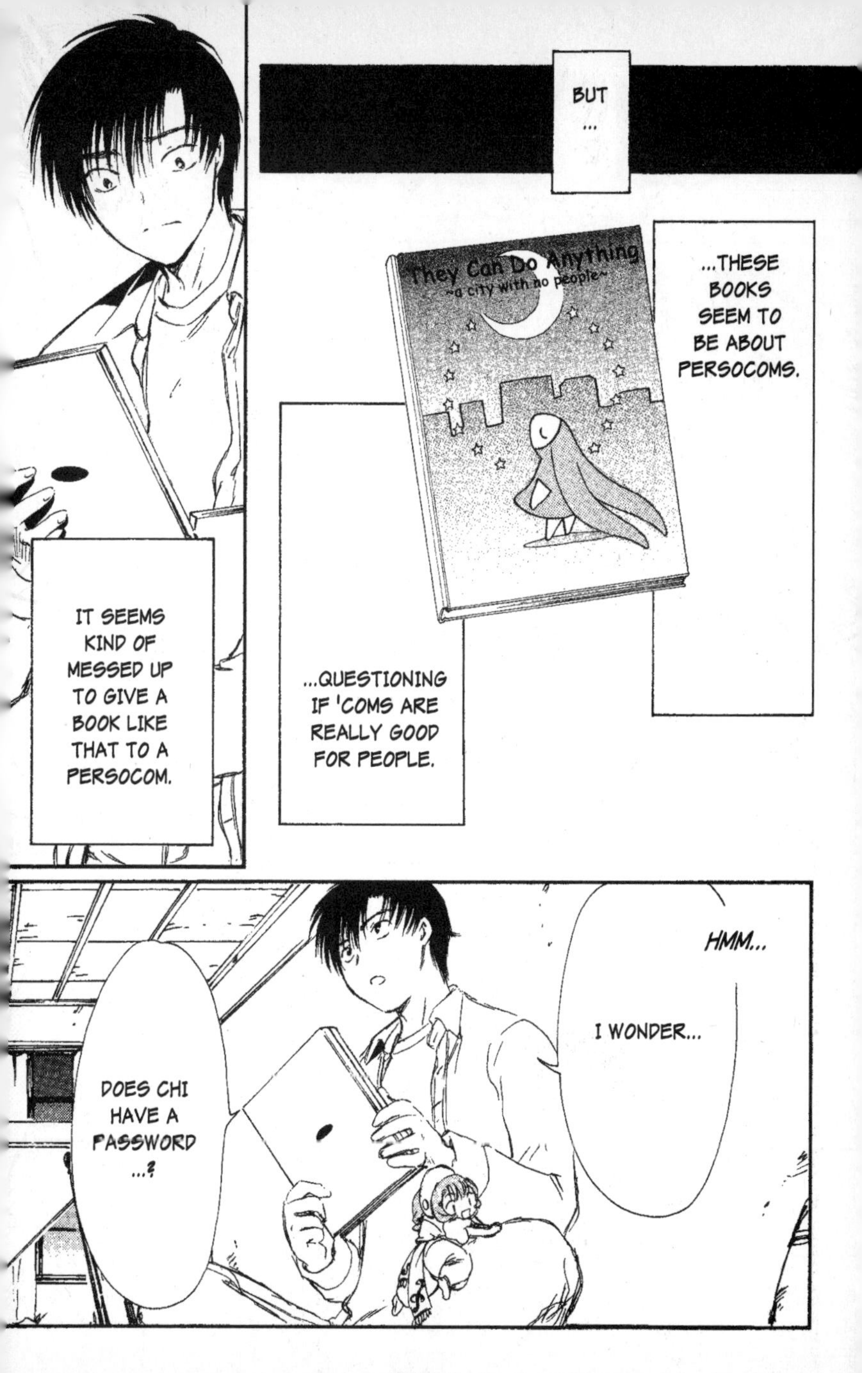
BUT ...
They Can Do Anything
~a city with no people~
...THESE BOOKS SEEM TO BE ABOUT PERSOCOMS.
...QUESTIONING IF 'COMS ARE REALLY GOOD FOR PEOPLE.
IT SEEMS KIND OF MESSED UP TO GIVE A BOOK LIKE THAT TO A PERSOCOM.
HMM...
I WONDER...
DOES CHI HAVE A PASSWORD ...?

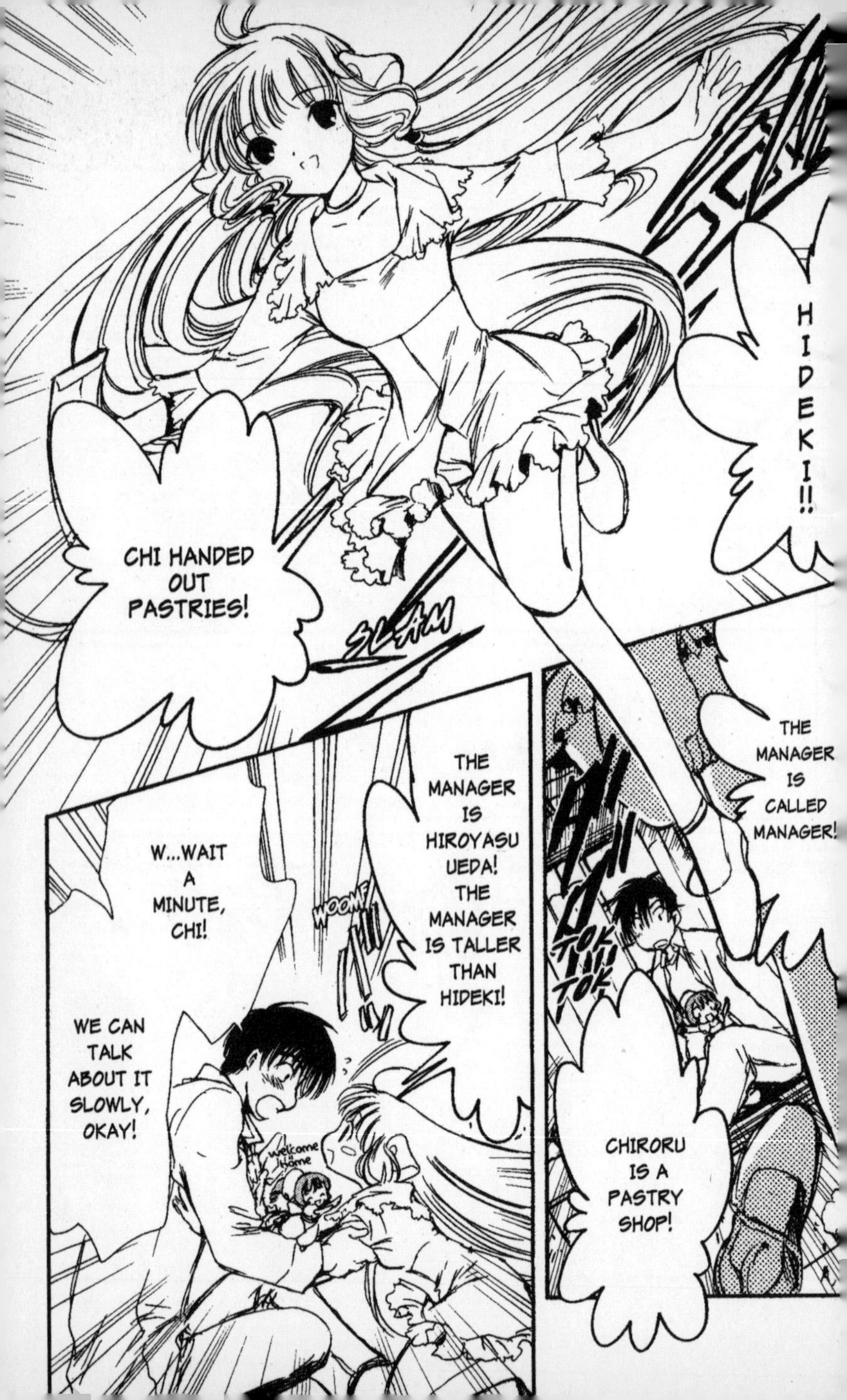
HIDEKI!!
CHI HANDED OUT PASTRIES!
SLAM
THE MANAGER IS CALLED MANAGER!
TOK TOK
CHIRORU IS A PASTRY SHOP!
THE MANAGER IS HIROYASU UEDA! THE MANAGER IS TALLER THAN HIDEKI!
WOOMF
W...WAIT A MINUTE, CHI!
WE CAN TALK ABOUT IT SLOWLY, OKAY!
Welcome Home

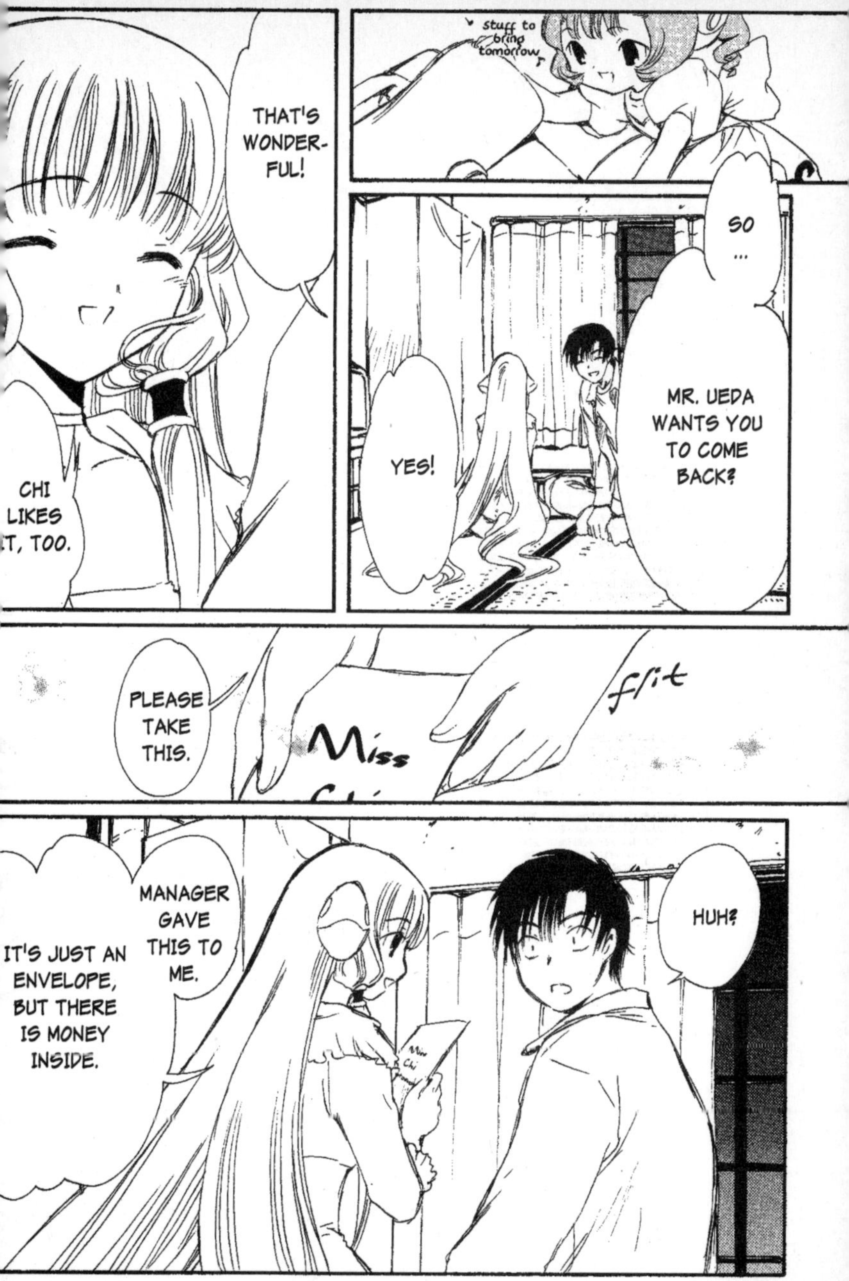
stuff to bring tomorrow
SO ...
MR. UEDA WANTS YOU TO COME BACK?
YES!
THAT'S WONDERFUL!
CHI LIKES T, TOO.
flit
Miss
PLEASE TAKE THIS.
HUH?
MANAGER GAVE THIS TO ME.
IT'S JUST AN ENVELOPE, BUT THERE IS MONEY INSIDE.
Miss Chi

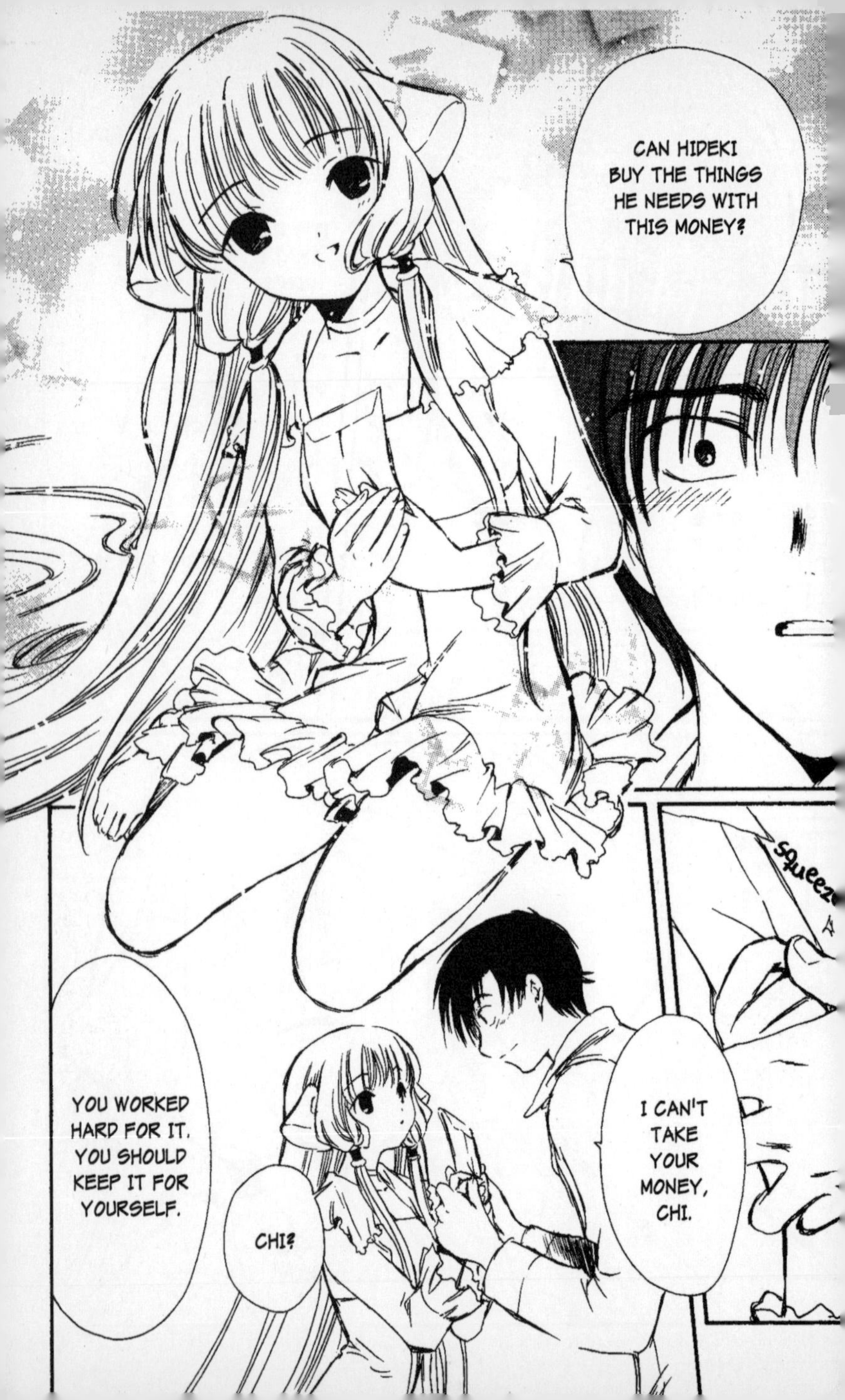
CAN HIDEKI BUY THE THINGS HE NEEDS WITH THIS MONEY?
I CAN'T TAKE YOUR MONEY, CHI.
CHI?
YOU WORKED HARD FOR IT. YOU SHOULD KEEP IT FOR YOURSELF.

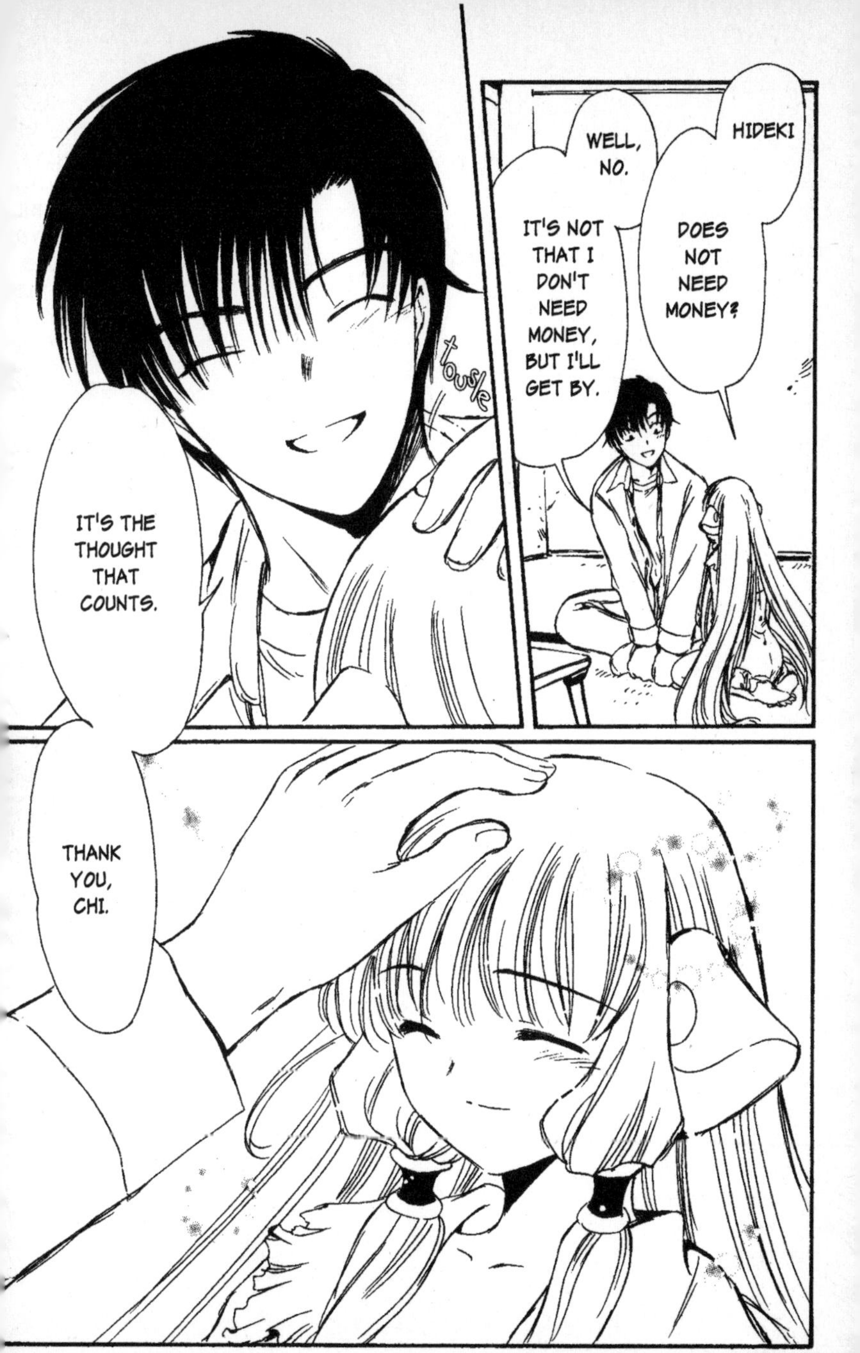
HIDEKI
DOES NOT NEED MONEY?
WELL, NO.
IT'S NOT THAT I DON'T NEED MONEY, BUT I'LL GET BY.
tousle
IT'S THE THOUGHT THAT COUNTS.
THANK YOU, CHI.

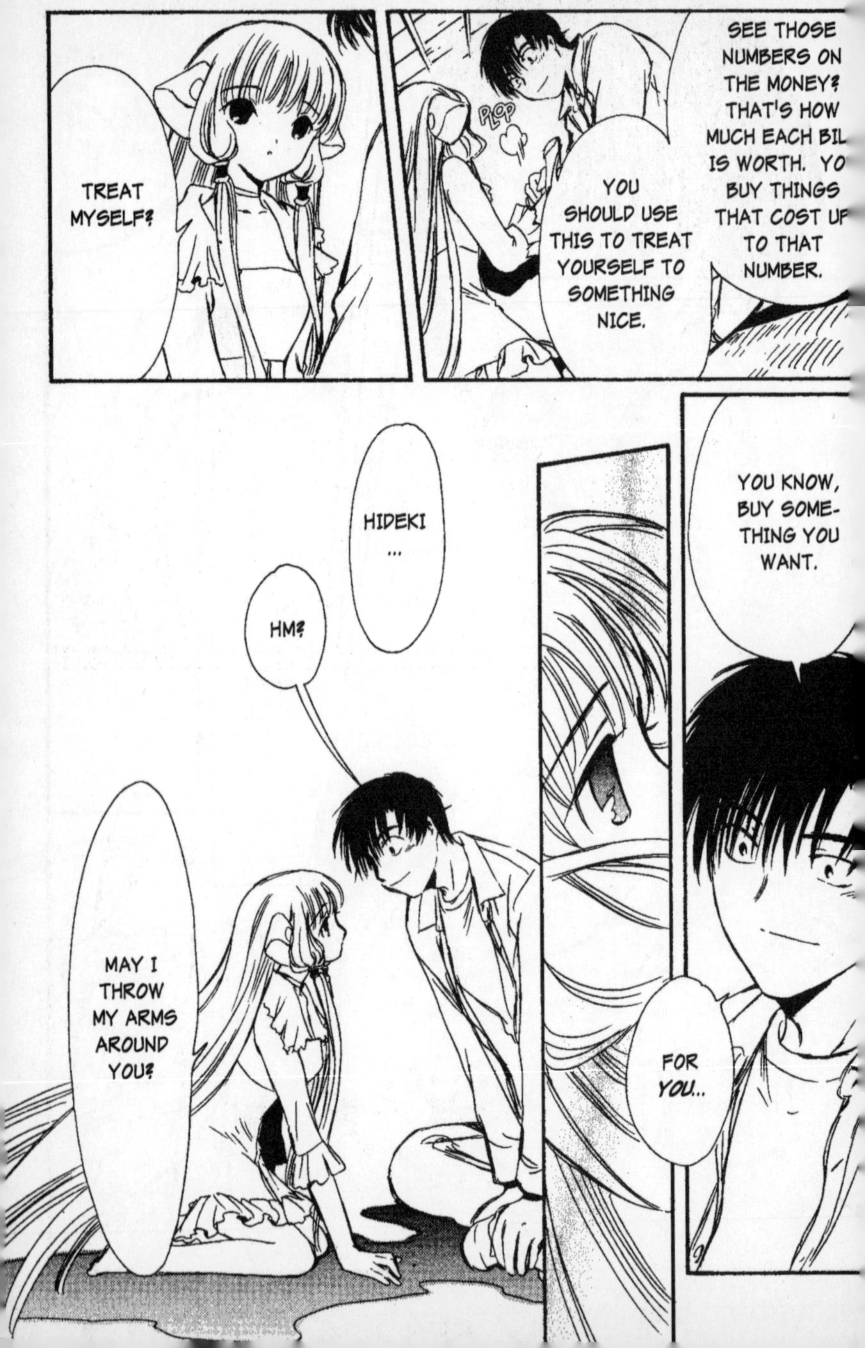
SEE THOSE NUMBERS ON THE MONEY? THAT'S HOW MUCH EACH BIL IS WORTH. YO BUY THINGS THAT COST UP TO THAT NUMBER.
PLOP
YOU SHOULD USE THIS TO TREAT YOURSELF TO SOMETHING NICE.
TREAT MYSELF?
YOU KNOW, BUY SOME-THING YOU WANT.
FOR *YOU*...
HIDEKI ...
HM?
MAY I THROW MY ARMS AROUND YOU?

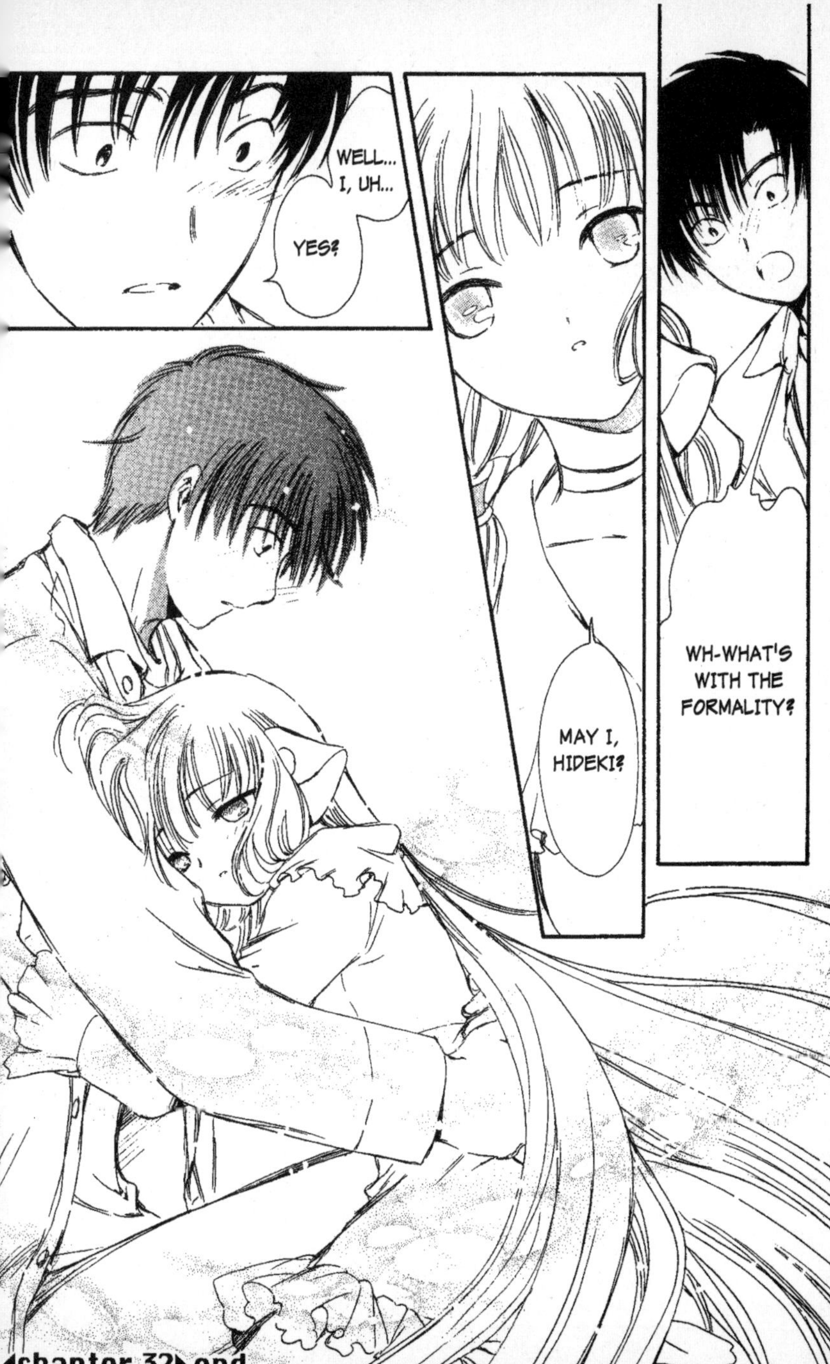
WH-WHAT'S WITH THE FORMALITY?
MAY I, HIDEKI?
WELL... I, UH...
YES?

◀chapter.32▶ end

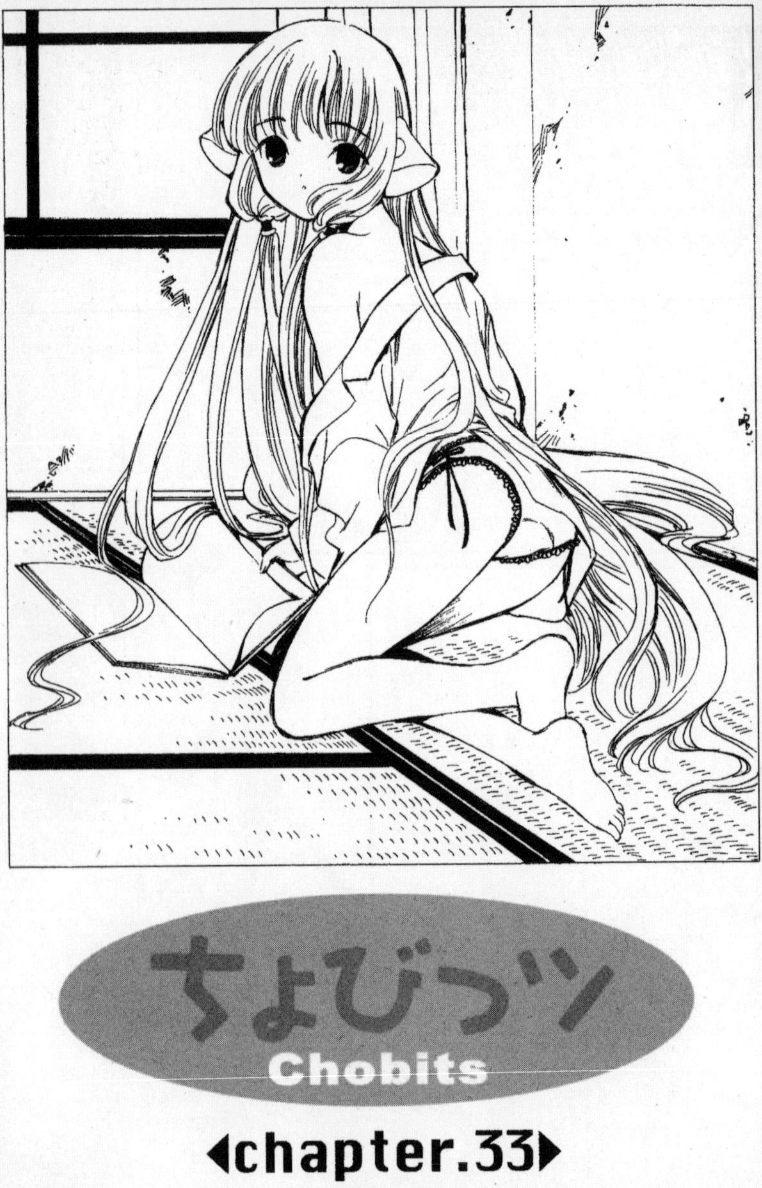

ちょびっツ
Chobits

◂chapter.33▸

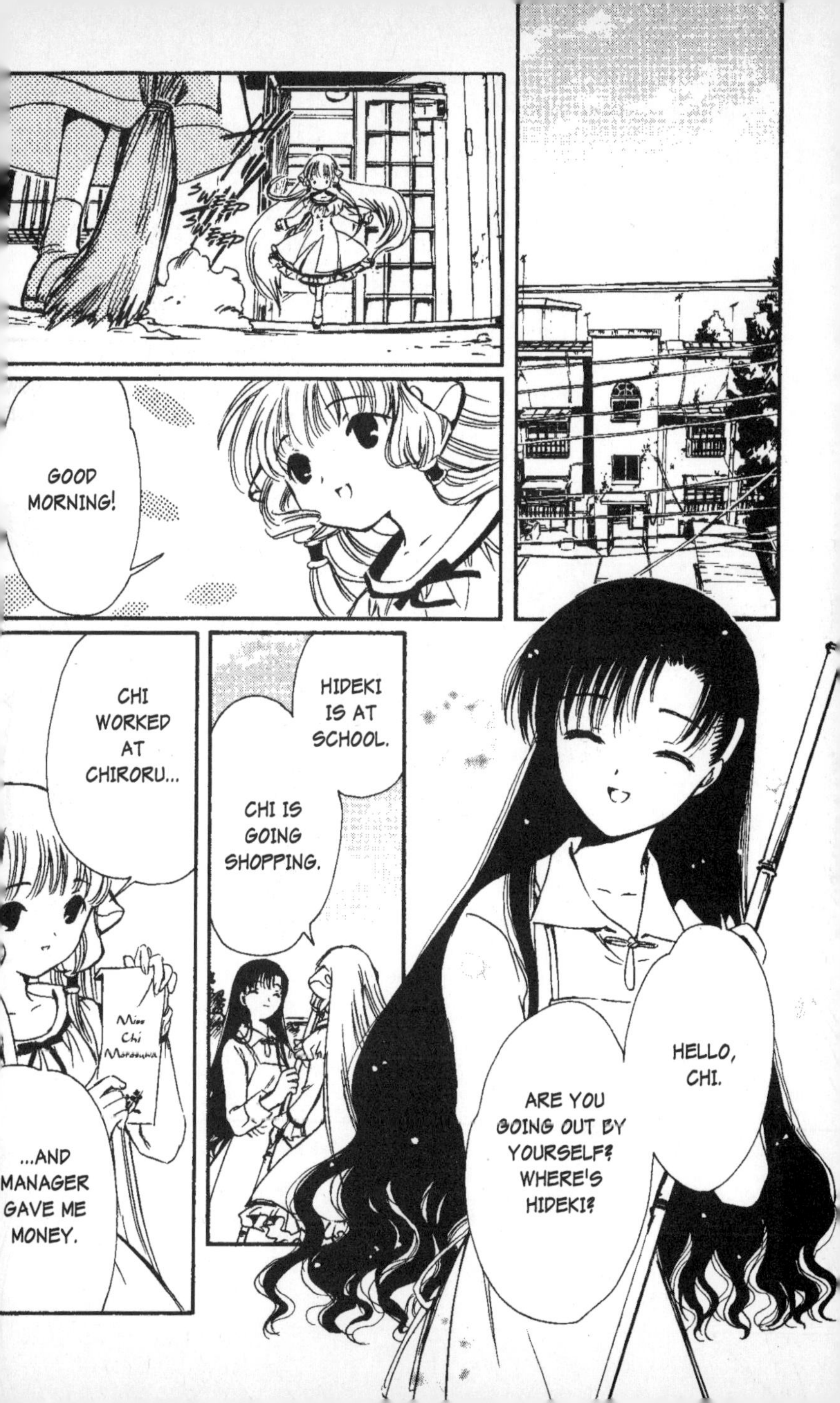
SWEEP
SWEEP
GOOD MORNING!
HELLO, CHI.
ARE YOU GOING OUT BY YOURSELF? WHERE'S HIDEKI?
HIDEKI IS AT SCHOOL.
CHI IS GOING SHOPPING.
CHI WORKED AT CHIRORU...
...AND MANAGER GAVE ME MONEY.

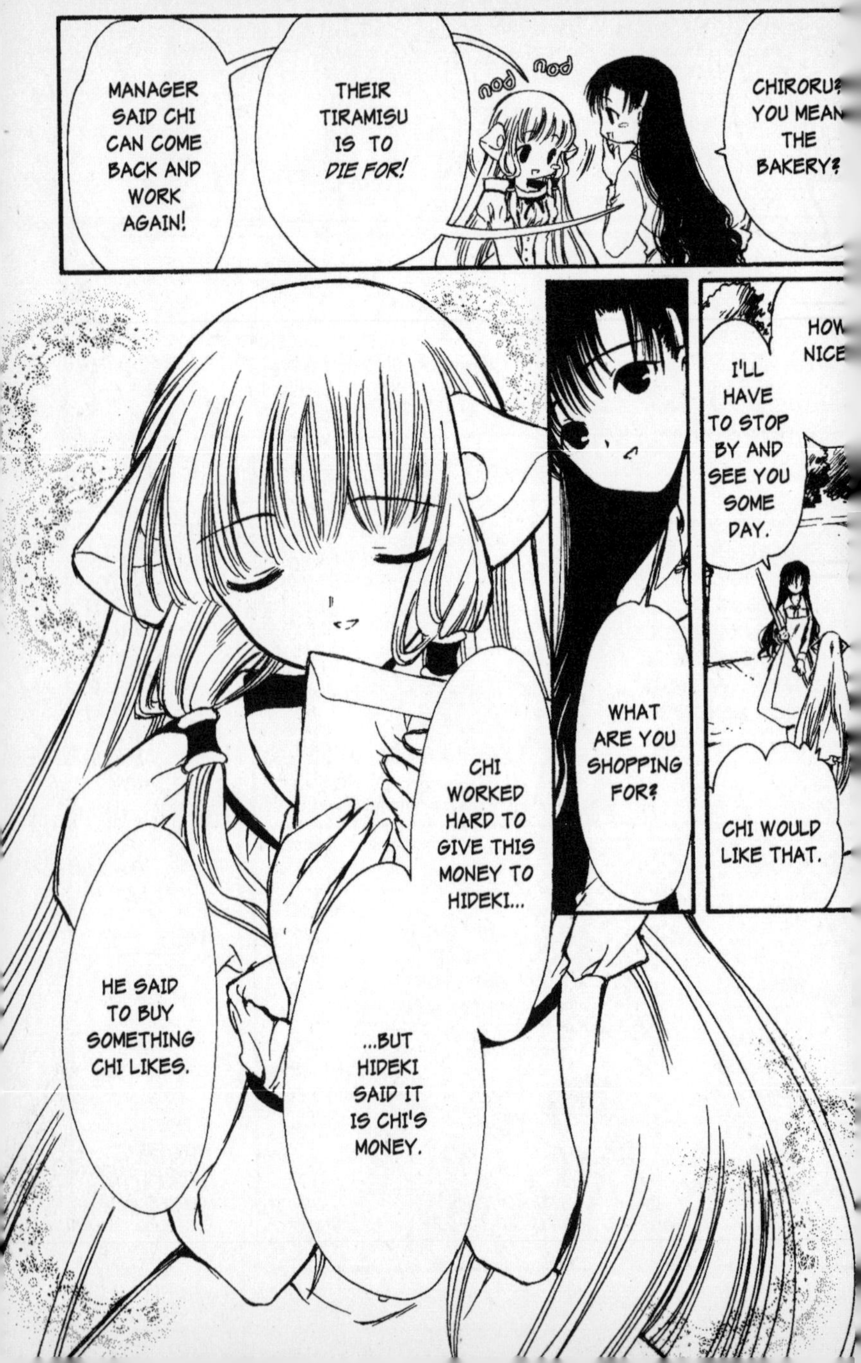
CHIRORU? YOU MEAN THE BAKERY?
nod nod
THEIR TIRAMISU IS TO *DIE FOR!*
MANAGER SAID CHI CAN COME BACK AND WORK AGAIN!
HOW NICE
I'LL HAVE TO STOP BY AND SEE YOU SOME DAY.
CHI WOULD LIKE THAT.
WHAT ARE YOU SHOPPING FOR?
CHI WORKED HARD TO GIVE THIS MONEY TO HIDEKI...
...BUT HIDEKI SAID IT IS CHI'S MONEY.
HE SAID TO BUY SOMETHING CHI LIKES.

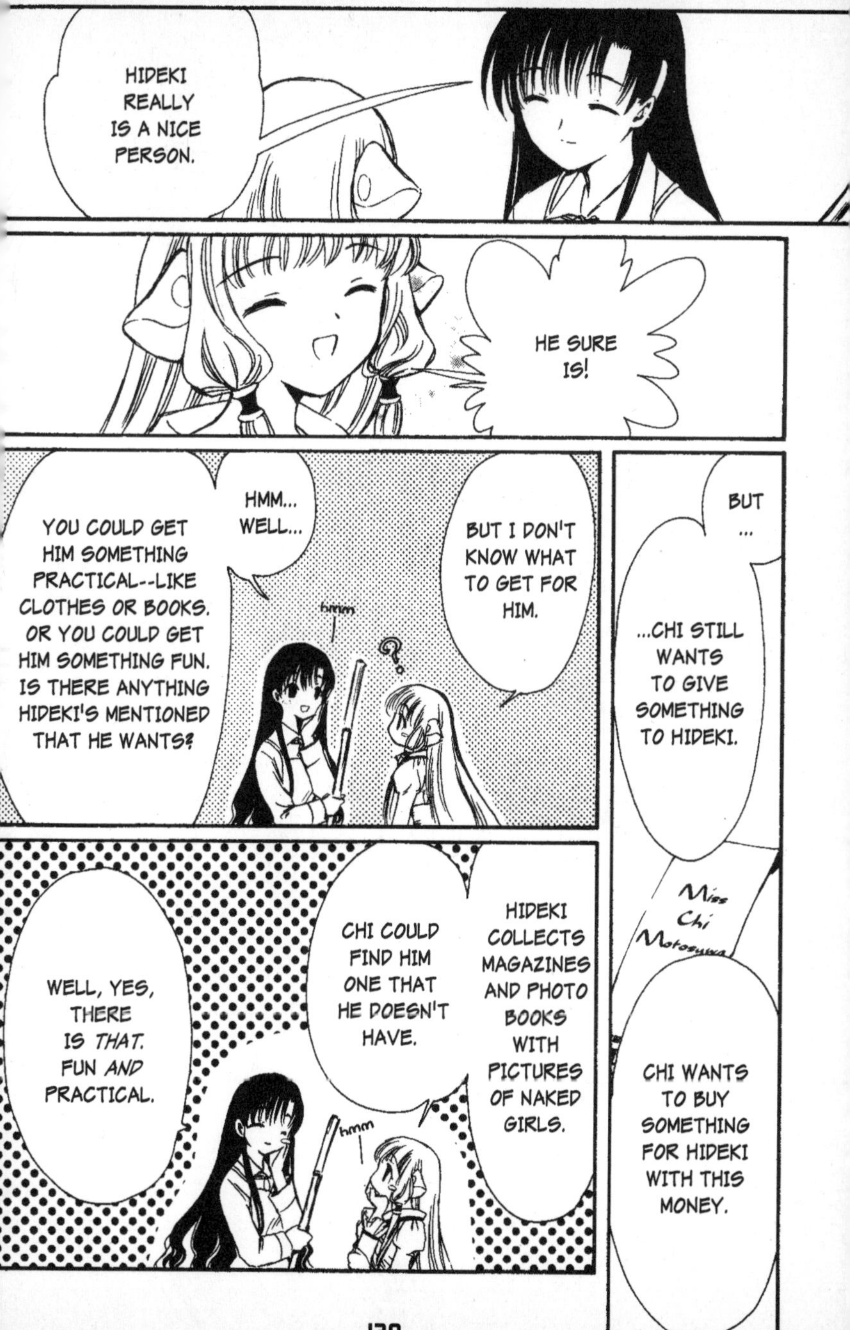
HIDEKI REALLY IS A NICE PERSON.
HE SURE IS!
BUT ...
...CHI STILL WANTS TO GIVE SOMETHING TO HIDEKI.
Miss Chi Motosuwa
CHI WANTS TO BUY SOMETHING FOR HIDEKI WITH THIS MONEY.
BUT I DON'T KNOW WHAT TO GET FOR HIM.
HMM... WELL...
hmm
YOU COULD GET HIM SOMETHING PRACTICAL--LIKE CLOTHES OR BOOKS. OR YOU COULD GET HIM SOMETHING FUN. IS THERE ANYTHING HIDEKI'S MENTIONED THAT HE WANTS?
HIDEKI COLLECTS MAGAZINES AND PHOTO BOOKS WITH PICTURES OF NAKED GIRLS.
CHI COULD FIND HIM ONE THAT HE DOESN'T HAVE.
hmm
WELL, YES, THERE IS *THAT*. FUN *AND* PRACTICAL.

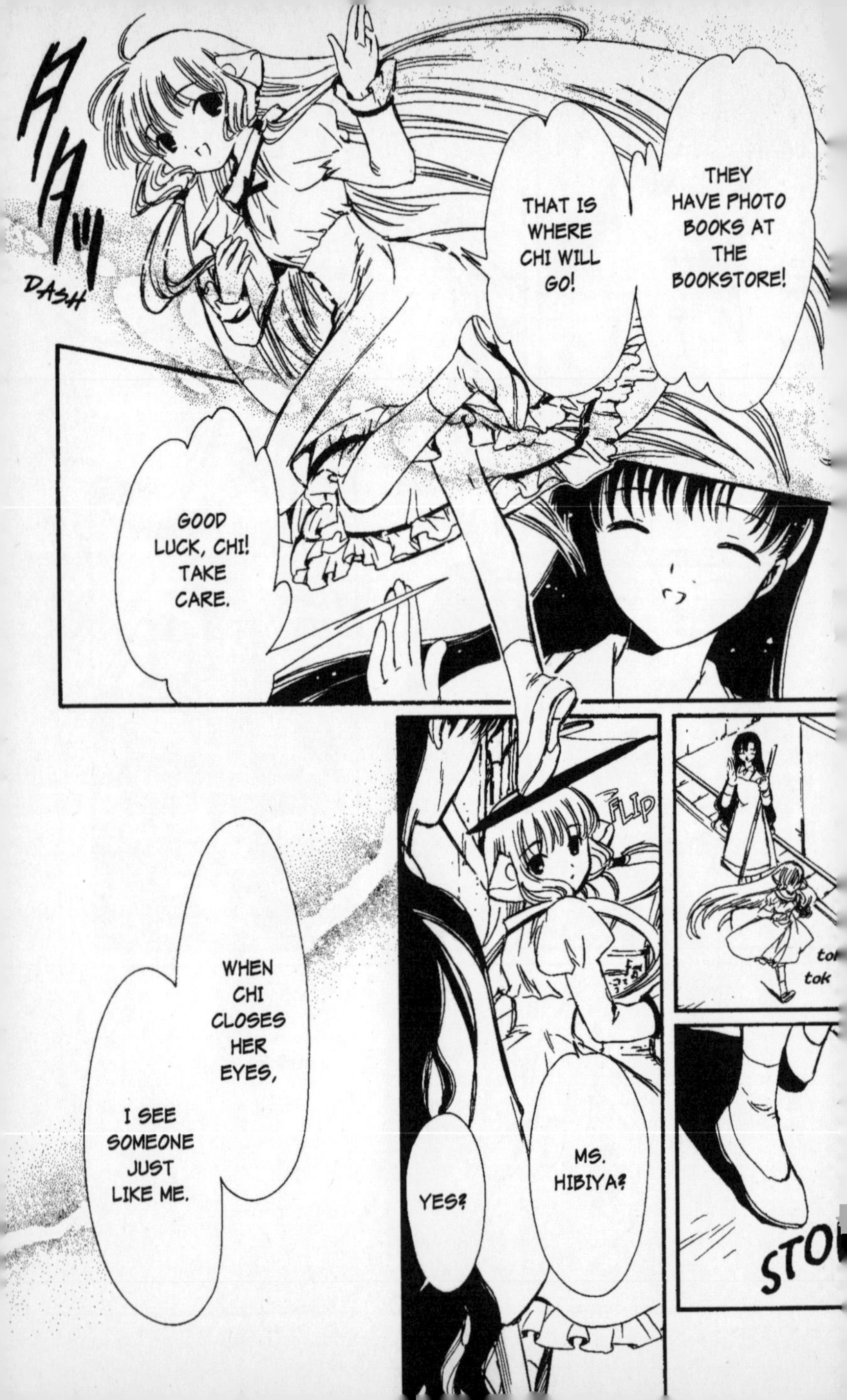
THEY HAVE PHOTO BOOKS AT THE BOOKSTORE!
THAT IS WHERE CHI WILL GO!
DASH
GOOD LUCK, CHI! TAKE CARE.
tok
STO
FLIP
MS. HIBIYA?
YES?
WHEN CHI CLOSES HER EYES,
I SEE SOMEONE JUST LIKE ME.

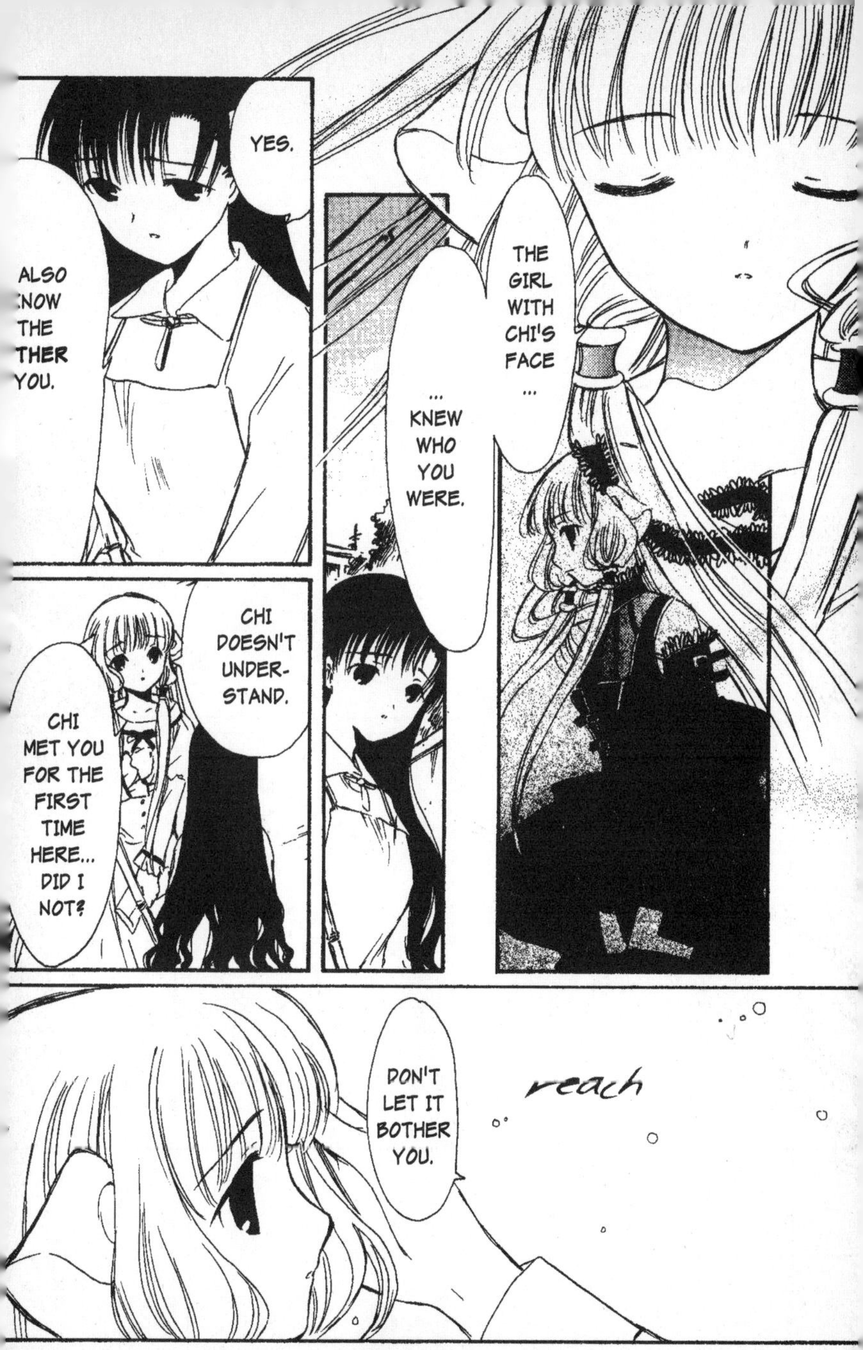
THE GIRL WITH CHI'S FACE ...
... KNEW WHO YOU WERE.
YES.
ALSO NOW THE THER YOU.
CHI DOESN'T UNDER-STAND.
CHI MET YOU FOR THE FIRST TIME HERE... DID I NOT?
DON'T LET IT BOTHER YOU.
reach

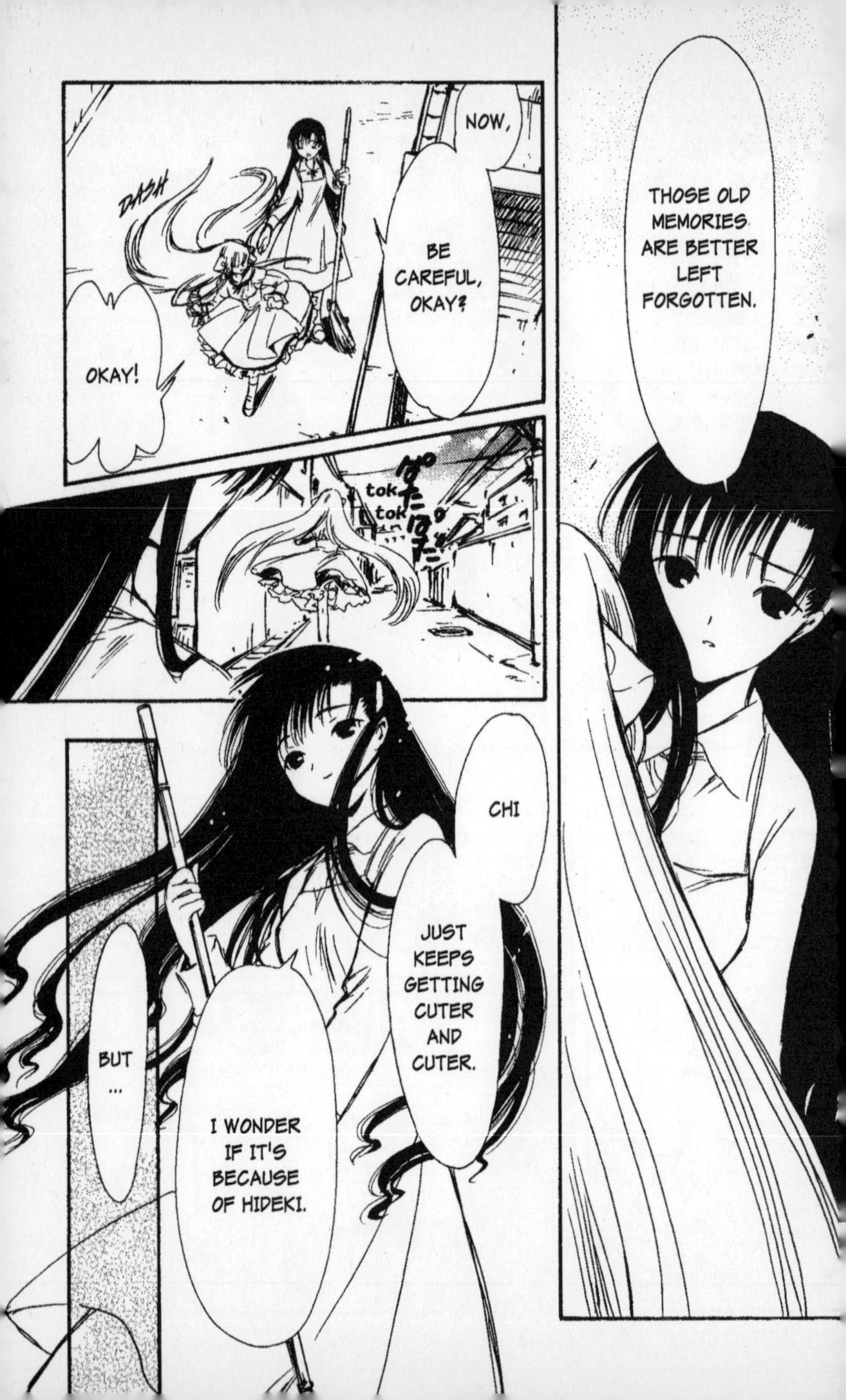
THOSE OLD MEMORIES ARE BETTER LEFT FORGOTTEN.
NOW,
BE CAREFUL, OKAY?
OKAY!
DASH
tok tok
CHI
JUST KEEPS GETTING CUTER AND CUTER.
BUT ...
I WONDER IF IT'S BECAUSE OF HIDEKI.

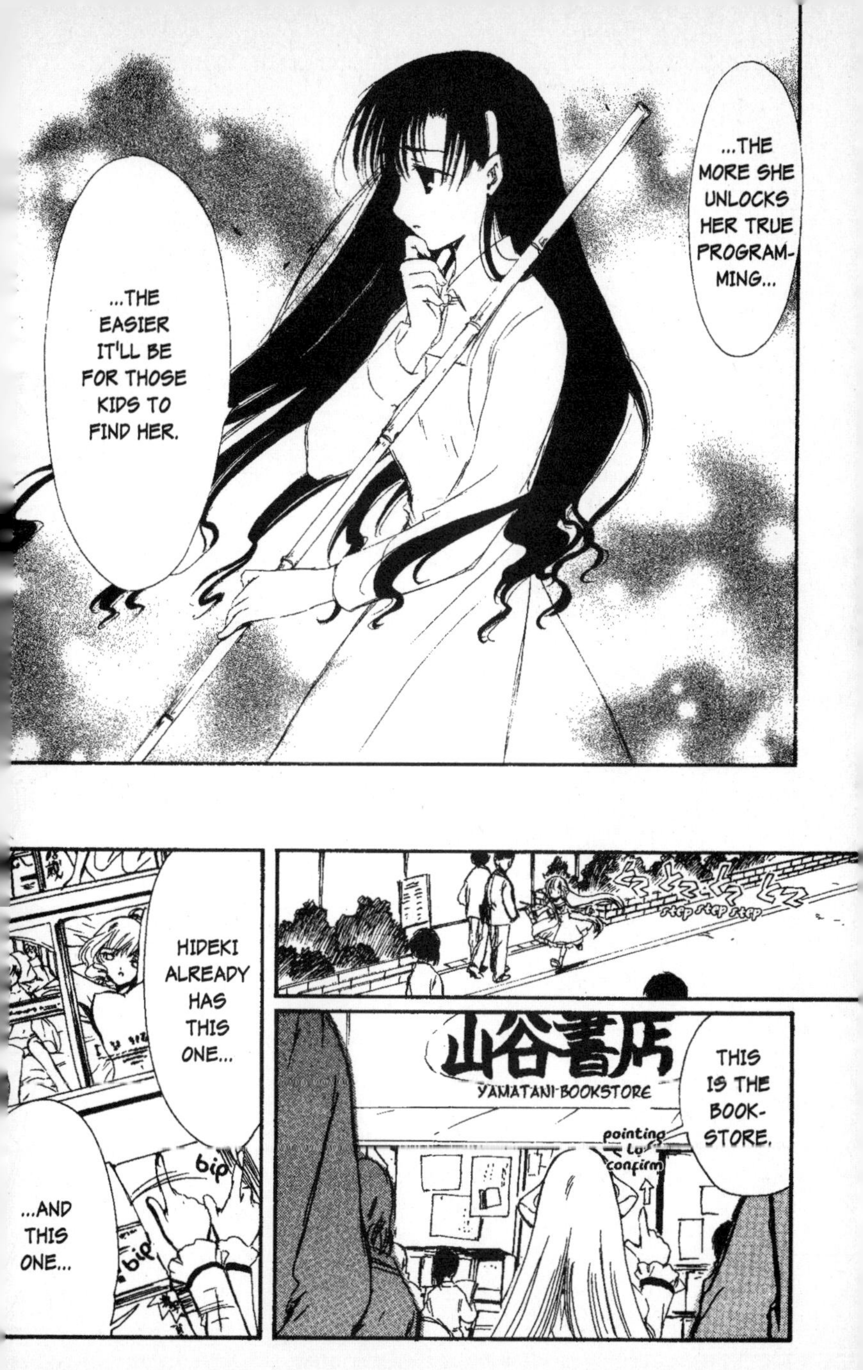
...THE MORE SHE UNLOCKS HER TRUE PROGRAMMING...
...THE EASIER IT'LL BE FOR THOSE KIDS TO FIND HER.
step step step
山谷書店
YAMATANI-BOOKSTORE
THIS IS THE BOOK-STORE.
pointing to confirm
HIDEKI ALREADY HAS THIS ONE...
bip
...AND THIS ONE...
bip

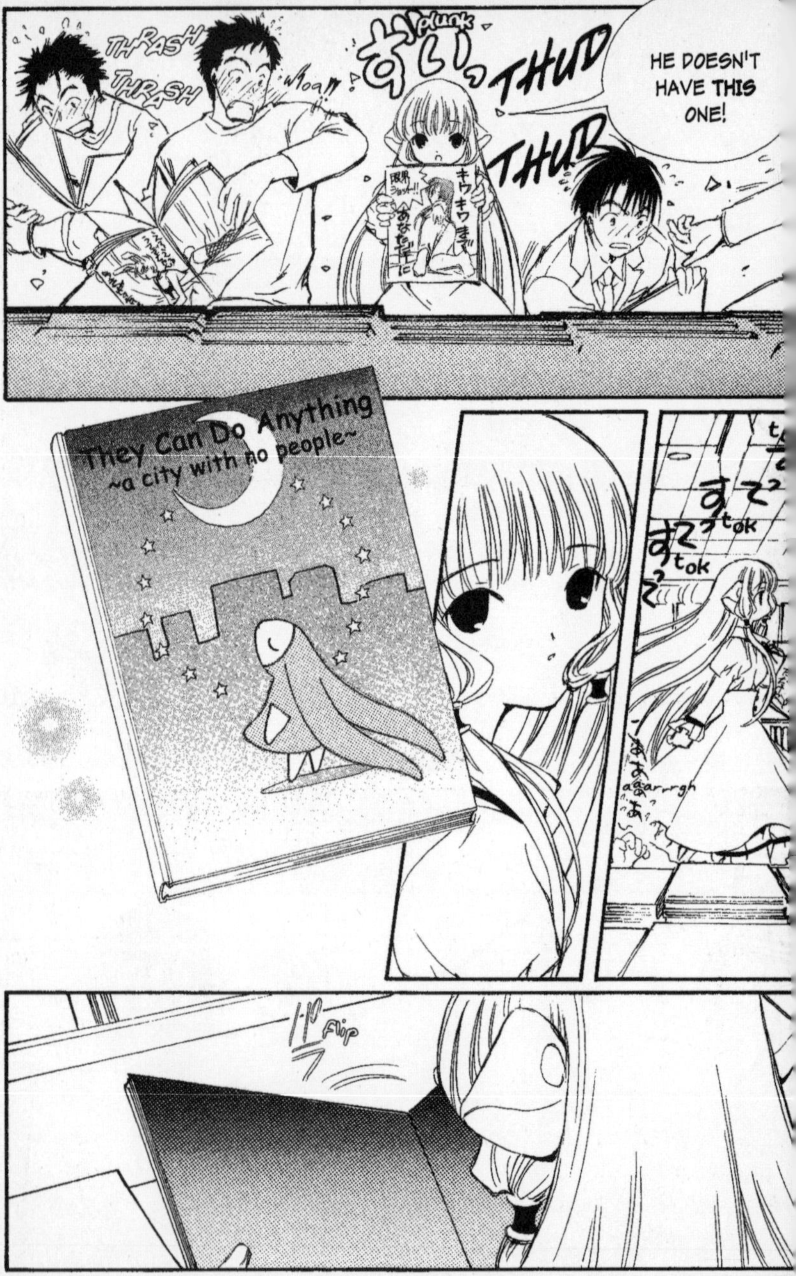
HE DOESN'T HAVE THIS ONE!
THUD
THUD
plunk
Whoa!!
THRASH
THRASH
tok
tok
aaarrrgh
They Can Do Anything
~a city with no people~
Flip

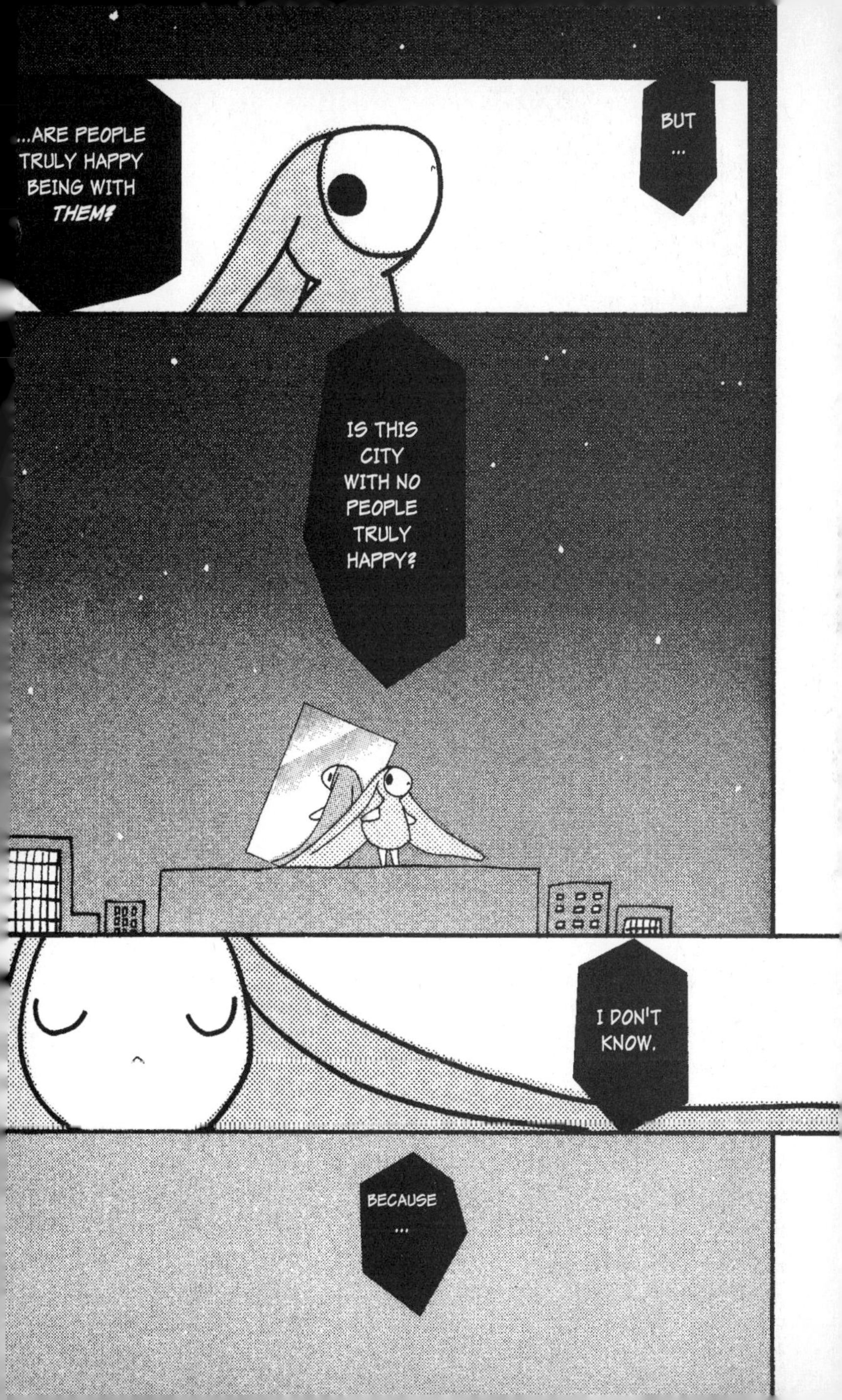
BUT ...
...ARE PEOPLE TRULY HAPPY BEING WITH *THEM?*
IS THIS CITY WITH NO PEOPLE TRULY HAPPY?
I DON'T KNOW.
BECAUSE ...

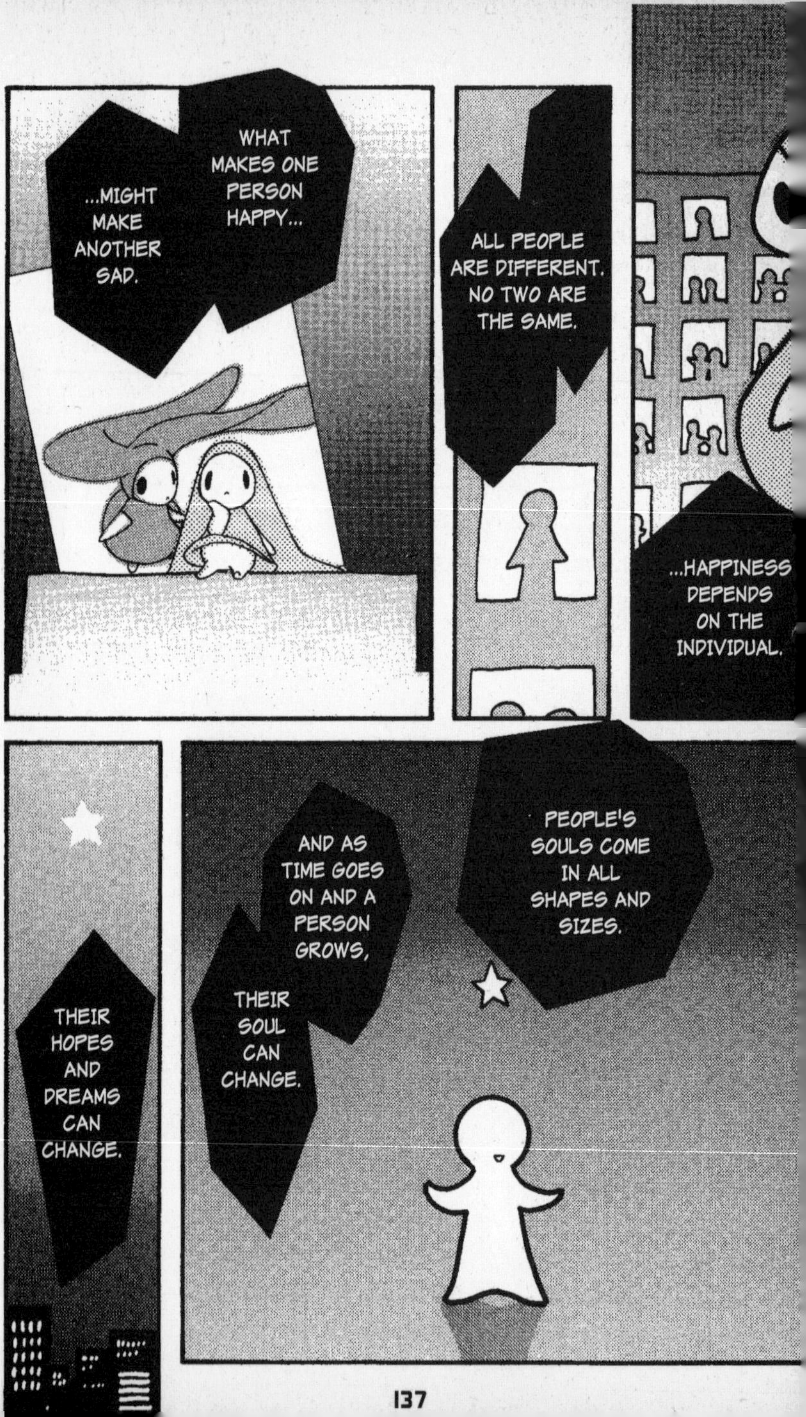
...HAPPINESS DEPENDS ON THE INDIVIDUAL.
ALL PEOPLE ARE DIFFERENT. NO TWO ARE THE SAME.
WHAT MAKES ONE PERSON HAPPY...
...MIGHT MAKE ANOTHER SAD.
PEOPLE'S SOULS COME IN ALL SHAPES AND SIZES.
AND AS TIME GOES ON AND A PERSON GROWS,
THEIR SOUL CAN CHANGE.
THEIR HOPES AND DREAMS CAN CHANGE.

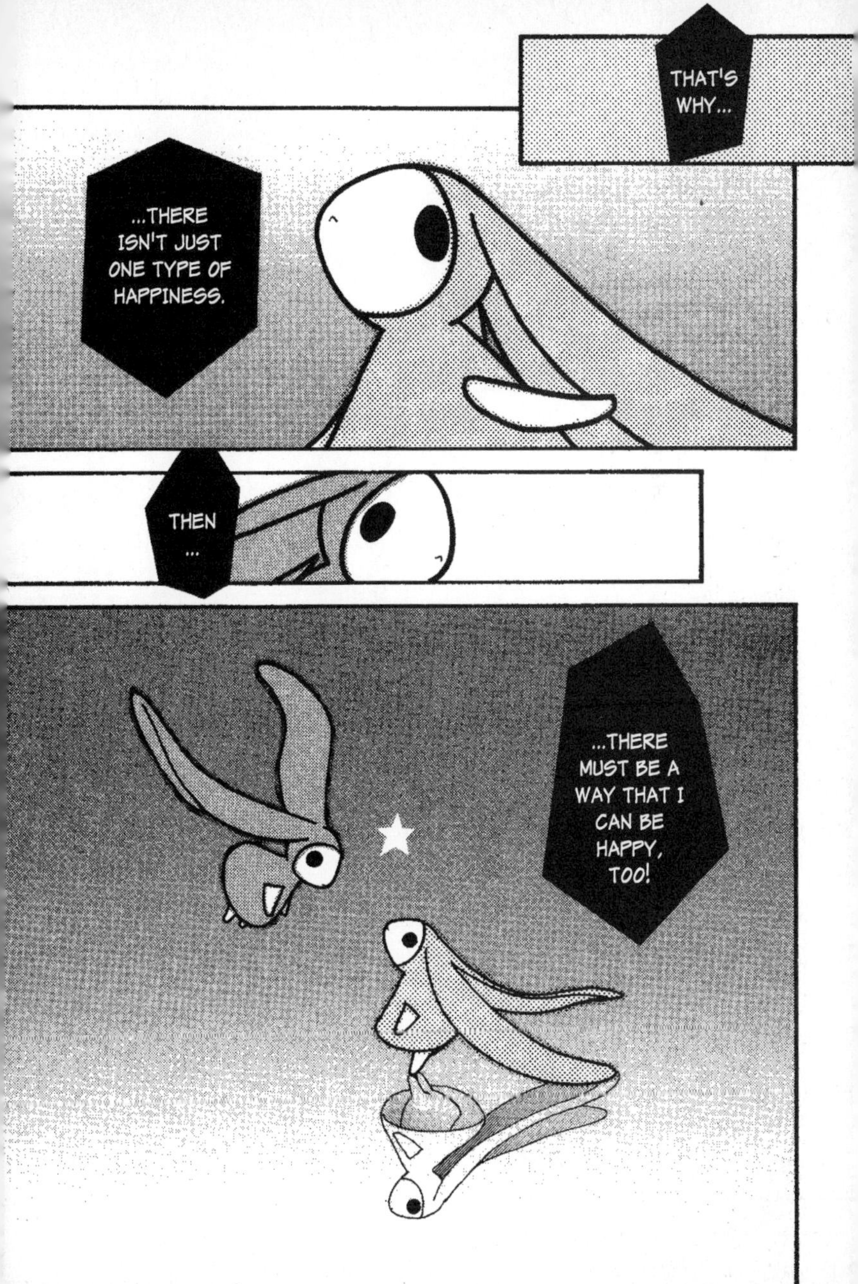
THAT'S WHY...
...THERE ISN'T JUST ONE TYPE OF HAPPINESS.
THEN ...
...THERE MUST BE A WAY THAT I CAN BE HAPPY, TOO!

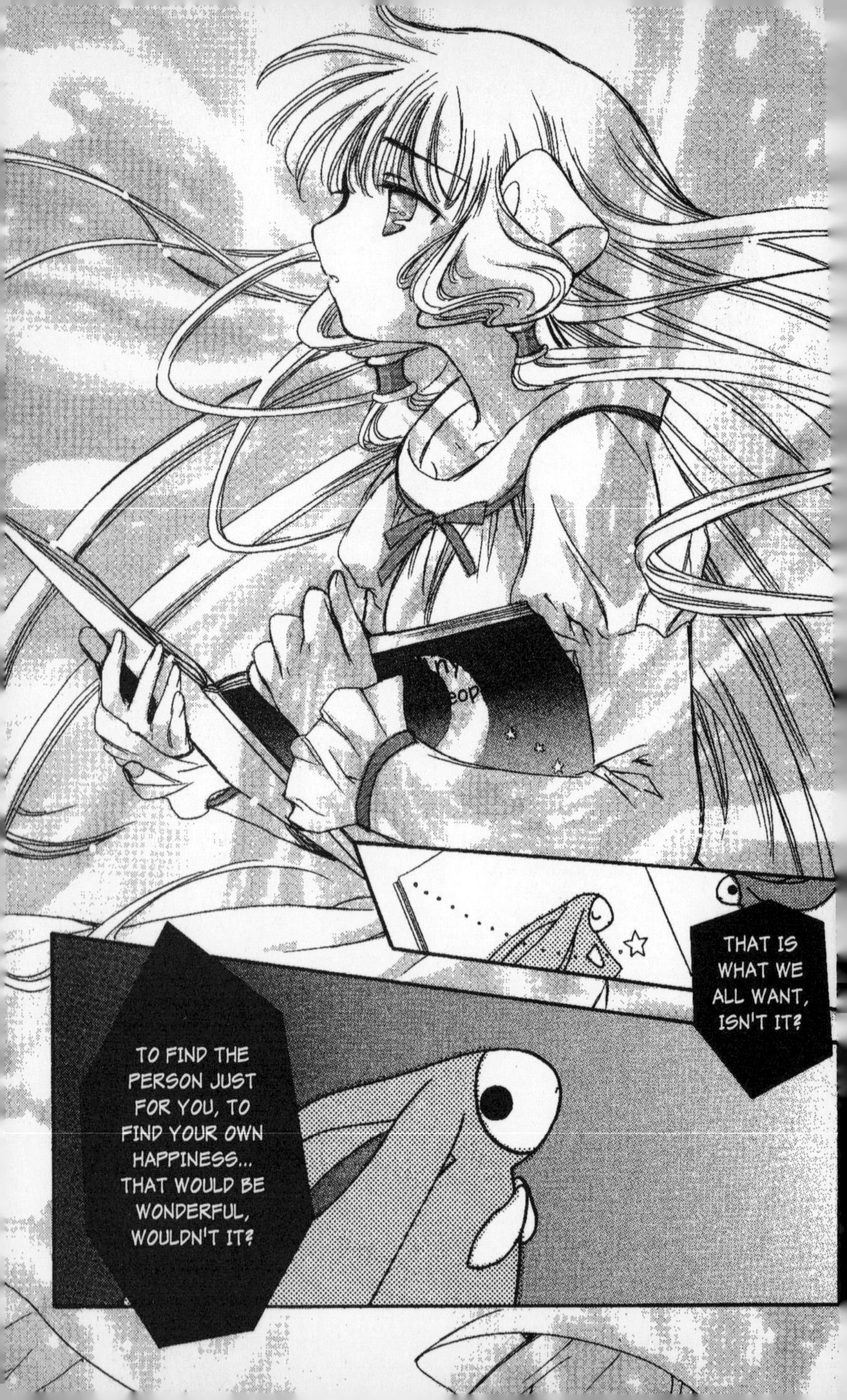
THAT IS WHAT WE ALL WANT, ISN'T IT?
TO FIND THE PERSON JUST FOR YOU, TO FIND YOUR OWN HAPPINESS... THAT WOULD BE WONDERFUL, WOULDN'T IT?

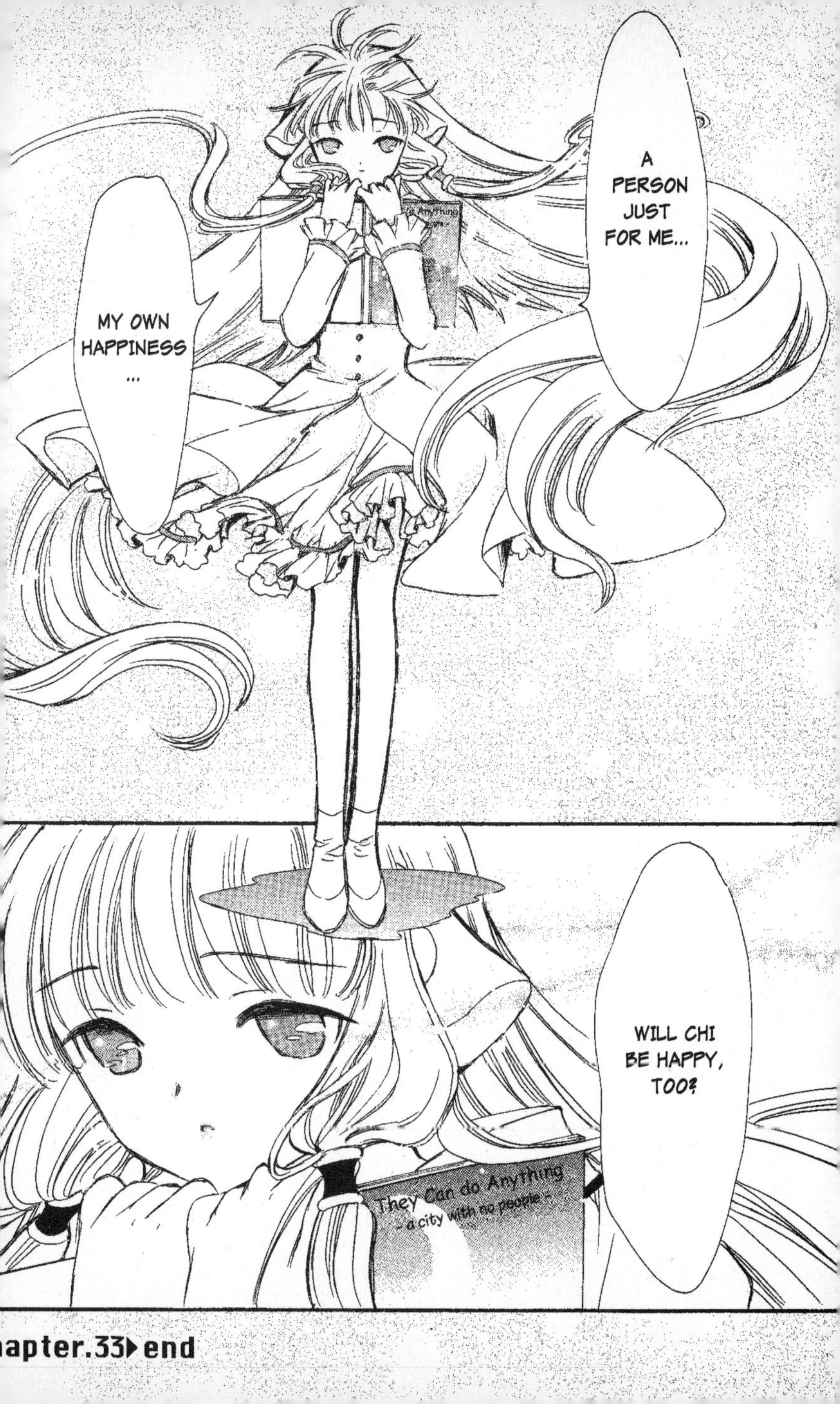
A PERSON JUST FOR ME...
MY OWN HAPPINESS ...
WILL CHI BE HAPPY, TOO?
They Can do Anything
- a city with no people -

apter.33 end

ちょびっツ

Chobits

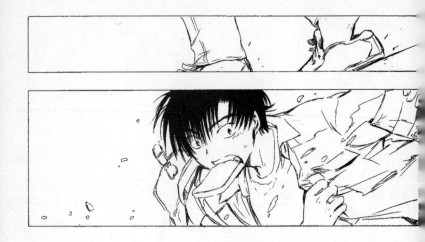

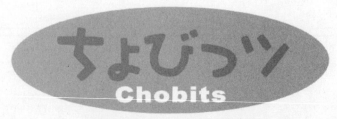

chapter.34

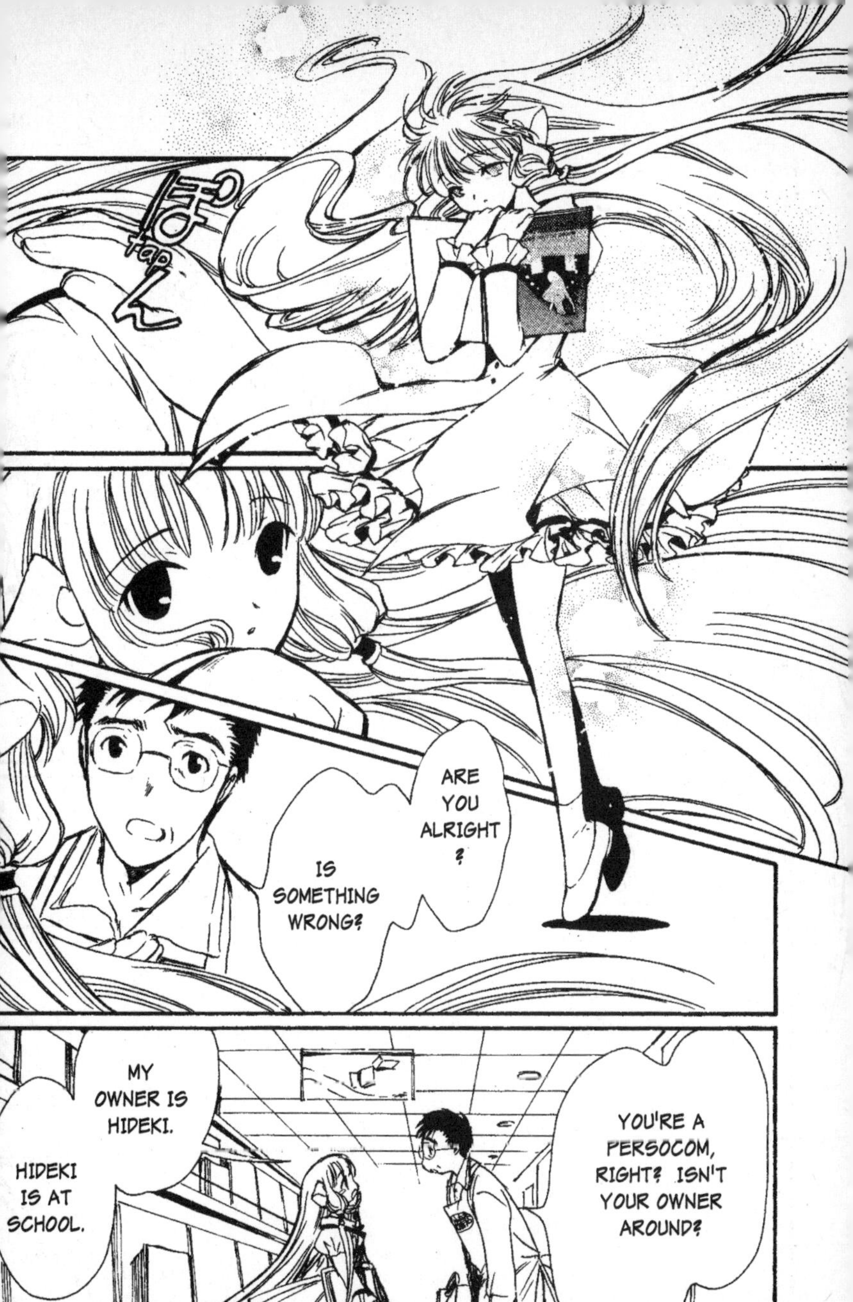
ぽん
tap
ARE YOU ALRIGHT?
IS SOMETHING WRONG?
YOU'RE A PERSOCOM, RIGHT? ISN'T YOUR OWNER AROUND?
MY OWNER IS HIDEKI.
HIDEKI IS AT SCHOOL.

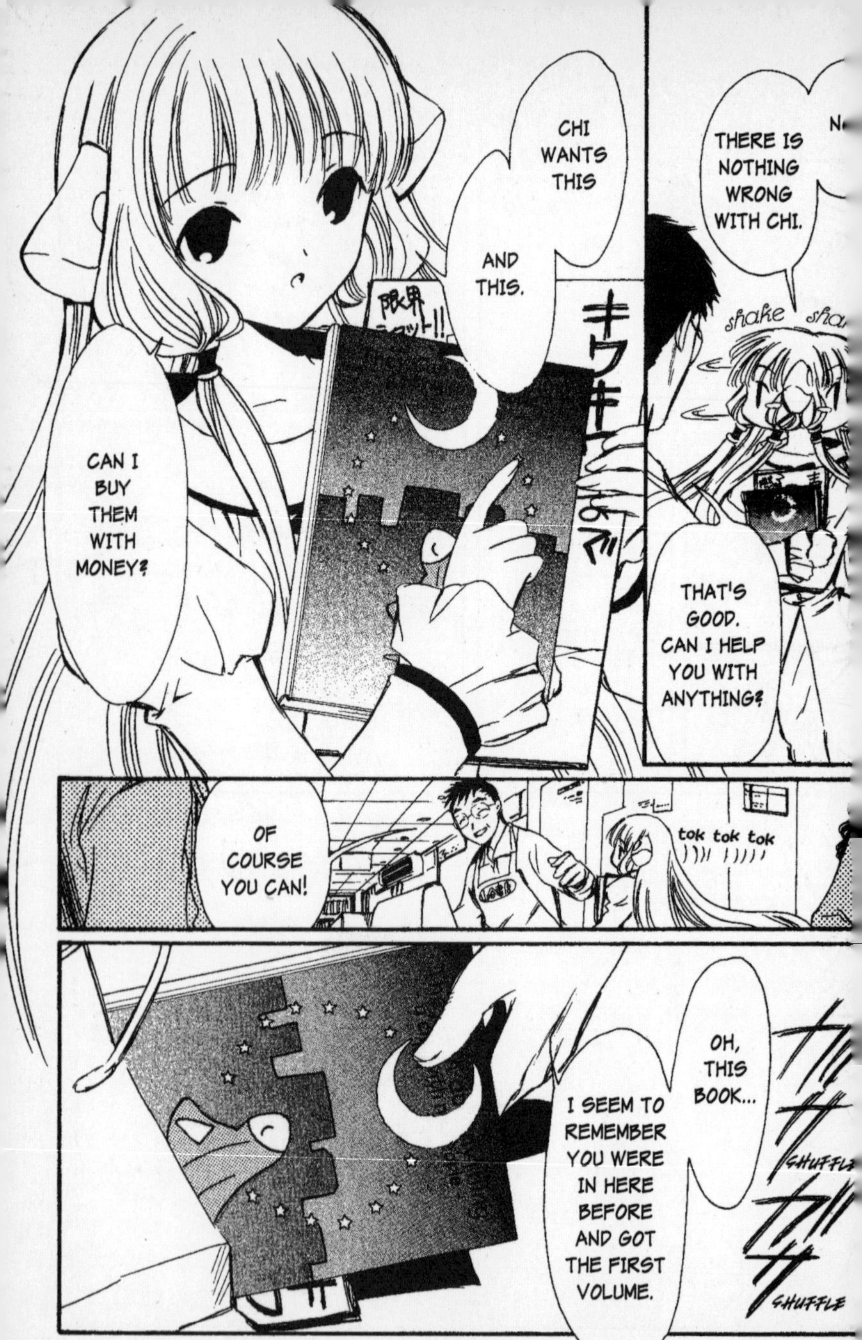
THERE IS NOTHING WRONG WITH CHI.
shake shak
THAT'S GOOD. CAN I HELP YOU WITH ANYTHING?
CHI WANTS THIS
AND THIS.
CAN I BUY THEM WITH MONEY?
tok tok tok
OF COURSE YOU CAN!
OH, THIS BOOK...
I SEEM TO REMEMBER YOU WERE IN HERE BEFORE AND GOT THE FIRST VOLUME.
SHUFFLE
SHUFFLE

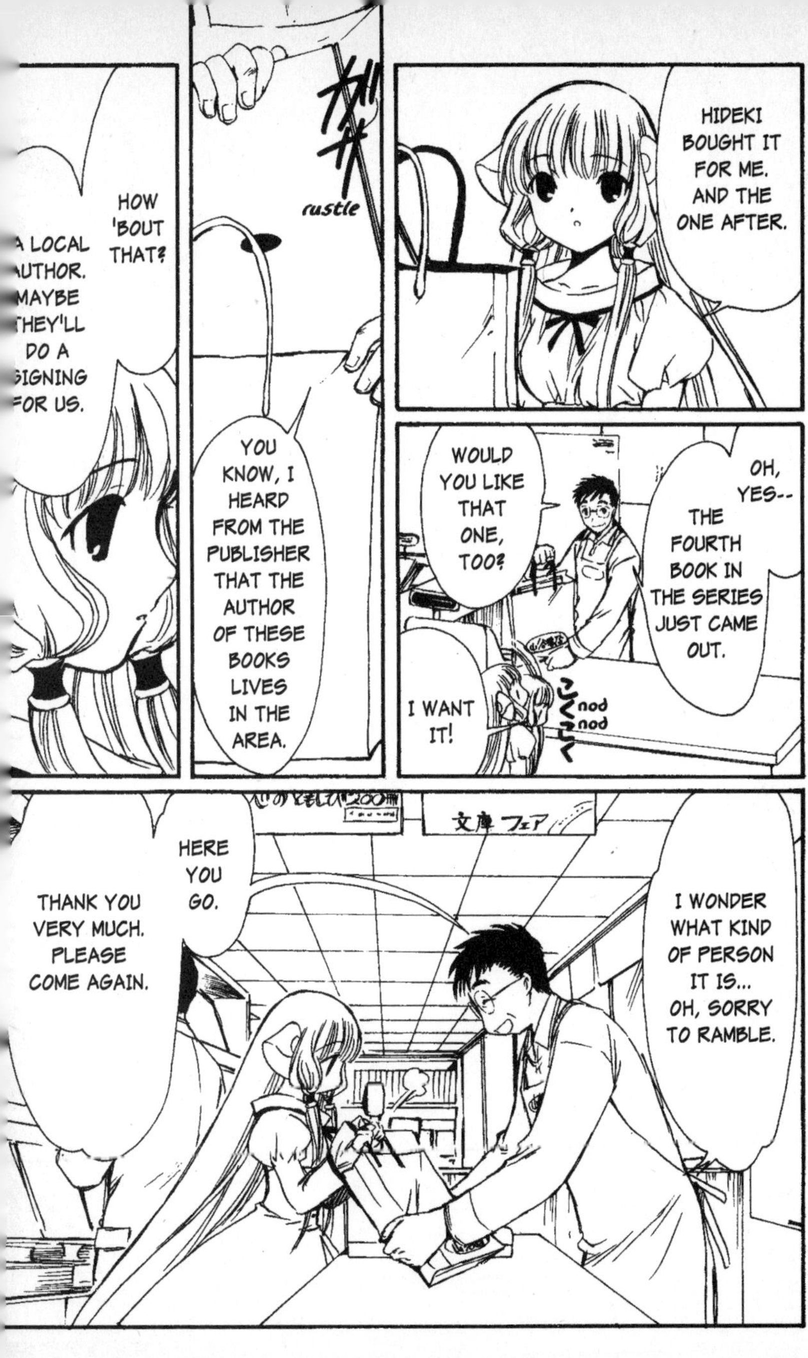
HIDEKI BOUGHT IT FOR ME. AND THE ONE AFTER.
OH, YES-- THE FOURTH BOOK IN THE SERIES JUST CAME OUT.
WOULD YOU LIKE THAT ONE, TOO?
I WANT IT!
nod nod
rustle
YOU KNOW, I HEARD FROM THE PUBLISHER THAT THE AUTHOR OF THESE BOOKS LIVES IN THE AREA.
HOW 'BOUT THAT?
A LOCAL AUTHOR. MAYBE THEY'LL DO A SIGNING FOR US.
文庫フェア
I WONDER WHAT KIND OF PERSON IT IS... OH, SORRY TO RAMBLE.
HERE YOU GO.
THANK YOU VERY MUCH. PLEASE COME AGAIN.

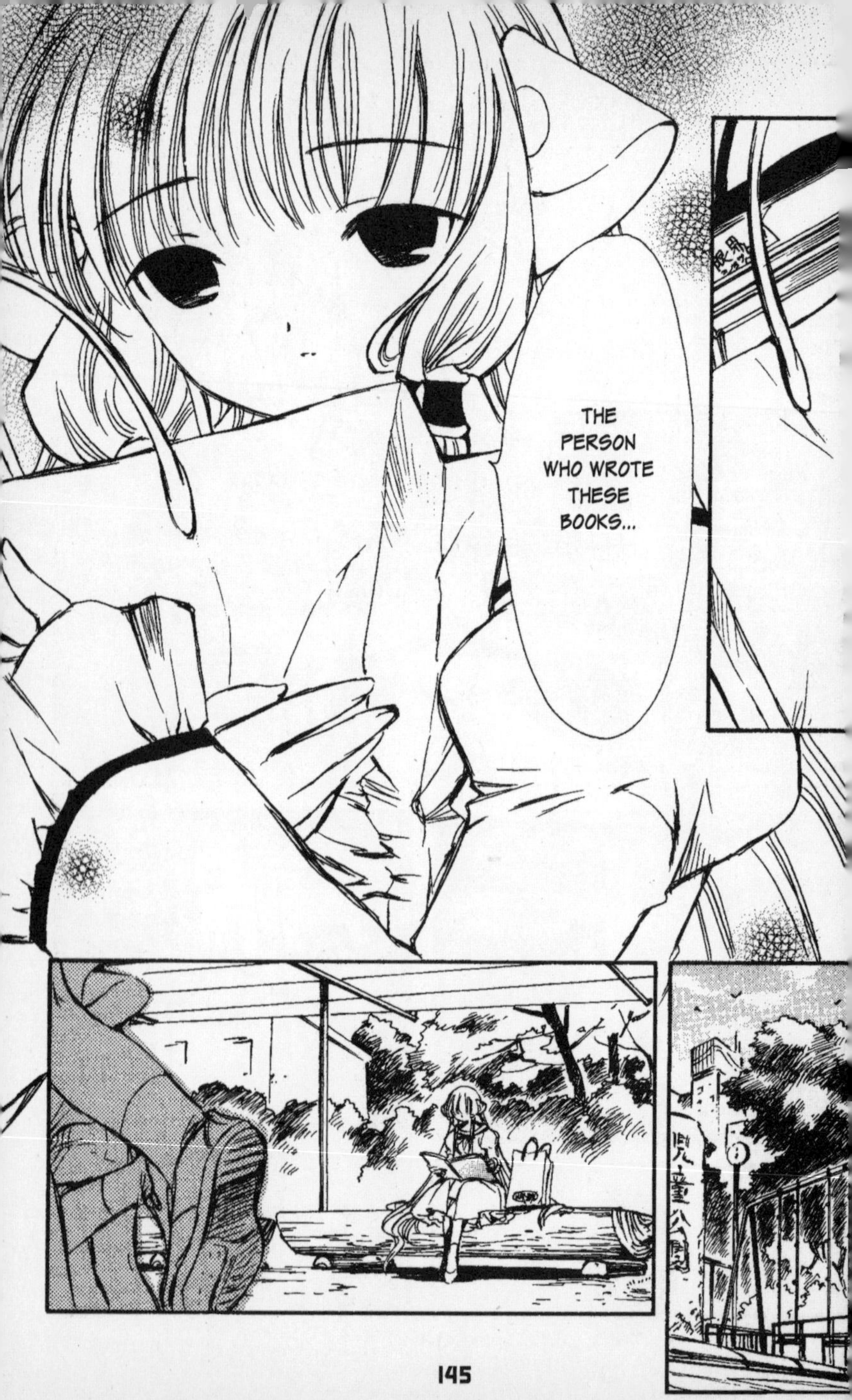
THE PERSON WHO WROTE THESE BOOKS...
児童公園

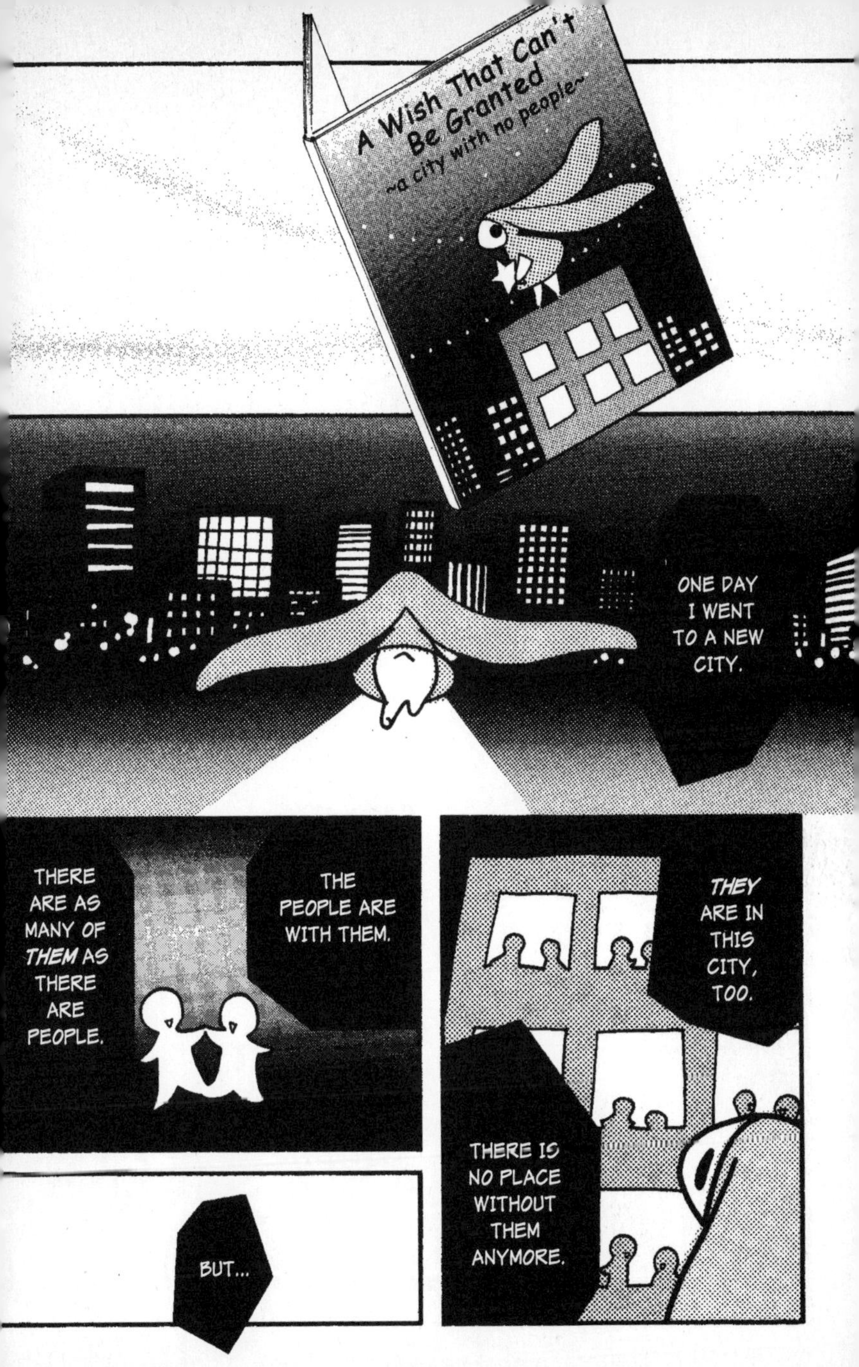
A Wish That Can't Be Granted
~a city with no people~
ONE DAY I WENT TO A NEW CITY.
THEY ARE IN THIS CITY, TOO.
THERE IS NO PLACE WITHOUT THEM ANYMORE.
THE PEOPLE ARE WITH THEM.
THERE ARE AS MANY OF *THEM* AS THERE ARE PEOPLE.
BUT...

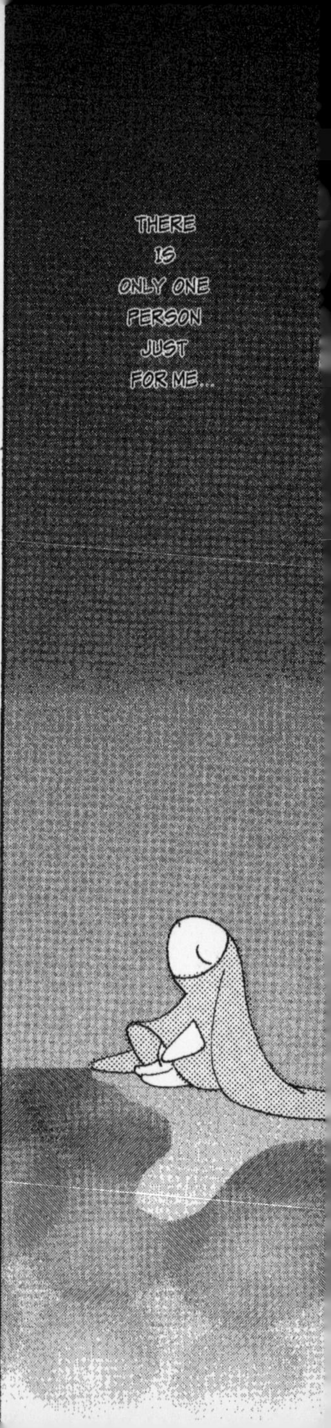
THERE IS ONLY ONE PERSON JUST FOR ME...

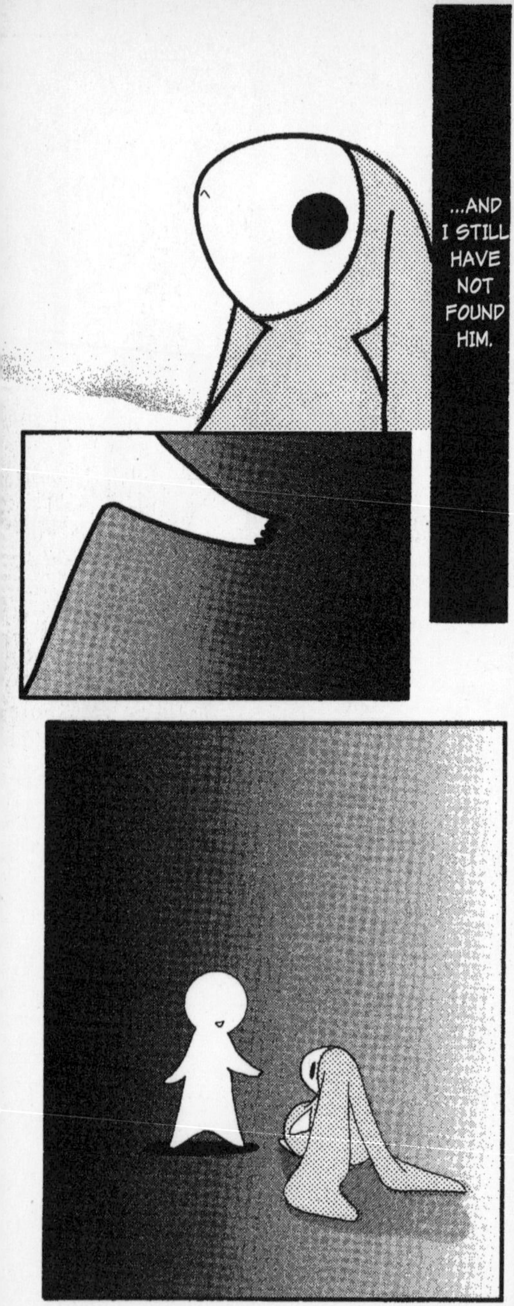
...AND I STILL HAVE NOT FOUND HIM.

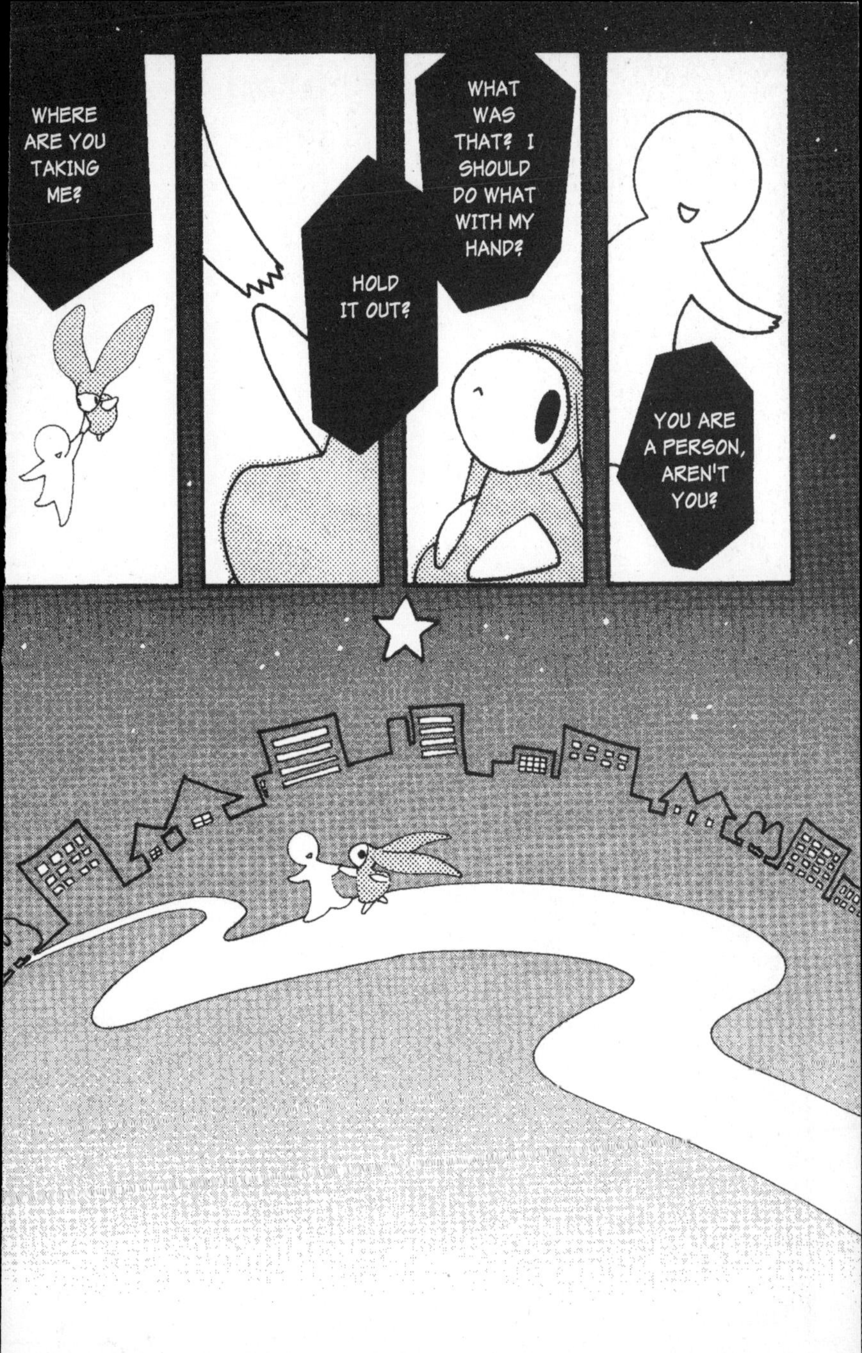
YOU ARE A PERSON, AREN'T YOU?
WHAT WAS THAT? I SHOULD DO WHAT WITH MY HAND?
HOLD IT OUT?
WHERE ARE YOU TAKING ME?

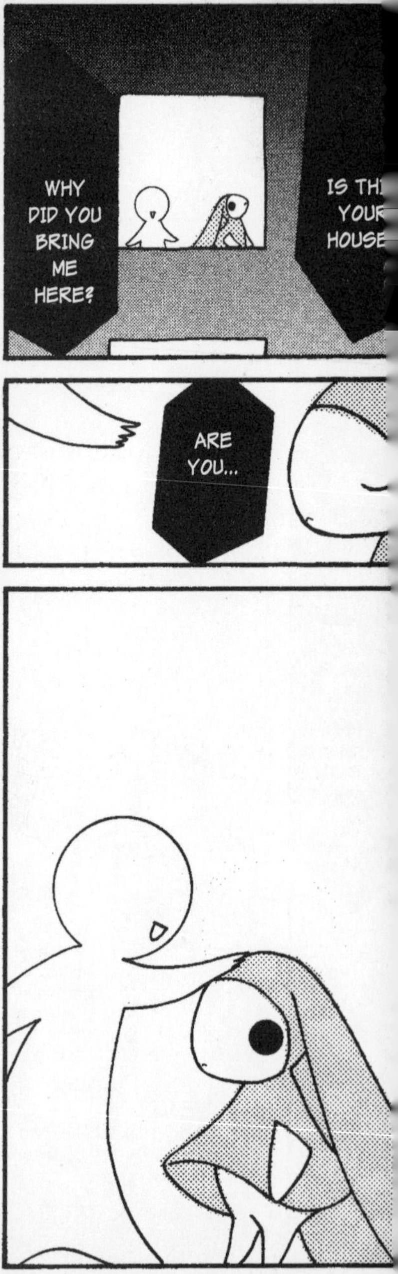
IS THI YOUR HOUSE
WHY DID YOU BRING ME HERE?
ARE YOU...

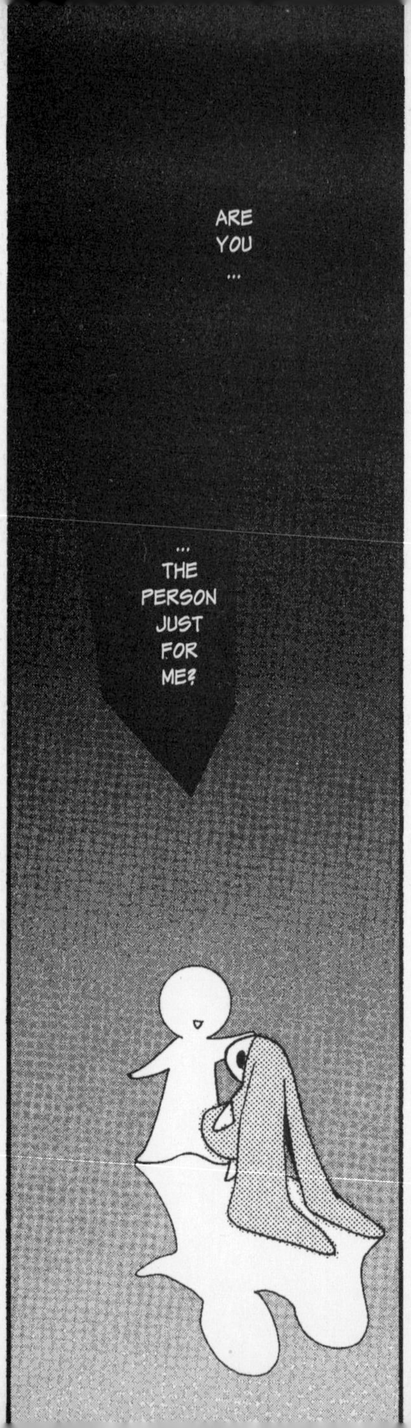
ARE YOU ...
... THE PERSON JUST FOR ME?

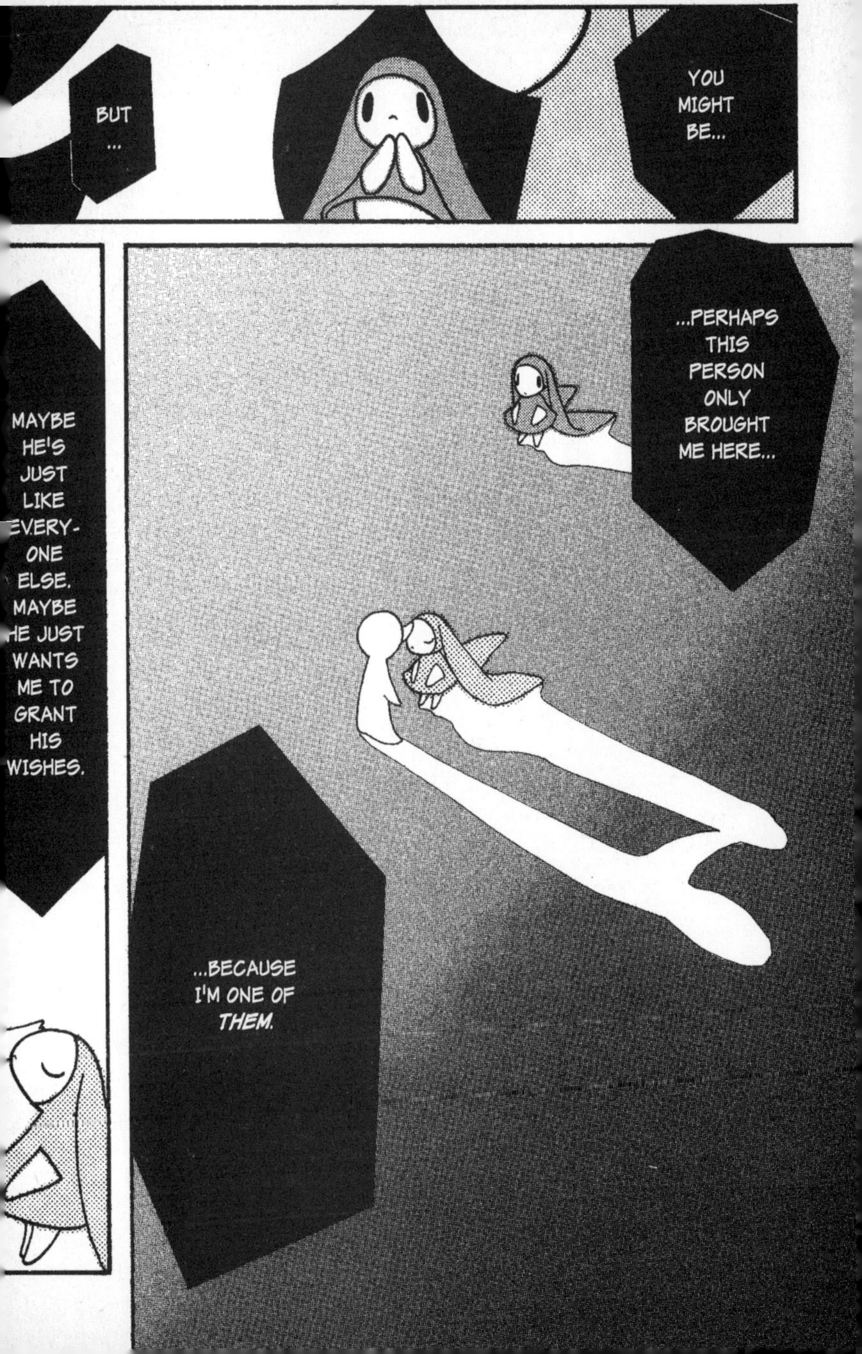
YOU MIGHT BE...
BUT ...
...PERHAPS THIS PERSON ONLY BROUGHT ME HERE...
...BECAUSE I'M ONE OF *THEM.*
MAYBE HE'S JUST LIKE EVERY-ONE ELSE. MAYBE HE JUST WANTS ME TO GRANT HIS WISHES.

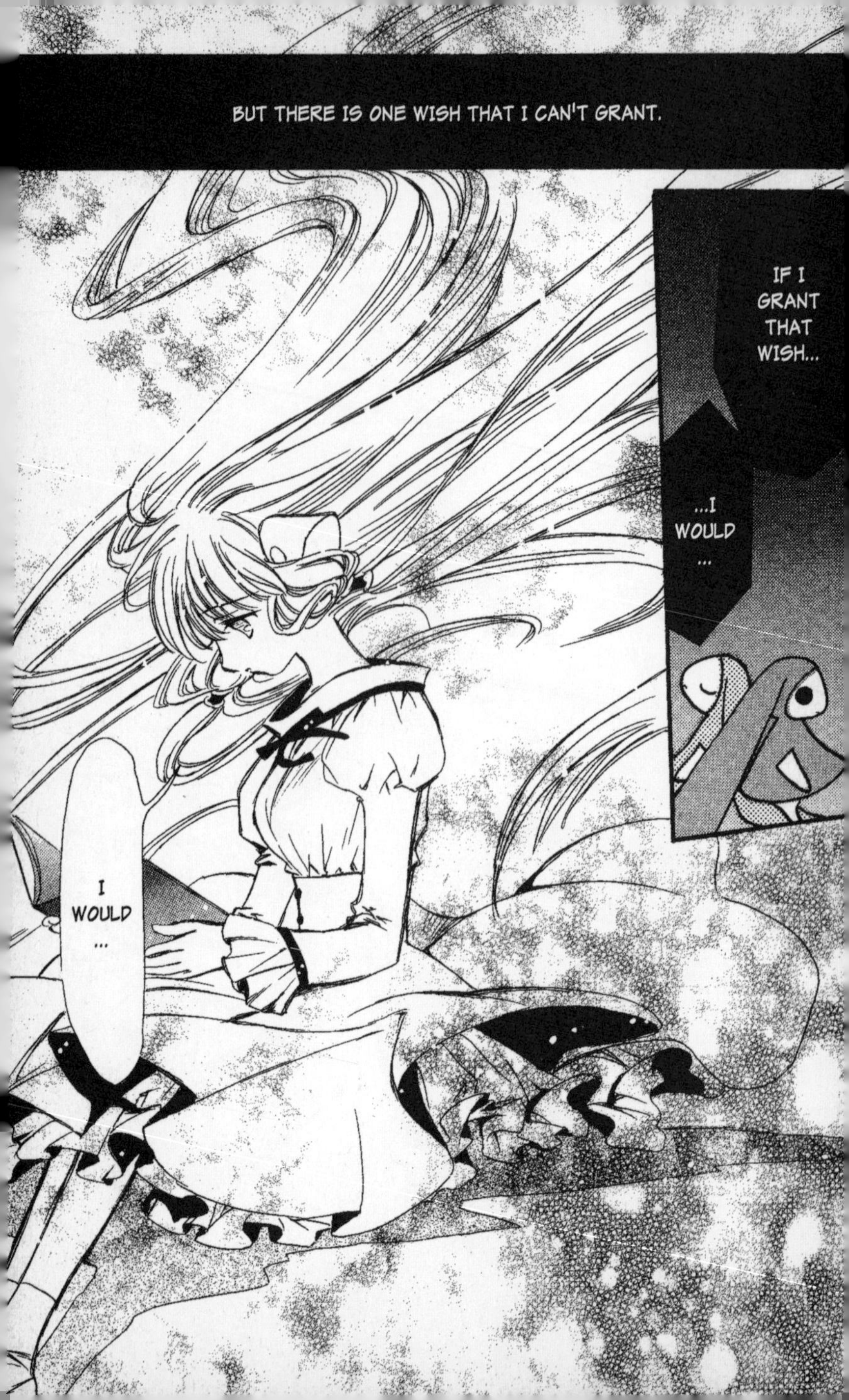
BUT THERE IS ONE WISH THAT I CAN'T GRANT.
IF I GRANT THAT WISH...
...I WOULD ...
I WOULD ...

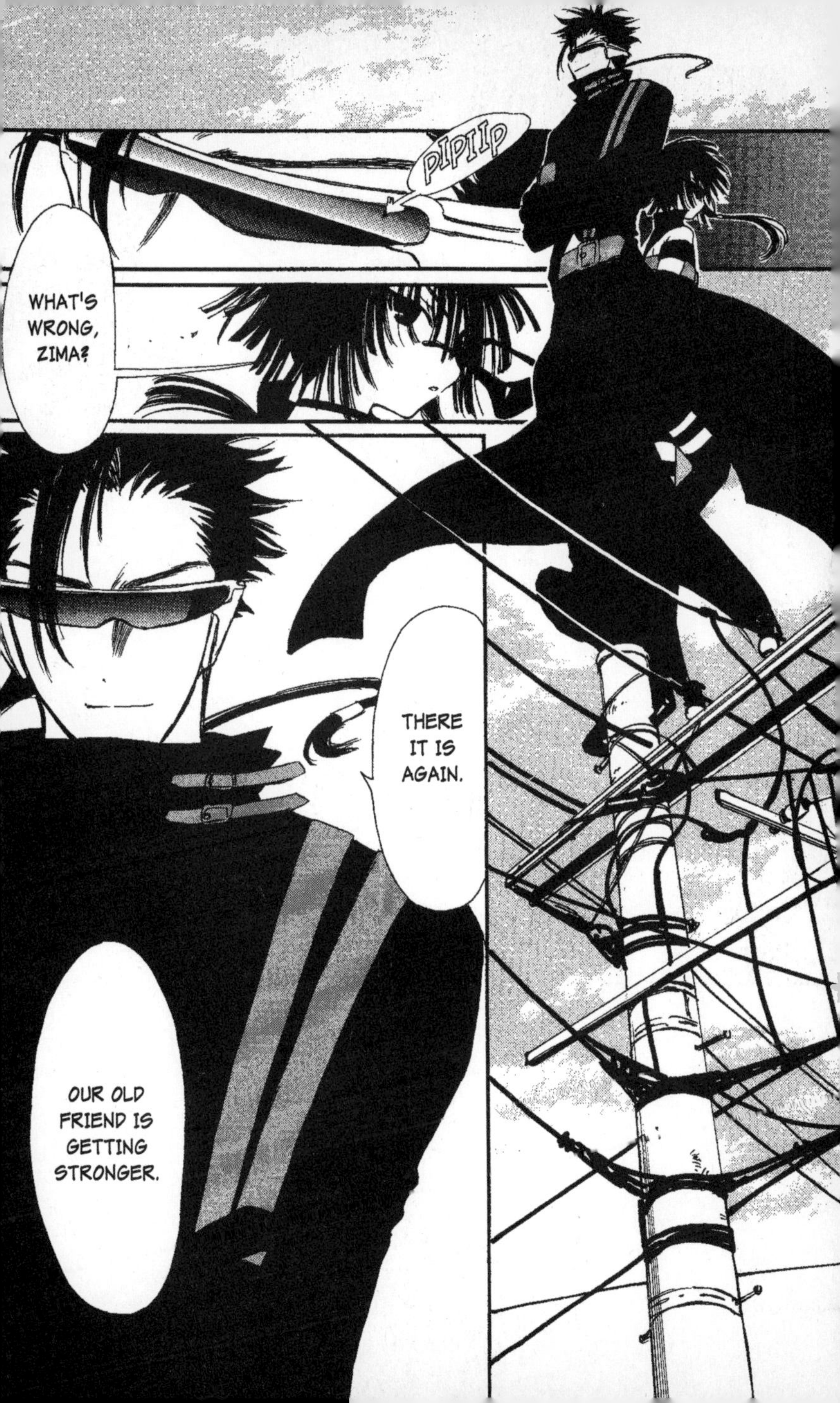
PIPIIP
WHAT'S WRONG, ZIMA?
THERE IT IS AGAIN.
OUR OLD FRIEND IS GETTING STRONGER.

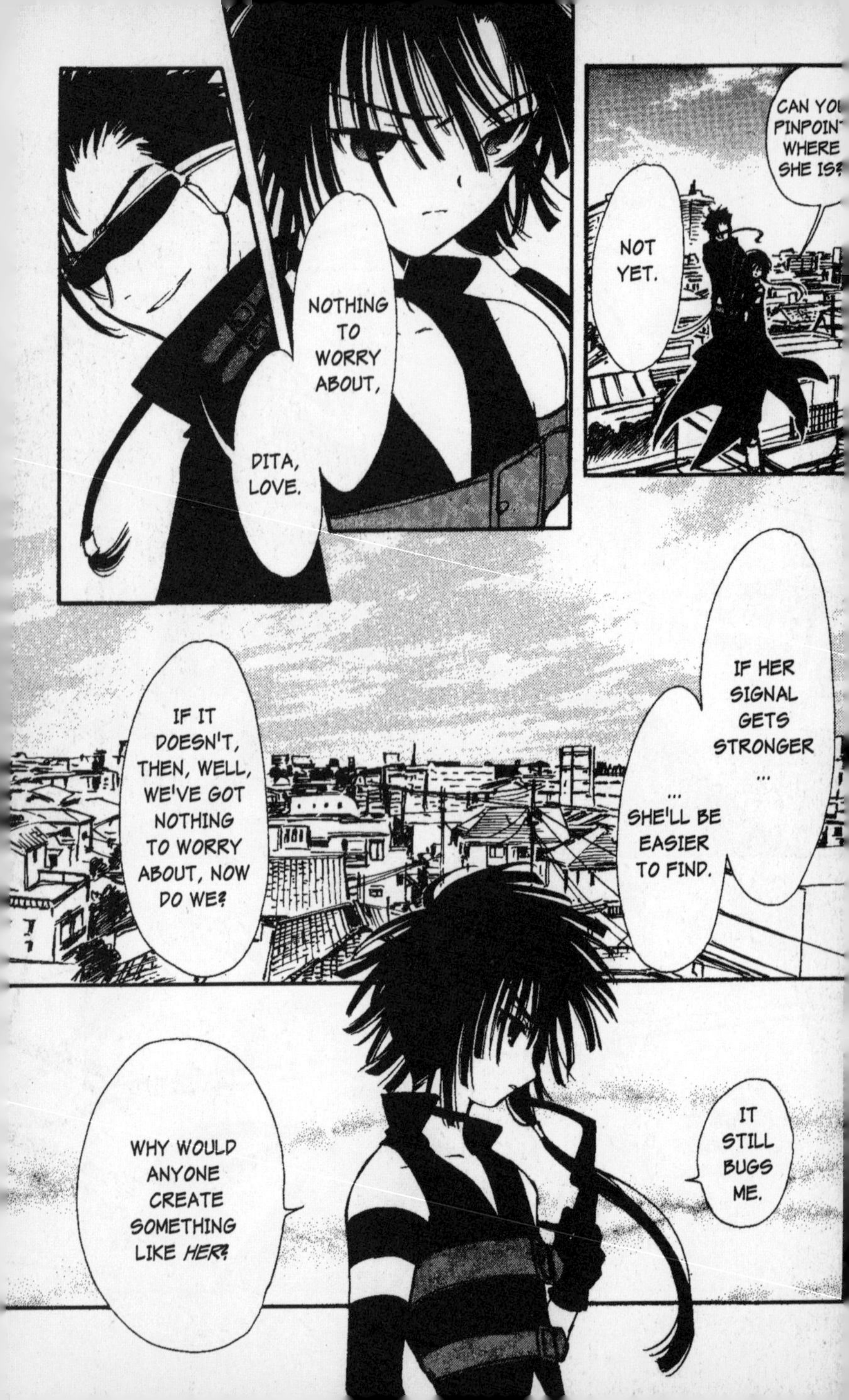
CAN YOU PINPOINT WHERE SHE IS?
NOT YET.
NOTHING TO WORRY ABOUT,
DITA, LOVE.
IF HER SIGNAL GETS STRONGER ...
... SHE'LL BE EASIER TO FIND.
IF IT DOESN'T, THEN, WELL, WE'VE GOT NOTHING TO WORRY ABOUT, NOW DO WE?
IT STILL BUGS ME.
WHY WOULD ANYONE CREATE SOMETHING LIKE *HER*?

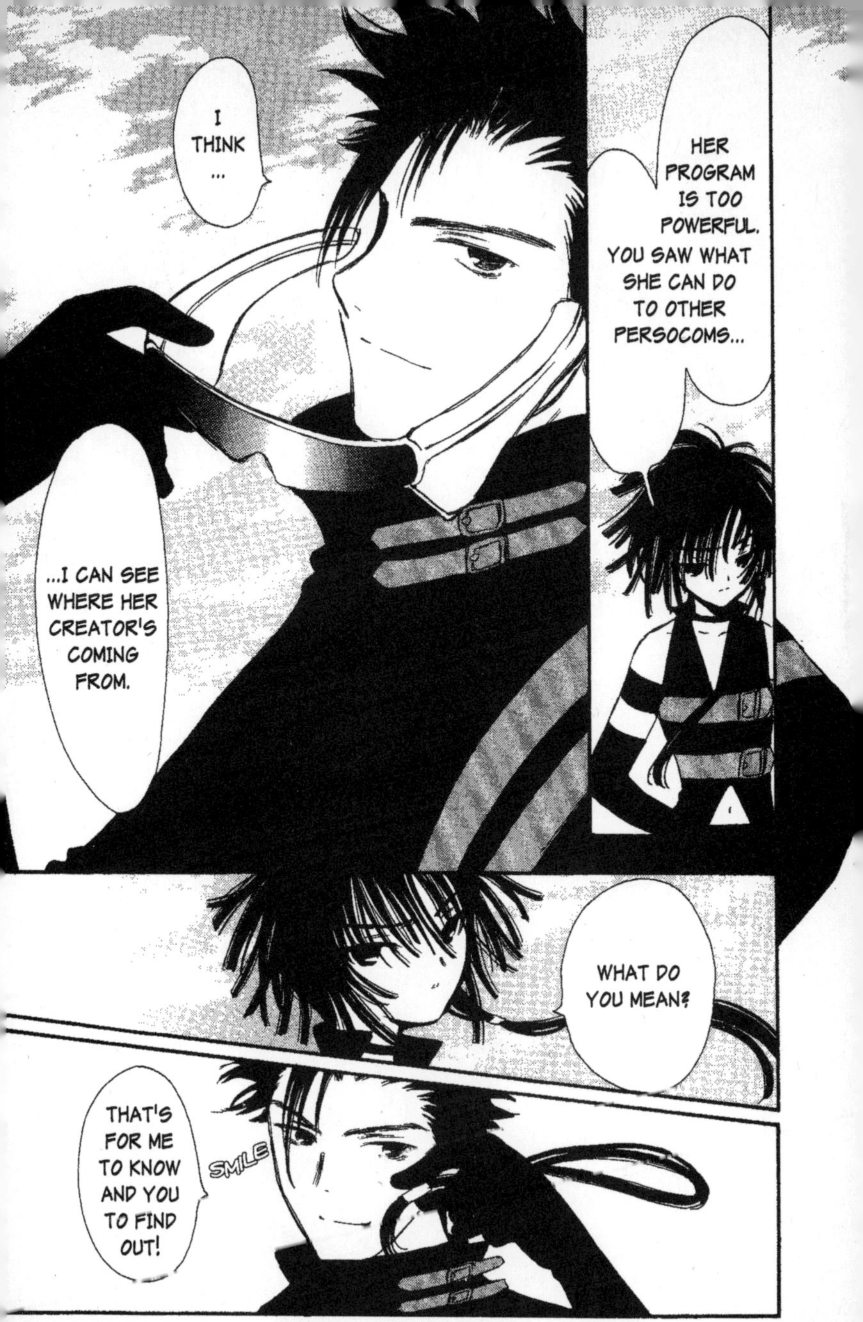
HER PROGRAM IS TOO POWERFUL. YOU SAW WHAT SHE CAN DO TO OTHER PERSOCOMS...
I THINK ...
...I CAN SEE WHERE HER CREATOR'S COMING FROM.
WHAT DO YOU MEAN?
THAT'S FOR ME TO KNOW AND YOU TO FIND OUT!
SMILE

chapter.34▸end

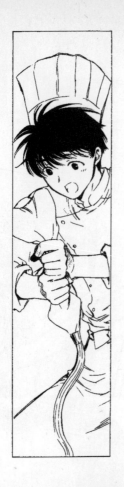
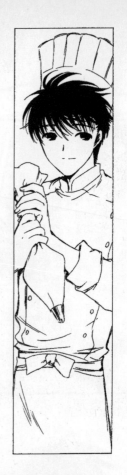

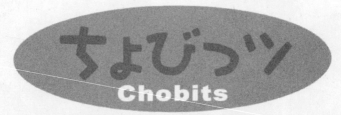

ちょびっツ
Chobits

◀chapter.35▶

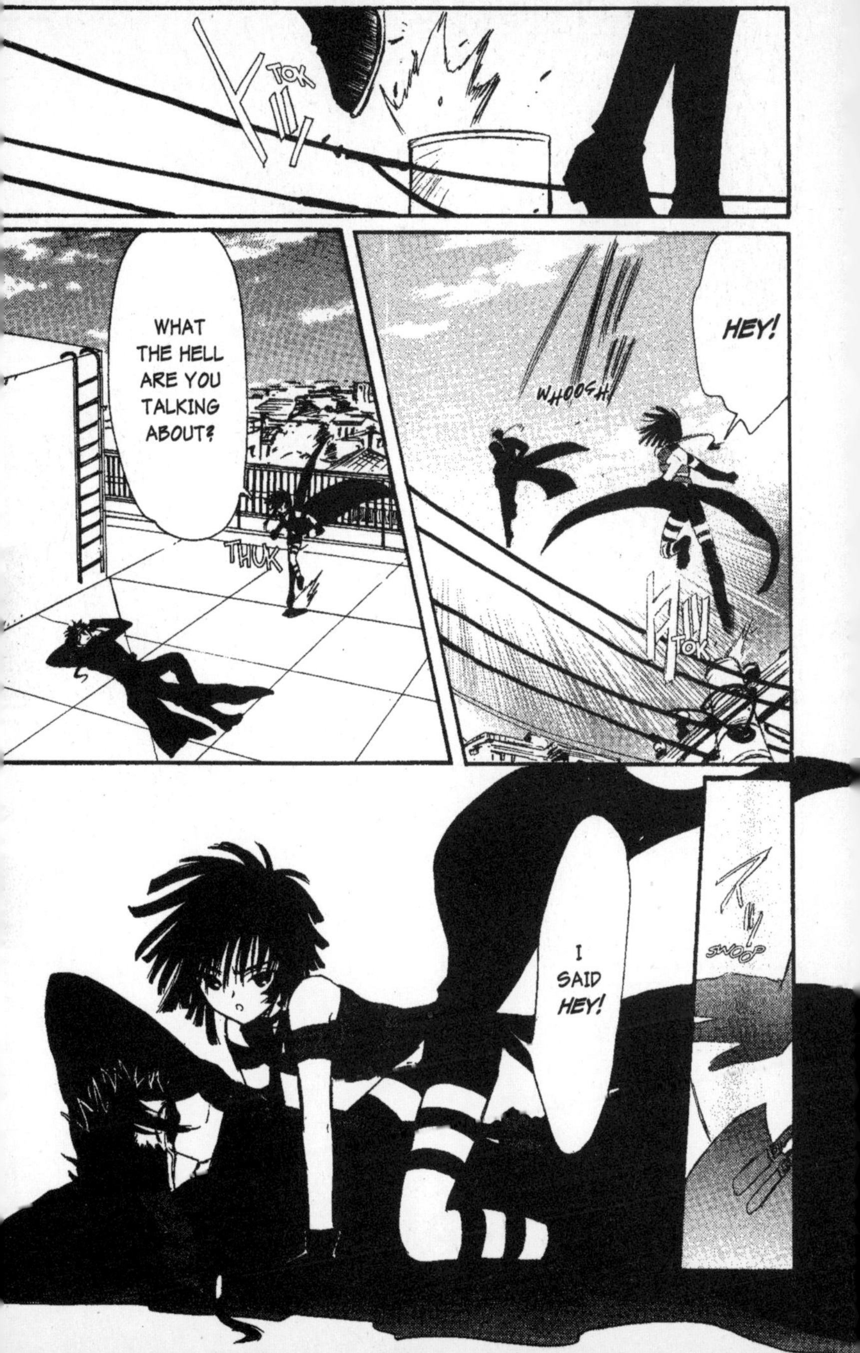
TOK
HEY!
WHOOSH
TOK
WHAT THE HELL ARE YOU TALKING ABOUT?
THUK
SWOOP
I SAID HEY!

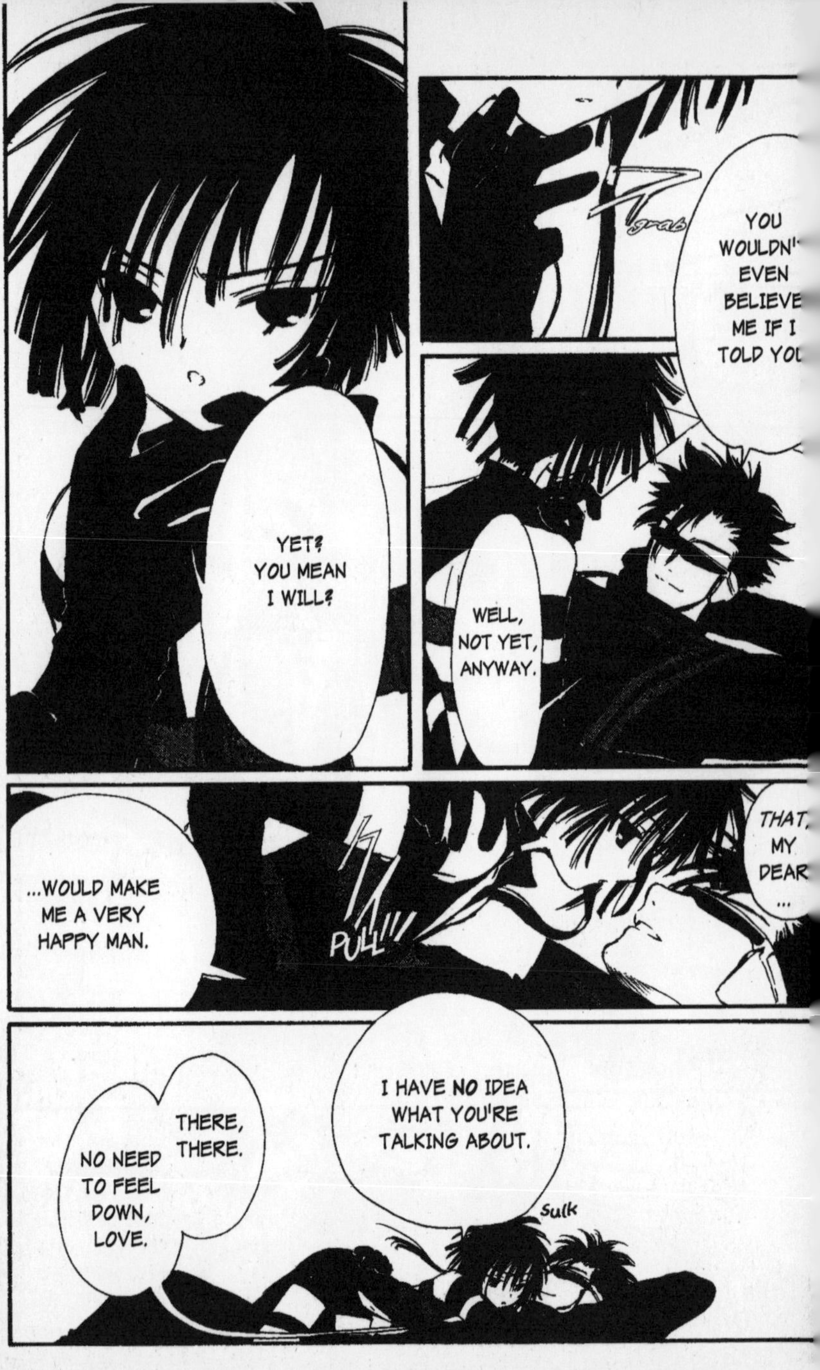
grab
YOU WOULDN' EVEN BELIEVE ME IF I TOLD YOU
WELL, NOT YET, ANYWAY.
YET? YOU MEAN I WILL?
THAT, MY DEAR ...
PULL
...WOULD MAKE ME A VERY HAPPY MAN.
I HAVE NO IDEA WHAT YOU'RE TALKING ABOUT.
Sulk
THERE, THERE.
NO NEED TO FEEL DOWN, LOVE.

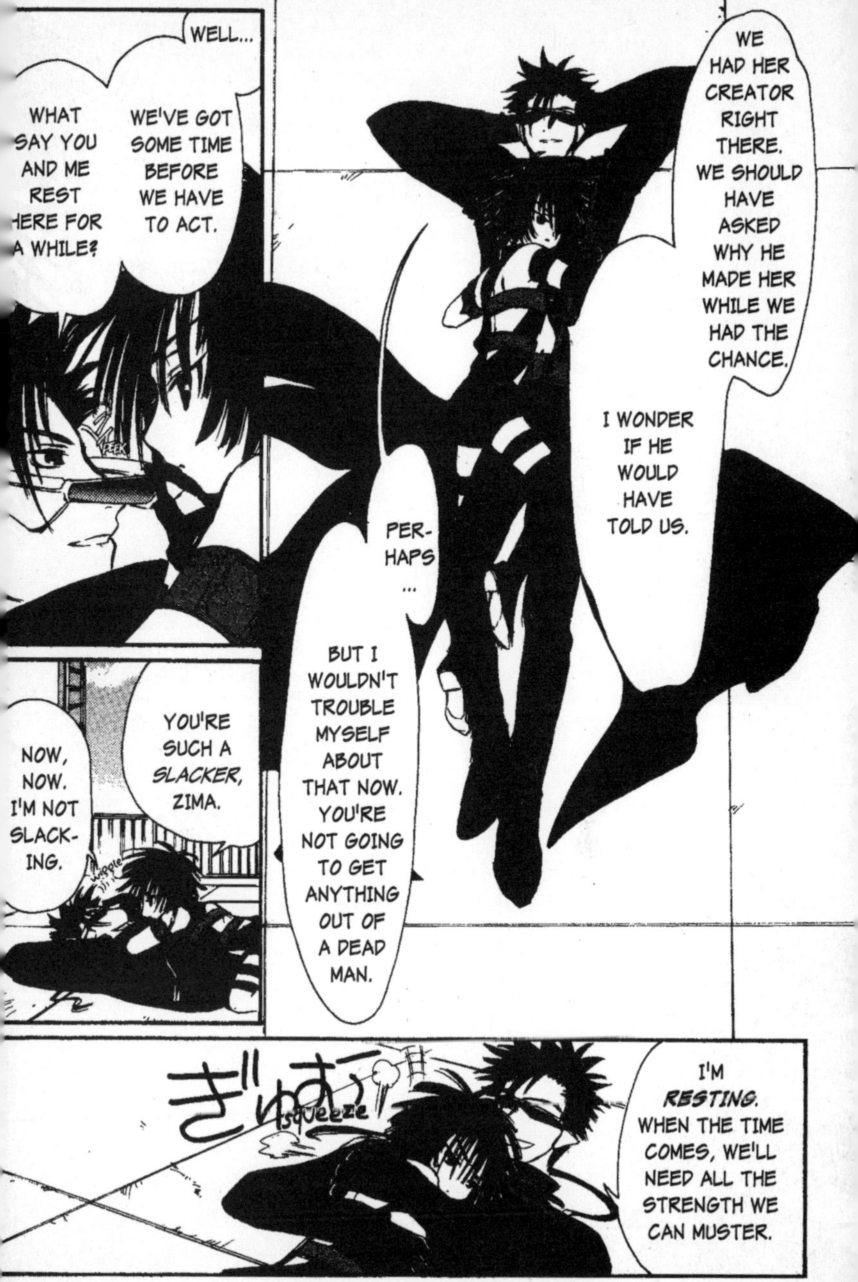
WE HAD HER CREATOR RIGHT THERE. WE SHOULD HAVE ASKED WHY HE MADE HER WHILE WE HAD THE CHANCE.
I WONDER IF HE WOULD HAVE TOLD US.
PER-HAPS...
BUT I WOULDN'T TROUBLE MYSELF ABOUT THAT NOW. YOU'RE NOT GOING TO GET ANYTHING OUT OF A DEAD MAN.
WELL...
WE'VE GOT SOME TIME BEFORE WE HAVE TO ACT.
WHAT SAY YOU AND ME REST HERE FOR A WHILE?
PEEK
YOU'RE SUCH A *SLACKER*, ZIMA.
NOW, NOW. I'M NOT SLACK-ING.
wiggle
I'M ***RESTING***. WHEN THE TIME COMES, WE'LL NEED ALL THE STRENGTH WE CAN MUSTER.
squeeze

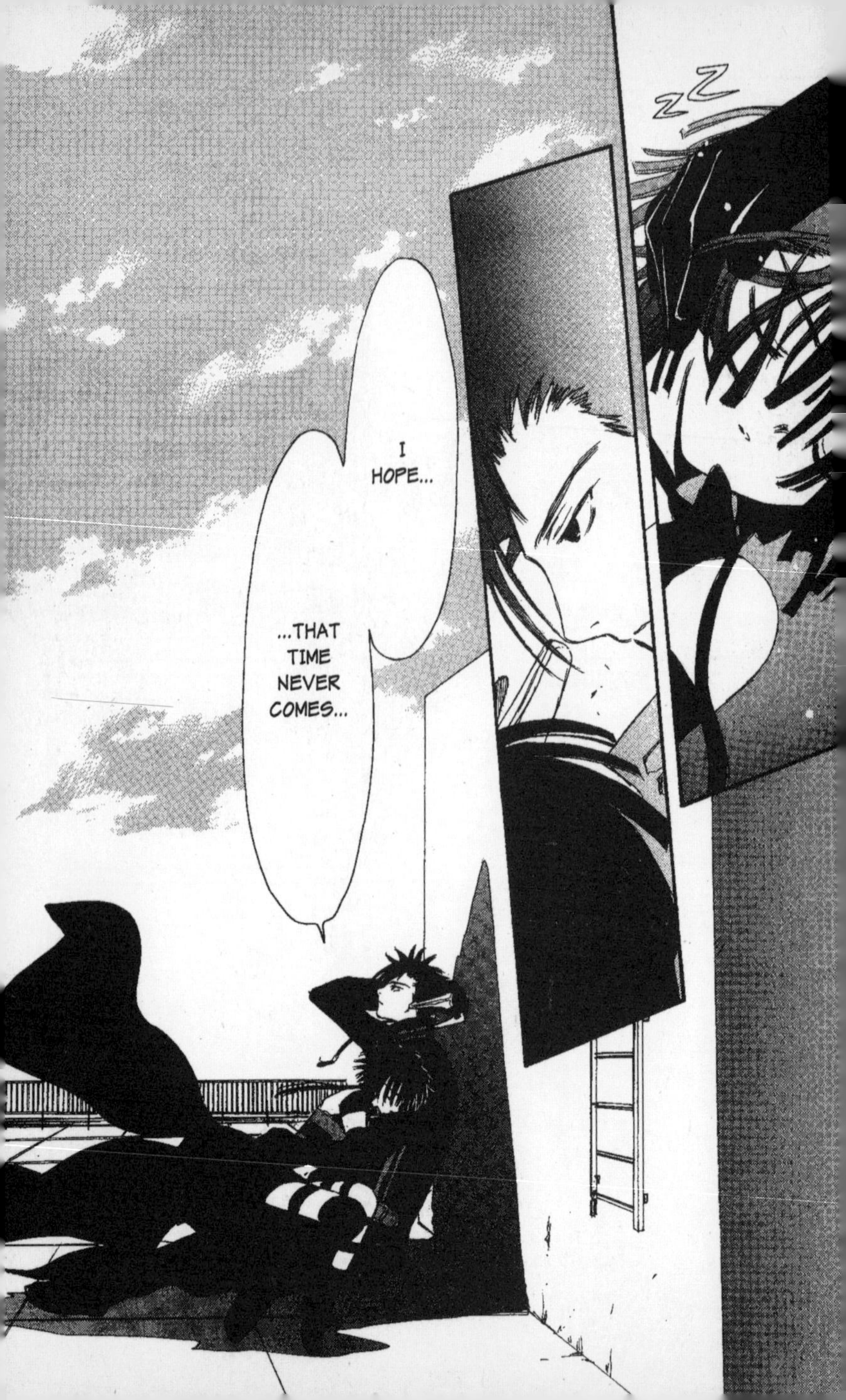
zz
I HOPE...
...THAT TIME NEVER COMES...

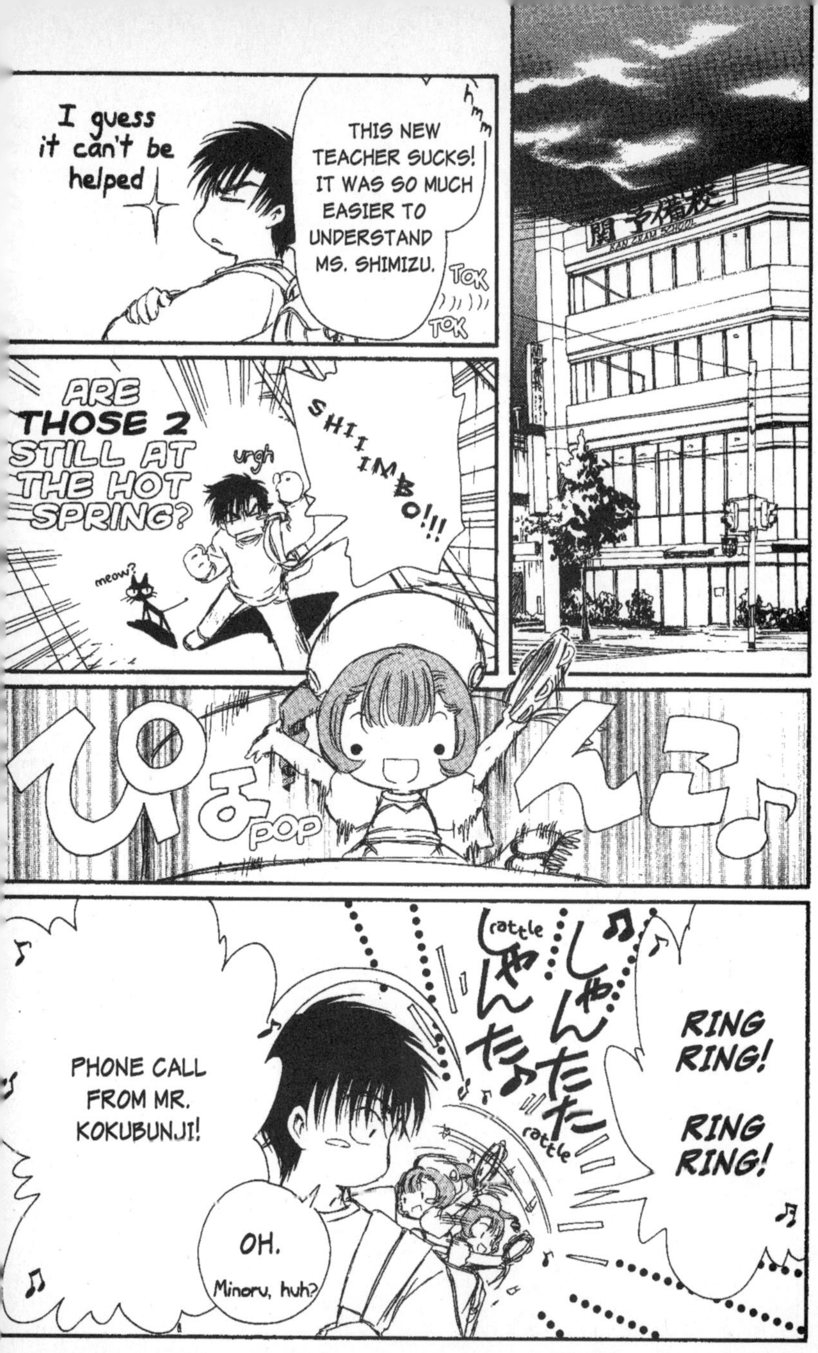
hmm
THIS NEW TEACHER SUCKS! IT WAS SO MUCH EASIER TO UNDERSTAND MS. SHIMIZU.
TOK
TOK
I guess it can't be helped
SHIIIMBO!!!
urgh
ARE THOSE 2 STILL AT THE HOT SPRING?
meow?
ぴょんこ♪
POP
RING RING!
RING RING!
しゃんたた
rattle
しゃんた♪
rattle
PHONE CALL FROM MR. KOKUBUNJI!
OH.
Minoru, huh?

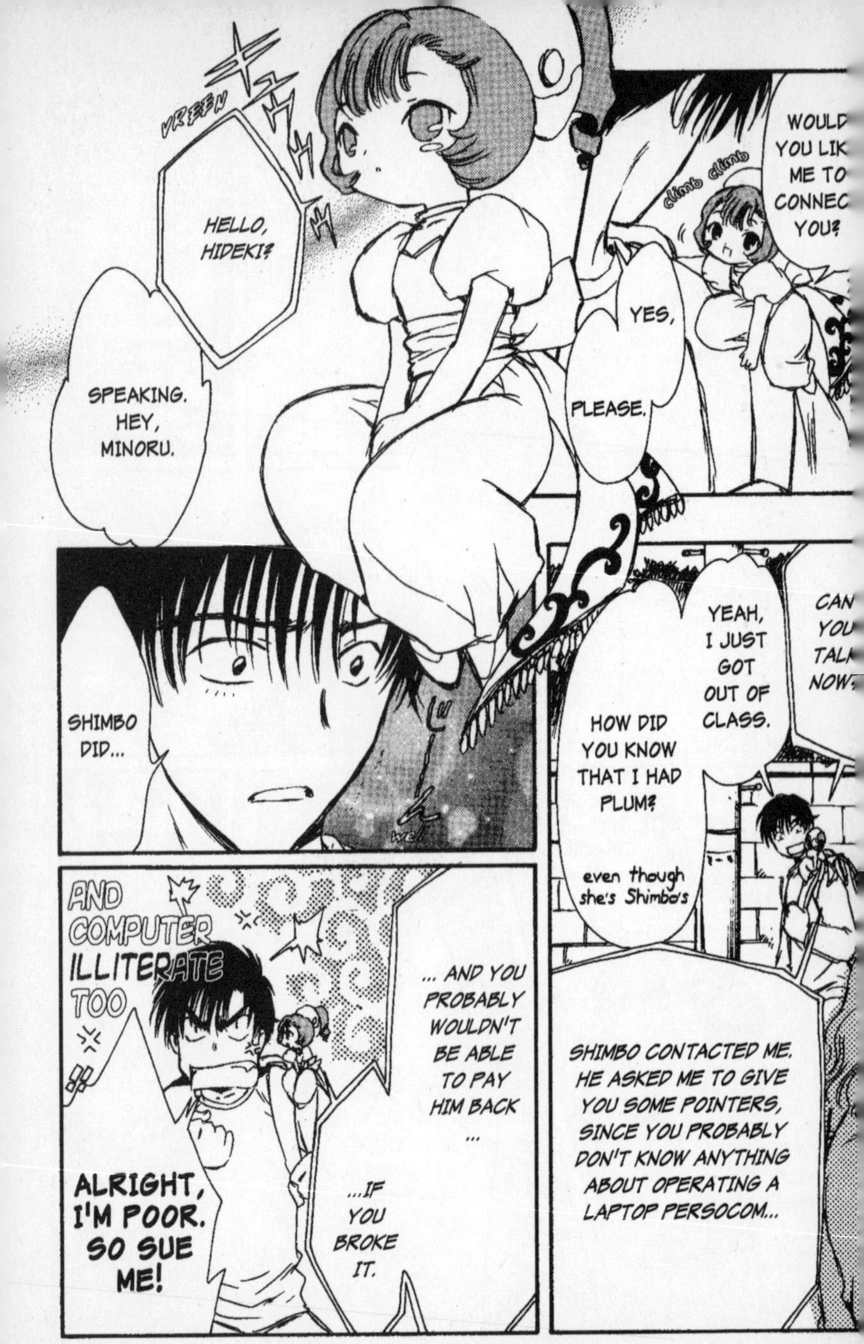

WOULD YOU LIK ME TO CONNEC YOU?
climb climb
YES, PLEASE.
VREEEN
HELLO, HIDEKI?
SPEAKING. HEY, MINORU.
CAN YOU TALK NOW?
YEAH, I JUST GOT OUT OF CLASS.
HOW DID YOU KNOW THAT I HAD PLUM?
even though she's Shimbo's
SHIMBO DID...
well
SHIMBO CONTACTED ME. HE ASKED ME TO GIVE YOU SOME POINTERS, SINCE YOU PROBABLY DON'T KNOW ANYTHING ABOUT OPERATING A LAPTOP PERSOCOM...
... AND YOU PROBABLY WOULDN'T BE ABLE TO PAY HIM BACK ...
...IF YOU BROKE IT.
AND COMPUTER ILLITERATE TOO
ALRIGHT, I'M POOR. SO SUE ME!

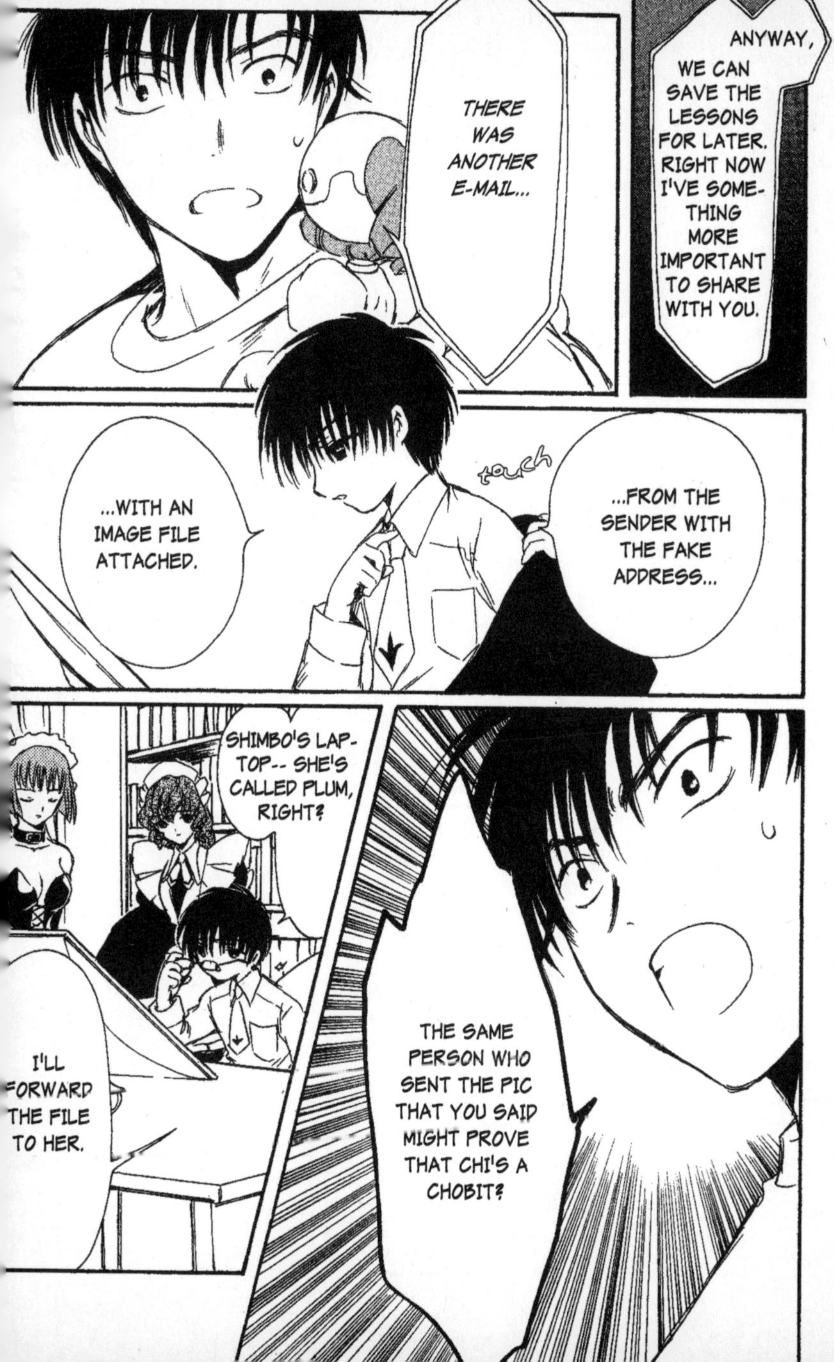
ANYWAY, WE CAN SAVE THE LESSONS FOR LATER. RIGHT NOW I'VE SOMETHING MORE IMPORTANT TO SHARE WITH YOU.
THERE WAS ANOTHER E-MAIL...
...FROM THE SENDER WITH THE FAKE ADDRESS...
touch
...WITH AN IMAGE FILE ATTACHED.
THE SAME PERSON WHO SENT THE PIC THAT YOU SAID MIGHT PROVE THAT CHI'S A CHOBIT?
SHIMBO'S LAPTOP-- SHE'S CALLED PLUM, RIGHT?
I'LL FORWARD THE FILE TO HER.

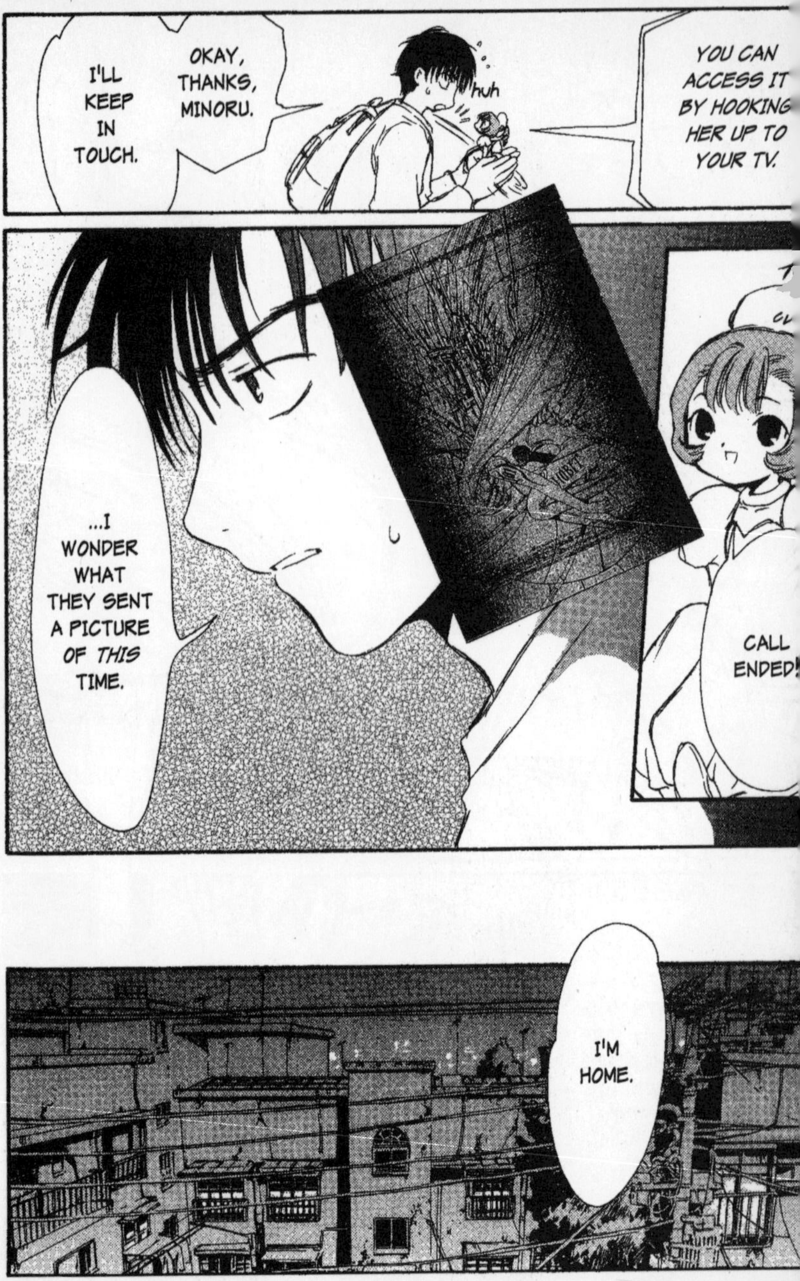
YOU CAN ACCESS IT BY HOOKING HER UP TO YOUR TV.
huh
OKAY, THANKS, MINORU.
I'LL KEEP IN TOUCH.
CALL ENDED!
...I WONDER WHAT THEY SENT A PICTURE OF *THIS* TIME.
I'M HOME.

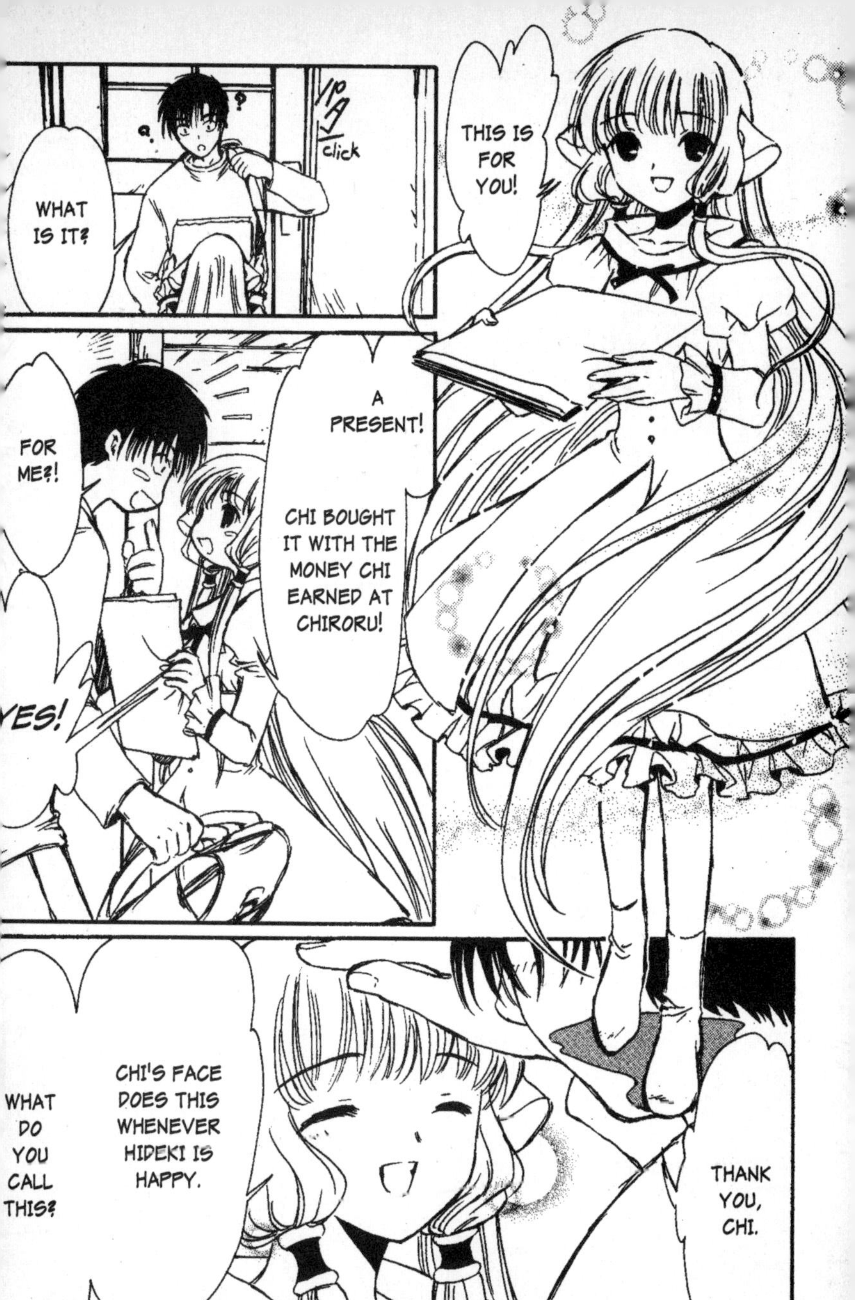
THIS IS FOR YOU!
click
WHAT IS IT?
A PRESENT!
CHI BOUGHT IT WITH THE MONEY CHI EARNED AT CHIRORU!
FOR ME?!
YES!
THANK YOU, CHI.
CHI'S FACE DOES THIS WHENEVER HIDEKI IS HAPPY.
WHAT DO YOU CALL THIS?

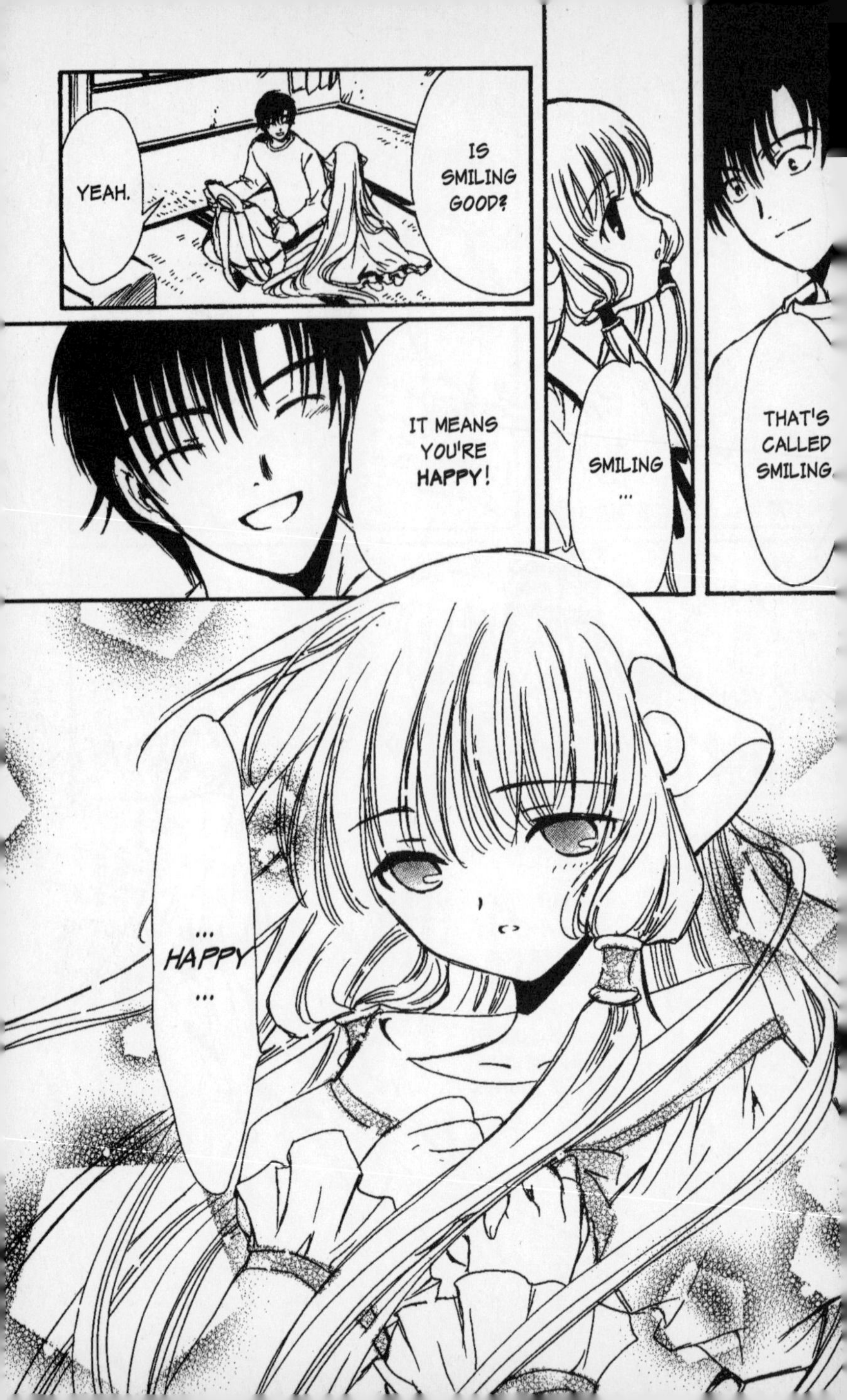
THAT'S CALLED SMILING.
SMILING ...
IS SMILING GOOD?
YEAH.
IT MEANS YOU'RE HAPPY!
... HAPPY ...

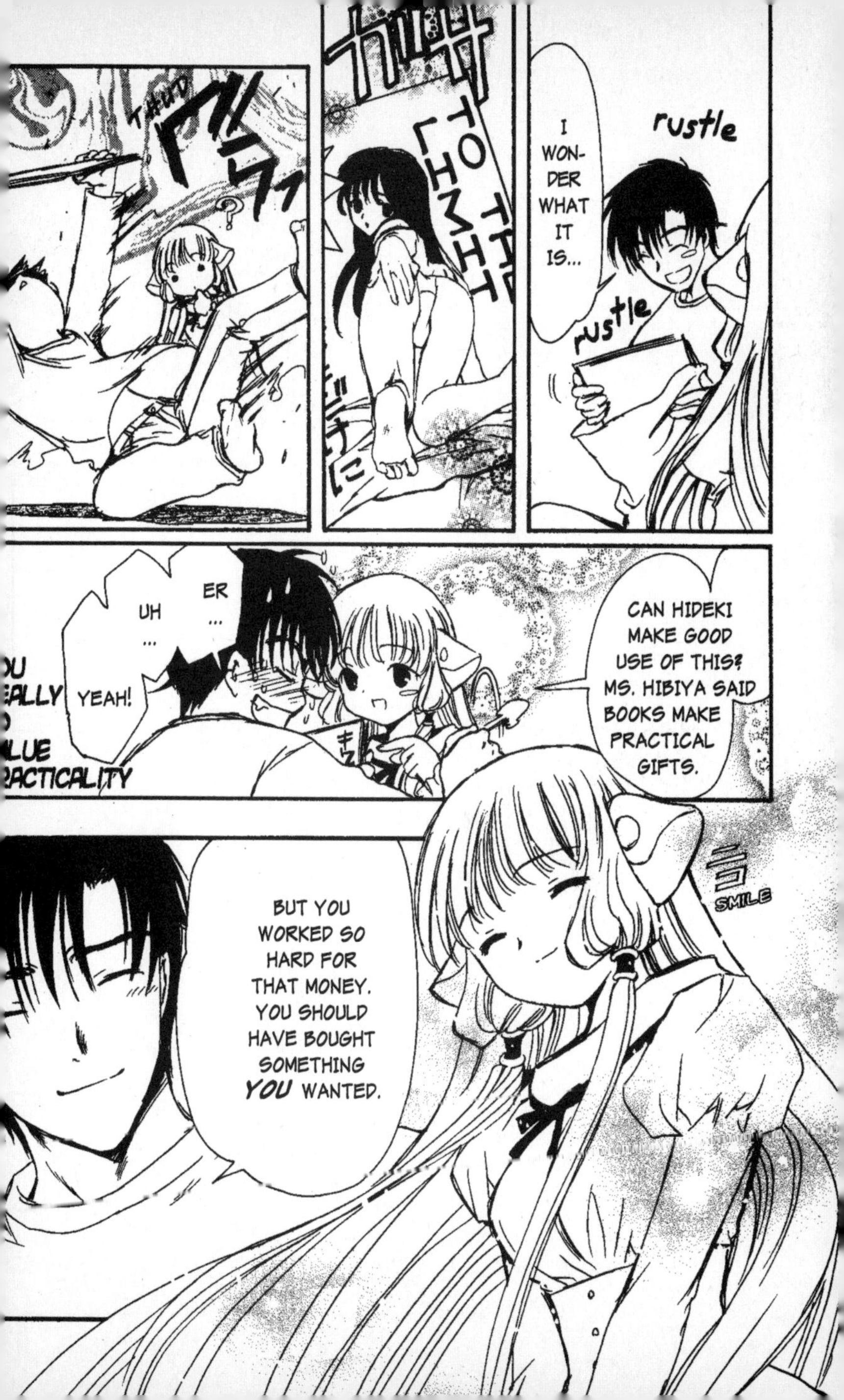
rustle
I WON-DER WHAT IT IS...
rustle
THUD
CAN HIDEKI MAKE GOOD USE OF THIS? MS. HIBIYA SAID BOOKS MAKE PRACTICAL GIFTS.
ER ...
UH ...
YEAH!
SMILE
BUT YOU WORKED SO HARD FOR THAT MONEY. YOU SHOULD HAVE BOUGHT SOMETHING *YOU* WANTED.

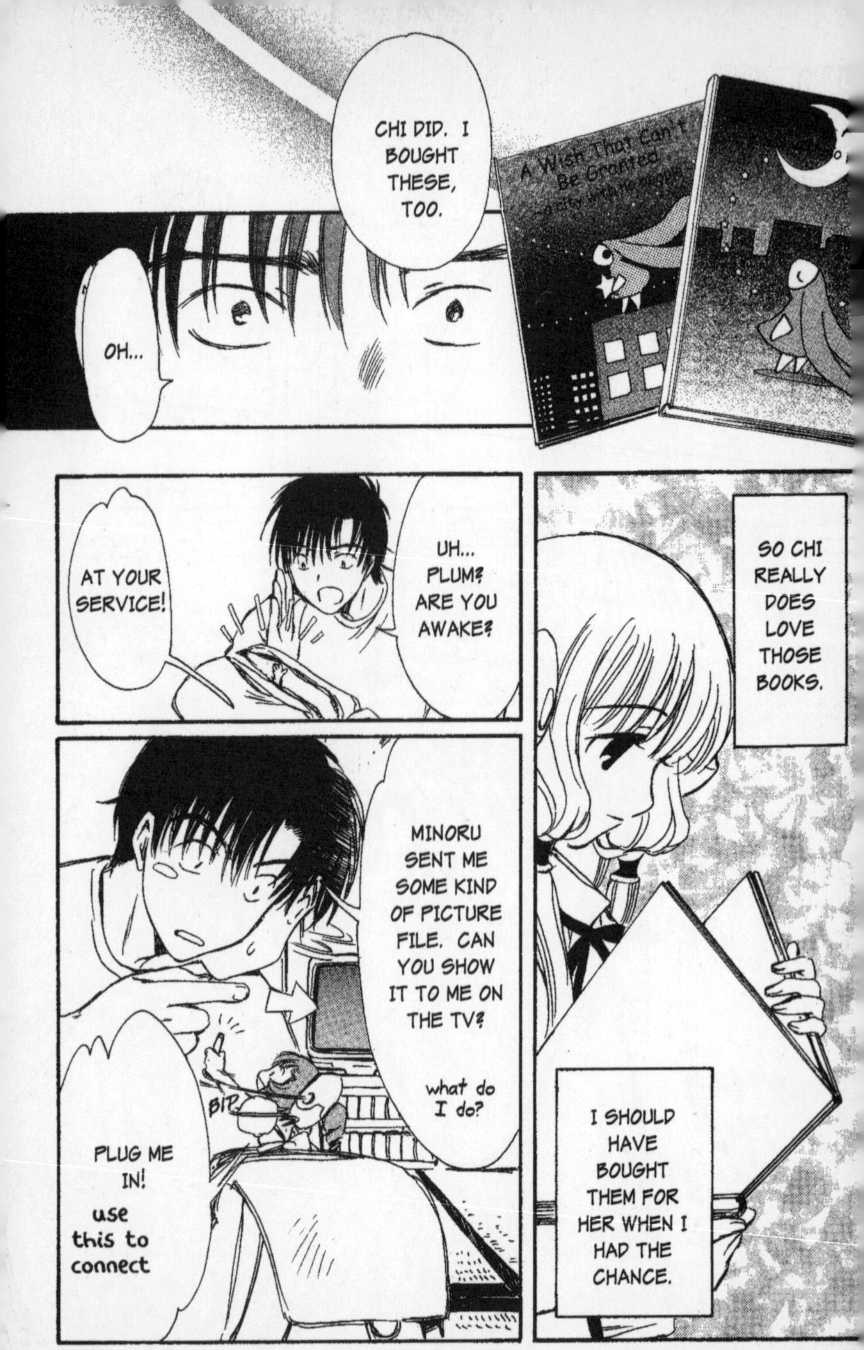
A Wish That Can't Be Granted
CHI DID. I BOUGHT THESE, TOO.
OH...
SO CHI REALLY DOES LOVE THOSE BOOKS.
I SHOULD HAVE BOUGHT THEM FOR HER WHEN I HAD THE CHANCE.
UH... PLUM? ARE YOU AWAKE?
AT YOUR SERVICE!
MINORU SENT ME SOME KIND OF PICTURE FILE. CAN YOU SHOW IT TO ME ON THE TV?
what do I do?
BIP
PLUG ME IN!
use this to connect

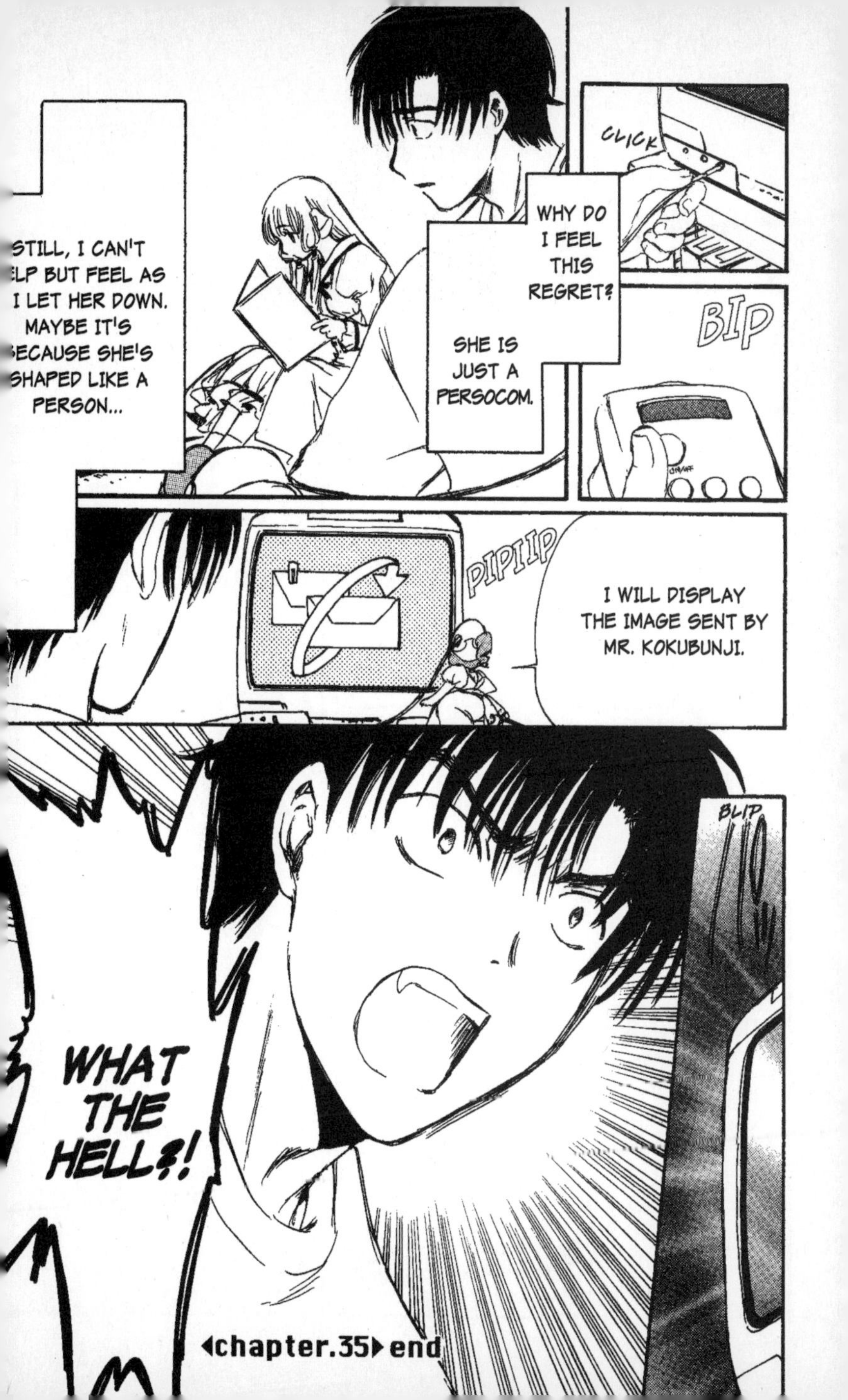
CLICK
BIP
WHY DO I FEEL THIS REGRET?
SHE IS JUST A PERSOCOM.
STILL, I CAN'T
ELP BUT FEEL AS
I LET HER DOWN.
MAYBE IT'S
ECAUSE SHE'S
SHAPED LIKE A
PERSON...
PIPIIP
I WILL DISPLAY THE IMAGE SENT BY MR. KOKUBUNJI.
BLIP
WHAT THE HELL?!
◂chapter.35▸ end

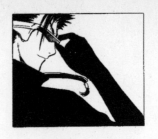

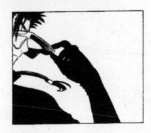

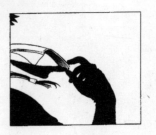

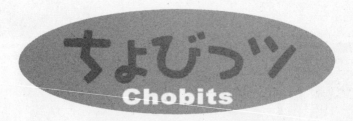

ちょびっツ

Chobits

◀chapter.36▶

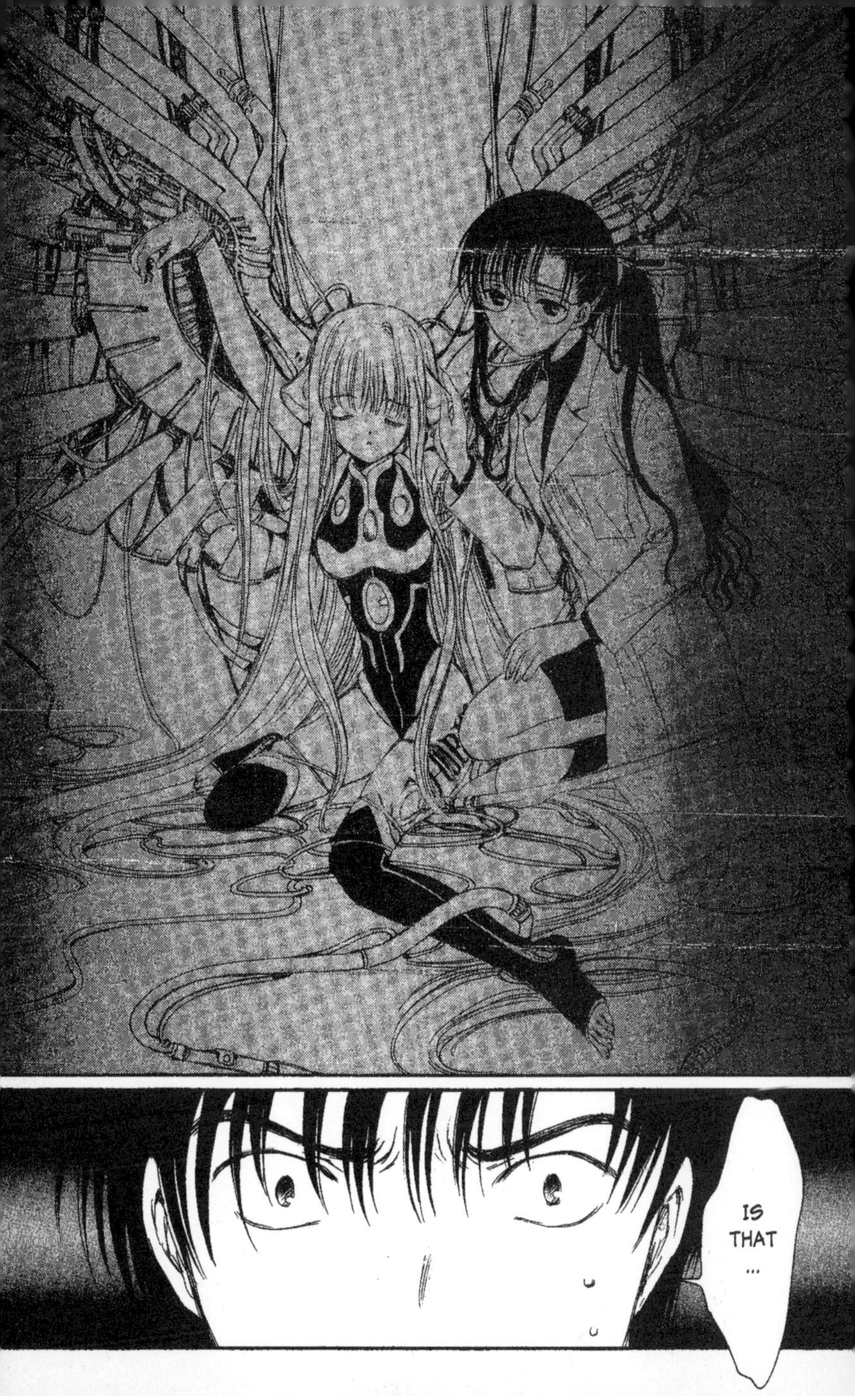
IS THAT ...

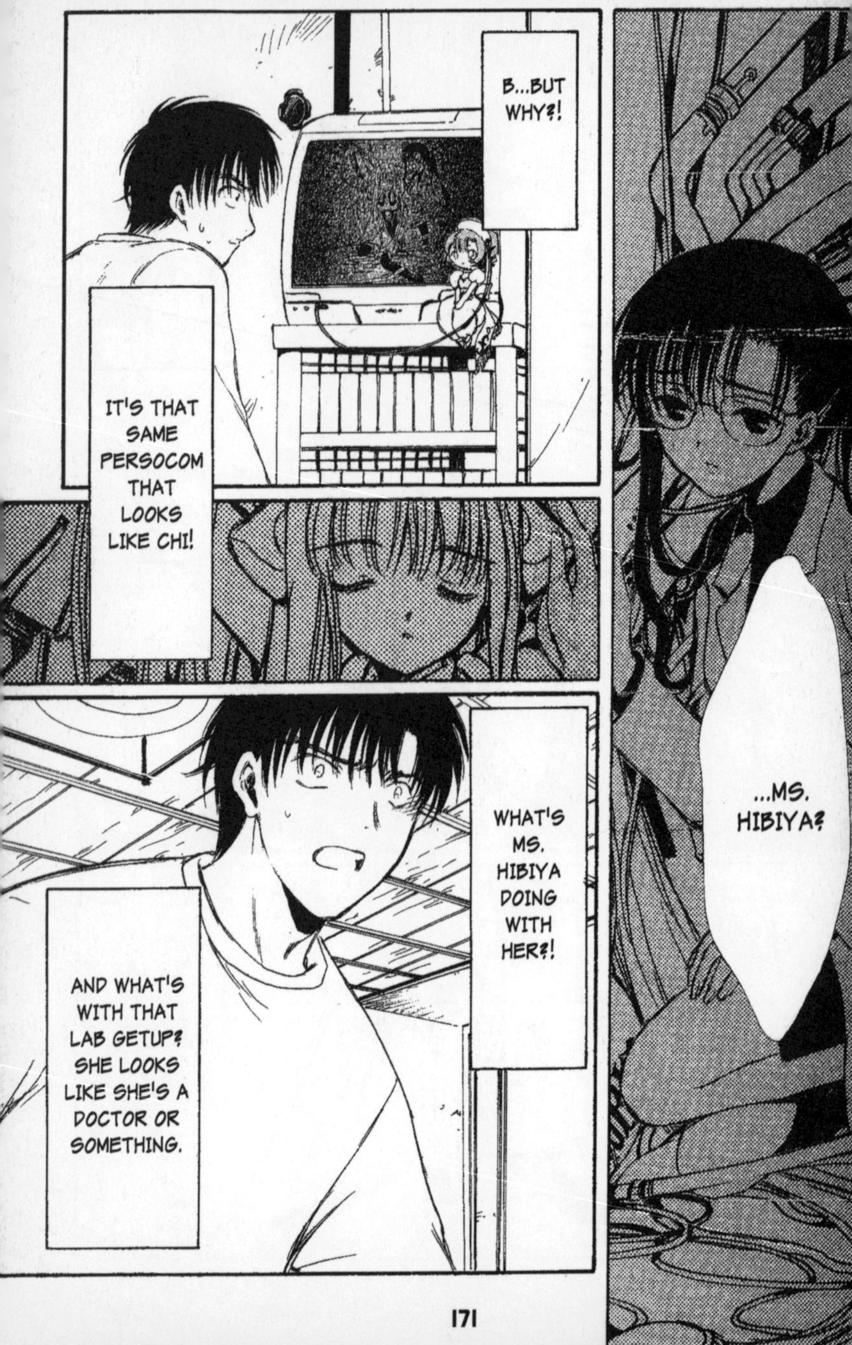
...MS. HIBIYA?
B...BUT WHY?!
IT'S THAT SAME PERSOCOM THAT LOOKS LIKE CHI!
WHAT'S MS. HIBIYA DOING WITH HER?!
AND WHAT'S WITH THAT LAB GETUP? SHE LOOKS LIKE SHE'S A DOCTOR OR SOMETHING.

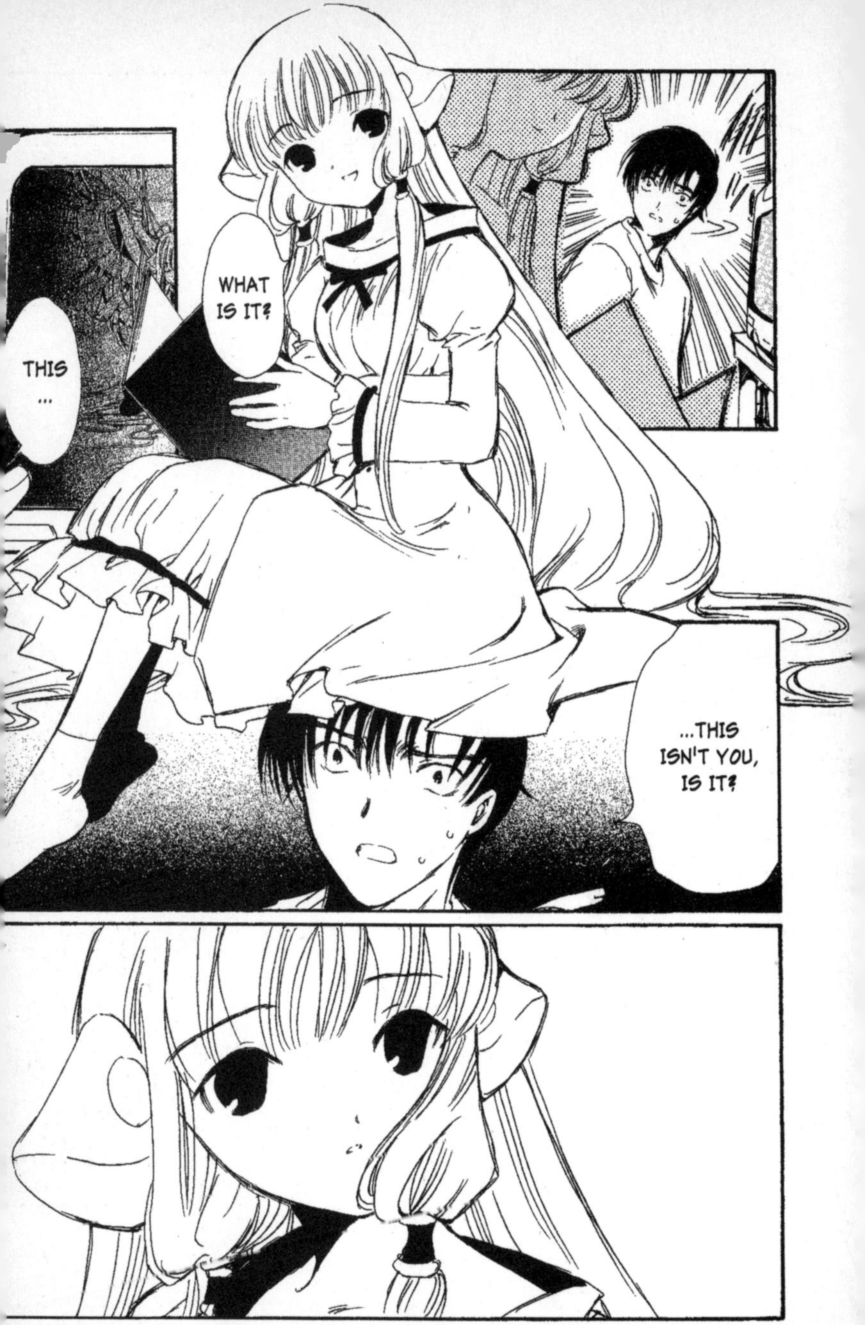
WHAT IS IT?
THIS ...
...THIS ISN'T YOU, IS IT?

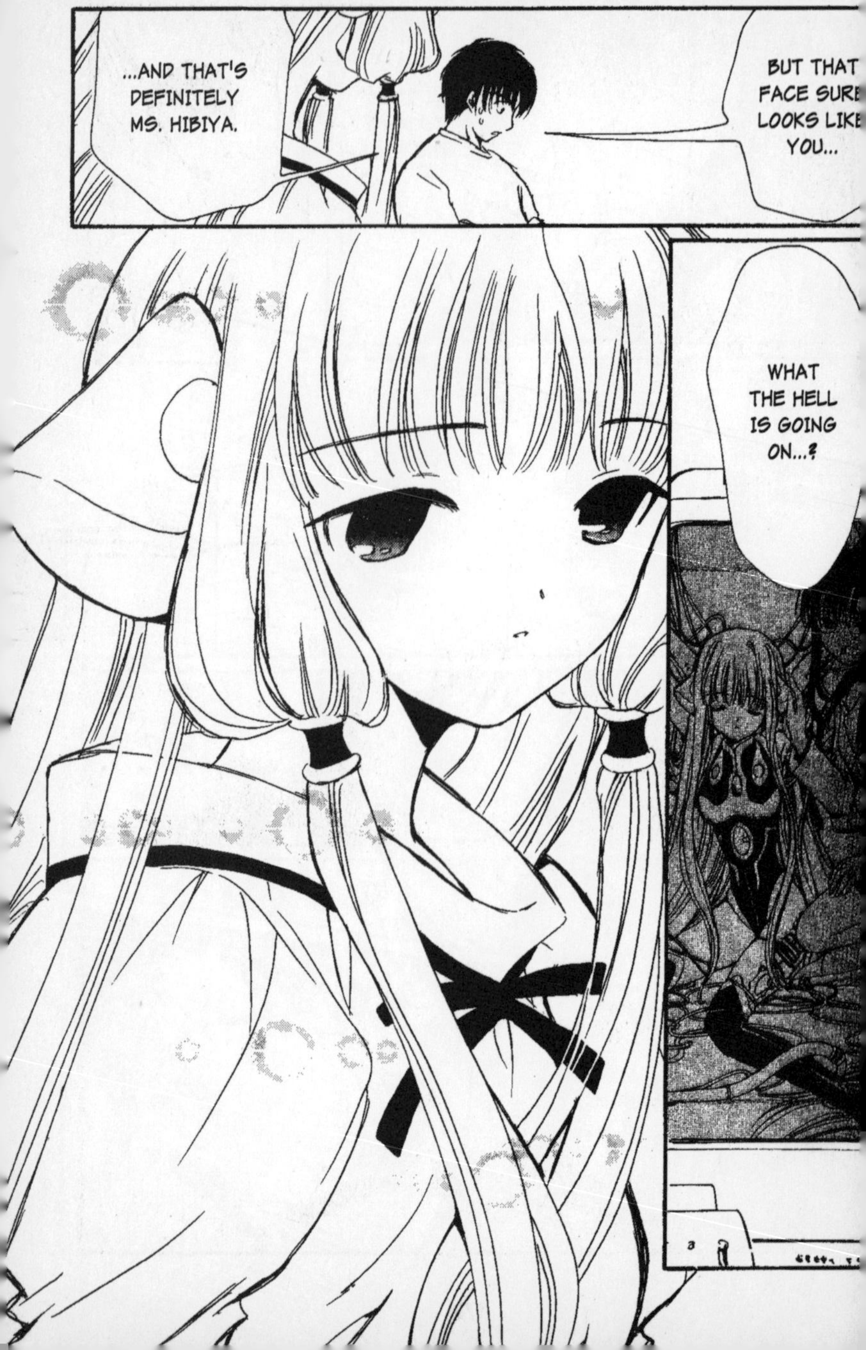
BUT THAT FACE SURE LOOKS LIKE YOU...
...AND THAT'S DEFINITELY MS. HIBIYA.
WHAT THE HELL IS GOING ON...?

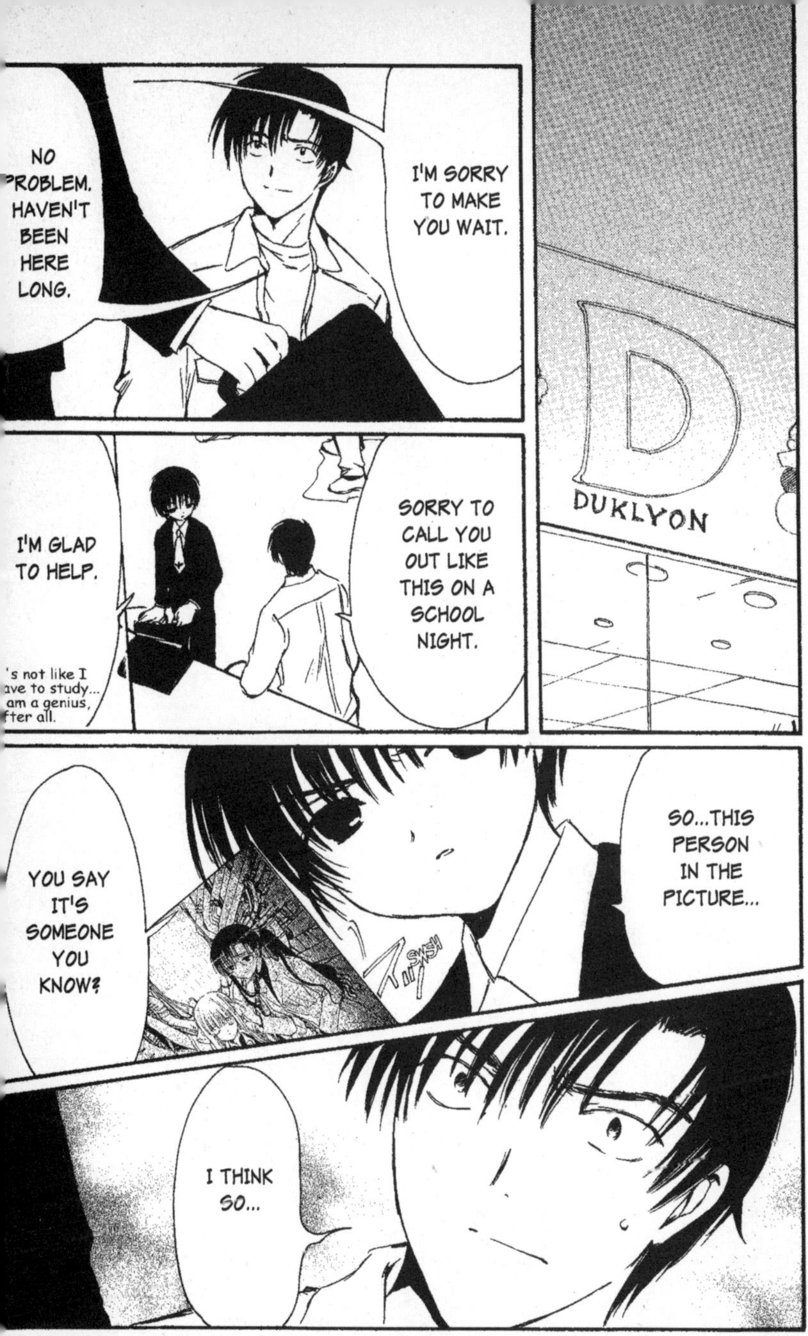
DUKLYON
I'M SORRY TO MAKE YOU WAIT.
NO PROBLEM. HAVEN'T BEEN HERE LONG.
SORRY TO CALL YOU OUT LIKE THIS ON A SCHOOL NIGHT.
I'M GLAD TO HELP.
's not like I ave to study... am a genius, fter all.
SO...THIS PERSON IN THE PICTURE...
SWSH
YOU SAY IT'S SOMEONE YOU KNOW?
I THINK SO...

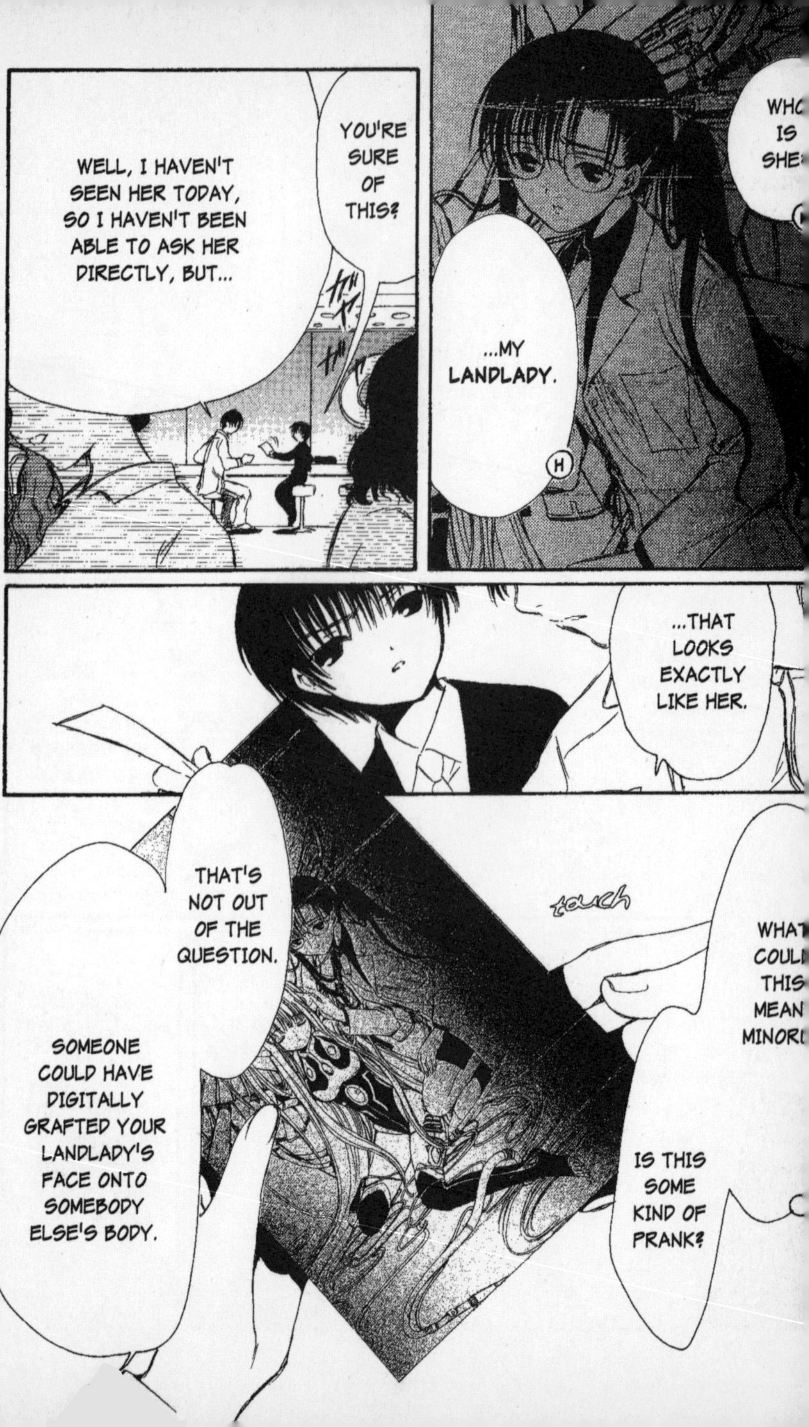
WHO IS SHE
...MY LANDLADY.
YOU'RE SURE OF THIS?
WELL, I HAVEN'T SEEN HER TODAY, SO I HAVEN'T BEEN ABLE TO ASK HER DIRECTLY, BUT...
...THAT LOOKS EXACTLY LIKE HER.
WHAT COUL THIS MEAN MINOR
touch
IS THIS SOME KIND OF PRANK?
THAT'S NOT OUT OF THE QUESTION.
SOMEONE COULD HAVE DIGITALLY GRAFTED YOUR LANDLADY'S FACE ONTO SOMEBODY ELSE'S BODY.

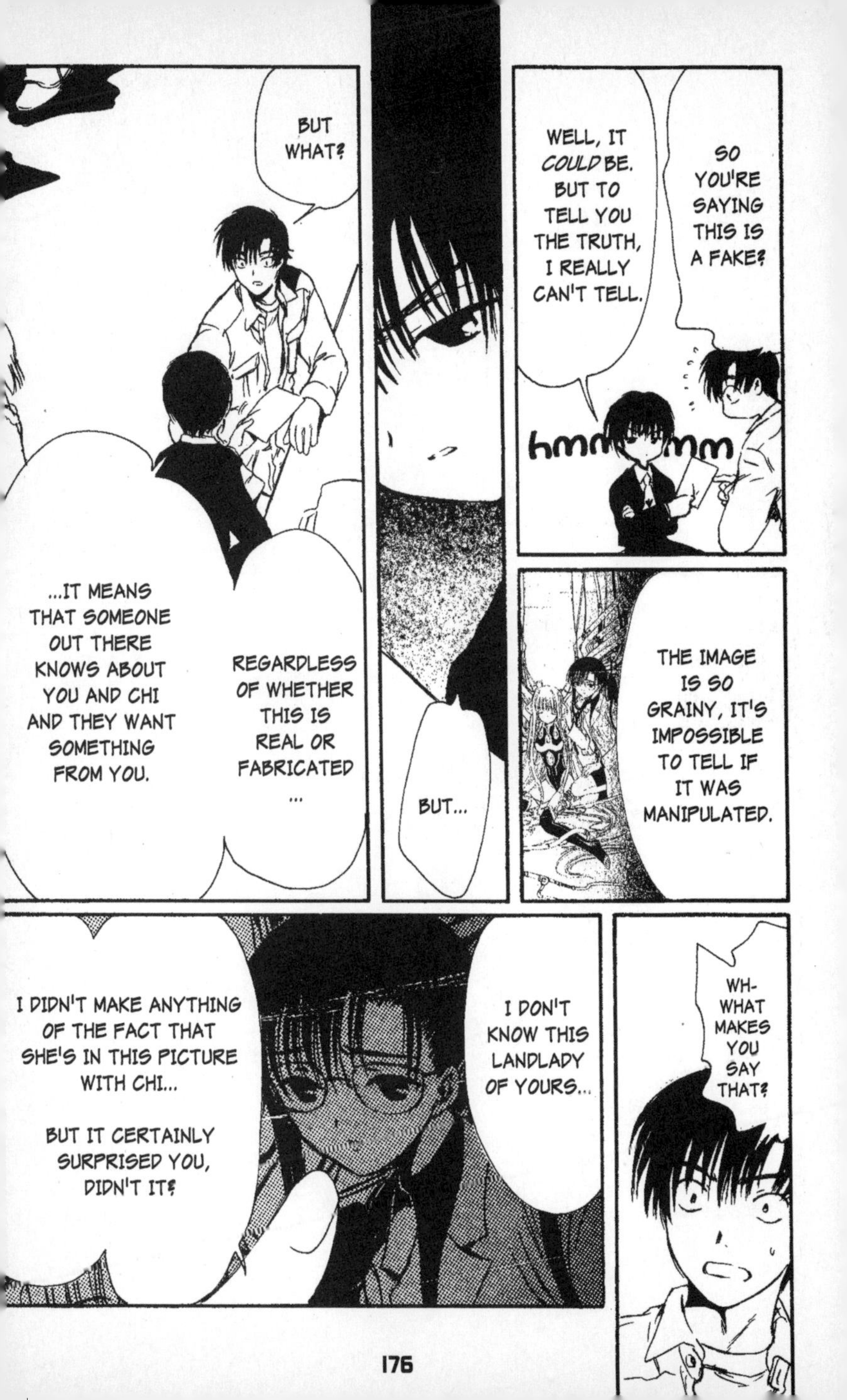
SO YOU'RE SAYING THIS IS A FAKE?
WELL, IT *COULD* BE. BUT TO TELL YOU THE TRUTH, I REALLY CAN'T TELL.
hmmmmm
THE IMAGE IS SO GRAINY, IT'S IMPOSSIBLE TO TELL IF IT WAS MANIPULATED.
BUT...
BUT WHAT?
REGARDLESS OF WHETHER THIS IS REAL OR FABRICATED ...
...IT MEANS THAT SOMEONE OUT THERE KNOWS ABOUT YOU AND CHI AND THEY WANT SOMETHING FROM YOU.
WH- WHAT MAKES YOU SAY THAT?
I DON'T KNOW THIS LANDLADY OF YOURS...
I DIDN'T MAKE ANYTHING OF THE FACT THAT SHE'S IN THIS PICTURE WITH CHI...
BUT IT CERTAINLY SURPRISED YOU, DIDN'T IT?

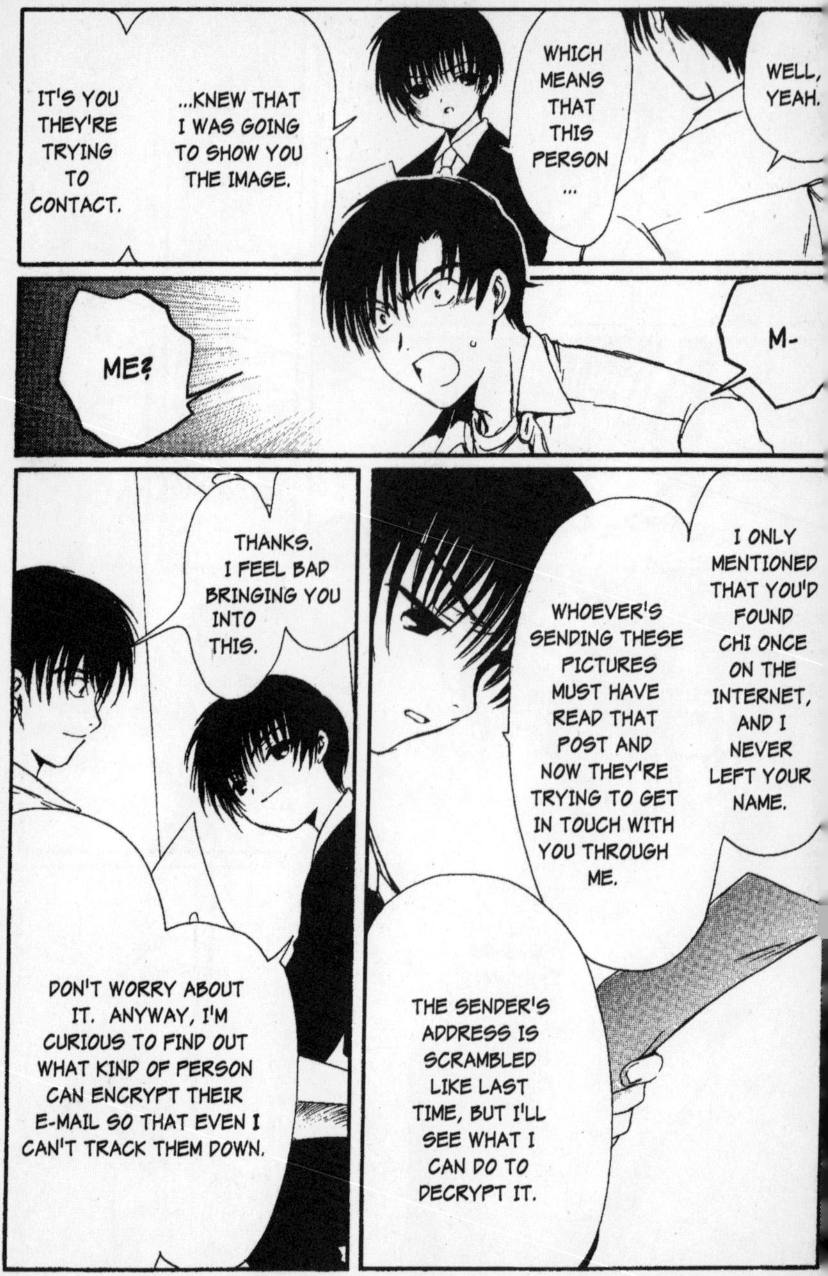
WELL, YEAH.
WHICH MEANS THAT THIS PERSON ...
...KNEW THAT I WAS GOING TO SHOW YOU THE IMAGE.
IT'S YOU THEY'RE TRYING TO CONTACT.
M-
ME?
I ONLY MENTIONED THAT YOU'D FOUND CHI ONCE ON THE INTERNET, AND I NEVER LEFT YOUR NAME.
WHOEVER'S SENDING THESE PICTURES MUST HAVE READ THAT POST AND NOW THEY'RE TRYING TO GET IN TOUCH WITH YOU THROUGH ME.
THE SENDER'S ADDRESS IS SCRAMBLED LIKE LAST TIME, BUT I'LL SEE WHAT I CAN DO TO DECRYPT IT.
THANKS. I FEEL BAD BRINGING YOU INTO THIS.
DON'T WORRY ABOUT IT. ANYWAY, I'M CURIOUS TO FIND OUT WHAT KIND OF PERSON CAN ENCRYPT THEIR E-MAIL SO THAT EVEN I CAN'T TRACK THEM DOWN.

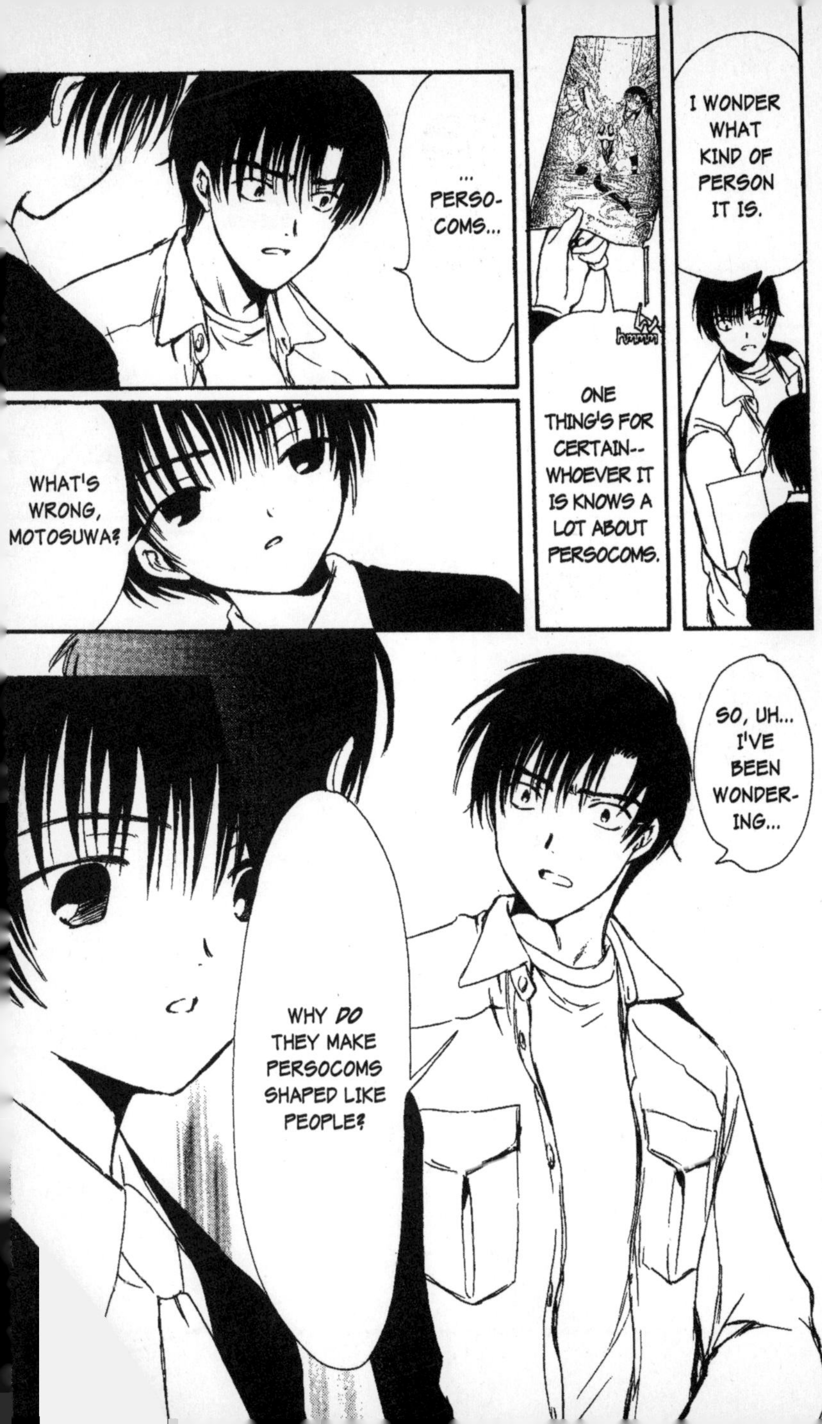
I WONDER WHAT KIND OF PERSON IT IS.
hmmm
ONE THING'S FOR CERTAIN--WHOEVER IT IS KNOWS A LOT ABOUT PERSOCOMS.
...PERSO-COMS...
WHAT'S WRONG, MOTOSUWA?
SO, UH... I'VE BEEN WONDER-ING...
WHY *DO* THEY MAKE PERSOCOMS SHAPED LIKE PEOPLE?

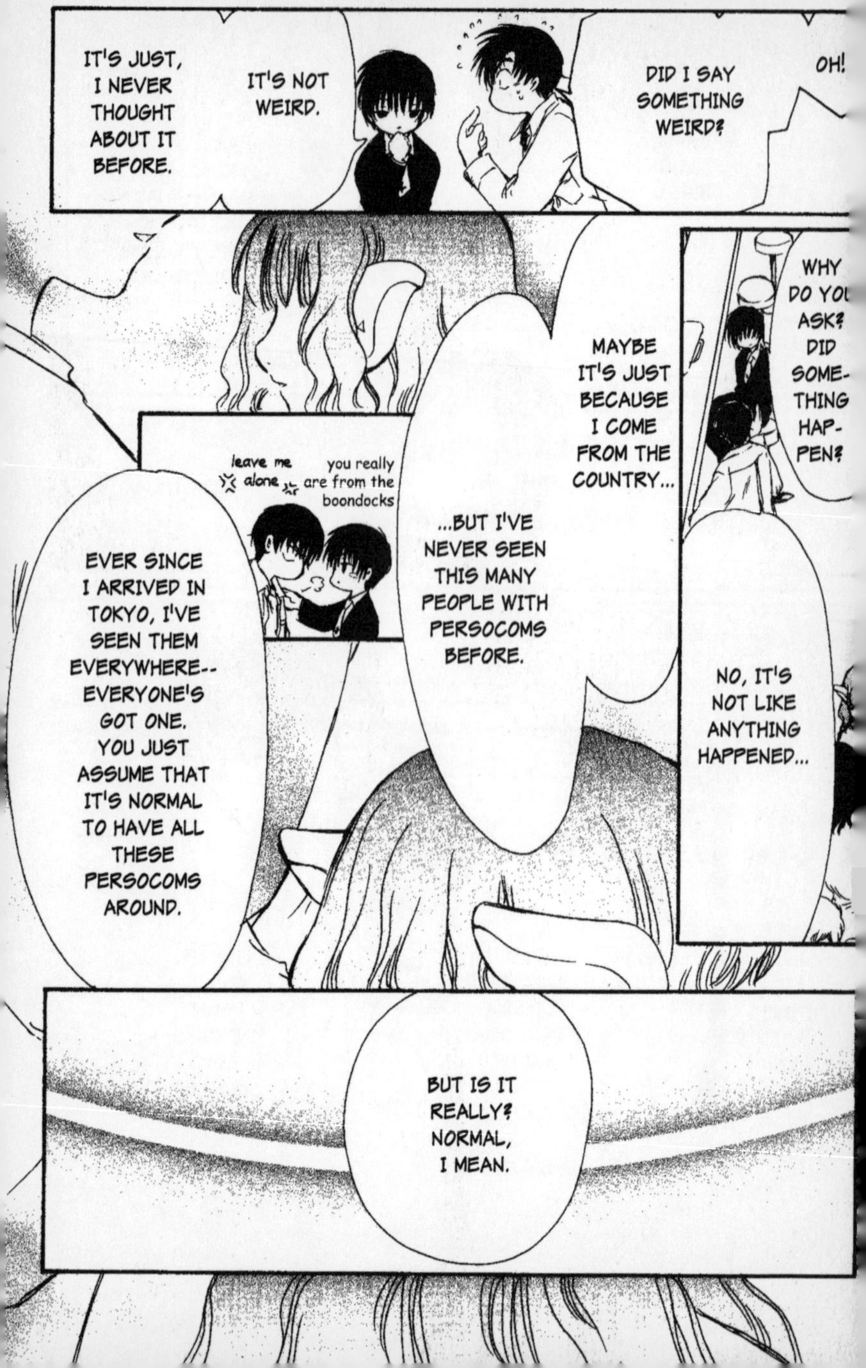
OH!
DID I SAY SOMETHING WEIRD?
IT'S NOT WEIRD.
IT'S JUST, I NEVER THOUGHT ABOUT IT BEFORE.
WHY DO YOU ASK? DID SOME-THING HAP-PEN?
NO, IT'S NOT LIKE ANYTHING HAPPENED...
MAYBE IT'S JUST BECAUSE I COME FROM THE COUNTRY...
...BUT I'VE NEVER SEEN THIS MANY PEOPLE WITH PERSOCOMS BEFORE.
you really are from the boondocks
leave me alone
EVER SINCE I ARRIVED IN TOKYO, I'VE SEEN THEM EVERYWHERE-- EVERYONE'S GOT ONE. YOU JUST ASSUME THAT IT'S NORMAL TO HAVE ALL THESE PERSOCOMS AROUND.
BUT IS IT REALLY? NORMAL, I MEAN.

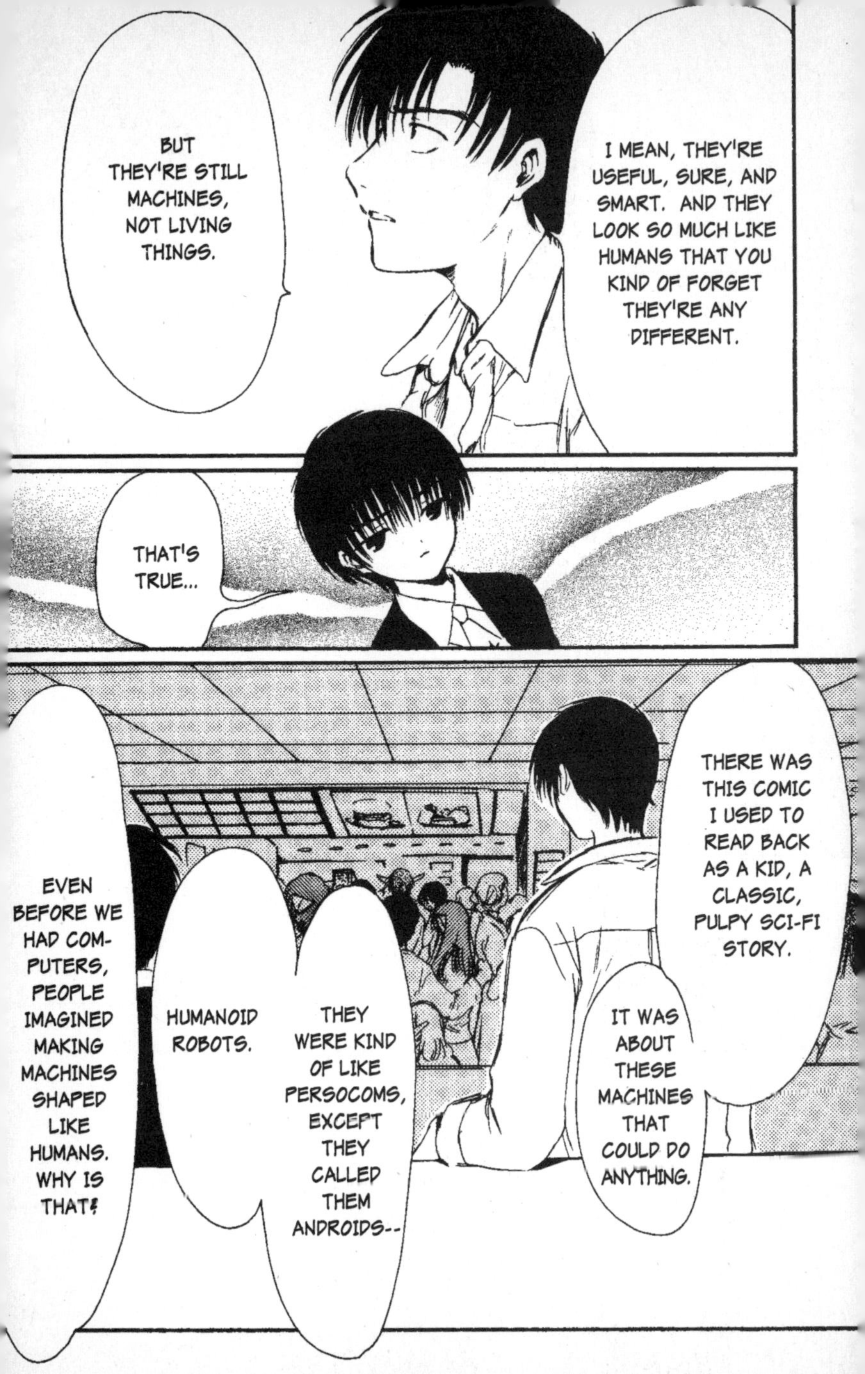
I MEAN, THEY'RE USEFUL, SURE, AND SMART. AND THEY LOOK SO MUCH LIKE HUMANS THAT YOU KIND OF FORGET THEY'RE ANY DIFFERENT.
BUT THEY'RE STILL MACHINES, NOT LIVING THINGS.
THAT'S TRUE...
THERE WAS THIS COMIC I USED TO READ BACK AS A KID, A CLASSIC, PULPY SCI-FI STORY.
IT WAS ABOUT THESE MACHINES THAT COULD DO ANYTHING.
THEY WERE KIND OF LIKE PERSOCOMS, EXCEPT THEY CALLED THEM ANDROIDS--
HUMANOID ROBOTS.
EVEN BEFORE WE HAD COM-PUTERS, PEOPLE IMAGINED MAKING MACHINES SHAPED LIKE HUMANS. WHY IS THAT?

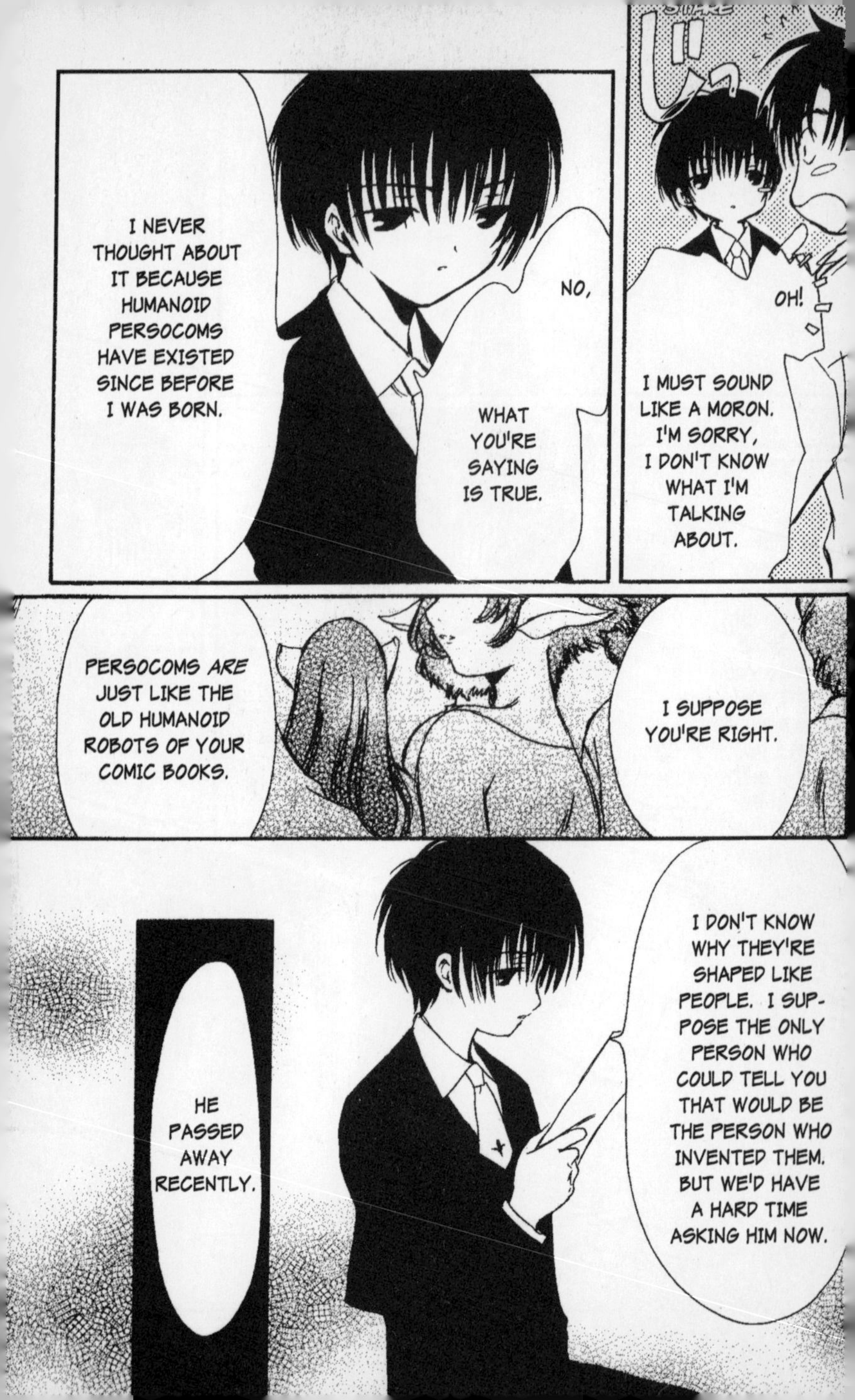
OH!
I MUST SOUND LIKE A MORON. I'M SORRY, I DON'T KNOW WHAT I'M TALKING ABOUT.
NO,
WHAT YOU'RE SAYING IS TRUE.
I NEVER THOUGHT ABOUT IT BECAUSE HUMANOID PERSOCOMS HAVE EXISTED SINCE BEFORE I WAS BORN.
I SUPPOSE YOU'RE RIGHT.
PERSOCOMS *ARE* JUST LIKE THE OLD HUMANOID ROBOTS OF YOUR COMIC BOOKS.
I DON'T KNOW WHY THEY'RE SHAPED LIKE PEOPLE. I SUP-POSE THE ONLY PERSON WHO COULD TELL YOU THAT WOULD BE THE PERSON WHO INVENTED THEM. BUT WE'D HAVE A HARD TIME ASKING HIM NOW.
HE PASSED AWAY RECENTLY.

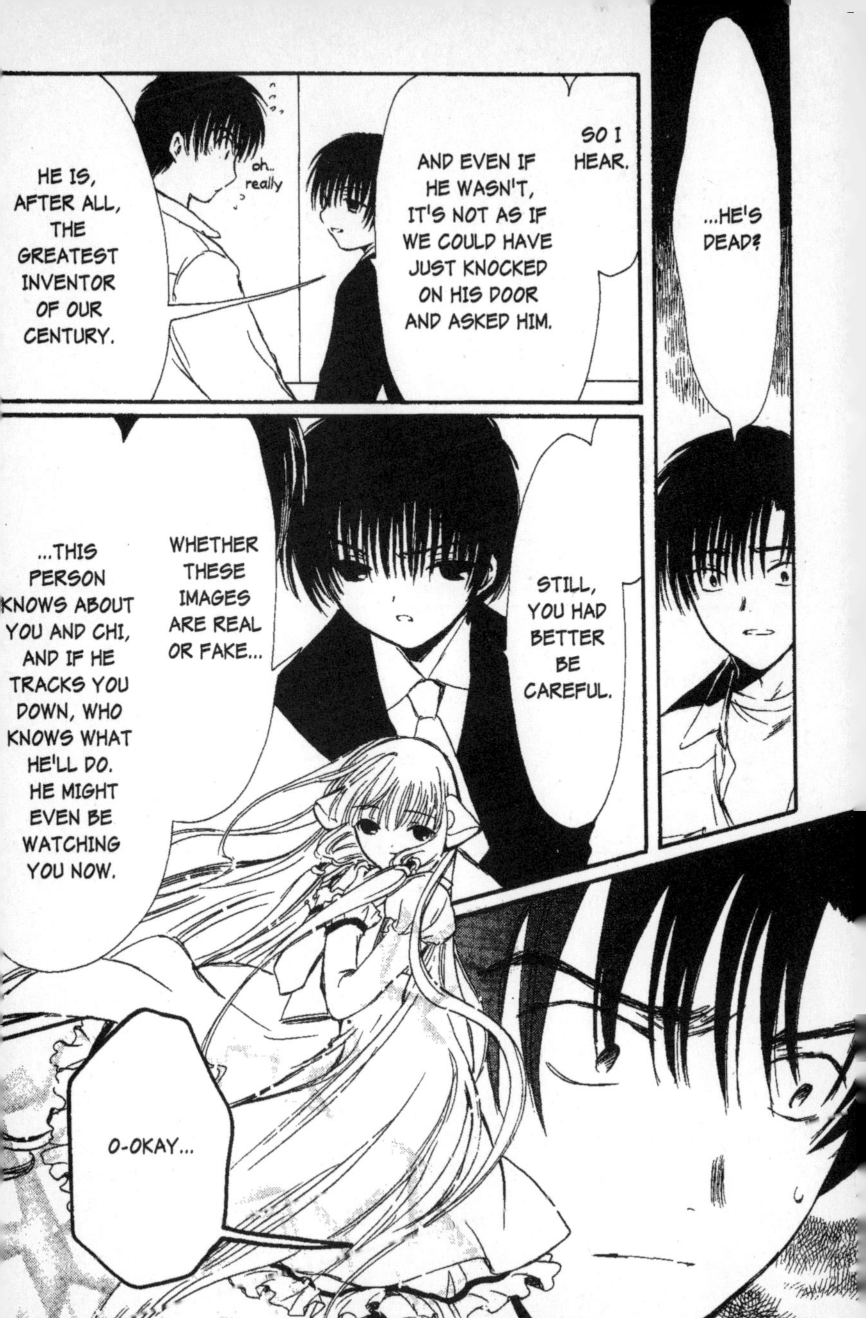
...HE'S DEAD?
SO I HEAR.
AND EVEN IF HE WASN'T, IT'S NOT AS IF WE COULD HAVE JUST KNOCKED ON HIS DOOR AND ASKED HIM.
oh.. really
HE IS, AFTER ALL, THE GREATEST INVENTOR OF OUR CENTURY.
STILL, YOU HAD BETTER BE CAREFUL.
WHETHER THESE IMAGES ARE REAL OR FAKE...
...THIS PERSON KNOWS ABOUT YOU AND CHI, AND IF HE TRACKS YOU DOWN, WHO KNOWS WHAT HE'LL DO. HE MIGHT EVEN BE WATCHING YOU NOW.
O-OKAY...

◀chapter.36▶ end

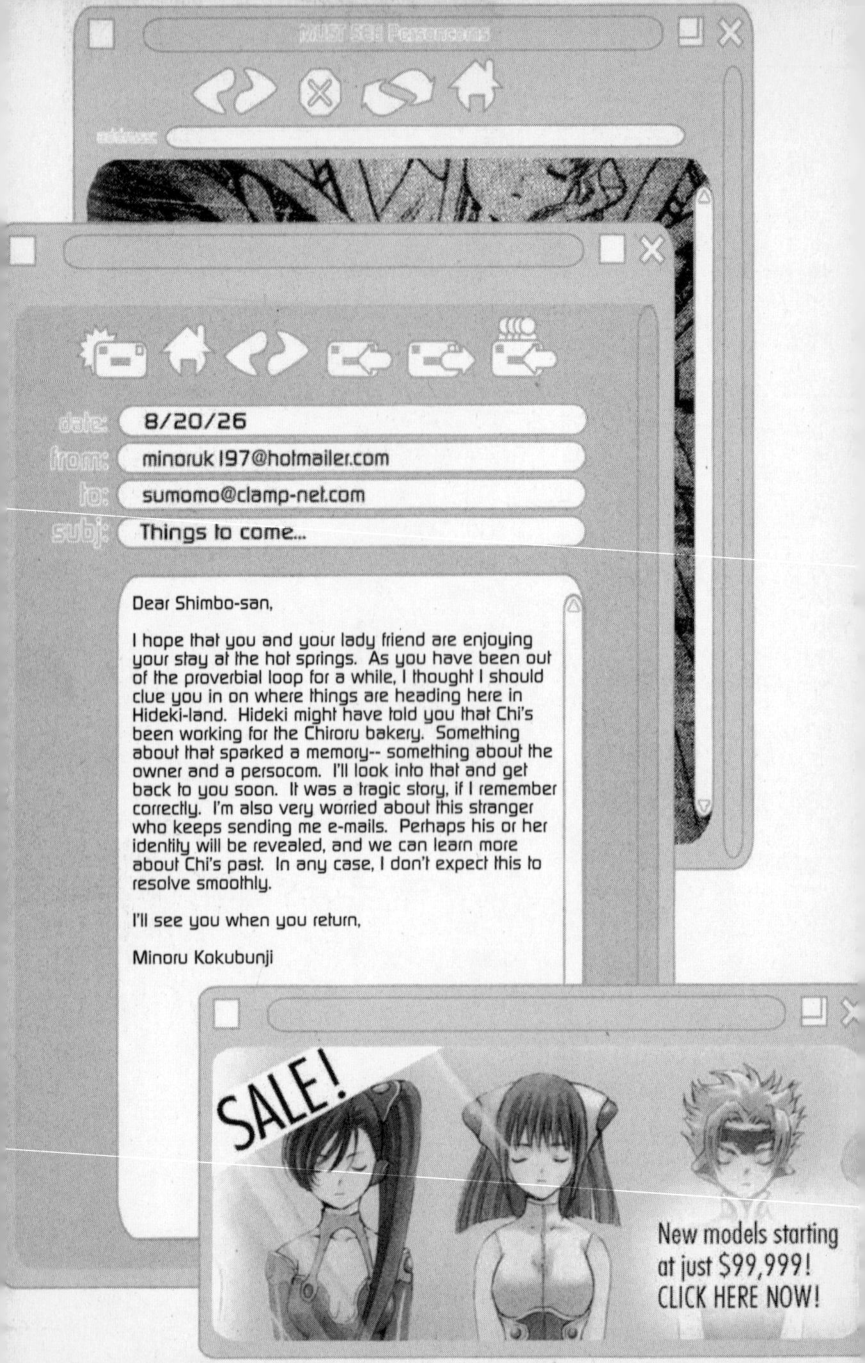
date: 8/20/26
from: minoruk197@hotmailer.com
to: sumomo@clamp-net.com
subj: Things to come...
Dear Shimbo-san,
I hope that you and your lady friend are enjoying your stay at the hot springs. As you have been out of the proverbial loop for a while, I thought I should clue you in on where things are heading here in Hideki-land. Hideki might have told you that Chi's been working for the Chiroru bakery. Something about that sparked a memory-- something about the owner and a persocom. I'll look into that and get back to you soon. It was a tragic story, if I remember correctly. I'm also very worried about this stranger who keeps sending me e-mails. Perhaps his or her identity will be revealed, and we can learn more about Chi's past. In any case, I don't expect this to resolve smoothly.
I'll see you when you return,
Minoru Kokubunji
SALE!
New models starting at just $99,999! CLICK HERE NOW!

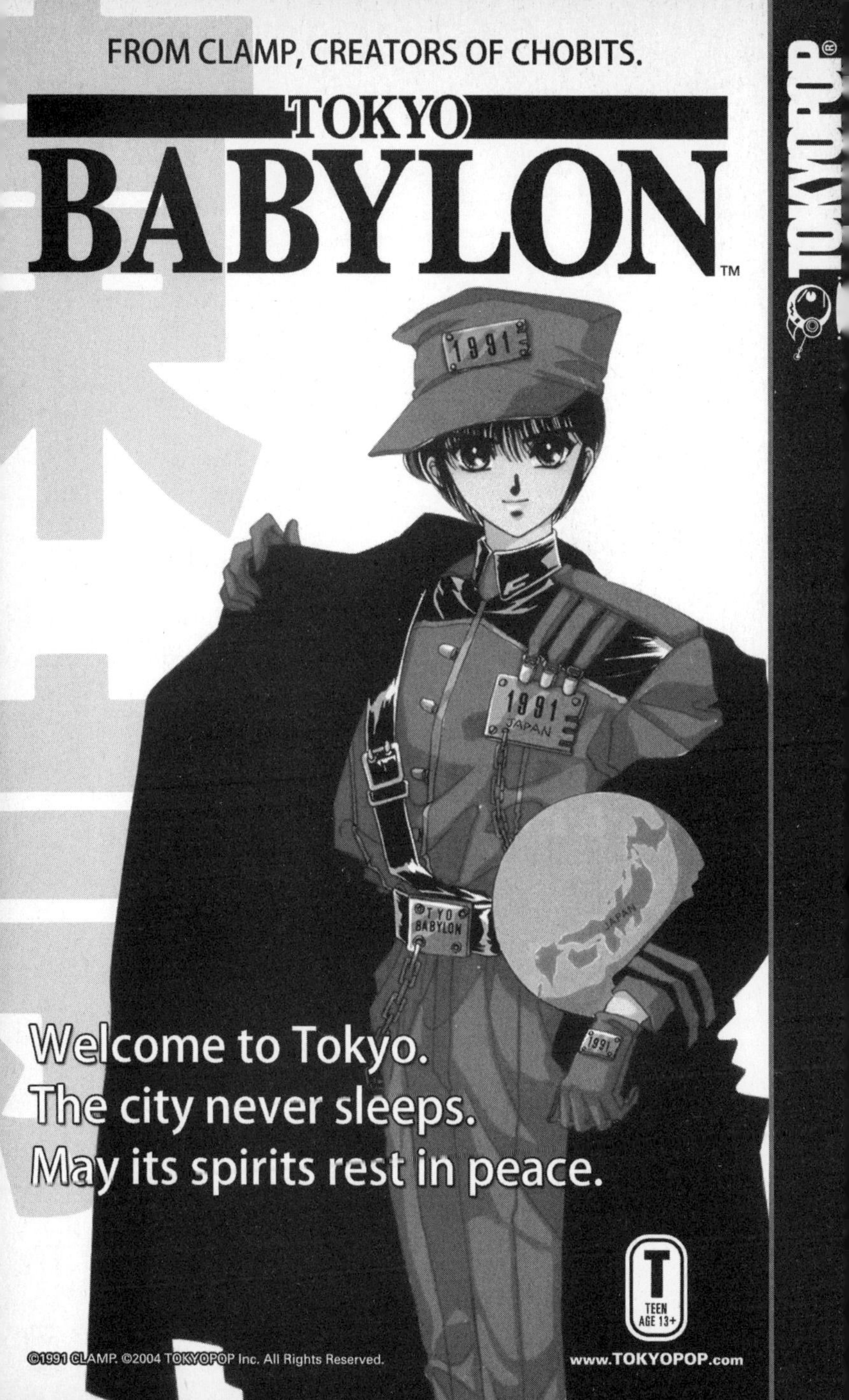
FROM CLAMP, CREATORS OF CHOBITS.
TOKYO BABYLON™
Welcome to Tokyo.
The city never sleeps.
May its spirits rest in peace.
T TEEN AGE 13+
TOKYOPOP®
©1991 CLAMP. ©2004 TOKYOPOP Inc. All Rights Reserved.
www.TOKYOPOP.com

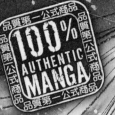

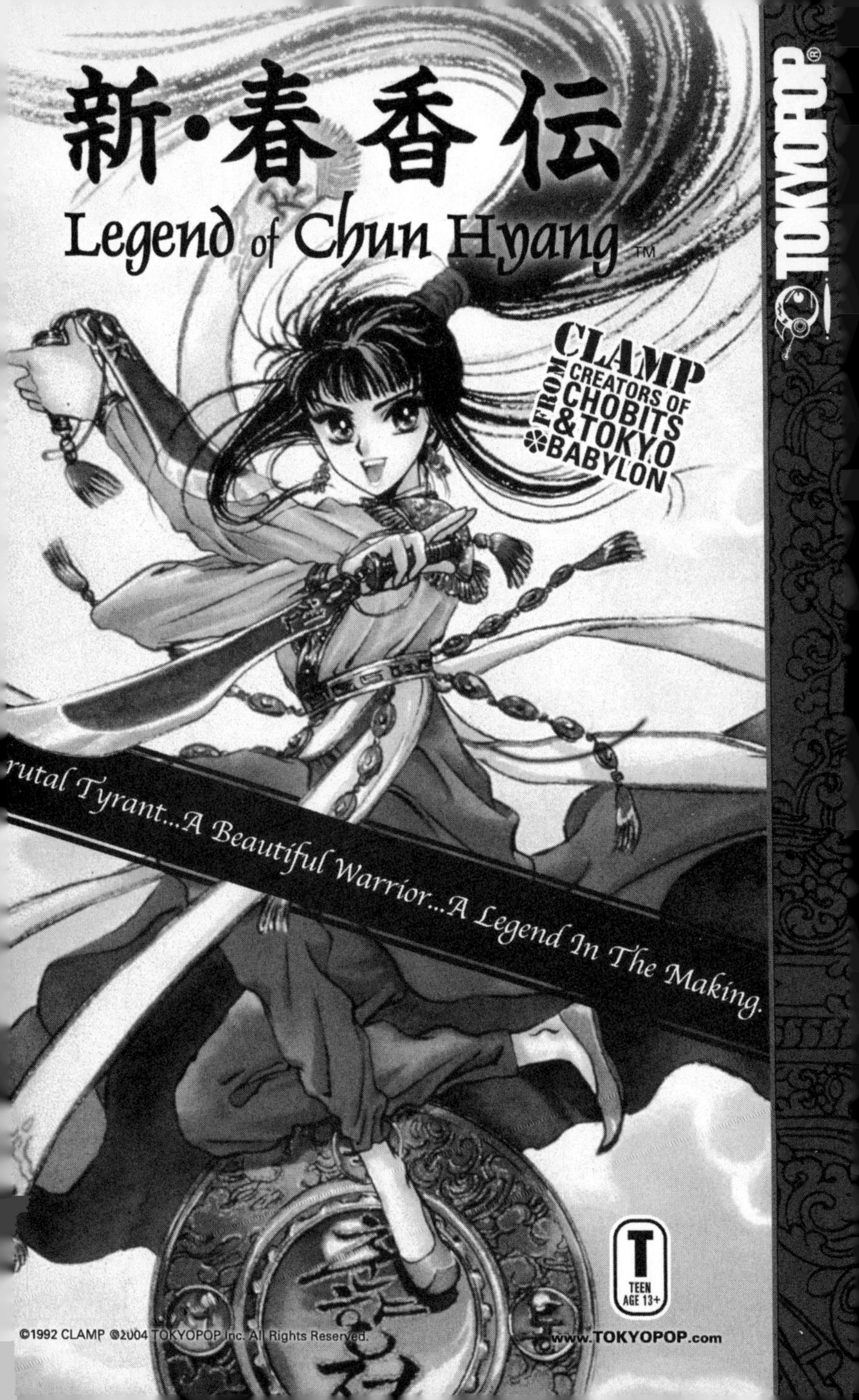
新・春香伝
Legend of Chun Hyang™
TOKYOPOP®
FROM CLAMP CREATORS OF CHOBITS &TOKYO BABYLON
rutal Tyrant...A Beautiful Warrior...A Legend In The Making.
T TEEN AGE 13+
©1992 CLAMP ©2004 TOKYOPOP Inc. All Rights Reserved.
www.TOKYOPOP.com

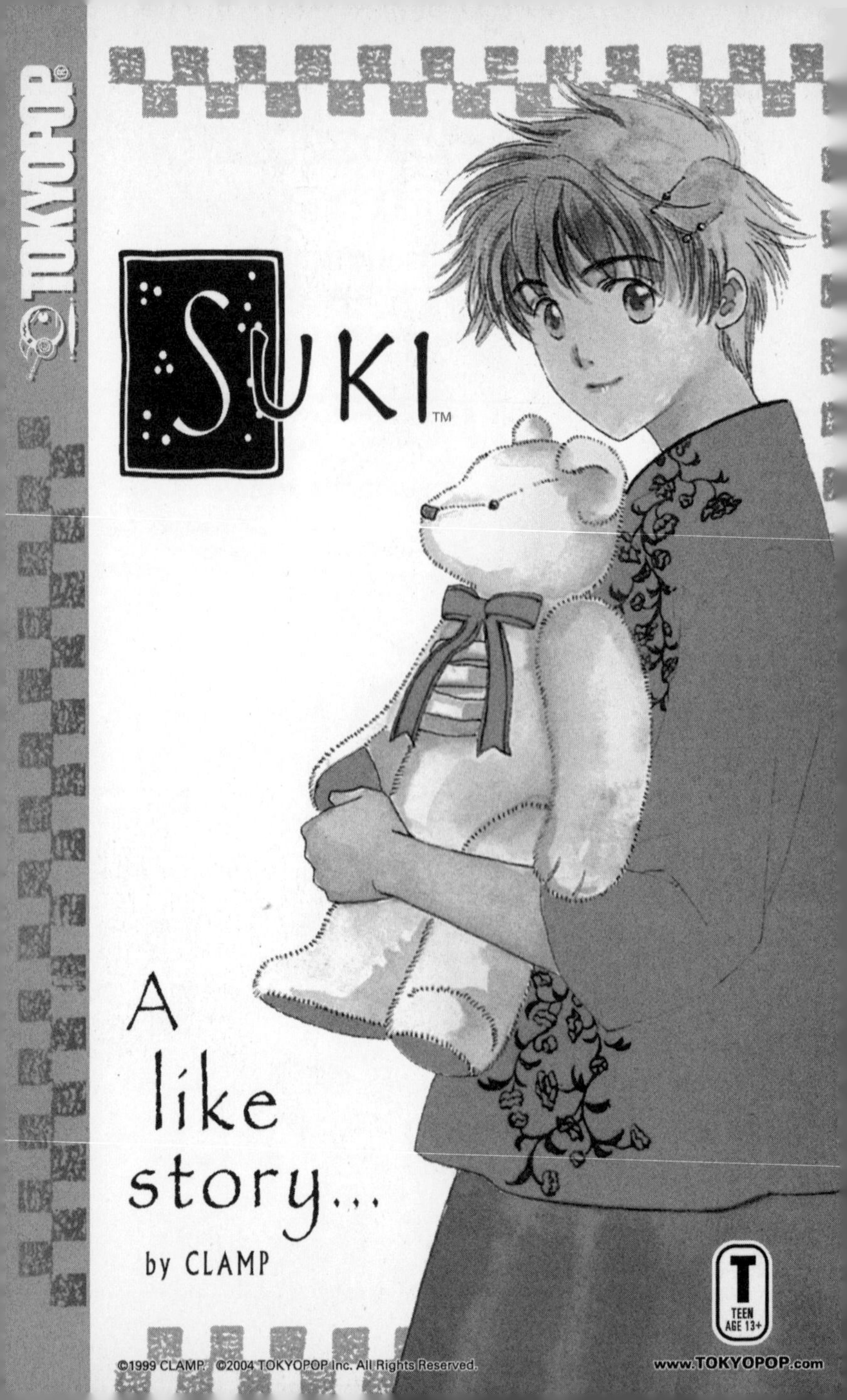
TOKYOPOP®
SUKI™
A like story...
by CLAMP
T TEEN AGE 13+
©1999 CLAMP. ©2004 TOKYOPOP Inc. All Rights Reserved.
www.TOKYOPOP.com

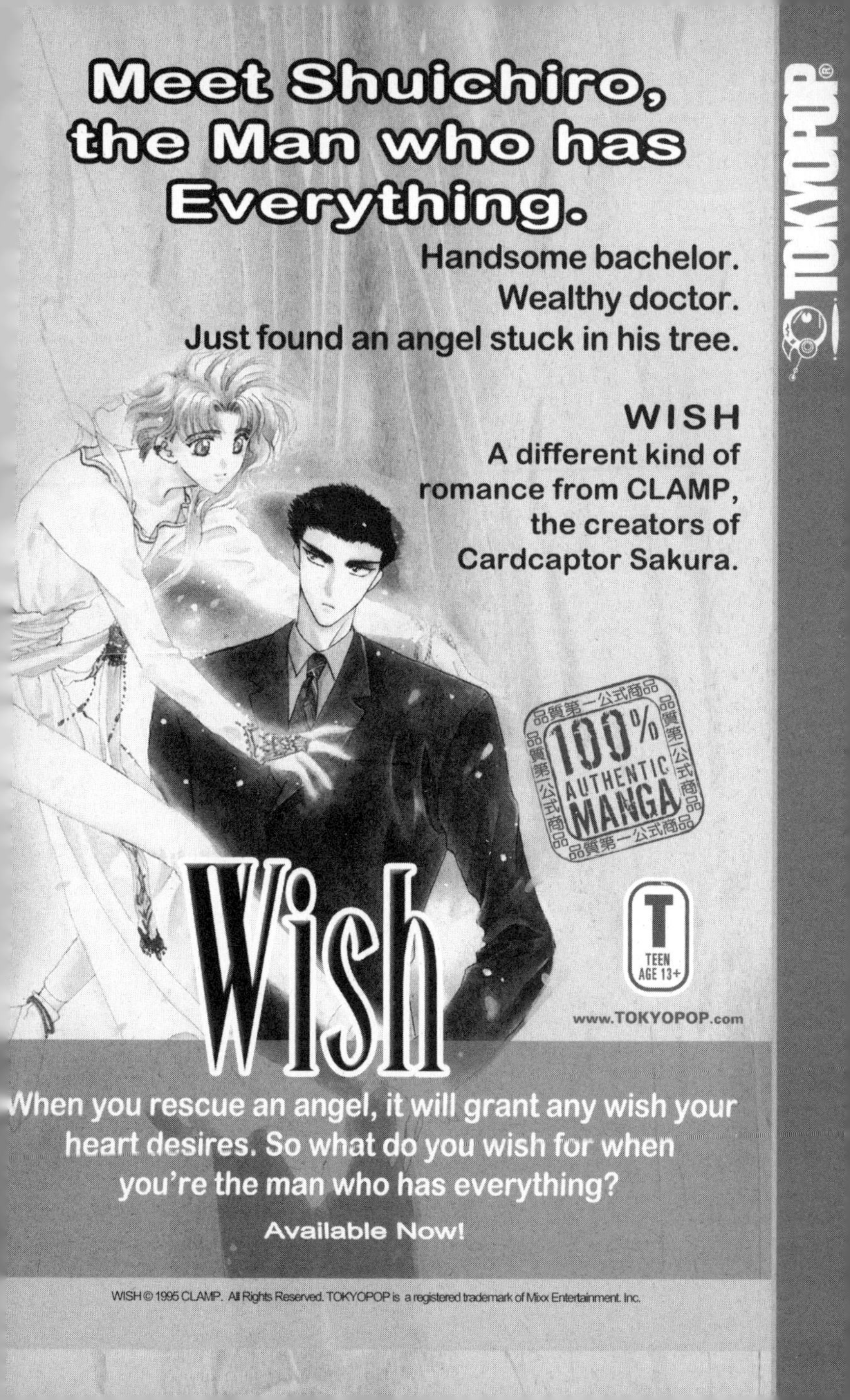
Meet Shuichiro, the Man who has Everything.
Handsome bachelor.
Wealthy doctor.
Just found an angel stuck in his tree.
WISH
A different kind of romance from CLAMP, the creators of Cardcaptor Sakura.
100% AUTHENTIC MANGA
品質第一公式商品
T TEEN AGE 13+
www.TOKYOPOP.com
Wish
When you rescue an angel, it will grant any wish your heart desires. So what do you wish for when you're the man who has everything?
Available Now!
WISH © 1995 CLAMP. All Rights Reserved. TOKYOPOP is a registered trademark of Mixx Entertainment, Inc.
TOKYOPOP

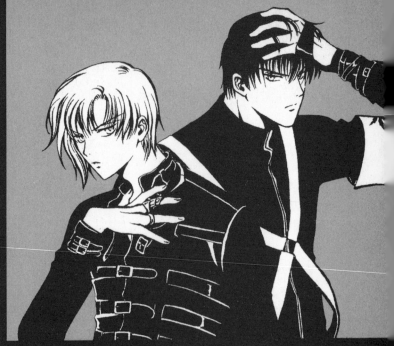

LEGAL DRUG ™

When no ordinary prescription will do...

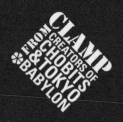

FROM CLAMP CREATORS OF CHOBITS & TOKYO BABYLON

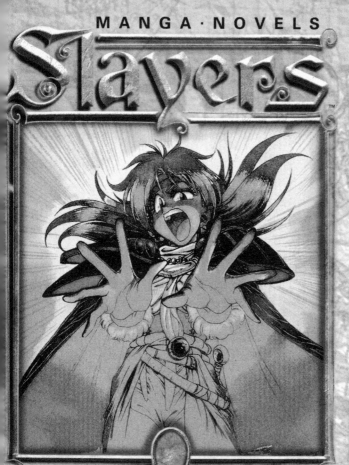

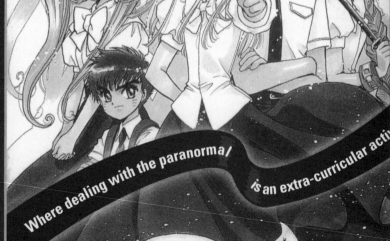

ALSO AVAILABLE FROM TOKYOPOP

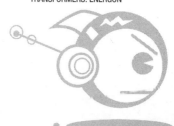

07.15.04T

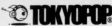

P9-EDQ-177

STOP!

This is the back of the book.
You wouldn't want to spoil a great ending!

This book is printed "manga-style," in the authentic Japanese right-to-left format. Since none of the artwork has been flipped or altered, readers get to experience the story just as the creator intended. You've been asking for it, so TOKYOPOP® delivered: authentic, hot-off-the-press, and far more fun!

DIRECTIONS

If this is your first time reading manga-style, here's a quick guide to help you understand how it works.

It's easy... just start in the top right panel and follow the numbers. Have fun, and look for more 100% authentic manga from TOKYOPOP®!

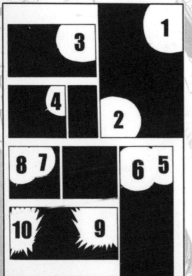

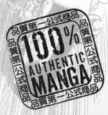